NATIONAL GEOGRAPHIC

TRAVELER

morocco

by Carole French

National Geographic
Washington, D.C.

CONTENTS

Pages 2–3: The kasbah of Aït Ben Haddou
Left: A shop in Marrakech's medina

TRAVELING WITH EYES OPEN

Alert travelers go with a purpose and leave with a benefit. If you travel responsibly, you can help support wildlife conservation, historic preservation, and cultural enrichment in the places you visit. You can enrich your own travel experience as well.

To be a geo-savvy traveler:

- Recognize that your presence has an impact on the places you visit.

- Spend your time and money in ways that sustain local character. (Besides, it's more interesting that way.)

- Value the destination's natural and cultural heritage.

- Respect the local customs and traditions.

- Express appreciation to local people about things you find interesting and unique to the place: its nature and scenery, music and food, historic villages and buildings.

- Vote with your wallet: Support the people who support the place, patronizing businesses that make an effort to celebrate and protect what's special there. Seek out shops, local restaurants, inns, and tour operators who love their home—who love taking care of it and showing it off. Avoid businesses that detract from the character of the place.

- Enrich yourself, taking home memories and stories to tell, knowing that you have contributed to the preservation and enhancement of the destination.

That is the type of travel now called geotourism, defined as "tourism that sustains or enhances the geographical character of a place—its environment, culture, aesthetics, heritage, and the well-being of its residents." To learn more, visit National Geographic's Center for Sustainable Destinations at *www .nationalgeographic.com/travel/sustainable.*

NATIONAL GEOGRAPHIC TRAVELER

morocco

ABOUT THE AUTHOR

British-born **Carole French** is an award-winning BBC-trained news journalist, travel guidebook author, magazine editor, and former UK newspaper business editor. Specializing in world travel, she is a member of the British Guild of Travel Writers and has traveled extensively throughout the world. Her love for Morocco was founded many years ago when, from the deck of a cruise liner, she first glimpsed the skyline of Casablanca, the gold facade of the huge mosque dedicated to Hassan II glinting in the early morning sunshine. French, who lives on the Mediterranean island of Cyprus, has written many travel books, authored dozens of articles for leading organizations such as the Association of British Travel Agents (ABTA), and provided expert consultation on world destinations for television.

Charting Your Trip

From the cosmopolitan cities of Tanger, Casablanca, Marrakech, and Rabat, which celebrate both their history and the latest cultural trends, to the modern city of Agadir and the deep south's kasbahs where time appears to have stood still, Morocco is a country that will capture the imagination. It offers a rich landscape of high mountains, deep river valleys, gorges, and vast deserts where the climate is as varied as the flora and fauna.

Opportunities Abound

Whether it's haggling over a glass of mint tea for a much admired piece of ceramic ware and enjoying the humor of the souk owner, or taking a trek with like-minded adventurers across the desert sand dunes on a camel, you are sure to find an activity that thrills you in Morocco. Perhaps you plan to scale the heights of Morocco's highest mountain, Jebel Toubkal, surf the waves of the Atlantic Ocean, hike in a river canyon, or bird-watch to see some of the world's rarest species? Maybe you're looking for a more relaxing way to spend your time, such as enjoying the sunshine at a chic Tanger seafront café looking out over the Mediterranean Sea? All of this and more can be enjoyed in this varied country. However, no visit to Morocco would be complete without spending time in the very heart of its cities, its medinas. Dating back centuries, medinas are atmospheric places of narrow streets lined with homes, souks, mosques, and *medersas* (universities). Every city has a new district full of shiny office blocks and buzzing with trendy restaurants, but the medina is where you will mingle with locals and where your memories of Morocco will be made.

A traditional painted clay *tagine*

How to Get Around

While it is possible to fly from Europe into Agadir for beach-style holidays and into Marrakech for a short cultural experience, and even visit Tanger by ferry or plane from Spain, by far the largest number of flights into Morocco land at Casablanca's Mohamed V International Airport. From here the country's national carrier, Royal Air Maroc (*www.royalairmaroc.com*), operates flights to towns and cities like Essaouira, Meknès, Nador, and Al Hoceima, or the southern cities of Ouarzazate, Laâyoune, Dakhla, Goulimine, and Tan-Tan, which are generally inexpensive and run most days. As Morocco is a large country with many miles between its cities, flying may be the best option for you if time is a constraint. In the north of the country, there is a good rail network, run by the national rail operator ONCF *(www.oncf.ma),* that links Tanger with the cities of Rabat and Casablanca along the Atlantic Ocean coast and, in turn, with the inland cities of Fès and Marrakech. Trains are modern, air-conditioned, and efficient. If you are driving, you'll find the highways are well maintained, although smaller roads can be a challenge. If you are planning to visit desert regions, it is unwise to go off-road without a guide, even if your vehicle is a 4x4. Once in the towns and cities, you will find taxis everywhere for getting around, as well as buses—while not the most comfortable mode of transport, they will give you the chance to sample everyday life.

If You Have a Week

If this is your first visit to Morocco, then you will probably want to see the sights and get a taste of the mountain and desert scenery. As most flights arrive in Casablanca, we'll begin to chart our trip from here. **Casablanca** offers lots of sights to see. On Day 1, make your way by taxi along the **boulevard Sidi Mohamed ben Abdallah.** Ahead of you will be the **Hassan II Mosque,** the city's highlight. Its *zellij* tile-covered minaret is one of Morocco's tallest. You can take a guided tour. Next, make your way to the **old medina,** worth spending a couple of hours at to absorb the atmosphere. Continue on to the **Parc de la Ligue Arabe** to visit the **Cathédrale Sacré-Coeur.** If you climb up the uneven steps of its tower, you will be rewarded with a panoramic view of the whole city.

On Day 2, before leaving Casablanca, stroll along the **boulevard Mohamed V** to see some of the art deco buildings for which the city is famous. Then take the midday Royal Air Maroc flight from Casablanca to **Marrakech.** It takes just 40 minutes, leaving you the afternoon to explore Marrakech. Head for the **Djemaa el Fna** market square in the medina and the vast **Koutoubia Mosque.**

Spend a little more time in Marrakech on Day 3 before driving or taking an excursion to the city of **Ouarzazate,** known as the gateway to the Sahara. Along the way you will see mountains, desert, and kasbahs. The journey may

Visitor Information

A bounty of helpful travel information can be found at *www.visitmorocco.com,* the website of the Morocco National Tourist Office. The extensive site includes details on local events, festivals, places to stay, shop, and dine, and includes an excellent transportation planner to help you chart your travels around the country. Once in Morocco, be sure to visit the regional tourist information offices, found in all major cities and towns, which offer ideas for things to see and do locally.

Currency

The currency of Morocco is the dirham (MAD), which is divided into 100 centimes. You will need to exchange your foreign currency into dirhams at a bureau de change or a bank when you arrive, and then change any remaining notes or coins on departure. It is strictly forbidden to import or export dirhams.

take you a couple of hours or more, so be sure to leave enough time to retrace your steps back to Marrakech before nightfall.

Take the early morning flight from Marrakech to Casablanca on Day 4, and then make your way by road to **Rabat.** It will take around an hour to drive the 60 miles (160 km), but you might like to stop for lunch at the seaside resort of **Mohammedia.** Arrive in Rabat late afternoon and explore the **Oudaïa Kasbah,** Morocco's first official historic monument. Relax now at your hotel or in one of the fashionable restaurants for which Rabat is known.

Start Day 5 with an early breakfast and make for Rabat's **Hassan Tower.** Be sure to be there at 7 a.m. sharp to see one of the city's most spectacular ceremonies, the changing of the guards. When the ceremony is over, spend some time exploring the tower. If the 12th-century ruler Sultan Yacoub el Mansour hadn't died and left it uncompleted, it would have been the world's largest. Just across the square is the **Mausoleum of Mohamed V,** one of the city's highlights.

On Day 6, take the train, hire a private taxi, or drive to **Meknès,** which is about 80 miles (130 km) away. Spend the day exploring this compact, exciting city. See the **Ville Impériale,** a manicured city created by Sultan Moulay Ismail in the 17th century. About 20 miles (32 km) away is the ancient Roman site of **Volubilis.**

Fès is less than an hour's drive from Meknès, so on Day 7 make an early start and you'll be in the city in good time to explore its sights. See **Fès el Bali** and **Fès el Jedid**—the two atmospheric old medinas—as well as the **tanneries** and the spectacular **Bou Inania Medersa,** a school founded in the 14th century. Be sure to allow time to shop in the souks.

If You Have More Time

If you have extra time, you might decide to linger in and around one of your favorite cities during the trip. Casablanca, Rabat, Fès, and Agadir all work as excellent base camp cities for longer day-trips. From Casablanca, the **Boulaouane vineyards** are less than a two-hour drive south by car. The rosé wine made in this region is almost as famous as the falconry that has been practiced in the kasbah since 1710. If you decide to spend one more night in Casablanca, stop in **Oualidia** (along the

When to Visit

Morocco has such a varied climate that choosing when to go depends largely on the activities you plan to do. Ideal temperatures for a mountain trek would be quite different from those hoped for by visitors on a beach holiday, for example. In general, spring and fall are ideal for coastal and city visits, as well as treks into the mountains where in winter routes can be impassable because of snow. The Mediterranean and Atlantic resorts are popular in the summer months, while the inland Saharan regions experience temperatures above 104°F (40°C) in summer, with cooler spring, fall, and winter months.

Street scene in the blue-walled town of Chefchaouene

Atlantic coast two hours southwest of Casablanca) on the drive back to sample the fresh, salty local oysters.

Bird lovers will want to spend an extra night in Rabat to visit the coastal bird sanctuary at **Merjda Zerga Biological Reserve.** The adjacent town, **Moulay Bousselham,** is one hour north from Rabat by car. There are thousands of waterfowl to spot, including the rare African marsh owl.

Talassemtane National Park, a hundred miles (160 km) or so north of Fès, offers enough gorges, forests, and mountains in to keep outdoor adventurers busy for a few days. When you long for the water again, head northwest from Talassemtane another hundred miles (160 km) and spend some remaining nights in **Tanger,** on the coastal A1. From here you can overlook the **Straight of Gibraltar** and spy on Spain.

Another option, if you've spent most of your trip exploring northern cities and want to change regions, is to take the hour-long flight from Casablanca to the sandy beaches of **Agadir** on the Atlantic. Agadir is also a great launching off point for a drive south to the Sahara. Within a couple of hours you will be in the town of **Goulimine,** set amid vast desert plains. From here, the intrepid traveler can drive south another seven hours to **Laâyoune,** where camel treks and and the classic sand dunes of **Western Sahara** await you.

History & Culture

Morocco's cultural mix is at times almost overpowering.

Morocco Today

With cities that combine cosmopolitan modernity with ancient palaces, medinas, and mosques; sleepy Berber villages sitting high in the mountains and untouched by time; a long coastline bordering the Mediterranean Sea and the Atlantic Ocean; and a multicultural population of 32 million people, Morocco is an eclectic Muslim country with a distinctly international feel.

Morocco occupies Africa's far northwest corner, lying less than 10 miles (15 km) south of Spain, just across the narrow Strait of Gibraltar. The ease with which it can be reached from cities throughout Europe and beyond has helped to make it a popular holiday destination, and today it provides many visitors with their first

Shopping at a souk in Marrakech's timeless medina

introduction to Africa. Though it is often regarded as a country at a crossroads—between Africa and Europe, Islam and Christianity, modernity and tradition, and, perhaps most fancifully, between the pragmatic West and the exotic, romantic East—Morocco has a distinct character all its own. Travelers drawn here by the handful of exotic tableaus for which the country is famed—the chaotic bustle of the medina, the great sweeps of *Lawrence of Arabia*-esque sand dunes—are often surprised by the sheer variety of experiences it has to offer. Morocco has something for everyone: wide sandy beaches to relax on, plenty of history and culture to explore, great scenery in the plains and the High and Middle Atlas mountain ranges, and fine restaurant dining, especially in the fashionable cities of Marrakech and Fès, plus accommodations that run the gamut from atmospheric Moroccan houses with court-

> **Today's population is an eclectic blend of genes, cultures, cuisines, and languages, most joined by the national religion of Islam.**

yards (known as *riads*) to luxury, top-name hotels.

In today's Morocco, modern influences combine with the historic cultures of a wide mix of ethnic groups to give rise to great diversity. The native people of North Africa (often referred to as Berbers by outsiders, although Amazigh is more correct), who for millennia have inhabited the continent from Morocco's Atlantic coast to Egypt's western desert, have been joined by Arabs from the Arabian Peninsula, Africans from areas south of the Sahara, and thousands upon thousands of Muslims and Jews who fled from Andalusia in southern Spain during periods of unrest. As a result, today's population is an eclectic blend of genes, cultures, cuisines, and languages, most joined by the national religion of Islam.

This rich cultural legacy is in evidence everywhere. The country's official language is Arabic, but you may also hear people speaking French (particularly in the business community), Spanish (Morocco has two Spanish enclaves on its coast), and various distinct but related Berber tongues, which have been kept alive over the centuries by the native people against some stiff linguistic competition.

Culture, Crafts, & Dress

Morocco's intense cultural brew can be felt at every turn, in dress styles, crafts, and cuisine, but also in the Berber- and Arabic-influenced music. Everyday life is accompanied by music, and the frenetic atmosphere of the souks is enlivened by rhythmic African and Arab pop sounds that give a lift to every step taken within the labyrinths of goods. In the cities of Meknès, Fès, and the northern coastal cities of Tanger and Tétouan, people favor a classical style of music that has its origins in Andalusia.

Festivals are held throughout the year, and these, too, feature various types of music, among them the rhythmic *daqqa*. In rural areas, Berber musical styles are popular, such as the *abouach*, which tells stories of local life accompanied by tambourine sounds, while *chaabi*, a genre that has a more Western sound, is all the rage in the cities.

The Moroccan style of dress is an eclectic mix of colors and fabrics that varies according to region, as well as by the ethnic orientation and social status of the wearer. A popular garment for women is the kaftan. It is usually worn full-length with a collarless

A young woman dries her henna-painted hands and chats with friends in Marrakech.

neck opening and wide sleeves, and secured by an embroidered gold or silver belt. Most women wear simple cotton kaftans of a single color, but those of a higher social status, or attending a special occasion, may wear brightly colored garments made from more lavish materials such as silk or brocade embroidered with floral or geometric patterns.

Both men and women sometimes wear a full-length robe with a pointed hood called a *djellaba*, although men in urban areas usually opt for Western dress. The djellaba is usually a plain or striped garment made of wool or cotton, with layers beneath to keep the wearer warm in the often cold mountainous regions. In the High Atlas, women wear caps to identify their tribe, while the Zemmour women of the Middle Atlas traditionally wear a colored plaited belt over their kaftan.

In the far south toward the Sahara, where Morocco becomes a desert dotted with oases, the traditional dress for women takes the form of a light, often richly colored full-length kaftan, generally made of cotton for coolness, with a black or white shawl to cover the head. Jewelry is important to the residents of southern Morocco, and on special days and for festivals they wear elaborately crafted pieces made of beads.

Leatherworking is a prime industry in the major cities, and the tanneries of Fès and Marrakech are among the leaders in their field. Visitors can see tanners cleaning a hide, dyeing it, and embellishing it with gold leaf before cutting and sewing it into garments such as slippers (known as *babouches*), belts, and handbags in workshops around the medinas. There are also woodworking workshops where furniture and souvenirs are created using cedar, citrus wood, walnut, and rosewood from the forests of the Rif and Atlas mountain ranges.

> **Leatherworking is a prime industry in the major cities, and the tanneries of Fès and Marrakech are among the leaders in their field.**

Ceramic jugs, bowls, and plates, which make nice gifts or souvenirs and are also used in everyday life by locals, are created in view of passersby in medina workshops. Their shapes and designs evoke Arabic, Berber, and Andalusian styles, with a few regional variations. In Fès, one of the major ceramic centers, for instance, pottery is typically white with blue decorative motifs.

Other crafts—such as the fashioning of copper and brass into household items and decorative architectural features for buildings, and the creation of the beautiful carpets for which Morocco is renowned (see sidebar p. 51)—are on display everywhere. All exhibit distinct influences from the country's various ethnic groups.

City Life

For many travelers, Morocco's greatest attraction is its cities. Indeed, 56 percent of the population resides in urban areas, creating the great buzz of life and commerce that visitors will encounter in towns and cities, especially among the labyrinthine streets of the medinas. Rabat is Morocco's administrative and political center, and its seat of royalty. It is also, along with Marrakech, Fès, and Meknès, one of four "Imperial Cities," so named because each has at one time been the capital of the country and the home of the ruling dynasty. Fès was the capital as far back as the eighth century and retained its premier status throughout three dynasties. It gave way to Marrakech during the Saadian period, and then Meknès and currently Rabat have been given the honor during the present ruling Alaouite dynasty.

Each of these cities has its charms: Rabat is famed for the picturesque 17th-century Oudaïa Kasbah, its Royal Palace, and the mighty Muhammad V Mausoleum; Marrakech for its lavish riads and souks that cluster enticingly around its main square, Djemaa el Fna; Fès for its Fès el Bali medina, the largest in the world and a UNESCO World Heritage site; and Meknès for its magnificent palaces and mosques, many of which were the follies of Sultan Moulay Ismail who reigned in the 17th and 18th centuries.

The country's largest urban center, however, has no imperial heritage. Morocco's financial hub, Casablanca, is a sprawling, densely packed city of art deco and neo-Moorish buildings, ancient souks, chic restaurants, and a bustling harbor.

Friday prayers at a mosque in Djemaa el Fna, Marrakech

But it isn't just Casablanca and the Imperial Cities that excite. Morocco's culture can be felt in its other great metropolises, too, such as Tanger with its dazzling white kasbah, the attractive city of Tétouan filled with Andalusian-influenced architecture, and the traditional cities of Chefchaouene, Salé, and Asilah where you can observe the fascinating spectacle of the Moroccan people going about their everyday lives.

Medina Life

One of the most memorable—if a tad overwhelming—experiences for any visitor to Morocco is a visit to a medina, the old Arabic quarter found in many North African towns. A medina (which means "city" in Arabic) can often appear chaotic but is, in fact, built to a quite regimented format. Enclosed within a defensive wall, the medina is a dense maze of tiny alleyways that have distinct areas for home and work. Within the work areas, types of goods are grouped together in souks. For example, spices will be in one souk—and will draw visitors in by their aroma—while ceramics, copper and brass ware, and leather slippers will be in another.

At the center of the medina is its spiritual heart, the grand mosque, while surrounding it are thick defensive walls lined with lookout towers where soldiers once sat watching for pirates or threatening armies during periods of unrest. A fortified gateway provides the entrance.

Like all of Morocco's medinas, the bustling car-free Fès medina has streets lined with houses, craft work-shops, and food vendors' stalls. The largest medina in the world, the Fès el Bali (meaning "Fès old city"), traces its heritage back to the eighth century.

Elsewhere, Safi, famous for its ceramics and tex-tiles, the stronghold of El Jadida, and elegant Tafraout with its pink, terra-cotta, and honey-colored houses dotting the hillside are all worthy excursions. The for-tified Taroudant and Ouarzazate, plus the enchanting city of Zagora located in the Jebel Anaouar foothills in the heart of the Drâa Valley, are also must-sees—each has a unique character.

Rural Life & the Economy

Beyond the cities, many visitors come in search of sand, be it on the wide beaches lining the Atlantic and Mediterranean coasts or piled in vast sand dunes stretching out over the Saharan horizon. Those wishing to channel Lawrence of Arabia should note that Morocco is well geared to the needs of desert tourism.

With 13.5 million Moroccans living in the country's rural areas and 44 percent of the workforce involved in agriculture, many of Morocco's inhabitants can be seen going about their business in the countryside. Self-sufficient in food production, Morocco's main products are barley, wheat, citrus, wine, vegetables, olives, and livestock. Recent economic reforms, including the $2-billion National Initia-tive for Human Development (INDH) introduced by King Mohamed VI in 2005, have led to increasingly higher agri-cultural growth rates and a more stable economy in general, despite the global recession and the decline in the price of oil, one of Morocco's main exports. Morocco's entrance into a free trade agreement with the United States in 2006 and the advanced status granted it by the European Union in 2008 have also boosted Morocco's economic prospects.

Morocco is a captivating country and its people are welcoming and hospitable. Whether you wish to go hiking in the mountains or the Sahara, indulge in water sports off the coast, mix with locals in the spice-scented souks, take a safari to the oases, study archaeological treasures, or relax in a spa, in a gourmet restaurant, or on a golf course, the Morocco of today will meet every visitor's need. ∎

At the center of the medina is its spiritual heart, the grand mosque.

Morocco's Cultural & Religious Festivals

The Moroccan festival calendar includes both traditional agricultural festivals, which celebrate harvests, and religious festivals known as *moussems*, but visitors can also attend music concerts and displays of horsemanship called *fantasias*. All provide a great way of interacting with local communities.

Gnaoua musicians perform atop Essaouira's ramparts during the summer music festival.

Ramadan is perhaps the best known Muslim religious festival. It lasts for a full month, the ninth according to the lunar calendar (which means the dates of Ramadan vary each year according to calendars based on solar movements), and is a time of reflection and prayer. During Ramadan, participating Muslims fast and refrain from indulgences between dawn and sunset.

Other major religious festivals include Aïd el Seghir, which takes place at the end of Ramadan, when Muslims celebrate the breaking of their fast; Aïd el Kebir, known as the "grand festival," which marks the culmination of the Hajj, the annual pilgrimage to Mecca; Ashorou,

a celebration of music, when people in villages throughout the country gather to feast and dance; and Aïd el Mawlid, which commemorates the birth of the Prophet Muhammad.

In addition to these countrywide events, many cities, towns, and villages also have their own religious festivals. These moussems are held in honor of a local saint or holy man and usually take the form of a pilgrimage, with people coming from miles around to pay homage at the tomb of the honored individual. Days of festivities follow.

Moussems

Hundreds of moussems take place every

year. Some are small and welcome just a handful of pilgrims, while others are large-scale, boisterous affairs that may be celebrated with a national holiday. Among the largest of these are the Moussem of Sidi Ben Aissa in Meknès (see sidebar below); the Moussem of the Regraga, which passes through several provinces, including Essaouira; and the Moussem of the Wax Candle in Salé, which focuses on the Grand Mosque. Others include the Moussem of Sidi Muhammad Ma el Aïnin in Tan-Tan, the Moussem of Moulay Abdallah ibn Brahim in Ouezzane, and the Moussem of Moulay Idriss II in Fès, which takes the form of a tribute to the city's founder.

On July 20 each year, the Feast of the Throne celebrates the day when King Mohamed VI came to the throne in 1999. The Royal Palace hosts receptions for dignitaries, while families gather, feast, and dance in towns and villages all across the country. Traditionally it is a day when the King addresses the people and the country unites.

Moroccans also celebrate harvests, both generally and at events dedicated to specific crops. These include the Cotton Festival in Beni Mellal, the Rose Festival in Ouarzazate, and the summer Cherry Festival in the old walled city of Sefrou, near Fès. There is also a Fig Festival in Bouhouda, near Taounate, and several that acclaim the success of the country's honey production industry; one of the largest is the Honey Festival in Imouzzer des Ida Ou Tanane, near Agadir. In October hundreds of riders, dressed in their finery, take part in the Tissa horse fantasia.

Music & Film Festivals

Musical festivals showcase various genres from jazz, opera, religious, and classical music to modern rock and electro sounds. One of the largest festivals is the Boulevard des Jeunes Musiciens, held over four days every year in Casablanca, when concerts are put on by both local and visiting musicians. Essaouira rocks to the Gnaoua Music Festival every summer. *Gnaoua* music is characterized by its upbeat drum and castanet *(garagab)* sounds and originated in the sub-Saharan region of Africa. In Tanger, jazz musicians are brought together for the Tanjazz International Festival, and in Fès the World Festival of Sacred Music is held over a week each summer. The annual International Mediterranean Film Festival in Tétouan each spring showcases little-known films in the vintage cinemas (including Cinema Espanol) for which the city is famed.

Festivals, whether religious or cultural, are a time when the people of Morocco come together to reflect, honor, and enjoy.

EXPERIENCE: Moussem of Sidi Ben Aissa

Most of Morocco's moussems are relatively quiet events, but others take on the air of a music and dance festival. The largest is the Moussem of Sidi Ben Aissa (see www.worldreviewer.com/destination/west-morocco/), which commemorates the founder of the ancient Aissoua Sufi Brotherhood in Meknès and is centered on the city's place el Hedime.

Most moussems are held in the summer to coincide with harvest festivals, but the Moussem of Sidi Ben Aissa takes place in spring. The square in Meknès is transformed with conical white tents that host jugglers and illusionists. Between the tents, riders on horseback fire guns into the air. While it may all look rather chaotic, it is very well organized.

During the moussem, musicians play traditional tunes, dancers perform folkloric dances, and souks sell all manner of crafts. The party atmosphere of the event offers the rare opportunity to mingle, relax, laugh, and dance with locals.

Food & Drink

Morocco's delicious and often fiery cuisine has been shaped by the country's long history of colonization. Its classic dishes have their roots in Berber, Moorish, and Arabic cuisine—using herbs and spices, nuts, dried fruits, raisins, olives, honey, and citrus fruits—but they also bear other influences. The result is a heady concoction of flavors, textures, and colors.

The staple ingredient of most dishes is meat, typically beef, lamb, or chicken, usually cooked in an unhurried fashion until it's tender enough to "melt" in the mouth. Increasingly fish and seafood are also finding their way into Moroccan cuisine and may be served grilled or in a *tajine*. Be sure to try the oysters from Oualidia (see p. 65), which are considered a delicacy and feature on the menus of many top restaurants. The country's Mediterranean climate of mild winters and hot summers ensures that vegetables grow freely and that fruits such as oranges, figs, cherries, and apples are almost always available.

The Main Meal

The main meal of the day is served around midday, except during the month of Ramadan, when Muslims eat and drink only after sunset and before dawn. It can be quite a feast, comprising several courses, so most Moroccans take only a light breakfast. The midday meal typically starts with a selection of hot and cold vegetable salads—such as garlic-marinated eggplant, finely chopped onions, diced cucumbers and tomato, and honey-coated carrots and chickpeas—or a thick soup made with vegetables, meat, and rice. The most famous Moroccan soup is *harira*, a medley of tomatoes, lentils, and rice flavored with coriander, which is traditionally served at the end of the day during the month of Ramadan. Two favorite salads are *chakchuka,* made with tomatoes and green peppers, and *ihzina*, a colorful selection of olives and slices of orange topped with a sprinkling of paprika.

Next up comes a more hearty dish, such as *bstilla*, formed of layers of paper-thin flaky pastry, known as *ouarka*, and filled with meat, eggs, and almonds and dusted with sugar. Alternatively, a hot tajine may be served. This slow-cooked dish of meat, fruits, and vegetables takes its name from the funneled earthenware pot in which it is prepared. Both dishes are flavored with spices such as saffron, turmeric, cumin, and ginger, which are an intrinsic part of the cuisine's Middle Eastern character. For an everyday meal, just one of these dishes will be served, but for a special feast they are likely to form the second and third courses. The main course of a meal will be accompanied by a large helping of couscous, a staple of the Moroccan diet.

A vendor serves myriad dishes at a food stall in the Djemaa el Fna souk, Marrakech.

Glossary of Moroccan Dishes

Beghrir: Pancakes, fried puff pastry

Bocadillos: Baguette sandwiches with meat or fish and salad fillings

Briouats: Triangular pastries with either sweet or savory fillings

Bstilla: Layers of filo pastry filled with poultry, eggs, and almonds

Chakchuka: A salad of tomatoes and green peppers

Chebakyas: Whirls of fried pastry flavored with honey and spices

Couscous: Granules of semolina coated with ground wheat flour

Faqqas: Almond-flavored biscuits

Halwa shebakia: Honey cake

Harira: A thick soup of meat, rice, tomatoes, beans, and lentils

Harsha: Fried semolina bread

Kefta: Meatballs, usually made with lamb

Kefta magawara: A tagine of kefta served with tomatoes and eggs

Kesra: Flat bread

Kseksu bidawi: A delicacy of couscous and seven vegetables, sometimes also served with meat

Lhzina: A salad of olives, orange, and paprika

Ma'amoul: Shortbread filled with nuts and figs

Mechoui: Roasted lamb

Merguez: A spicy lamb sausage

Mezé: A meal comprising many small dishes

Milk pastilla: An almond-and-vanilla-flavored milk pudding

Mrouzia: A sweet lamb dish made from raisins, honey, and almonds

Pastili: A pastry dessert filled with nuts and honey

Rfisa: Chicken and beghrir pancake

Seffa: Sweet couscous with spices and fruit, such as raisins

Sfenj: A dough ball or hoop covered in sugar and honey

Tajine: A slow-cooked dish of meat and vegetables

Zaalouk: A tomato-and-eggplant dish

Bread will also be provided with every meal. Moroccans like to cook several different types, which are often packed with fennel seeds to aid digestion. The best known is the flat bread *kesra*.

While Morocco hasn't really embraced the notion of vegetarian dining, the cuisine's reliance on fresh vegetables, salads, and fruits, as well as breads and couscous, means that there is usually a good choice of dishes available for nonmeat-eaters in restaurants.

Dessert

The main meal will be followed by a tempting array of desserts. Pancakes, biscuits, and delicious pastries crammed with nuts and fruits and drenched in honey are key parts of most meals. Be sure to try *kaab ghzahl*, also known as *cornes de gazelle*, a crescent-shaped pastry containing ground nuts, sugar, orange-flavored water, and cinnamon, or milk *pastilla*, an almond-and-vanilla-flavored milk pudding. Other favorites include *briouats*, small triangular sweet pastries made with almonds and orange, and delicious *chebakyas*, which are whirls of fried pastry, honey, and spices.

A platter of fruits will follow the pastries and conclude the meal. At the same time, you will be offered mint tea, known locally as *thé à la menthe*. Whether dining in a Berber's tent or a top-quality hotel, tea, the most popular drink for Moroccans, will be served with much ritual in small, often elaborately decorated glasses. Making mint tea, the most widely consumed variety, has become something of a national art form. The tea leaves are placed in the pot and covered with boiling water to remove their bitterness. More leaves and sugar are added and left to infuse the water for a few minutes before a small amount of the liquid is poured and tasted. This may be repeated several times until the host is satisfied the tea is perfect. Loose tea can be found in most souks. Moroccans also enjoy coffee. It is always strong and served with milk *(café au lait)*, unless black *(qahwa kahla)* is specifically requested.

Fast Food

Like many countries, Morocco is embracing the notion of fast food, and big international names serving burgers and snacks are becoming commonplace. You'll also find plenty of traditional places turning out homegrown fare, such as kebabs of skewered meat and *bocadillos*—baguette sandwiches filled with salad and meat. Most bazaars have stalls selling freshly baked breads, often flavored with olives, fruit, and spices, or sweet snacks like the almond-flavored biscuits called *faqqas*, dough balls covered in sugar and honey known as *sfenj*, and *halwa shebakia*, a cake made with honey. Food stalls can be found in the souks of all the major towns. For one of the best introductions to Moroccan street food, pay a visit to the place Djemaa el Fna in Marrakech, which becomes a huge open-air eatery every evening, with mesmerizing aromas filling the air.

Alcohol

Observant Muslim Moroccans refrain from consuming alcohol, but a wide choice of beers, spirits, and wines is available to visitors in hotels, restaurants, shops, and supermarkets. Morocco's wine-producing regions (around Fès and Meknès, and to the north of Casablanca and Ouidja) offer some very drinkable red, white, and rosé vintages. Among the most popular wines are Les Trois Domaines Guerrouane (available as both a white and a rosé) and the red Ksar Beni M'Tir. ■

A waiter pours a glass of traditional mint tea in a Moroccan teahouse.

Land & Environment

With lush palm groves, seemingly endless sand dunes, rugged coastlines, soaring mountains, plunging valleys, and winding rivers, the landscape of Morocco—and the flora and fauna it supports—is spectacularly diverse.

Morocco stretches from the Atlantic Ocean to Algeria, and from the Mediterranean Sea to the western Sahara in the south (see sidebar). Large parts of the interior are mountainous, occupied by the mighty Rif Mountains, which stretch across the north of Morocco east of Tanger and Tétouan, and the High and Middle Atlas ranges, which have been occupied by Berber tribes for millennia and run from southwest to northeast. Southern Morocco is characterized by huge expanses of formidable desert, interspersed by rivers that support fertile growing areas on their banks and oases thick with palm trees.

The Sahara

The western Sahara, to the south of Morocco, is a land of endless sand dunes that supports very few human inhabitants. The indigenous population of the area is the Sahrawis, a tribal people with a Berber-Arab nomadic Bedouin culture. Despite its desolate appearance, the desert is home to a surprisingly wide range of wildlife, including hares, rabbits, hedgehogs, moles, bats, and gazelles, as well as pelicans, ostriches, herons, and shearwaters.

Climate

Morocco's extremely varied topography gives it a particularly mixed climate. Its northernmost region, from Tanger and Tétouan to Oujda, and its Atlantic coast south to Agadir enjoy temperate conditions with temperatures typically reaching around 82°F (28°C) in summer and 64°F (18°C) in winter. Evenings tend to be chilly throughout the year except in the height of summer. The north experiences heavy rainfall, although generally only during the winter months. In sharp contrast, the south is largely dry, arid, and windswept. Inland, the plains and cities such as Fès, Marrakech, and Meknès are scorching hot in summer, but much cooler in winter, when the Atlas ranges can be positively frigid, with subzero temperatures and sometimes heavy snowfall. Don't travel unprepared!

Rif Mountains

At 8,034 feet (2,448 m) high, Mount Tidighine is the highest peak in the Rif mountain range, which forms part of a geological region known as the Gibraltar Arc. The Rif offers a number of lush and fertile landscapes that may surprise anyone expecting Morocco to be largely made up of desert. The high peaks are blanketed in pine forests that rise above the middle-altitude mountains, and in the rainy season, cascades of water tumble into pools. The Jebala district, which is named for a Berber tribe, is one of the best places to see these. The range's lower reaches are crisscrossed by deep gorges that have been created over millions of

Tourists enjoy camel travel in the western Sahara desert near Merzouga.

years (Oued Laou is a particularly good example) and steep valleys sprinkled with almond trees that blaze with pink blossoms each spring.

This region experiences some of Morocco's highest levels of rainfall, which allows a wide range of plants and wildlife to thrive. Its forests contain the only remaining swath of Moroccan fir, as well as dense growths of deciduous holm oak, cork oak, and the large Atlas cedar that can grow to a height of more than 130 feet (40 m). The endangered Barbary macaque makes its home among the pine and cedar forests of the range's middle altitudes. The Rif's lower slopes are blanketed with thick clumps of evergreen pines, including maritime pine and Aleppo pine, which are offset in spring and summer by rich carpets of colorful flowers. In the winter the region is much less verdant, but no less beautiful, with all the peaks, slopes, and plateaus dusted with snow, which accumulates to several feet deep in some places.

Atlas Mountains

Morocco's other mountain range, the Atlas, is divided into the main Middle Atlas and High Atlas ranges, plus the smaller Anti Atlas and Tell Atlas. The latter is known for its dramatic rock formations. Collectively, these peaks stretch from the

Sheep graze in a lush, green valley in the Rif Mountains.

far northeast through the inner core of the country to the southwest. Like the Rif Mountains, the Atlas ranges have their own distinct geography and ecology. The Middle Atlas range, which runs to the west of the High Atlas, is famed for its beautiful lakes, including the almost impossibly gorgeous Aguelmane Sidi Ali. Surrounded by mountains, cedar trees, and rushes and lying at an altitude of some 6,600 feet (2,000 m), the lake supports large populations of trout, salmon, and pike. The plentiful supply of water trickling down from the mountain peaks allows agriculture to thrive, at least in summer. The winter months bring freezing weather and a good deal of snow, which provides a different set of opportunities. One of the largest cities in the region, Ifrane, has in recent times become a popular ski resort.

> **The plentiful supply of water trickling down from the mountain peaks allows agriculture to thrive, at least in summer.**

Despite its sometimes unforgiving climate, the Middle Atlas has a good mix of flora and fauna. It is the domain of wild boar, deer, polecats, and endangered Barbary leopards. In summer, birdsong fills the air. This region is home to one of the largest forests of cedar in the world. Some of the trees, such as the Atlas cedar, are endemic to the region—and protected. Only

when they fall as a result of natural causes can they be used by craftsmen to make the woodcarvings and furniture seen in the cities' souks. This is also where you'll find the celebrated Tazzeka National Park, which lies near Taza. Its forests of cork oak and holm oak, and the habitats created for an abundance of wildlife by its caves, valleys, and lakes, make it one of the most important ecological areas in Morocco.

The High Atlas range extends for some 450 miles (750 km) and boasts scores of peaks higher than any found elsewhere in Morocco or, indeed, in the whole of North Africa. Some of the most notable include l'Ouenkrim and l'Aksoual, the summits of which have been sculpted by nature into a series of long ridges. The range's highest point is the great mass of Jebel Toubkal, 13,675 feet (4,167 m) high and surrounded by the Toubkal National Park. Set among the peaks of the High Atlas are deep valleys flanked by soaring rock faces. The most dramatic of these are the Taghzout and the Aqqa-N'Tazart gorges, which appear as great ravines snaking across the landscape. Perhaps the most beautiful is Aït Bouguemez, a long, narrow valley full of walnut trees that is accessible only in the summer.

The High Atlas is a formidable terrain, and it supports an unparalleled biodiversity. Among its forests of cedar, pine, walnut, oak, and juniper trees live endangered Barbary macaques, Barbary sheep, countless wild boar, and numerous bird species, including woodpeckers, Moussier's redstarts, several species of wheatears, thrushes, warblers, finches, and eagles.

A spectacular waterfall cascades in the Gorges de l'Ouzoud, east of Marrakech.

As might be expected, this enormous mountain range has no single climate. The eastern slopes, which face the desert, are dry and warm, while the western extremity, bordering the Atlantic Ocean, is cooler and fresher, even in summer. In the winter months, the peaks, especially those around Ouarzazate, are covered with snow as the temperatures plummet well below freezing.

Coast & Desert

To the north and south of the mountain ranges, the climate and terrain are quite different. The swath of land lying along Morocco's northern coastline has a Mediterranean climate of hot summers and cool winters. The Atlantic Ocean coast, which runs down the western side of the country, teems with migratory birds. One of the best places to see them is at the picturesque village of Moulay Bousselham, near Rabat, home to the famous Merdja Zerga lagoon and wetland. This was one of the last places where slender-billed curlews—now possibly extinct—were seen in the last years of the 20th century. The region is also renowned for the abundance of migratory birds it attracts during the spring and fall, and for its wintering shorebirds.

In the coastal waters of the Mediterranean Sea and Atlantic Ocean, there is a wealth of marine life. Dolphins and large fish, such as marlins, can often be spotted weaving their way through the warm waters. The fish and seafood caught by the many boats that ply these areas are some of the best in Morocco. Indeed, the oysters hauled ashore are considered nothing short of legendary.

In southern Morocco lie plateaus of scrubland and pre-Saharan steppes, beyond which are the often hostile sands of the western Sahara desert itself. Enlivening the landscape are oases of palm trees with bunches of bright orange fruit and other lush vegetation. Golden jackals, dorcas gazelles, and houbara bustards are among the inhabitants of this challenging environment.

Environmental Concerns

In the last ten thousand years, Morocco's environment has undergone some profound changes. Some of these are entirely natural. The savanna that once blanketed much of the area has now largely disappeared as a consequence of an ongoing process of desertification that began at the end of the last ice age. Population increase, however, has also put tremendous pressure on the land. A combination of overgrazing (particularly during dry periods), overhunting, deforestation (and consequent soil erosion), and the diversion of natural watercourses for agricultural irrigation has taken its environmental toll on the land and led to the disappearance of a number of native species, including the Barbary lion, and put many more on the endangered list. ■

Saving the Northern Bald Ibis

With its bald head, scruffy bronze-green plumage, and long down-curved beak, the northern bald ibis is not one of the world's most attractive birds—but it is one of the rarest. Because 95 percent of the world population of 500 lives in Souss Massa National Park north of Agadir, a particular conservation onus fell on Morocco, and the country rose to the challenge. In the 1990s, scientists studied the behavior of the ibises, locals were recruited to discourage disturbance by people and predators, and drinking water was provided for the thirsty birds. Although the species is still considered critically endangered, there was an increase in breeding numbers—now up to about 100 pairs—in the decade leading up to 2008.

History

With its imperial cities, palaces, souks, mosques, and ancient sites, Morocco is a living museum that offers tantalizing glimpses into a rich history. Some believe the country is referred to in ancient Greek mythology as Atlas, after the god of the same name. What is certain is that this land has been inhabited since antiquity by the Berber people.

Phoenician colonizers, followed in turn by the Romans, Byzantines, Islamic settlers, and Europeans, all left a distinct legacy that helped shape the country we see today. Though there have been power struggles over the centuries—between Berber tribes and Arabs, the dynastic sultans and kings, the native population and European invaders—present-day Morocco is a largely united state.

Ancient History

Archaeological evidence suggests that Morocco has been inhabited since at least Paleolithic times. The first settlers, known as the Capsian people, arrived between 10,000 and 6000 B.C., shortly after the end of the last ice age. The enormous climatic change that melted the glaciers of Europe had profound effects on North Africa. Rainfall declined dramatically and the Sahara, until then a fairly lush environment, began to dry out and become the great expanse of desert it is today. The vast Sahara and the Atlas Mountains effectively cut off a huge swath of northwest Africa from the rest of the continent, forming a region that the Arabs would later call the Maghreb, meaning "farthest west" or "place of sunset." In the post-ice-age period, the landscape was largely made up of grassy savanna, especially along the coastal plains, which proved to be extremely fertile and ideal for the cultivation of crops and the rearing of cattle.

> Though there have been power struggles over the centuries . . . present-day Morocco is a largely united state.

It is from these earliest inhabitants that the Berber people are believed to have descended. Mostly they inhabited the coastal areas across North Africa and evolved into different tribes. Collectively known as the Imazighen peoples (Imazighen is the plural of Amazigh), their name may be derived from a word for "free men" or "nobles," which suggests that they may well have been nomads who subsequently joined to form settled tribes. They originally inhabited most of the land that makes up present-day Morocco, although over time they began to congregate in the mountainous regions as a precaution against marauding foreign invaders.

When the Phoenicians arrived around 1000 B.C. and began colonizing the country, Morocco began to absorb cultural influences from its close Mediterranean neighbors. The Phoenicians had spent several centuries building up an extensive power base in the Mediterranean before Morocco caught their eye. They saw it as a gateway from Europe

Berbers are thought to be descendants of the ancient Caspian people.

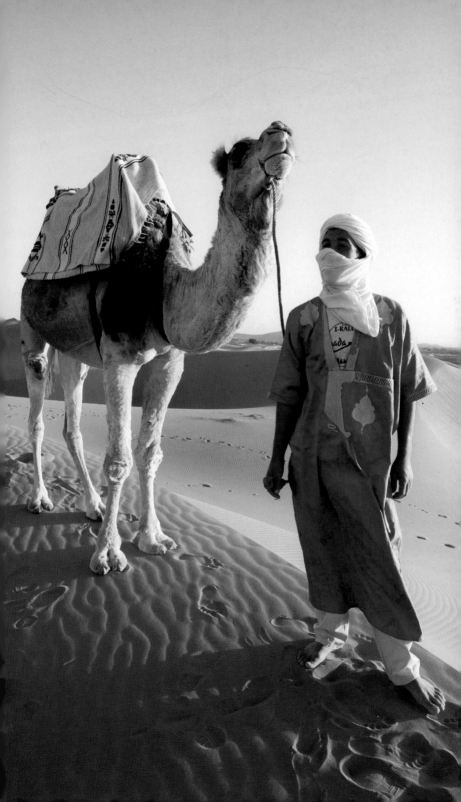

The ruins of the basilica at Volubilis, one of the best preserved Roman sites in Morocco

into Africa and began establishing trading centers for ore and salt along the coastal plains and in the mouths of the country's many rivers. Trading links were formed with other countries, and industries such as ironworking were introduced, bringing prosperity to the country.

This, in turn, spurred the creation of a number of new cities, including Chellah on the banks of the Oued Bou Regreg river, just south of present-day Rabat, and Liks (or Lixus) on the Mediterranean coast at the point where the Oued Loulous river meets it. Today this ancient city is known as Larache. The largest of all the Phoenician cities in Morocco was Mogador on the site of present-day Essaouira on the Atlantic coast. Protected by an island from the strong winds that blow off the ocean, Mogador was seen as a safe harbor for the Phoenicians' fleet. Though Phoenician power grew, the Berbers had not been entirely usurped and remained largely safe from incursions in their remote mountain hideaways. Indeed, by around 400 B.C. Berber tribes had established affiliations with the rulers in Carthage, the Phoenician capital, near Tunisia's present-day capital of Tunis, and had begun uniting to form kingdoms, including what was to become the powerful Kingdom of Mauretania.

The power of Carthage reached its peak in the fourth century B.C. when it was probably the richest city in the entire Mediterranean region. However, decline followed swiftly thereafter. The Carthaginian empire would come under increasing pressure over the next couple of centuries, first from the Greeks and then—and much more seriously—

from the new great force of the region, the Romans. In 146 B.C., following a series of conflicts, the Romans defeated the Phoenicians and razed Carthage.

Roman & Byzantine Era

As the Kingdom of Mauretania—and the Moroccan lands it contained—grew in strength from its new trading partnerships with settlements around the Mediterranean, it began attracting Rome's attention, with inevitable consequences.

Contrary to their modern warlike reputation, the Romans built their empire as much through negotiation as conflict. For example, having conquered the Berber kingdom of Numidia (which covered present-day Algeria and Tunisia), the Romans brought its young heir, Juba II (46 B.C.–A.D. 23), to Rome to be educated and allowed him to rule neighboring Mauretania as a client-king.

Berber by birth, Juba II was a prolific scholar and author of history, art, and geography books, as well as a loyal ally of Rome. Indeed, his wife and queen was Cleopatra Selene II, daughter of the famous Roman Mark Antony and Cleopatra VII of Egypt. Together, Juba II and his queen helped to develop the region's sciences and performing arts and are considered key figures in the ancient history of Morocco. The couple are entombed in the Royal Mausoleum of Mauretania near Algiers in Algeria.

In A.D. 23 Juba II died, leaving the kingdom to his son Ptolemy. When Ptolemy died in A.D. 40, the Romans divided it into two provinces: Mauretania Caesariensis, centered more or less on modern-day Algeria, and Mauretania Tingitana, which contained much of what is now northern Morocco, as well as Volubilis near Meknès, parts of the south, and the future Spanish cities of Ceuta and Melilla on its Mediterranean coast. They maintained their power in Mauretania Tingitana not through military force, but by drawing on their good relations with the Berber tribes, and delegated much of the day-to-day responsibility for running the province to Berber leaders.

This policy of delegation meant that, although they were the province's official overlords, the Romans kept a rather low-key presence there, largely leaving the Berber tribes alone. They founded just a handful of outposts, known as *coloniae*, in their new province, mostly on the coast as the great Rif and Atlas Mountains made access to the interior all but impossible. The most notable were Iulia Campestris Babba, Iulia Constantia Zilil, Iulia

> **As the Kingdom of Mauretania . . . grew in strength . . . it began attracting Rome's attention, with inevitable consequences.**

Velantia Banasa on the southern bank of the Oued Sebou, and Chellah on the Atlantic coast, then known as Sala Colonia, near the site of Rabat.

Nonetheless, the province proved particularly valuable to the Romans, largely because of its strategic location and strong Mediterranean trading links. It exported fruit, pearls, grain, fish, and crafted wooden furniture to other parts of the empire, most notably Italy and Spain. Its coinage was also highly sought after in Europe. Its most important export, however, was a purple dye harvested from shellfish that thrived in its waters, which was used for making ceremonial garments manufactured in Europe. Mauretania Tingitana's capital, Tingis, became a major trading center for the dye. Tingis would eventually evolve into the present-day city of Tanger.

One of the most significant legacies of the Roman period was the introduction of Christianity. In addition to adopting the culture and traditions of the Roman Empire, the communities of Mauretania Tingitana were steadily converted to Christianity from the early third century A.D. onward. The new religion spread rapidly, and by the end of the fourth century, much of the population, other than the substantial Jewish communities, were Christians, including many members of the Berber tribes.

In the fifth century, Morocco was invaded and conquered by the East Germanic tribes, the Visigoths and the Vandals. Their rule was short-lived, however, and they were swiftly removed from power in 540 by the Greek-speaking Byzantines, whose influence had grown in the Mediterranean following the collapse of the Western Roman Empire. Each of the new colonizing groups concentrated its presence on Morocco's coastal areas, which was fortuitous for the Berber tribes who continued to live peacefully in its mountainous interior.

The Introduction of Islam

The country's history changed course again from the late seventh century onward as Arab conquerors swept into Morocco, bringing with them the new religion of Islam. The population soon began to convert, although for the Berbers this was often a slow process. At first the tribes were reluctant to accept the new belief system, but over time began to embrace it, although they retained many of their own traditions and laws.

Still, Islam proved a good deal more durable than many of the Arab rulers who introduced it. The initial advances of the Arab armies in the late seventh century saw them take control of much of Morocco's northern coastal areas, where they set about creating new communities. Over time these grew to become important kingdoms. However, the Berbers did not take kindly to their new overlords, and in 683 the Arabs were forced out of the country by the Berber chieftain Qusayla. A second period of Arab rule, beginning around 710, fared better, lasting until 740, when the Berbers once again rebelled and the Arab leaders were again forced to flee.

> The country's history changed course again from the late seventh century onward as Arab conquerors swept into Morocco, bringing with them the new religion of Islam.

Idrisid Dynasty

In 788, the country came under the control of Idriss I, who ruled until 791 and founded the Idrisid dynasty. Though his reign proved brief, he is seen by history

The Holy City of Zerhoun (now Moulay Idriss) was founded by Idriss I in the eighth century.

scholars as a key figure in shaping Morocco into an Islamic country. Born in Syria, Idriss I was a direct descendant of the Prophet Muhammad. However, when the Abbasid caliphs sought to eliminate Idriss's family in 787 as rivals to the caliphate, he was forced to flee west, arriving in the ancient city of Walila, site of Roman Volubilis, which was then the home of a Berber tribe, the Awraba. As a descendant of Muhammad (he was the great-great-grandchild of Ali, the Prophet's cousin), Idriss was welcomed by the tribe, who believed him to have divine guidance. He married Kanza, the daughter of the tribal chief, Ishaq ibn Muhammad, and together they had a son who would later succeed him to become the ruler Idriss II (791–828).

It was during the reign of Idriss I that a large swath of northern Morocco was conquered and the city of Fès, not far from Volubilis, was founded. Idriss I's power grew to the point where Morocco felt able to declare itself independent of the governing Abbasid Caliphate, much to the fury of the then caliph, Harun el Rashid. Harun sent an assassin to kill Idriss I, who died from poisoning in 791.

Idriss II was born just months after his father's death, and although he immediately inherited the title of ruler of the Idrisid dynasty, it wasn't until 805, when he was 13 years old, that he was officially declared the king. Until then he was cared for by the Awraba tribe in what proved to be a period of great instability for the country. The young king soon established his rule, however, making Fès the country's new capital, seat of royalty, and commercial hub. In time, Idriss II came to be regarded as a great ruler, uniting the country, increasing its independence, encouraging the spread of Islam, and overseeing a period of growth. Under his reign the population expanded hugely as thousands of refugees from the politically unstable Islamic cities of Córdoba in Spain and Kairouan in Tunisia sought a new life in Morocco.

Islamic Berber Dynasties

Upon the death of Idriss II in 828, his power was divided among his 12 sons. Each ruled a small emirate, which weakened the dynasty and ultimately led to its demise. The ninth and tenth centuries were characterized by factional infighting with various dynasties vying for control, but none was able to establish itself for any significant period of time.

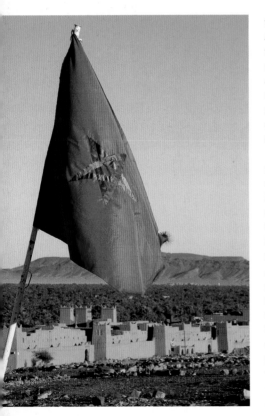

The national flag of Morocco waves over Ksar Zagora, site of an 11th-century fortress.

This instability would be ended in the mid-11th century by the rise of the Almoravids, an Islamic Berber dynasty from the northern Sahara. It oversaw a period of astonishing growth and took around a hundred years to gain dominance over much of North Africa, as well as the areas of present-day Western Sahara, Mauritania, and parts of Spain, Portugal, Algeria, Senegal, and Mali.

The Almoravid dynasty can trace its roots back to the work of a young Muslim missionary and lawyer, Abdallah ibn Yasin. He came from the Sanhaja tribe of the northern Sahara and practiced Sunni Islam, the most popular form of the religion. Encouraged by his chief, Yahia ibn Ibrahim, to take his teachings to the masses, Abdallah ibn Yasin and his followers began preaching to the Berber communities of the western Sahara from around 1054 onward. However, he was forced to retreat back across the desert when the Berbers did not take kindly to the harshness of his proposed regime. Nonetheless, he perse-vered and soon the Berbers were on the march throughout southern and central Morocco. Covering their faces as they rode

Moroccan Timeline

10,000–6000 B.C.	Capsian people arrive in Morocco
1000 B.C.	Phoenicians begin colonizing Morocco's coast
400 B.C.	Berber tribes form Kingdom of Mauretania
A.D. 40	Roman province of Mauretania Tingitana established
5th century	Vandals and Visigoths arrive, ending Roman rule
6th century	Byzantines establish authority over Morocco
7th century	Arab conquests bring Islam to Morocco
788–791	Idriss I founds the first major Islamic dynasty
791–828	Reign of Idriss II
1061	Youssef ibn Tachfin (R. 1061–1106) founds Almoravid dynasty, establishing Marrakech as capital
1145	Start of Almohad dynasty
1195	Marinid dynasty established
1492	Christians conquer Granada, the last Muslim kingdom in Spain, prompting exodus of Andalusian Muslims to Morocco
1554	Under Muhammad ash-Sheikh, the Saadi dynasty takes control of Morocco
1666	Morocco ruled for first time by Alaouite dynasty
1884	Spain creates protectorate in coastal areas of Morocco
1912	Morocco becomes French protectorate under Treaty of Fès, with Spain retaining its coastal possessions
1927	Reign of Sultan Mohamed V begins
1956	French protectorate ends, although Spain retains its enclaves; Mohamed V declared Morocco's first king
1961	Death of King Mohamed V; his son, Hassan II, succeeds him
1973	Algerian-supported Polisario movement formed to create an independent state in Spanish-controlled area of Sahara
1975	Spanish Sahara, now known as Western Sahara, comes under joint Moroccan-Mauritanian control, but Algeria objects and Morocco occupies the territory
1976	War in Western Sahara between Moroccan and Algerian troops, as Morocco and Mauritania divide Western Sahara
1991	Cease-fire in Western Sahara, but control still undecided to this day
1999	King Hassan II dies and is succeeded by his son, Mohamed VI
2007	Morocco submits an autonomy blueprint for Western Sahara to United Nations to which Polisario movement raises objections
2007	Morocco unsuccessfully demands return of Spanish enclaves

The 14th-century Shrine of Moulay Idriss II in Fès

through the desert on their devastating campaigns of war, they became known as "the veiled ones."

From 1061, under Abdallah ibn Yasin and the dynasty's first ruler, Youssef ibn Tachfin (R. 1061–1106), the Almoravids conquered the desert trade route from the Sahara and made headway into the country as far as Adhmet, near the site of present-day Marrakech. In 1062, Marrakech was founded as the Almoravids' capital city. They went on to capture Fès in 1069, Tanger a few years later, and by 1086 had crossed the Mediterranean to take the Spanish cities of Córdoba, Granada, and Seville. The empire, unified by Sunni Islam, continued to grow in size and power, stretching from Barcelona in Spain in the north to deep into the Sahara in the south.

Almohad, Marinid, & Saadian Dynasties

By the 12th century, the Almoravid dynasty was more Andalusian than Moroccan, and as a result of a weakening grasp of power, it was replaced by the Almohad dynasty in 1145 following campaigns by two formidable characters: a religious hard-liner, Ibn Toumart, who was intent on restoring Islamic purity to a country he perceived as having become wayward; and one of his powerful followers, the warrior Abd el Mu'min (1094–1163).

Abd el Mu'min assumed power on the death of Ibn Toumart, establishing one of the greatest dynasties the Maghreb had ever seen. At its peak, all the Moroccan cities of the Almoravid dynasty and much of Muslim Spain, as well as parts of Libya, Algeria, and Tunisia, were under his control. The dynasty lasted well over a hundred years and, through the work of Abd el Mu'min and his successors, the period saw unparalleled social and economic growth. Universities were built, a navy was formed, and an enhanced infrastructure was put in place. This was also a time of great architectural achievements, particularly under the rule of Abd el Mu'min's grandson Yacoub el Mansour, also known as Moulay Yacoub, who oversaw the creation of the great Koutoubia Mosque in Marrakech and the Hassan Tower in Rabat.

Mansour's reign, which ended in 1199, probably marked the high-water mark of Almohad control. However, in the following decades a series of battles weakened the dynasty's grip on power. First, the Battle of Las Navas de Tolosa in 1212 proved the tipping point of the Reconquista, the centuries-long campaign fought by the Christian rulers of the Iberian Peninsula—who at that time included King Alfonso VIII of Castile (1155–1214), King Sancho VIII of Navarre (1157–1234), King Pedro II of Aragon (1178–1213), and King Alfonso II of Portugal (1185–1223)—to claim back their territory and evict the Berber Muslim Almohads from the peninsula. This was followed by a series of battles and tribal uprisings in Africa, leading to the loss of territories and ultimately the fall of the Almohad dynasty.

The Marinid dynasty, which ruled from the late 13th century to the mid-15th century, began from a much lower base than its predecessor. The Almohads' demise had seen their territory divided up, with the Marinids left in charge of Morocco only. Despite this, and the fact that they failed to conquer any new territories, the Marinids' achievements were considerable. Denied the chance of military honors, they concentrated instead on architectural achievements. They built some fabulous structures in Fès, their capital city, including a magnificent royal palace, for which they established an entire new district, Fès el Jedid, just outside the existing city walls to give them more space. Their structure

> **Abd el Mu'min assumed power on the death of Ibn Toumart, establishing one of the greatest dynasties the Maghreb had ever seen.**

had its own fortifications, Koranic schools and universities, souks, parks, and homes, plus a *mechouar*, a huge square designed for ceremonial events. Over time, however, the Marinids gradually saw their power decline until they became a target for other Berber, Arab, and Christian dynasties keen on taking control. First it was the Wattasids, followed by the powerful Saadians, who claimed descent from the Prophet Muhammad and came to power under ruler Sultan Mohamed ash-Sheikh (R. 1554–1557) in the early 16th century. Their period of rule lasted until the mid-17th century, during which time

Morocco successfully defended itself against Ottoman and Portuguese invaders. In 1541, the Portuguese were evicted from Agadir, and they were later conquered in the Battle of the Three Kings near Tanger in 1578.

The Saadians came from Tagmadert in the Drâa Valley, where the city of Taroudant was their capital. But, like their Berber-dynasty predecessors, they soon adopted Marrakech as their seat of government and the hub of their empire. The first sultan to rule from Marrakech was Zidan Abu Maali (R. 1603–1627). Saadian-dynasty rule came to an end in 1659. Tombs dating back to the Almoravid, Almohad, and Saadian dynasties can be seen in Marrakech today.

Alaouite Dynasty

In the 17th century, Morocco came to be ruled by the Alaouite dynasty. Founded by the Sultan of Tafilalt, Moulay Ali Cherif, the dynasty started from an even more lowly position than the Marinids, ruling just the Drâa Valley and southern areas of the country, including the Sahara region. But when Moulay Ali Cherif's son, Moulay el Rashid, succeeded to power, he seized the opportunity to increase the dynasty's power. He took Taza, a city in northern Morocco, and then Fès. Finally, he took Marrakech and the mountains. Alaouite power in Morocco became absolute around 1666. Despite periods of tribal disturbances, the country's unity was largely maintained for the next 150 years.

Nationalist unrest increased after World War II, eventually resulting in the reinstatement of an independent Morocco in 1956.

In the 19th century, the Maghreb once again caught the eye of European powers. The Portuguese and French attempted to take control of large swaths of North African territory, including Morocco. The country's eastern neighbor Algeria fell to the French in 1830 and, although Morocco managed to retain its independence, it was a time of great unrest. In 1859–1860, a simmering dispute over Ceuta, an enclave on Morocco's coast that Spain had long held as an autonomous territory, erupted. Spain declared war, seizing further territory around Ceuta as well as Tétouan, another city on Morocco's Mediterranean coast. In 1884, Spain created a protectorate of its coastal areas of Morocco.

France also kept up its interest in (and pressure on) Morocco, which eventually resulted in the establishment of a French protectorate in the country in 1912, under the terms of the Treaty of Fès, which allowed Spain to retain control of its coastal areas. The protectorate lasted through the reign of Sultan Yusef (1882–1927) and into that of Sultan Mohamed V (1927–1961), who was later forced into exile. Both men, however, found their roles were now subordinate to that of the governor, appointed directly by France. French rule brought its benefits, including a massive program of infrastructure improvement, which saw new roads and railways built and entire new towns, known as villes nouvelles, created alongside the city's old medinas. But it was hugely resented by the native population, particularly the Berbers, who fought a long campaign of resistance.

Nationalist unrest increased after World War II, eventually resulting in the reinstatement of an independent Morocco in 1956. Mohamed V was brought back from exile and declared king to great popular acclaim—this period would become known as "the

King Hassan II (center right) on a visit to France—ties between the countries remain strong.

Revolution of the King and the People" (in Arabic, *Taourat el malik wa shaab*) and is celebrated on August 20 each year. In 1961, King Mohamed V died. He was succeeded by his son, King Hassan II (1929–1999), who went on to become the Arab world's longest serving monarch.

The 1970s witnessed the formation of the Algerian-supported Polisario movement, which sought to create an independent state in the formerly Spanish-controlled area of Western Sahara. Extensive negotiation resulted in the area coming under the joint control of Morocco and Mauritania. When Algeria objected, Morocco occupied the territory. War erupted between Moroccan and Algerian troops, before Morocco and Mauritania proposed that they divide Western Sahara between them. Although a ceasefire was eventually declared in 1991, the status of the region remains unresolved.

Today Morocco is ruled by King Mohamed VI, who is a direct descendant of the Alaouite dynasty's founders. During his reign, the King has addressed human rights issues under the commission Instance Equité et Réconciliation and has overseen negotiations for free trade agreements with the European Union and the United States. He has immense power and can call and dissolve parliament, as well as create new laws. One such law, the Mudawana, came into effect in 2004, giving more rights to women. He has also made commitments to address many of the other problems facing modern Morocco, such as poverty, corruption, and illiteracy, and the conditions of those living in the country's many slums. ■

The Arts

From literature and theater to films and music, not to mention indigenous crafts such as ceramics, copperwork, and leatherwork, Morocco has a vibrant artistic heritage. The modern arts scene boasts influences dating back to ancient Berber times, which have been added to and augmented over the centuries by Arabic, French, and Spanish traditions.

Literature

Of all the arts, Moroccan literature is perhaps the one with the richest tradition, drawing on a long history of scholars and poets writing in Arabic. Moroccan writers first gained recognition during the great learning periods of the Almoravid and Almohad dynasties from the 11th to 13th centuries. This era saw writers emerging through two principal channels: from within the palaces of the sultans, who were keen to promote high levels of learning and culture within their courts, and, perhaps more remarkably, from the general populace of Morocco and Andalusia.

The Andalusian-Arab Ibn Bajjah (1095–1138) was one of the most noted writers of the period. A respected astronomer, philosopher, and scholar of mathematics and medicine, he worked in the offices of the Almoravid administration. Although few examples of his work have survived, he is credited with greatly influencing the understanding of physics and astronomy in early Islamic dynasties.

Qadi Ayyad ibn Musa (1083–1149) was a contemporary of Ibn Bajjah, and one of the most famous and prolific scholars of the Sunni Islam school of Maliki law. Such was his influence, especially in the city of Marrakech, that the University of Marrakech (the Qadi Ayyad) is now named after him. The university, along with museums such as the Musée Dar el Batha in Fès and the Musée de Marrakech, has exhibits of early works by Qadi Ayyad and his fellow writers. Books from the period tended to be leather-bound and embossed or decorated with gold.

The Almohad dynasty promoted learning not just among serious scholars but also for the masses. It was during this period that the great Koutoubia Mosque in Marrakech

Street theater group from Salé performing in the streets of Rabat

Literary Milestones

- **12th century:** *Hayy ibn Yaqdhan,* the first Arabic novel, is written in Moroccan-controlled Spain by the philosopher and physician Ibn Tufail.
- **1377:** Ibn Khaldoun's historical record, the *Muqaddimah,* is published. It is considered one of the pioneering works of the philosophy of history and economic theory.
- **18th century:** *El Hawd (The Reservoir)* by Muhammad Awzal is believed to be the first published Berber-language work.
- **1980:** Leila Abouzeid publishes *Aam al-Fil (Year of the Elephant),* one of the first novels published in Arabic by a Moroccan woman, about the aftermath of colonialism, independence, and the changing position of women in Moroccan society.

American author and composer Paul Bowles (left) exercises with Moroccan author and artist Mohammed Mrabet (whose works Bowles translated).

was built, with a library capable of holding around 25,000 books and manuscripts. Sultan Abu Yaqub Yusuf is credited with founding one of the first public libraries, spearheading a program of building schools and universities, and sponsoring the education of poor scholars. The philosophers Ibn Rushd (1126–1198), known in Europe as Averroes and seen as one of the greatest thinkers of his generation, and Ibn Tufail (1105–1185), who is best known for his novel *Hayy ibn Yaqdhan*, were two of the most prominent writers to emerge at this time.

In the 12th century, the University of Fès, also known as El Qarawiyyan University, became a center for the development of literature, while the Bou Inania Medersa, also in Fès and built to complement the university, was erected on the orders of Sultan Abu Inan during the reign of the Marinids. It provided both an education and a cultural and religious grounding for the many resident scholars and became one of the most highly esteemed universities in the country.

Noted scholars from Fès include the North African polymath, astronomer, and historian Ibn Khaldoun (1332–1402), a pioneer of modern economics. He is best known for his magnum opus, the *Muqaddimah*, published in 1377, which is a pioneering work on the philosophy of history and the rise and fall of civilizations. Other scholars of the period include the Berber Muslim academic and prolific travel writer Abu Abdullah Muhammad ibn Abdullah el Lawati el Tanji ibn Battuta, also known more simply as Ibn Battuta (1304–1368), whose works on travel included *Rihla (Journey)*. His life, which took him as far afield as China, India, and the Maldives, as well as throughout Africa and Spain, formed the basis of the 2009 film *Journey to Mecca*.

In the 16th and 17th centuries, Moroccan literature was given a boost by the Saadian ruler Ahmed el Mansour, who proudly published works by his court of poets. More libraries were opened under the Saadian dynasty, most notably at Taroudant, and works in the Berber language were pioneered by Muhammad Awzal, a 17th-century religious poet. He wrote *El Hawd (The Reservoir)*, which is believed to be the first Berber-language work.

Modern Moroccan literature took off in the 20th century, as educated Moroccans came into contact with modern European literary genres and techniques, giving a new impetus to Moroccan fiction, poetry, and drama. In the 1950s, when the sociopolitical scene changed dramatically following independence and centers of education were founded alongside traditional schools, Moroccan writers came increasingly to the fore and began to be known beyond the country's borders. Indeed, international names in litera-ture and film soon came flocking to Morocco, seeking inspi-ration. Among the big names of the period were Muhammad Choukri (1935–2003), who is best known for his two-volume autobiographical work *For Bread Alone* (1987) and *Streetwise* (1996). Both were written in Arabic but have been widely translated. His contemporaries included Driss Chraibi (1926–2007), whose most famous work is the French-language novel *Le Passé Simple (The Simple Past)*, published in 1954; Tahar ibn Jelloun (b. 1944), who wrote *L'Enfant de Sable (The Sand Child)*, published in 1988; Muhammad Berrada (b. 1938), whose work *The Game of Forgetting* was published in 1996; and the novelist Mohamed Zafzaf (1942–2001), after whom one of Morocco's most prestigious literary awards is named. Among his works is the award-winning 1990s novel *The Rooster Egg*.

> **The most famous cinematic repre-sentation of the country, *Casablanca*, was fictitious, . . . having been filmed entirely on a Hollywood sound stage.**

Of the international literary elite to be inspired by Morocco, Paul Bowles (1910–1999) is one of the most prominent. The American writer and musician first visited Tanger in 1947 and was so captivated by what he saw that he stayed for the next 52 years until his death. He is best known for his critically acclaimed work *The Sheltering Sky*, published in 1949 and set in North Africa. Many Moroccan literary works have been adapted for cinema and theater and are celebrated at festivals, such as the Amazigh Theatre Festival in Casablanca.

Cinema

As international air travel became more widely available in the second half of the 20th century, Morocco's majestic, sweeping sand dunes and raucous, chaotic medi-nas began drawing more and more foreign filmmakers. The most famous cinematic representation of the country, *Casablanca*, was fictitious, however, having been filmed entirely on a Hollywood sound stage in 1942. But films seem to have a way of creating their own reality. There may not have been a "Rick's Café Américain" in World World II Casablanca, but there are plenty of them now. One of the earliest genuine portrayals of the country came a few years later, in 1949, when Orson

(continued on p. 50)

Moroccan Architecture

Over the past thousand years, there have been two principal influences on Moroccan architecture: Islam (Morocco's architecture forms part of a wider Islamic tradition), and the tastes of its rulers, be they native dynasties or colonial overlords.

It was the Almoravids, whose empire encompassed Andalusia in Spain, who first introduced the decorative plasterwork and arches of Moorish architecture to Morocco in the 11th century. Their successors, the Almohads, also favored the Spanish style, but were perhaps more concerned with scale, overseeing the construction of a series of monumental structures, including Marrakech's Koutoubia Mosque and the Grand Mosque in Salé. This building spree was supposed to culminate in the construction of the world's second largest mosque (after Mecca's) in Rabat in the late 12th century. But the death of the scheme's patron, Sultan

Yacoub el Mansour, put an end to the project and the mosque was never built.

One of the most distinctive features of the towns and cities built in Morocco in the Middle Ages is their impressive fortifications. Almost every urban settlement of importance boasted thick walls encircling a kasbah (fortress), which could only be entered through a small number of ornamental gates known as *bâbs*. Some of the finest examples of these gates can be found in Rabat (Bâb Oudïaa) and Meknès (Bâb Mansour).

Palaces & Mosques

As dynastic power became entrenched, however, the royal families turned their attention from military to domestic architecture, erecting enormous palaces designed to inspire awe in all who entered them. The Marinids were the first to indulge in palace construction on a major scale. Deciding that their capital, Fès, was too small for their purposes, they had an entire new town, Fès el Jedid, laid out for their palace complex in the 13th century. Of course, the royals also made sure they offset all their schemes of personal aggrandizement with acts of religious devotion, ordering the construction of mosques in Fès, Mèknes, Marrakech, and Salé.

The early Moroccan dynasties controlled great empires, the spoils from which largely paid for their lavish building projects. But as the power of the later dynasties shrank, so too did their architectural ambitions. There was the odd flurry of construction here and there, particularly in the late 17th century under the Saadians (the highlight being the El Badi palace in Marrakech) and in the early 18th century when the Alaouite sultan Moulay Ismail adorned his capital, Meknès, with many fine buildings,

Minarets

Minarets are distinctive crowned columns that form a key feature of all mosques. Moroccan mosques usually boast a single minaret that is square with four equal sides, a major exception being the octagonal minaret of the mosque in Chefchaouene. This contrasts with the rest of the Muslim world, where minarets often have a conical or bulbous "onion" shape. Minarets have a gallery that provides a platform from where Muslims are called to prayer five times a day: at dawn, midday, mid-afternoon, sunset, and night. Notable Moroccan minarets include the tower of the Koutoubia Mosque in Marrakech, the highest building in the city, which was built by the Almohads in 1150–1190, and the Hassan II Mosque in Casablanca, which has the tallest minaret in the world, standing 689 feet (210 m) high.

Le Jardin Majorelle in Marrakech: modern architecture influenced by mosque curves and patterns

including a palace, stables, and more than 25 miles (40 km) of walls. Generally, however, the sultans of the 18th and 19th centuries were too busy fending off the incursions of acquisitive foreign powers to match the artistic endeavors of their illustrious predecessors.

Modern Influences

The next major influence on Moroccan architecture occurred in the early 20th century during the first decades of the French protectorate. The French set about a massive program of urban renewal creating *villes nouvelles* (new towns) alongside the traditional medinas in towns and cities across the country. Most of these were designed in a Hispano-Moorish style, although in the 1930s a form of Moroccan art deco emerged that proved particularly popular in Casablanca. Indeed Casablanca has been the site of numerous architectural innovations over the past 50 years, culminating in the creation of the massive Hassan II Mosque in the 1990s. Among Marrakech's exciting new buildings are the Banque Commerciale du Maroc (Abdeirahim Sijelmassi, 1985), Douar Ahiad housing development (Charles Boccara, 1992), and Marrakech Airport's Terminal 1 (CR Architects, 2008).

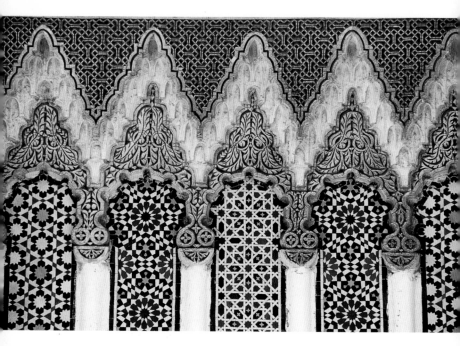

Intricate Moroccan zellij mosaic tilework

Welles filmed his version of *Othello* in the ports of Essaouira, Safi, and El Jadida. The film went on to win the Palme d'Or prize at the Cannes Film Festival under the Moroccan flag. This was followed by a number of other Hollywood projects, including Alfred Hitchcock's *The Man Who Knew Too Much* (1955), starring James Stewart, which featured scenes filmed in Marrakech's medina; the 1962 classic *Lawrence of Arabia*, starring Peter O'Toole, Omar Sharif, and the country's dramatic stretches of desert; and *The Man Who Would Be King* (1975), starring Sean Connery and Michael Caine, in which Morocco stood in for Afghanistan. Morocco provided the scenic backdrop for the 1985 blockbuster *The Jewel of the Nile*, starring Michael Douglas and Kathleen Turner, as well as Ridley Scott's Oscar-winning *Gladiator* (2000), in which some scenes were filmed in Ouarzazate.

Morocco's domestic film industry took a little longer to get off the ground, with the first full-length feature films not appearing until the late 1960s. While foreign directors concentrated on showcasing the country's exoticism, Moroccan filmmakers focused more on contemporary social issues. Notable releases include 1975's *El Chergui (The Violent Silence)*, which tackled such issues as polygamy and women's rights; *Alyam Alyam (Oh the Days*, 1978), a study of peasant life; and *Le Coiffeur du Quartier des Pauvres (The Hairdresser from a Poor District*, 1982). In 2009, director Bruce Neilbur made the fascinating, award-winning documentary *Journey to Mecca*, which traced the story of Ibn Battuta, who undertook a perilous hajj, a pilgrimage to the city of Mecca, in 1325. Morocco hosts a number of international film festivals, including Marrakech's International Film Festival and the International Mediterranean Film Festival of Tétouan.

Theater

Theater has been deep rooted in the culture of Morocco since the ancient days of the shadow theater when itinerant puppet-show performers would travel from town to town. Traditional Moroccan theater is known as *halqa* (meaning "the circle") and takes the form of spontaneous, impromptu open-air performances, put on wherever and whenever an audience (which forms the circle implied by the name) can be found and often comprising comedy, tragedy, music, and dancing.

Though outdoor performances of halqa are still given—there's a famous halqa stage in place Djemaa el Fna in Marrakech—modern Moroccan theater increasingly follows Western traditions with most shows now taking place inside purpose-built venues. Here you can also see *bsat*, a form of comic, satirical theater made popular in the 18th and 19th centuries, as well as performances of Shakespeare and adaptions of modern international literary works.

There are theaters in all the major cities, and new venues are being planned as the Moroccan administration continues to encourage the development of theatrical culture. The new CasaArt complex in Casablanca's place Mohamed V, which is due to be completed in 2015, will encompass an area of some 6 acres (25,000 sq m), making it the largest theater in Africa and the Arab world.

Traditional Crafts

Morocco is rightly famous for its traditional crafts, especially those using stone, wood, plaster, metal, clay, and leather. The skills required to carve handmade furniture, work motifs into leather, or cast intricate patterns in ironwork have been passed from generation to generation—and the results can be seen in souks and on the exteriors of buildings in every town and city. Three crafts that have been incorporated into the fabric of Moroccan towns are intricately crafted woodwork, carved plasterwork, and *zellij* mosaic tilework, featuring zigzags, triangles, squares, and stylized animals and birds, on great mosques and small homes alike. ∎

The Art of Carpet Weaving

Carpet weaving is a traditional craft practiced throughout Morocco, but the styles and techniques can differ greatly between the regions. Carpets made by Berber tribes are usually long with simplistic geometric designs and are often fringed, while those made in Casablanca and Rabat, for example, are more intricate and symmetrically patterned. In Marrakech, carpets are usually knotted to create highly colorful patterns. Weaving a carpet is a time-consuming exercise. Typically, women will wash the wool and then untangle and align the threads with a pronged instrument rather like a comb. This process is known as carding. The wool is then spun into yarn, dyed, and woven on a loom. Most looms take the form of a square frame, onto which vertical strands (the warp) are densely threaded to the size of the intended finished carpet. Wool is then either knotted around the warp or threaded horizontally by hand. As each line is completed, it is pressed down tightly with a comb. You will find weavers at work around the souks in any major city. In Marrakech, visit the Moulay Hfid Weaving Association (*2nd Floor, Fondouk Moulay Hfid, Essebtiyne*) to see carpets being made.

Big, brash, and always on the move, Morocco's most cosmopolitan face, laced with some places of real tranquility

Casablanca & the Coast

The Hassan II Mosque dominates the skyline.

Casablanca & the Coast

Casablanca is a city that thrills you the moment you see it. Whether viewed from the window of a plane or the deck of a cruise ship, its sprawling skyline stretches as far as the eye can see and will capture your imagination and entice you into exploring its streets, squares, and structures which can, at times, even overpower the senses.

Casablanca is a city of huge contrasts. This historic and yet cosmopolitan city and port is the financial, industrial, and commercial hub of Morocco. It is the largest city in Morocco, with a population of over 3.6 million. It is second in stature only to the country's governmental capital Rabat. Major names from around the world adorn offices and factories in the city, while its port—through which everything from grains to textiles are traded—is the largest in North Africa and a leading port of the world.

Each of the city's eight administrative districts has its own vibe. In the west is the relatively peaceful Anfa, a residential area where many of Casablanca's wealthier inhabitants live; near the center are the bustling areas of downtown, including the busy intersection of place des Nations Unies, the nearby medina, Mers Sultan, Ben Slimane, and to the northeast, the industrial port area at Sidi Belyout. South of downtown is the Quartier des Habous, home to the new city (ville nouvelle) built by the French in the 1930s in imitation of local architectural styles.

Casablanca, which originated as a small Berber settlement in the seventh century, today has an architectural mix that suits its status as one of Africa's most cosmopolitan and influential cities. High-rise buildings, such as its twin business center towers, define the city, along with its mosques, its neo-Moorish homes, and its sprawling working-class districts (bidonvilles). Another reminder of the city's variety is its Jewish Museum, probably the only one in the Islamic world.

Add to this vibrant mix top-class hotels and trendy restaurants along elegant, palm-tree-lined boulevards radiating from huge squares, beaches such as those at the holiday resort of Aïn Diab, vast areas of parkland, and lanes ripe for exploration and you have a city of immense variety. All this can be enjoyed in a Mediterranean climate with little seasonal variation. It is comfortably warm in summer and relatively mild in winter.

Along the Coast

If you visit Casablanca, don't stop your exploration at the city limits. To its southwest and northeast, visitors can enjoy many activities on the coast and inland. There are more than 17 miles (28 km) of sandy beaches to

---

NOT TO BE MISSED:

explore close to Casablanca and, for sporting enthusiasts, lots of opportunities for sailing and golf. Forests, such as the mighty Ziaïdas cork oak forest, provide hiking and walks among an abundance of plant and animal life. Along the coast to the west lies a series of coastal towns, each fascinating in its own way. The largest of these, El Jadida, is about 50 miles (80 km) from Casablanca. Very popular with Moroccan vacationers because of its wide sandy beaches, this large town boasts a famous fortress built by the Portuguese in the 16th century to protect their developing trade routes and was the scene of furious battles two centuries later. A few miles from El Jadida, the smaller fortified settlement of Azemmour seems unchanged by the influence of tourism and offers a great insight into the character of a typical small Moroccan town. Its medina of narrow,

winding streets is a big attraction, and there are some good restaurants and hotels. Farther west along the coast is the enchanting little town of Oualidia Bay, famous for its beach-fringed lagoon and its oyster fishing. And then there is the port and industrial city of Safi—with its own large Portuguese fortress—which is not without its own charm if you can ignore the phosphate factory and other signs of industrial activity.

Heading Inland

Inland, and to the south of Casablanca, the traveler is soon well off the tourist trail, but there are many hidden delights. Boulaouane is famed for its vineyards, which produce delicious rosé wine, and its kasbah, perched high above a bend in Morocco's longest river. Falconry has been practiced here for more than 200 years.

The plains and rolling hills between bustling Settat and Beni Mellal form a breathtaking landscape that gets even more exciting near the Middle Atlas Mountains. And for those wishing to get a more intimate taste of the mountains, Beni Mellal, in the shadow of Jebel Tassemit, is a great base for hiking. ■

Central Casablanca

Casablanca is one of North Africa's most forward-thinking cities. It has been sculpted in spectacular fashion by architects over the past hundred years. Today, modern business centers occupied by high-tech companies and banks sit comfortably around Casablanca's ancient ramparts and the art deco and neo-Moorish homes of its burgeoning population. This vibrant city is, without doubt, the face of modern Morocco.

The Ancienne Medina clock tower looms over bustling evening traffic at place des Nations Unies.

Growth of the City

Casablanca is a new city, yet can trace its origins back more than a millennium to when it was little more than a small Berber settlement known as Anfa, nestling on the slopes of the Anfa Hills. Anfa retained its independence in the early Islamic era, but its strategic location on the west coast of Morocco attracted foreign interest. The first to conquer Anfa were the Almoravids in the 11th century, followed by the Marinids in the 14th century.

The Portuguese invasion of Anfa in 1468 caused widespread destruction to the town, and a fortress was built around which numerous small white buildings grew up. This gave the city its name: *Casa* means "house," and while the Portuguese word for white is *branca,* this was changed to the Spanish *blanca* when the city came under Spanish influence in the 16th and 17th centuries.

Casablanca came to the fore in the 18th century under the sultanate rule of Mohamed ibn Abdallah, as a major trading post for wool, tea, sugar, and grains. A devastating earthquake in 1755 hampered the city's development for a while, but it continued to grow in importance nonetheless.

The city as we see it today owes much to the French protectorate of the 20th century. The first resident-governor of French Morocco, Gen. Hubert Lyautey (1854–1934), wanted to establish Casablanca as Morocco's financial and commercial center. He engaged architects, town planners, and hundreds of construction teams to rebuild vast areas.

The reshaping of Casablanca began around 1912 and went on for more than 50 years, even after the country became independent from France in 1956. The result is a showcase of art deco and neo-Moorish architecture and one of the best examples of colonial urban planning in the world.

Heart of the City

Casablanca is a metropolis with a rich past. At its heart are two squares, the place des Nations Unies and, about 0.5 mile (0.8 km) to the south, the place Mohamed V. These are linked to each other and the rest of the city by a network of wide, busy boulevards. The **place des Nations Unies** (United Nations Square) was once a small marketplace that was remodeled in the 1920s to become a fashionable area of arcades, trendy restaurants, and hotels. In contrast, the **place Mohamed V** is the administrative and business center of the city. Many

(continued on p. 60)

Casablanca

⚠ 55 B2, 59

Visitor Information

✉ Moroccan National Tourist Board, 55 rue Omar Slaoui
☎ (0522) 27 11 77

✉ Syndicat d'Initiative, 98 boulevard Mohamed V
☎ (0522) 22 15 24

✉ Mohamed V International Airport, Office National des Aeroports, Casa-Oasis, BP 8101
☎ (0522) 53 90 40

✉ Compagnie de Transports au Maroc Buses, 23 rue Léon L'Africain
☎ (0522) 45 13 84

✉ ONCF Railroads
☎ (0890) 20 30 40
www.oncf.ma/index_en.aspx

Casablanca Conference

In January 1943, during World War II, a meeting was held in the now demolished Anfa Hotel, Casablanca, which has since entered the history books. It was between U.S. President Franklin D. Roosevelt (1882–1945) and British Prime Minister Winston Churchill (1874–1965). The agenda finalized plans to liberate Italy and Sicily and delayed a cross-Channel invasion until 1944. The Germans, who heard about the meeting in advance, translated information about its location and mistakingly thought it was taking place in the White House in Washington, D.C., and not Casablanca (which means "white house" in Spanish) in Morocco. The meeting went ahead and was a resounding success.

A Walk Through Central Casablanca

Casablanca is a sprawling city, but a walk around its center and out to the great Hassan II Mosque along the harborside boulevards is pleasurable and takes in some of the city's great squares and its outstanding architecture.

The Palais de Justice in Casablanca's place Mohamed V

Start from the **Villa des Arts** ❶ (see p. 61), an art gallery housed in a beautiful 1930s art deco building. A short walk along boulevard Brahim Roudani brings you to the **Parc de la Ligue Arabe** ❷ (see p. 60), with its palm trees offering welcome shade, and—just to the north—the **Cathédrale Sacré-Coeur** ❸ (see p. 60). From here it is another short walk along boulevard Rachidi to **place Mohamed V** ❹ (see p. 57).

Head north along boulevard Hassan II to arrive at **place des Nations Unies** ❺ (see p. 57), the city's commercial hub. The main area of historic interest is to the north, but it is worth wandering a little way to the east along **boulevard Mohamed V** ❻, a 1-mile (1.6 km) stretch of art deco buildings with wonderful designer fashion and specialty craft shops. Return to place des Nations Unies. This large square has some impressive build-

NOT TO BE MISSED:

Cathédrale Sacré-Coeur • The old medina • Hassan II Mosque

ings, such as the 1930s city hall. Designed by French architect and town planner Henri Prost (1874–1959), it has elements of Venetian and Moroccan styling and a huge bell tower.

From here, enter the **old medina** from avenue de l'Armée Royale—it lies between place des Nations Unies and boulevard des Almohades. The old medina is surrounded by the remains of ramparts. Work your way through the busy old Jewish quarter or *mellah* ❼, and then look out for the **Jamaâ Chleuh** ❽, a garrison-style building dating from the 14th century, and the **Sidi Kairouani**

Sanctuary ❾, where the remains of the city's patron saint Sidi Allal el Kairouani lie. A bastion in the ramparts known as **Sqala** ❿ is also well worth a look. Continue toward boulevard des Almohades, turn left along boulevard Sidi Mohamed ibn Abdallah and you will be greeted by the astonishing sight of the mighty **Hassan II Mosque** ⓫ (see p.

61), the perfect place to end your walk. Stand in its front courtyard to admire its elaborate marble facade with echoes of Marinid styling, its magnificent *zellij*-adorned minaret, and its sheer enormity before stepping inside to be dazzled by its glass floor, high ceilings, and 200-yard-long (183 m) Prayer Room which can hold up to 25,000 people.

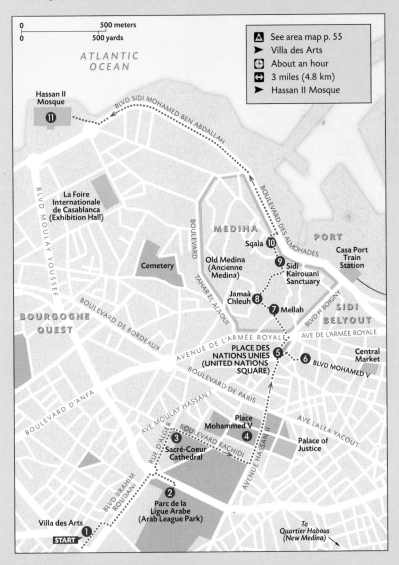

0	500 meters
0	500 yards

ATLANTIC OCEAN

▲ See area map p. 55
► Villa des Arts
🕐 About an hour
↔ 3 miles (4.8 km)
► Hassan II Mosque

Hassan II Mosque ⓫

BLVD SIDI MOHAMED BEN ABDALLAH

La Foire Internationale de Casablanca (Exhibition Hall)

BLVD MOULAY YOUSSEF

MEDINA

Sqala ❿

PORT

Cemetery

Old Medina (Ancienne Medina)

BOULEVARD

TAHAR EL ALAOUI

❾ Sidi Kairouani Sanctuary

Casa Port Train Station

Jamaâ Chleuh ❽

BOULEVARD DES ALMOHADES

❼ Mellah

SIDI BELYOUT

BLVD H BOIGNY

BOURGOGNE OUEST

BOULEVARD DE BORDEAUX

AVENUE DE L'ARMÉE ROYALE

AVE DE L'ARMÉE ROYALE

PLACE DES NATIONS UNIES (UNITED NATIONS SQUARE) ❺

❻ BLVD MOHAMED V

Central Market

BOULEVARD DE PARIS

BOULEVARD D'ANFA

AVE MOULAY HASSAN I

RUE D'ALGER

BOULEVARD RACHIDI

Place Mohammed V ❹

AVE LALLA YACOUT

AVENUE HASSAN II

Palace of Justice

❸
Sacré-Coeur Cathedral

BLVD BRAHIM ROUDANI

❷
Parc de la Ligue Arabe (Arab League Park)

Villa des Arts ❶

START

To Quartier Habous (New Medina) ↘

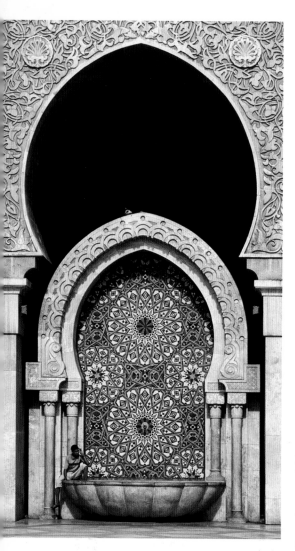

Towering mosaics at Hassan II Mosque

Cathédrale Sacré-Coeur

✉ Corner of rue d'Alger and boulevard Rachidi

☎ (0522) 26 73 37

www.sacred-destinations.com/morocco/casablanca

shops can be found. Continue along this boulevard and you will come across the **Central Market,** with its colorful fruits and vegetables, where crafts, spices, and other souvenirs make shopping a delight.

Just southwest of place Mohamed V, and not far from anywhere in the city center, is the city's largest public park, **Parc de la Ligue Arabe** (Arab League Park), designed by French architect Albert Laprade (1883–1978). Here, locals and visitors can be seen strolling along the palm-lined pathways.

A few years after the park was completed, in 1930, work began on a Moorish-style neo-Gothic-inspired cathedral just to the north. It became known as the **Cathédrale Sacré-Coeur** (Cathedral of the Sacred Heart) and was the work of French architect Paul Tournon (1881–1964). Although used as a church for many years, it is now a cultural center. If you visit, make sure you climb the cathedral's tower to enjoy a panoramic view of Casablanca, although the ascent up the uneven steps is not for the faint-hearted.

To the north of the place des Nations Unies lies the fabulous old medina, known locally as the **Ancienne Medina,** an area characterized by a labyrinth of tiny streets contained within the remains of ramparts. It is one of the oldest parts of the city and is quite different from other medinas in Morocco in that its architecture has colonial influences rather than Arab-Muslim ones.

outdoor cafés line its edges, providing good spots from which to watch city life. Linking the two squares is **avenue Hassan II,** while heading east from the place des Nations Unies is the **boulevard Mohamed V,** along which the city's smartest

The medina stretches toward the harborside, where a restored fortified bastion can be found with the **Sidi Kairouani Sanctuary** (rue de Tnaker, tel 0522/99 49 40), a tomb containing the remains of Casablanca's patron saint, Sidi Allal el Kairouani.

No visit to Casablanca would be complete without a visit to the **Hassan II Mosque**, the fifth largest mosque in the world. It dominates the city skyline. It lies on a 5-acre (2 ha) promontory looking out over the Atlantic Ocean, and it is said that 3,300 craftsmen created the mosque from the designs of French architect Michel Pinseau (1924–1999). Most notably, it has the tallest minaret on the planet, which stands 689 feet (210 m) high. Non-Muslims are allowed entry only as part of a guided tour.

Just east of the mosque, and adjacent to the old medina, in the **Sidi Belyout** district, is Casablanca's huge port. And a little to the south of the city center is the **Villa des Arts**, which exhibits contemporary Moroccan and international art.

Neighborhoods

Beyond the immediate center of Casablanca are some fascinating neighborhoods; each has its own distinctive character. **Bourgogne** and **Anfa** lie to the west and are notable for long, wide boulevards lined with plush mansions screened by palm trees that give them an exclusive feel. Also to the west, about 4 miles (6 km) from the center, is **Aïn Diab**. Stretching along the Atlantic waterfront, this district is packed with hotels, restaurants, clubs, and bars where wealthy and chic young Casablancans hang out. In **l'Oasis**, a 15-minute cab ride south of the center, is the excellent **Musée du Judaïsme Marocain** (Museum of Moroccan Judaism), which presents Moroccan Jewish films, dance, music, and art.

The **Quartier Habous** is perhaps the most intriguing area away from the center. Featuring arcades of shops, homes, markets, and large public squares contained within walls, it was laid out beginning in the 1930s in the style of a traditional medina, using what was then the most modern building techniques. Within its boundaries visitors can watch age-old Moroccan crafts such as pottery, leatherwork, furniture, and carpets being produced. ■

Hassan II Mosque

✉ boulevard Sidi Mohamed ibn Abdallah
☎ (0522) 99 49 40
🕓 Closed Fri. and Sun. Open to non-Muslims only as part of a guided tour.
$ $$$

Musée du Judaïsme Marocain

✉ 81 rue Chasseur Jules Gros
☎ (0522) 99 49 40
$ $

Villa des Arts

✉ 30 boulevard Brahim Roudani
☎ (0522) 29 50 87
🕓 Closed Sun.–Mon.
$ $

Art Deco

Art deco is the name given to a design style that was popular from the 1920s through the early 1940s. Art deco captured the world's senses and was represented in both architecture and fashion, as well as interior design. It is based on geometric shapes that are simple but bold, and convex and concave shapes became avant garde. Casablanca's architects embraced this new movement during a period when the city was undergoing dramatic expansion. However, Moorish influences also crept in, and the result is Casablanca's unique and interesting architecture: lavish buildings adorned with *zellij* tilework and stucco surfaces that depict flowers and swirls, with elaborate stone or wrought iron balconies, arches, and domes.

Around Casablanca

Casablanca lies on a stretch of Atlantic coastline known for its fabulous beaches, their resorts endowed with a range of tourist facilities. There are also picturesque fishing ports and ancient kasbahs and medinas. Inland, vineyards and orange groves stretch toward the Middle Atlas.

Fishing in the Atlantic from the shore a few miles west of Casablanca

Mohammedia

🅰 55 B2

Around Casablanca, the hot summers are tempered by cooling breezes from the Atlantic Ocean, while the winters are pleasantly warm. The climate, similar to that around the Mediterranean, is suitable for olive and pomegranate cultivation on the fertile coastal plain.

To the northeast and southwest of Casablanca, the coastline is dotted with resorts offering golf (see sidebar opposite), windsurfing, sailing, surfing, or simply sun-warmed beaches. Ancient coastal towns vie with modern settlements for the attentions of the traveler.

Falling very much into the second category is the city of

Mohammedia, about 15 miles (24 km) northeast of Casablanca and worth a visit if your itinerary is not too tight. The town can be reached along the coastal road or by a 20-minute rail journey from Casablanca's downtown station, Casa Port *(boulevard Moulay Abderrahmane, tel 0522/24 38 18)*. Mohammedia, often called by its former name of Fedala, is a popular beach resort and home to many of the region's most luxurious hotels, a casino, a yacht club, and a racecourse. Mohammedia's tree-lined boulevards are famous for their profusion of flowers, which have helped give rise to the city's affectionate name of *madinate lwouroude wa riyada,* meaning "city of flowers and sports." If you are tempted to stay and enjoy the beach life, there are many hotels and restaurants. However, note that Mohammedia is also a major port city, with plenty of industry.

Toward Safi

If your time is more limited, leave Casablanca to the southwest, where the coastline offers a more varied selection of resorts and old towns. Avoid the temptation of the fast A5 or N1 roads, which follow an inland course, in favor of the coastal route through Dar el Maizi.

Azemmour: This town, 75 miles (120 km) from Casablanca, sits on the banks of Morocco's longest river, the Oued Oum er Rbia, just inland from the Atlantic coast. An ancient and atmospheric city, Azemmour's origins go back to the 15th century and earlier. Within its towered walls (access from place du Souk) is crammed the **old medina,** whose square white buildings date from the period of Portuguese occupation in the 16th century, as does its castle. The latter hides something even older—the remains of a mosque—and the **old synagogue** is also worth a visit (a key is a available from the keeper).

For a real taste of Morocco, **rue Moulay Bouchaib** should be savored in the evening, its mix of traditional stores and small

Azemmour
🅰 55 B2

EXPERIENCE: Playing Golf at the Royal

One of the highlights for golfing enthusiasts visiting Casablanca is playing at the **Anfa Royal Golf Club** (Hippodrome d'Anfa, tel 0522/35 10 26), which lies due west of the city. A 9-hole, par-35 course, it has been designed around attractive hillside gardens from which the minaret of the Hassan II Mosque can be seen. It offers a practice range, golf club rental, and golf carts, and although a shorter course than most, its design is challenging. Trees and flowerbeds line the fairways and collect wayward balls. The clubhouse overlooks the course and gardens. The Anfa Royal accepts male and female players with a maximum handicap of 24.

Keen golfers will find other high-standard courses nearby, too. At Mohammedia, visitors and wealthy Moroccans enjoy golf at the super 18-hole, par-72 golf course, the **Mohammedia Royal Golf Club** (BP 12, Mohammedia, tel 05235/32 46 56), set beside the sea. Designed in the 1930s with straights and bunkers that at times experience strong coastal crosswinds, it is said by many to be one of the most challenging courses in this region.

Between Rabat and Casablanca, there is also the smaller 9-hole, par-35 **Bouznika Bay Golf Club** (km 22, route secondaire de Bouznika Plage, Bouznika, tel 0537/62 53 71), surrounded by beach, and there is a 9-hole, par-37 course at **Settat University Royal Golf Club** (km 2, route de Casablanca, BP 575, Settat, tel 0523/40 21 31), located 43 miles (70 km) south of Casablanca. The **El Jadida Royal Golf and Spa** (km 7, route de Casablanca, BP 542, El Jadida, tel 0523/35 22 51) is an 18-hole, par-72 course set in a spectacular location on the Atlantic coast 60 miles (97 km) south of Casablanca.

El Jadida

⛺ 55 B2

Visitor Information

✉ Syndicat
d'Initiative,
33 place
Mohamed V

☎ (0523) 34 47 88

🕐 Closed Wed.

Citerne Portugaise

✉ place Mohamed
Ahchemi Bahbai,
El Jadida

💲 $

🕐 Closed Sat.–Sun.

restaurants enticing the visitor at every step. And for daytime activities, **El Haouzia beach,** just a 15-minute walk north of the town center, is the place to be. Kitesurfers, surfers, and bodyboarders are drawn here. If you are interested in something more sedate, the mouth of the estuary is a good place for bird-watching, or you can just relax in the sun. La Perle restaurant (tel 0523/34 79 05) is recommended for its locally caught fish. There are good accommodation options, including

was a 16th-century outpost of the Portuguese empire, and the architectural influences of that period are still obvious. The part-fortified city is famous for its old ramparts and bastions—and its role in evicting the occupying Portuguese in 1769. Then known as Mazagan, the town was given back to local Moroccan tribes by the ruler Sidi Muhammad.

El Jadida's major attractions include its 10-mile (16 km) beach and chic promenade, lined with bars and cafés, and the **Citerne Portugaise,** a fabulous underground reservoir built by the Portuguese in the 16th century. When light shines on the water, it illuminates the vaults in spectacular fashion. Orson Welles used the location for scenes in his 1952 film Othello.

Two locals with falcons, World Heritage site of El Jadida

Oualidia

⛺ 55 A1

Safi

⛺ 55 A1

Visitor Information

✉ Délégation du
Tourisme, 26 rue
Imam Malik

☎ (0524) 73 05 62

🕐 Closed Sat.–Sun.

www.safi-ville.com

the **Riad Azama** (17 impasse Ben Tahar, Medina, tel 0523/34 75 16, www.riadazama.com).

The town is surrounded by olive groves and terraces of pomegranate trees, which in summer lend it green and red hues.

El Jadida: West of Azemmour lies the next city of note, the World Heritage site of El Jadida. Like Azemmour, this busy city

Oualidia & Safi: Continue along the coast road to the village of Oualidia, which is famous for its oysters (see sidebar opposite). If you fancy trying them firsthand, you could do worse than to visit one of the oyster farms.

A few miles southwest stands the large fishing port of **Safi,** 130 miles (208 km) from Casablanca. Safi's modern buildings blend with ancient ramparts and the 16th-century Kechla Citadel, which houses the **National Ceramics Museum** (Citadelle de la Kechla, Safi, tel 0524/46 38 95, $). The museum has a fine collection of traditional sculpted and engraved ceramics. Its port is where the country's sardine trade is based.

EXPERIENCE: Oysters & Bird-watching in Oualidia

Oualidia is a small village on the coast between Casablanca and Safi, and although unassuming, it is known for its fabulous beaches, coves of crystal-blue waters, world-famous bird habitats, and, most important, renowned oyster farms.

No visit to the Casablanca region should be without a meal of delicious Oualidia oysters. Seafood lovers are said to regard them as a gastronomic delicacy.

With their large tanks and beds, oyster farms are a common sight in Oualidia. Several types of oysters are farmed here, including those also found in the Marennes-Oléron region of France (and regarded as a particular delicacy in Europe), along with the Pacific cupped oyster, often called the Japanese oyster, and the Gasar cupped oyster.

Oysters were first brought to Oualidia in the 1950s when Morocco was under the French protectorate. At first the farms were primitive, but the oysters harvested were so highly regarded that the industry grew rapidly over the next few decades. Today, the farms are strictly regulated according to European standards of health and hygiene procedures. Their large purification tanks, calibration equipment, and operational procedures are modern, and technological innovation is making the industry ever more efficient.

Visiting a farm and sampling some of its oysters, followed by a stroll along the beach and taking in the

The oysters of Oualidia are renowned throughout Morocco.

many islands that dot the seascape, is a great way to spend an afternoon. The farms are clearly signposted from the center of Oualidia, and many offer the chance to tour the beds. A highly recommended restaurant is **l'Araignée Gourmande** (*Oualidia Lagoon, tel 0523/ 36 64 47, www.araignee -gourmande.com*).

Bird-watching

For enthusiasts of bird-watching, Oualidia's sandy beaches, reefs, wetlands, and salt pans host a magnificent range of species—one of the finest in Morocco. A visit at any time of the year will be productive, but be sure to bring your binoculars.

Look for gatherings of pink flamingos, providing a colorful spectacle, while

long-necked cormorants can be seen stretching and drying their wings. Along the shore, redshanks delicately wade in the shallows, along with black-and-white avocets and black-winged stilts, godwits, elegant storks, terns, egrets, and orange-billed oystercatchers probing among rocks.

If your visit is during spring or fall, expect the unexpected, because at these times of year many thousands of birds will be migrating either from sub-Saharan Africa to Europe, or vice versa. Bee-eaters, wheatears, great spotted cuckoos, and a variety of warblers will join the cast of avian attractions. If your interest is in birds of prey, watch for marsh harriers, booted eagles, and ospreys.

Boulaouane

🗺 55 B1

Settat

🗺 55 B2

From Safi you can either retrace your route back to Casablanca or head inland to experience something very different.

Heading Inland

To experience the varied countryside inland from the Atlantic coast, head toward Settat, 35 miles (57 km) due south of Casablanca. If you are in a hurry, take the A7 highway, but if you have more time on your hands and are feeling adventurous, follow a more circuitous route from Safi: take the road east to Bouguedra, pick up the N1 to Khemis Zemamra, then drive east again through Sidi Bennour to **Boulaouane.** In this area, vineyards dot the countryside and yield the delicious orange-tinted rosé wine, Gris de Boulaouane. Just south of the town,

Boulaouane Kasbah overlooks the Oued Oum er Rbia river on a dramatic bend. The landscape hereabouts is peppered with towns and small villages set in a semiarid landscape. Drive east along the R316 to reach Settat, the capital and administrative center of the Chaouia-Ouardigha region.

Settat is dominated by the large 18th-century **Ismailiya**

EXPERIENCE: Trekking at Jebel Tassemit

At 7,372 feet (2,247 m), Jebel Tassemit is not the highest peak in the Middle Atlas, but it is challenging nonetheless. Its summit can be reached in around a day or so by experienced climbers, and the route to the top passes through widely different landscapes, from valleys and steep gorges to continuous rock terrain. Along the way, hikers will see the ruins of homes and churches. Most treks start at Beni Mellal.

As when preparing for any trek in Morocco's mountains, care should be taken to ensure your safety. Be sure you have adequate insurance and take with you a strong pair of comfortable walking boots. Pack both lightweight clothing and some warm items, as temperatures can plummet in the mountains. You will also

need first-aid equipment and a tent if you are planning an overnight outing, and pack plenty of water and food supplies.

It is a good idea to join an organized tour, as guides understand the routes, terrain, and weather. Treks into the Middle Atlas will often have one or more donkeys to carry baggage. Always stay with your guide, or if traveling alone, make sure someone knows of your whereabouts and plans.

Companies specializing in treks include **Olive Branch Tours** (35 rue Eloraibi, Jilali, Casablanca, tel 0522/26 14 16, www .olivebranchtours.com) and **S'Tours** (4 rue Turgot, Quartier Racine, Casablanca, tel 0522/36 07 73, www.stours.co.ma), and **Receptours** (tel 022/98 57 57), all based in Casablanca.

While children look on, Berber women prepare a meal in a village near Beni Mellal.

Kasbah, which was built by Moulay Ismail (d. 1727). Today a modern city, Settat flourished under French rule and enjoyed rapid growth through the 20th century. It now boasts a university and the international-standard Settat University Royal Golf Club (see sidebar p. 63). Apart from the kasbah, it is worth soaking up the atmosphere of the attractive pedestrianized areas off the **place Hassan II.** Settat has places to stay that will suit all budgets, and it is a good base from which to explore the landscape toward the Middle Atlas Mountains.

To get closer to the mountains, take the road to Berrechid, then the N11 to Beni Mellal, which sits on the fertile Tadla Plain in the foothills of the Middle Atlas. This area is blanketed by orange groves that produce especially delicious fruit, olive groves, and fields of grain. Much of this produce is sold at the market in **Beni Mellal,** which today revolves around the 17th-century **Kasbah Bel Kush.** The city is of little interest to most travelers apart from serving as a base for mountain hikers.

If you have time, go into the hills to the south; the kasbah of **Ras el Ain** and the nearby spring and gardens of **Ain Asserdoun** (get a bus from Beni Mellal medina) are worth a visit. A few miles to its south lies the track to 7,372-foot (2,247 m) **Jebel Tassemit** (see sidebar opposite). And nearby are the lush **Oued Derna Valley** and the **Tarhzirte Gorge,** another popular hiking route and home to Barbary macaques. ■

Beni Mellal

⊠ 55 C1

Visitor Information

✉ Délégation du Tourisme, avenue Hassan II, Beni Mellal

☎ (0524) 48 97 29

A modern, cosmopolitan capital filled with potent reminders of the past—plus easy access to the great forests and beaches of the region

Rabat

A Rabat water-seller in traditional dress

Rabat

As Morocco's capital and seat of government, Rabat's influence is matched only by that of the country's financial center, Casablanca. It has the feel of a grand imperial city, with a fascinating historic center filled with splendid sultans' palaces, inspiring mosques, and centuries-old ramparts. These are complemented by neat modern buildings housing political offices, foreign embassies, and university faculties.

Rabat lies on the country's Atlantic coast at the mouth of the Oued Bou Regreg (Bou Regreg River), 140 miles (225 km) south of the Strait of Gibraltar. Its twin city of Salé, now in effect a suburb of Rabat, sits on the opposite bank of the river. Rabat enjoys a mild climate of warm summers and slightly cooler winters, making it a popular destination for both city breaks and longer vacations. Typically, temperatures reach around 82°F (28°C) in summer and 64°F (18°C) in winter, although evenings tend to be on the chilly side whatever the time of year. Spring and autumn are the most comfortable times to visit.

The pace of life seems slower in Rabat than

in many Moroccan cities, despite the fact that Rabat and Salé together make up one of the most densely populated areas of the country. Things are certainly much less fast-paced than in bustling Casablanca, just along the coast. This leisurely approach to life hasn't always been the case, however. Rabat has a long history of invasions and endured a spectacular period in the 17th century when pirates ruled not only the city but also the seas around its coast.

Modern Rabat has plenty to offer visitors, from the chance to relax in neatly tended gardens and explore the medina (which is considerably less chaotic and intense than those of Morocco's other imperial cities) to the opportunity to spend time in the Marché Central, with its heady smell of spices, and enjoy a meal in one of the numerous cafés lining the broad tree-filled avenues of the French-built *ville nouvelle* (new town).

The must-sees are the Oudaïa Kasbah, perched strategically above the estuary, with its celebrated 12th-century gate and mosque, the brilliant-white Mausoleum of Mohamed V, and the unfinished mosque and minaret of the 12th-century sultan Yacoub el Mansour. Rabat is also famed for its great medieval ramparts, which still dominate the skyline, winding for 3 miles (5 km) around the kasbah, medina, and new town. They are punctuated by five great, ornamental gates known as *babs*.

To the south of Rabat's center is the Chellah Necropolis, on the site where the city began. The weed-strewn ruins lie in marked contrast to the gleaming facades of the city's Royal Palace and government and commercial buildings.

Rabat can easily be explored in a few days;

its history may, however, take longer to digest. Be sure to visit some of its museums, which are among the best in the country. The Musée Archéologique provides a fascinating overview of Morocco's ancient past and holds numerous examples of statues, ceramics, and bronze implements recovered from the Roman settlements of Volubilis, Lixus, and Sala Colonia (modern-day Rabat). The Musée des Oudaïa, meanwhile, housed in the Oudaïa Kasbah, is dedicated to the Moroccan arts with displays of ceramics, jewelry, musical instruments, and traditional costumes.

Excursions

Rabat also offers easy access to a host of other attractions. Around half an hour's walk from central Rabat, across the river, lies Salé, once the region's dominant urban center, but now subsumed into the greater Rabat area. Its well-preserved center boasts plenty of fascinating architectural treats, including the Bab el Mrisa (Gate of the Sea), which leads to a thriving, bustling medina filled with traditional craft workshops.

The cities of Casablanca, Meknès, and Fès are all also within reachable distance for excursions, as are the attractive resorts of Temara and El Harhoura Beach, as well as a number of smaller towns, including Kenitra. Inland, toward the foothills of the Middle Atlas mountain range, lies the cork-oak and eucalyptus-rich Mamora Forest, which is a real hikers' paradise. ■

Central Rabat

Rabat is a bustling metropolis of government buildings, offices of major financial and commercial companies, and elegant modern hotels that sit among centuries-old souks, aged kasbahs, and ramparts with imposing gates decorated with arabesque floral motifs. It is a thrilling mix of contemporary and ancient architecture, and the new and the old are more integrated and interwoven than in most Moroccan cities.

The houses and mosques of the city rise above the Oued Bou Regreg.

Rabat

🅰 71 A1

Visitor Information

✉ Corner of rue Oued El Makhazine & rue Zalaga-BP

☎ (0537) 67 39 18

www.visitmorocco.com

Rabat Today

As most of Rabat's main tourist sites lie within (or just beyond) the city walls, the city is an easy place to navigate your way around. Its environs have been inhabited continuously since Roman times, when it was known as Sala. Very little remains from this period of Rabat's history—earthquakes and local builders carried away the Roman town's monumental buildings centuries ago—but traces can still be seen around the town's main thoroughfare, which was created as the Decumanus Maximus in the first century A.D.

After the Romans left, the town's population migrated to nearby Salé, and it was not until around a thousand years later that Rabat began to be rebuilt. At first, this new town was a peculiar place—half necropolis and half fortress—but in time the living returned to the Oued Bou Regreg river's southern bank.

The engine that drove Rabat's development was piracy, an unglamorous but lucrative trade in people and goods seized from ships passing the coast on their way back from the Americas, sub-Saharan Africa, or the Indies. Despite attempts to stop it, the trade continued well into the 19th century, earning the city several retaliatory bombardments from European navies.

In 1912, the city was subdued by the French colonial administration, which built a grand *ville nouvelle* (new town) on the outskirts of the old city. Rabat was made into the new capital city, and it kept this prestigious status after Morocco gained its independence in 1956.

Modern Rabat is home to nearly two million people, most of whom are engaged in the construction, textile, and food-processing industries. The population is boosted throughout the year by visiting foreign dignitaries on government business and thousands of vacationing visitors attracted by Rabat's rich history, relaxed atmosphere, and pleasant coastal climate.

Linking the old town with the new is the city's main artery, the avenue Mohamed V. Along this broad street, you'll find Rabat's main train station, its central post office, and many of the city's major hotels and restaurants. Large public squares and parks lie on either side, including the city's largest green space, the Garden Nouzat Hassan, which stands in the shadow of the medina's walls.

Oudaïa Kasbah

The Oudaïa Kasbah, with its mighty honey-colored ramparts and watchtowers dominating the skyline, occupies the city's northern tip on the banks of the Oued Bou Regreg. The kasbah is named for the Oudaïa, an Arab tribe that settled on the Atlantic coast in the 17th century and played a key role in defending the city from Spanish invaders during the reign of Sultan Moulay Ismail.

Oudaïa Kasbah differs from examples found elsewhere in Morocco in that it is not simply a fortress or a palace, but a small, heavily fortified town—a medina

Rabat Bus Stations
- Gare Routier, place Zerktouni
- (0537) 79 58 16

- CTM, avenue Hassan II
- (0537) 79 51 24 or (0537) 79 58 16

Oudaïa Kasbah
- 77
- Off boulevard Tarik el Mersa, via Bab Oudaïa

Summer Olympics?

Rabat could see massive investment in its sports, leisure, and hotel infrastructure over the next few years if its bid to host the 2020 Summer Olympics proves successful. New stadiums and sporting facilities have been earmarked for a large area to the east of the capital's center, between the Quartier Administratif and the Oued Bou Regreg. The International Olympic Committee is expected to announce its decision in 2013.

Bab Oudaïa
🏛 77
✉ place Souk el Ghezel

El Atika Mosque
✉ rue Jamaa el Atiq, Oudaïa Kasbah

within the medina—complete with its own mosques, souks, and museums.

The kasbah is entered via the **Bab Oudaïa** on place Souk el Ghezel, an imposing ocher-colored gatehouse built in the 12th century and widely considered one of the finest surviving examples of its type in the country. Reached by a broad, gently sloping staircase, the Bab Oudaïa is watched over by two large defensive towers. Despite its obvious defensive purpose, the Bab Oudaïa is a beautiful example

can display their works.

The town within these imposing walls is characterized by narrow residential streets, lime-washed in soft shades of blue and white, which open out onto squares and courtyards. For those interested in traditional Islamic architecture, the Oudaïa Kasbah is a delight. At its center is the 12th-century **El Atika Mosque** (Old Mosque) also known as the Jamaa el Atiq, which can be found on the rue Jamaa. It's been the city's main place of prayer for centuries, and the mosque's well-preserved

Mausoleum of Mohamed V

A magnificent structure, the Mausoleum of Mohamed V (see p. 81) was commissioned on the death of King Mohamed V (1909–1961), the first king of the modern state of Morocco and a long-standing veteran of the independence movement. This imposing structure houses his white-onyx sarcophagus, along with those of his sons, King Hassan II (R. 1961–1999) and Prince Moulay Abdullah (1935–1983).

The renowned Vietnamese architect Vo Toan designed the building and, with the help of around 400 local craftsmen, began its construction in 1962 using white Italian marble and onyx imported all the way from the Hindu Kush mountains

in Afghanistan. The mausoleum stands on a platform with staircases leading up to a series of terraces that surround the pavilion building itself. Inside, it is decorated with granite, marble, and onyx. The complex also holds a museum telling the (official) story of the current ruling Alaouite dynasty.

One of the most distinctive features of the building is a series of marble columns through which guards can pass to the doors of the mausoleum. Its walls are adorned with Maghrebi calligraphy script, ornate carvings, and *zellij* tilework. It is one of the most popular attractions in Rabat.

of Almohad architecture, and complex abstract patterns radiate out from a huge but elegantly proportioned keyhole arch. Within the arch sits a massive pair of bronze-plated doors, covered in lines of rivets and interestingly weatherworn. Today the gate's entrance passageway serves as an exhibition area where local artists

minaret can be seen for miles.

Another feature that has a prominent place in the Rabat skyline is the watchtower, **Plateforme du Sémaphore** (Signal Platform), that sits at the northern tip of the kasbah. This was once used as a signal tower for communicating with the city's pirate ships as they left port. Like

Children play in an alleyway in the Oudaïa Kasbah.

several features of the kasbah's northern fortifications, the watchtower was designed in the 18th century by a man called Ahmed al Inglizi (Ahmed the English, also known as Ahmed el Alj—Ahmed the Renegade), an engineer who had converted to Islam and joined the significant population of European pirates living and working out of Rabat.

At the southeastern corner of the kasbah lies the palace of Moulay Ismail, which was extensively restored during the French protectorate period. This grand building now houses the **Musée des Oudaïa.** This museum holds a delightful collection of local folk art and traditional crafts, including examples of jewelry, woodcarvings, ceramics, musical instruments, and costumes. The palace's main exhibition areas lie around an attractive inner courtyard.

Next to the palace, also within the walls of the kasbah, is the beautiful **Andalusian Garden.** Designed in a Moorish style with mature trees, box hedging, and lawns, the garden's main focal point is a waterwheel, known as a *noria,* which is used to irrigate the shrub beds. Enclosed within walls, the gardens make a peaceful retreat from the bustle of the city outside. While you're in this area, be sure to stop off at the **Café** *(continued on p. 78)*

Musée des Oudaïa

🅐 77

✉ Oudaïa Kasbah

☏ (0537) 72 61 64

🕒 Closed Tues.

 $

Andalusian Garden

🅐 77

✉ Off boulevard Tarik el Marsa, via Oudaïa Kasbah

Walk: Central Rabat

This walk takes in many of central Rabat's finest historical sites, by way of some of its liveliest and most atmospheric districts, including the Marché Central.

The Bab Oudaïa, the ornately carved 12th-century gate of the Oudaïa Kasbah

The **boulevard Hassan II** is a landmark thoroughfare running right through central Rabat. The extensive **Garden Nouzat Hassan ❶**, which lies along the boulevard's southern boundary, is a great place to start a walk around the city center. From here, turn left to visit the **Bab el Had ❷**, a large gateway with 19th-century towers standing on either side, that provides access to the city's teeming **Marché Central** (Central Market) **❸**. In the market you can buy a huge range of items, from textiles to aromatic spices.

If markets aren't your thing, then from the park you can instead head straight for the **Rabat Medina ❹** along the **rue Sidi Fatah** opposite. With its wider than normal streets and recently renovated homes, this medina has a different, more modern feel than many of Morocco's other medinas. It lies protected by ramparts built during the Almohad and the Andalú periods, not far

NOT TO BE MISSED:

Marché Central • Oudaïa Kasbah • Mausoleum of Mohamed V

from the Oued Bou Regreg river. The Jewish quarter of the medina, the **Mellah ❺**, is filled with charming, traditional homes interspersed by narrow lanes, and it is a pleasure to explore.

The medina continues to the **boulevard Tariq el Marsa,** where you will find the **Ensemble Artisanal**—here, carpets and other goods are displayed in a government-run showroom. Turn left and head toward the river mouth. On your right you will find the **Andalusian Garden** and the impressive **Musée des Oudaïa ❻** (see p. 75), hidden behind the ramparts of the **Oudaïa Kasbah**

7 (see pp. 73–79). The kasbah was given the honor of becoming the first official historic monument in Morocco during the French protectorate period. Entrance to the kasbah is by the **Bab Oudaïa** (see p. 74) an intricately decorated gateway built on the orders of Sultan Yacoub el Mansour in the 12th century. The gate has a somewhat checkered past, having been used to hold prisoners captured by marauding Barbary pirates, many of whom were sold at slave markets. A small stone staircase at the back leads down to dungeons where the prisoners were kept. The Oudaïa Kasbah itself is a gem. Within, look out for the oldest mosque in Rabat, the **El Atika Mosque.**

Retrace your steps on boulevard Tariq el Marsa and continue on to place Sidi Maklouf, then turn south onto avenue Alaouiyine, where you will find the **Mausoleum of**

More Walks

The Moroccan National Tourist Office has a number of guided tours of the city available. Visit the tourist information office on the corner of the rue Oued El Makhazine and the rue Zalage in Agdal to pick up a route leaflet.

Mohamed V 8 (see sidebar p. 74). The final stop is at the nearby **Hassan Tower 9** (see p. 81), site of Sultan Yacoub el Mansour's ultimately failed attempt to create the largest mosque in the world.

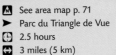

▲	See area map p. 71
►	Parc du Triangle de Vue
⏱	2.5 hours
↔	3 miles (5 km)
►	Hassan Tower

The stunted columns and half-completed minaret, the Hassan Tower, of the Unfinished Mosque

Ensemble Artisanal

✉ boulevard Tariq el Marsa

☎ (0537) 73 05 07

Place Souk el Ghezel

✉ rue des Consuls

🕐 Closed Mon. & Wed.

Maure (Oudaïa Kasbah, close to Andalusian Garden) where you can indulge in some local delicacies while watching boats bobbing about in the Bou Regreg river.

Medina

Coming out of the Oudaïa Kasbah, the path leads past the walls of the Andalusian Garden to the entrance to the medina at the rue des Consuls, the main shopping street in the medina. One of the first things you'll see as you enter the medina is the huge **Ensemble Artisanal**—a government-sponsored boutique where local artisans sell their wares at fixed prices. These places can be found in every reasonably large town in Morocco and offer an expensive but hassle-free way to shop for local crafts.

For a more authentic shopping experience, head farther down the road to the **place Souk el Ghezel** (Square of the Wool Market), where a carpet auction takes place every Thursday (see sidebar opposite).

The square is a good place to begin exploring the city's busy medina. Its streets are filled with stalls selling spices, honey cakes, carpets, jewelry, crafts, and colorful textiles. Both the **rue Souika** and the **rue des Consuls** seem to carry everything and anything you could wish to purchase. Both are teeming with people at all times of day.

The medina's southeast corner is occupied by the mellah,

or Jewish quarter, where Rabat's once buoyant Jewish community lived. The Jewish population has now almost entirely left this district, and the neighborhood is fairly run-down. There were once around a dozen synagogues in this area, but they all have been converted to other uses. The city's only remaining active syna-gogue lies a few hundred yards/ meters away on the other side of the place du Mellah.

Ville Nouvelle

Rabat's business and residential district, the ville nouvelle (new town), lies in the city center, south of the medina. It was created during the early to mid-20th century, during the time of the French protector-ate, to house the city's financial and administrative buildings. A network of wide boulevards forms the basic layout of the new district, and the boule-vard Mohamed V is the main thoroughfare.

Interspersed along the various boulevards are green areas that have been planted with tropical flowers and laid out with lawns. The boulevards themselves are lined with residential buildings, government offices, and banks, which have been designed in

INSIDER TIP:

The Ensemble Arti-sanal, in boulevard Tariq el Marsa, is a good place to get an idea of the prices, quality, and variety of goods you may wish to haggle for elsewhere.

—CHIP ROSETTI
National Geographic contributor

Garden Nouzhat Hassan

🅰 77

✉ Off boulevard Hassan II

EXPERIENCE: A Carpet Auction

The region around Rabat is particularly famous for the quality of its carpets, which are usually woven from a striking red-colored wool and have a luxurious velvet-like feel. If you fancy buying a carpet as a souvenir of your stay in Rabat, or if you simply wish to enjoy the spectacle of a carpet auction, head for the **place Souk el Ghezel** on a Thursday morning. You'll find it in the medina just south of the Oudaïa Kasbah. Many of the Rabat carpets you find in stores throughout the country pass through this auction. The market can get crowded, so try to arrive early to guarantee yourself a good vantage point.

The carpet auction attracts locals and visitors alike, not to mention the hundreds of women who come from surrounding towns and villages hoping to sell the carpets that they have woven at home. The auctioneer in charge will be easy to spot, as he will almost certainly be wearing a loose, hooded garment known as a *djellaba*. He will raise his hand to accept bids until a carpet is sold. It is a bit of local culture that is well worth experiencing. Locals are not always happy to be bidding alongside visitors, however, so you may have to spend some of the time watching from the sidelines, which itself can be quite entertaining.

Postal Museum

77

✉ 196 boulevard Mohamed V

☎ (0537) 70 23 74

$ $

Cathédrale Saint-Pierre

⚠ 77

✉ place du Golan

☎ (0537) 72 23 01

Archaeological Museum

⚠ 77

✉ 23 rue Brihi, Quartier Hassan

☎ (0537) 70 19 19

🕐 Closed Tues.

$ $

Mausoleum of Mohamed V

⚠ 77

✉ avenue Alaouiyine

$ $

Royal Palace

⚠ 77

✉ Off avenue Yacoub el Mansour

🕐 Access only to méchouar and part of gardens

an attractive Hispano-Maghrebi style with elegantly decorated exteriors.

At the northern end of the ville nouvelle, bordering avenue Hassan II and opposite the south wall of the medina, is the **Garden Nouzhat Hassan,** the city's largest and prettiest park and a welcome oasis of green among all the stone and concrete.

A short distance west, the **Postal Museum** (Musée de la Poste), housed in the PTT building on boulevard Mohamed V, tells the history of the Moroccan postal system. From here, it's only a brief walk southeast to the 1930s-built **Cathédrale Saint Pierre,** one of the city's most striking modern buildings and one of just a handful of Catholic places of worship that can be found in the city.

The new town's main attraction, however, is undoubtedly the **Archaeological Museum** (Musée Archéologique), which lies to the south and has an important collection of prehistoric, Roman, and Islamic relics from the nearby ruins of Chellah. It's not the biggest museum of its type in the country, but it is

packed to the rafters with fascinating artifacts. The museum's collection of Roman bronzes is accessed through a different entrance to the main museum, and tickets must be bought separately. The information boards are mostly in French.

Royal Palace

Just southeast of the center, but still contained within the city's mighty walls, is the Royal Palace, a stately collection of buildings originally erected in the late 18th century, but largely remodeled by King Hassan II, who, among other things, had a private golf course added. It's very much a working palace today, with government

---

EXPERIENCE: Military Moments

Every day, Rabat witnesses a number of colorful military ceremonies, performed with lots of pomp and pageantry. The first is the changing of the guard at the Hassan Tower (see opposite), when you can watch members of the King's Royal Military Household, resplendent in their brightly polished uniforms. The mounted guards wear red in winter and white in summer, and their role is to protect the royal family. The ceremony starts precisely at 7 a.m. A few hours later, at 10:45 a.m., the ceremony to hoist the national flag takes place at the barracks of the Royal Guard. Visitors can enter the barracks at the Royal Palace to witness the event.

buildings, administrative offices, stables, and a mosque. The palace is the seat of government and the official home of King Mohamed VI and his family and, as such is closed to visitors, although you can explore the grounds. The best views are from the central *méchouar*, or parade ground.

Hassan Mosque

In the east of the city, not far from the banks of the Oued Bou Regreg, lies the Hassan Mosque complex. This consists of several interesting features. The first, and most obvious, is the **Hassan Tower** (Le Tour Hassan), a splendidly decorated minaret, built to adorn a great mosque that was never completed.

In the 12th century, Sultan Yacoub el Mansour embarked on a major construction program, which would see the creation of the Koutoubia in Marrakech and the Giralda in Seville. Sadly, the sultan died before most of the work could be completed. The tower we see today is the lower half of the planned minaret, but is nonetheless an impressive structure. It stands around 140 feet (44 m) tall, about half its intended height. Visitors can witness the early-morning changing of the guard here each day (see sidebar opposite).

Across from the mosque stands the **Mausoleum of Mohamed V** (see sidebar p. 74), which was added to the site in 1961.

Another notable feature of the site is the cluster of **200 columns** gathered around the base of the tower, the only part of Mansour's

Guarding the gates of Rabat's Royal Palace

monumental mosque that was built. This construction, known as the **Unfinished Mosque** (see sidebar p. 82), has become perhaps the best known landmark in the city.

Chellah Necropolis

The oldest part of the city, the Chellah Necropolis, lies to the southeast, beyond the city walls. Beautifully preserved, the burial

Hassan Tower
 rue de la Tour Hassan

Chellah Necropolis
✉ boulevard Moussa ibn Nossair
$ $

INSIDER TIP:

Pay a visit to Rabat's atmospheric Chellah Necropolis and try figuring out which ruins date from Roman times and which were added in the 14th century.

—TOM JACKSON
National Geographic contributor

site is entered through a huge gate dating from the time of the Almohads and sometimes called the **Arc de Triomphe.** Once inside, visitors will see a mixture of Roman and 14th-century ruins, the latter dating from the peroid of Sultan Abou al Hassan's development of the

site as a necropolis. A minaret covered in brightly colored tile mosaics towers over the site. The Roman ruins date back to the time when this area was part of the city of Sala Colonia and include what would have been a major road that linked the city with its port.

Although the first-century B.C. port is now covered by sand and gravel, excavations have identified its original location. From the viewing platform at the center of the site, visitors can see the remains of the Roman **Temple of Jupiter** alongside the much more recent ruins of the **Mosque of Abou Youssef.** Other structures from the Roman city still visible include the octagonal **Pool of the Nymph,** which once formed a part of the Romans' water

Yacoub el Mansour's Unfinished Mosque

No visitor to Rabat can pass up a trip to the Hassan Tower (see p. 81), which, had it ever been completed, would have formed part of one of the world's greatest mosques. The 12th-century ruler Sultan Yacoub el Mansour, founder of the Almohad dynasty, wanted to build a mosque so magnificent it would go down in history. He saw Rabat as the center of his empire and wanted a mosque that was befitting of its state of grandeur and consequence.

The mosque was designed by the Moroccan architect Jabir, who also designed the Koutoubia Mosque in Marrakech. It was to be built to a rectangular shape and would have incorporated a huge prayer room with a series of columns topped with capitals.

Its minaret would have stood some 260 feet (86 m) high, making it the tallest in the world. However, the sultan died in 1199 and construction stopped with just a couple hundred columns having been completed; the minaret stood little more than half its intended height.

Still standing, the unfinished square minaret and marble column stumps are a spectacular sight. Made of red sandstone, the minaret is highly decorated with a fretwork of arches. It overlooks the Oued Bou Regreg river and, although not open to the public, it is—along with the nearby Mausoleum of Mohamed V—one of the most visited landmarks in the city. The tower is currently being considered for UNESCO World Heritage site status.

The gardens in the Chellah Necropolis, near the Roman site of Sala Colonia

distribution system, and the **forum.** The site also has springs and gardens of hibiscus.

Beyond the Center

Rabat's long stretches of beach are a draw, too, along with leisure amenities such as the celebrated **Dar es Salam Royal Golf Club.** The golf club's signature par-73 course was designed by legendary English golf course architect Robert Trent Jones (1906–2000). It is here that the prestigious Hassan II Trophy is held every November.

Sandy beaches at the mouth of the Oued Bou Regreg face the Atlantic Ocean in one direction and Salé—across the river—in the other. Away from these beaches, Rabat's coastline becomes a dramatic jagged line of rocky outcrops and high cliffs, which at high tide are battered by the powerful waves of the North Atlantic. At the right time of day, however, the tide reveals a series of small beaches and coves. These precarious beaches are sometimes used by the brave surfers of the **Oudayas Surf Club,** a local group based on the beach near the kasbah. They offer English-language surfing and surfboarding lessons and surfboard rental to visitors. Unfortunately the water quality around Rabat is dubious enough to make many vistiors wary of riding the waves here. ■

Dar es Salam Royal Golf Club

 Km 9, avenue Mohamed VI, route des Zaërs Souissi, Rabat

☎ (0537) 45 58 64

www.royalgolfdar essalam.com/english

Oudayas Surf Club

✉ 3 plage de Rabat, Oudaïa Beach

☎ (0537) 26 06 83

www.ras.ma/ transitions/surfing/ index.html

Around Rabat

Rabat is the capital of the Rabat-Salé-Zemmour-Zaër region, one of the most heavily populated regions in the country. Most of its inhabitants, however, live in just a handful of urban areas—Salé, for example, has a population of more than three-quarters of a million—so the region also has its fair share of open spaces. There are great swaths of forest and long stretches of sandy beach where you can walk for miles without encountering another person.

The Festival of Candles in Salé

Salé

With its imposing city walls enclosing a maze of tiny whitewashed streets, Salé is a characterful former enemy of Rabat. Today it is very much a close friend and a key part of the Moroccan capital city.

In its time, Salé has had Phoenician, Roman, Vandal, Byzantine, and Arab rulers, and it was already a prosperous place when the Marinids fortified it with walls in the 12th century. As it grew into a thriving trading hub, it caught the attention of Barbary pirates, who made it their base in the 17th century. These "Salé Rovers," as they were known, joined forces with Rabat to form the Republic of Bou Regreg, which became a legendary force under the pirates' control. However, by the 18th century, sultan rule had returned to the cities and the pirates disbanded.

A period of decline followed, but Salé again found prosperity a couple of centuries later thanks to its rapidly expanding craft industry. It also benefited from the growing importance of Rabat, which was seeing unparalleled growth, first under the Alaouite rulers and then, when it regained its status as the capital of Morocco, during the French protectorate.

INSIDER TIP:

The pottery market of Salé offers an incredible array of local ceramics, from cups and bowls to *tagines* and planters—excellent decorative gifts for family and friends.

—SANAA AKKACH
National Geographic Books designer

City Center: Although there are few reminders of Salé's turbulent history today, visitors can get a sense of stepping back in time as they pass through the 13th-century **Bab el Mrisa** (Gate of the Sea), so called because it was the route taken to the harbor by its seafaring residents, not least the Salé Rovers. If you let your imagination run wild, you can still hear their cries of jubilation as they bring ashore their latest haul of gold.

From the Bab el Mrisa, go past the old *mellah*—Jewish quarter—and the new mellah, across the main thoroughfare, the rue Fondouq Abd el Hadi, and you'll arrive at the heart of the souk district.

Comprising just a few interlinked streets around the **Grand Souk,** the souk area is easy to navigate. Unlike the souks of Rabat, which have numerous themed areas, Salé's souks are nearly all dedicated to crafts. The ceramics, colored candles, and intricately patterned embroidery of the Souk el Merzouk have helped make Salé a key player in Morocco's craft industry.

Just beyond the souks is a small 14th-century *medersa* dedicated to the Marinid ruler, Abou el Hassan. Although the university's main building is closed to visitors, you can tour its inner colonnaded courtyard, where each column is decorated with *zellij* tilework in shades of brown and topped with floral plasterwork. Be sure to look up to admire the medersa's intricately carved wooden roof.

To the left of the medersa lies Salé's **Grand Mosque.** Most of what you see dates from the 12th century, although the minaret, which dominates the city's low-rise skyline, is of a more recent vintage. If you continue down toward the sea, you will come to the **Seaman's Cemetery,** which contains not just the resting places of many sailors but also the tombs

Salé
⚑ 71 A2

Salé Medersa
✉ rue de la Grande Mosque

Seaman's Cemetery
✉ Off boulevard Circulaire

Salé's Festival of Candles

Held ten days after the Muslim New Year, on the eve of Moulid an-Nabi, the anniversary of the birth of the Prophet, the Festival of Candles is one of the highlights of the Salé calendar. The people of Salé, in particular its boatmen, parade through the streets in elaborate costumes carrying large, intricately carved candles. They head to the tomb of Sidi Abdullah ibn Hassoun, the patron saint of Salé and its boatmen, upon which they place the candles to show gratitude to the saint for keeping those who work at sea safe. It's a spectacle not to be missed.

Moulay Bousselham
⚑ 71 B3

Kenitra
⚑ 71 B2

Mamora Forest
⚑ 71 B1, C1

of several holy men, known as *marabouts*. The first tomb you reach is that of Sidi Abdullah ibn Hassoun, the patron saint of Salé and the focal point of the famous Festival of Candles (see sidebar p. 85). Just beyond is the tomb of Sidi Ahmed ibn Achir, a 16th-century holy man who is said to have employed his special powers to help heal the sick and guide sailors in distress safely back into Salé's harbor.

INSIDER TIP:

Sabra is a linen made 100 percent from plants. A sumptuous mix of aloe, silk, raw linen, and satin wool, each piece of fabric is unique.

—CHRISTEL CHERQAOUI
National Geographic Books

Coastline North of Salé

Along the Rabat-Salé-Zemmour-Zaër region's coastline are several interesting towns and villages, including Kenitra, founded by the French in 1913 and once known as Port Lyautey, and **Moulay Bousselham,** famed for its Merdja Zerga lagoon—and, in particular, the lagoon's wealth of birdlife—which now lies within a protected nature reserve (see sidebar opposite).

Kenitra: Although the countryside around Kenitra shows signs of ancient occupation, the town we know today was founded only in the early 20th century during the early years of the French protectorate. In 1912, the resident general, Hubert Lyautey, chose the small settlement Kenitra, at the mouth of the Oued Sebou, as the site of a new military base. Under his command, a town was created. From 1932 to 1956, it was known as Port Lyautey, but when Morocco gained its independence, it reverted back to its original name.

It's a modern Moroccan town, its center filled with offices, banks, and restaurants lining pedestrianized squares. The surrounding landscape has been shaped by the principal regional industries of agriculture and producing pulp for papermaking. Fields of cereal crops, citrus groves, and forests of cork oak and eucalyptus can be seen everywhere. As a coastal town, Kenitra is also known for its fishing industry and sandy beaches. For the visitor, the town gives an intriguing taste of modern-day Morocco.

A few miles north of Kenitra near Sidi All ibn Ahmed are the ruins of the ancient Roman town of **Thamusida,** where you can see the remains of baths, a temple, city walls, and a praetorium.

Inland from Kenitra is **Mamora Forest,** known locally as the Forêt de la Mamora, where, along with the Forêt As-Sehoul and the Forêt des Zaërs, acres of cork-oak trees grow among scented pines, acacias, eucalyptus, and wild pear trees. In fact, about half of all the cork-oak trees that grow in Morocco are

EXPERIENCE: Bird-watching at Moulay Bousselham

The small, picturesque village of Moulay Bousselham lies in an idyllic coastal location and, although a popular holiday spot for Moroccans who travel here from Rabat or from the ancient towns of Larache and Asilah (see pp. 104–108) farther north, it is probably best known for flora and fauna, and in particular its amazing birdlife.

Moulay Bousselham occupies a stretch of land created by high sand dunes, with the waves of the Atlantic Ocean breaking on its shore on one side and the more tranquil Merdja Zerga lagoon (*École Nationale Forestière d'Ingénieurs, BP 511*) on the other. It lies at the mouth of the Oued Drader, a river that flows from the foothills of the Rif Mountains, to the northeast, and has some amazing beaches and wetlands where migrating birds gather.

Bird-watching enthusiasts can see wading shorebirds (including avocets, snipe, curlews, sandpipers, and plovers); herons and spoonbills; various species of wildfowl, especially during the winter and fall; and plenty of migrant passerine birds, notably in spring and fall when they are on the way to the Mediterranean and Europe—or on their way back again! Some of these are truly stunning: Check out the bee-eaters and rollers, for example, whose kaleidoscopic coloration can excite even those with little interest in the natural world.

Merdja Zerga lagoon became famous in the 1990s as one of the last known wintering locations of the critically endangered slender-billed curlew, but sadly these birds haven't been seen in recent years. Another of Merdja Zerga's special birds is the marsh owl.

Boat trips across the lagoon are available from the town's small fishing harbor (*negotiate fee and length of trip before embarking*).

The Merdja Zerga lagoon has been afforded protected status. If you are not a birder, it is said that the beaches nearby are some of the most beautiful in Morocco. Moulay Bousselham has few residents, but the mosque that lies in the middle of the village reportedly contains the tomb of a tenth-century holy man—Moulay Bousselham himself. The local population is swelled all year—by nature enthusiasts and by pilgrims visiting the tomb.

The black-winged stilt is just one of Moulay Bousselham's many attractive wading birds.

Sidi Yahya el Gharb
⚠ 71 B2

Sidi Moussa el Harrati
⚠ 71 B3

Mehyda
⚠ 71 B2

in the Mamora Forest. Lying between the Oued Sebou and the Oued Bou Regreg, this huge forest covers an area of more than 500 square miles (1,300 sq km).

Between the forested areas are dozens of small communities whose inhabitants live in traditional village homes and rely on the land for their livelihoods, raising crops and rearing cattle and sheep. To get an impression of the area's beauty, drive east from Kenitra to **Sidi Yahya el Gharb,** then take the R411 road toward **Sidi Moussa el Harrati.**

Mehdya: Around 10 miles (16 km) west of Kenitra on the coast is the small resort of Mehdya. With an attractive cluster of whitewashed houses beside a long, wide beach, it's a popular excursion from Kenitra and Rabat. Most of the town is modern, although it does boast a now largely ruined kasbah. You enter through a monumental gate built during the reign of Moulay Ismail, and then weave your way through the remains of a once glorious palace, a mosque, and a mazy network of narrow streets. Lying on

Moroccans on vacation enjoying the waters north of Rabat

INSIDER TIP:

Don't pass up an invitation for a home-cooked meal from a pleasant stranger you may meet. Be prepared to try everything and eat more at their kind urging.

—HEATHER PERRY
National Geographic contributor

the estuary of the Sebou river, Mehdya is a popular fishing harbor. You can see fishermen bringing their catches ashore most mornings.

Lac Sidi Bou Ghaba: Just south along the coast is a large freshwater lake known as the Lac Sidi Bou Ghaba, which provides a home to an abundance of birdlife, including crested coots, warblers, and teals. Wildflowers carpet the banks in springtime.

South of Lac du Sidi Bourhaba, heading toward Salé and Rabat, is the small, sleepy town of **Sidi Bouknadel,** site of an interesting little arts and crafts museum, the **Musée Dar Belghazi.** Gathered by three generations of the Belghazi family, the collection includes musical instruments, wood carvings, and jewelry. The beach at Sidi Bouknadel, sometimes known as **Plage des Nations,** is relaxed and friendly.

Nearby, on the main road through town, is the **Jardins Exotiques,** a garden full of tropical plants, most of which are found nowhere else in Morocco. It was created by a French horticulturist, Marcel François, in the 1950s as a private garden, but had become overgrown by the 1980s when the Moroccan authorities recognized its importance to horticulture and decided to restore it to its former glory. Today it contains more than a thousand different species of plants from around the world, planted in geographically themed areas, including a Japanese garden, an Andalusian garden, and a Polynesian garden.

Temara & Around

South of Rabat and Salé lie Temara and its neighbor, the quieter resort of Skhirat. Both are on a stretch of coast that in centuries past attracted the attention of successive waves of

Sidi Bouknadel
🗺 71 B2

Musée Dar Belghazi
✉ 55 Washington Route de Kenitra, Sidi Bouknadel
☎ (0537) 82 21 78
💲 $
museebelghazi.
marocoriental.com

Jardins Exotiques
✉ Route de Kenitra, Sidi Bouknadel
☎ (0537) 82 27 56
www.les-jardins-exotiques.com

Temara
🗺 71 A1

EXPERIENCE:
The Caves of Temara

The coastline that runs due south of Temara down to Casablanca is a cave enthusiast's paradise, offering a series of caverns that can be explored. The largest, the **Cave of El Harhoura** (see map p. 71 A1), is around 50 feet (16 m) high. Carved into the rock on the beach of El Harhoura, its gaping maw faces the sea.

The Cave of El Harhoura has been created over millions of years, and excavations have revealed evidence of human occupation from the Paleolithic and Neolithic Stone Age eras. Fragments of household pots and jugs, tools, weapons like ax heads, and jewelry are just some of the artifacts discovered in the cave, along with human and animal bones.

The training of Thoroughbred horses is big business in the region around Rabat.

Kasbah de Guiche Oudaïa
✉ rue la Plage, Temara

El Harhoura Beach
◭ 71 A1

invaders, including the Phoenicians, the Andalusians, the Spanish, and the Portuguese, all of whom helped shape its character.

Life now is centered around a sheltered harbor that becomes a hive of activity as fishermen bring their catches ashore. Most people live and work in and around the port, although more and more are now engaged in the tourism industry as hotels and restaurants grow in number. Several fishermen offer pleasure cruises out to sea. Many wealthy Rabat residents holiday in Temara, where they have plush villas looking out over the sand dunes to the ocean.

Temara can trace its roots back to the 12th century, when the then Alhmohad ruler, Sultan Abd el Mumin (1094–1163), established a mosque here.

Over the next few centuries, the town developed and, in the 17th century, acquired a kasbah, the impressive **Kasbah de Guiche Oudaïa,** named for the Oudaïa Arab tribe who settled there.

Four centuries on, Temara is best known for its string of sandy beaches, which stretch for some 7 miles (10 km) along the shoreline. **El Harhoura Beach,** famed for a large **sea cave** (see sidebar p. 89) that may have been inhabited as far back as Palaeolithic times, is the most popular. Away from the town, the beaches of **Sidi el Abed, La Falaise, Val d'Or,** and **Petit Val d'Or** are usually less crowded, but have fewer amenities. Relaxing on the soft sand in front of a forest backdrop while waves crash on the shore is a great way to spend an afternoon away from the throngs of central Rabat.

Not far from El Harhoura beach is the outdoor **Mohamed Kacimi Arena,** which is named after a famous Moroccan painter, Mohamed Kacimi (1942–2003), who lived in Temara. Cultural events are regularly held here and, if you are fortunate, you might catch one of the classical musical concerts for which Temara is becoming increasingly known. Nearby is the **Royal School of Cavalry** (see sidebar below), where several hundred horses are stabled and trained to appear in the *fantasias* (displays of horsemanship) that take place in most Moroccan cities.

Khemisset

Khemisset lies inland toward the cities of Meknès and Fès and is mainly populated by Berbers from the Middle Atlas region, many of whom work in its prosperous agricultural industry. Some, however, commute into Rabat or Meknès via the Rabat–Fès expressway, built in the 1990s to link the cities. It is the most convenient way for visitors to reach the city.

Although it has few visitor attractions, a walk around Khemisset gives an intriguing insight into day-to-day Moroccan life. It is most famous for being the site of an early narrow-gauge railway that ran from Rabat during the French protectorate period, although little remains of it today.

Lying between Khemisset and Meknès is the ancient town of **Tiflet,** which is believed to have been inhabited by Phoenicians and Romans from the first millennium B.C. Excavations have revealed remains of dwellings, primitive roads, and artifacts such as tools, jewelry, and pottery. In more recent times, Tiflet became known for its beekeeping cooperatives run by local women. These cooperatives still produce some of the country's most flavorful honey today, which is used for making traditional sweet pastries such as baklava. ∎

Mohamed Kacimi Arena

✉ rue el Harhoura, Temara

Khemisset

🅰 71 C1

Tiflet

🅰 71 B1

Royal School of Cavalry

✉ avenue Hassan II, Temara

☎ (0537) 74 11 74

🆂 $

EXPERIENCE: The Royal School of Cavalry

You know you have found somewhere special as you approach the magnificent entrance to the Royal School of Cavalry (École Royale de Cavalerie), just outside Temara. This lavishly decorated structure has three arches, beyond which is a long, wide driveway to a stable complex.

There are stables here for around 300 horses, ranging from Berbers' barbs and Arabian barbs to purebred Arabs and English Thoroughbreds. The school provides intensive training for both horses and riders. There are classrooms for teaching the theories of equine control and outside training areas where riders can put their lessons into practice. A saddler and workshops for producing fine riding clothes and boots are also on the site, along with a gallery area.

The school, which is signposted from the center of Temara, is open to the public and often hosts festivals for visitors at times when the horses are not performing in competitive riding events, or in the traditional *fantasia* shows of horsemanship for which Morocco is famous.

From endless beaches near Larache and Al Hoceima to the ghosts of Tanger's international zone, and beyond to the wild Rif Mountains

Tanger & the North Coast

Local women in traditional dress in one of Tanger's alleys

Tanger & the North Coast

The lush landscape of northern Morocco is not one many would associate with North Africa—when coupled with the architectural legacy of colonialism and the dizzying variety of languages spoken here, it can be hard to believe that you're in Morocco.

Despite the temperate climate and European cultural influence, this area is still indisputably Moroccan, and you do not have to venture far from the art deco streets of Tanger's *ville nouvelle* (new town) to find yourself in a landscape of isolated Berber villages where the women weave traditional fabrics in small village workshops, and of traditional fishing ports where the catch is cooked on big grills right on the docks. During the second half of the 20th century, Tanger, as well as the area around it, fell into a long period of governmental neglect and economic stagnation. Although the tourist industry and major infrastructure projects are improving the daily lives of the people in this area, they are gradually wearing away the untouched charm that currently

lures intrepid travelers to the region.

Although you'd never guess it standing dockside in Tanger with the day-trippers from Spain, this area of Morocco is one of the least visited parts of the country. While there is a constant stream of travelers on the "Marrakech Express" route to the south of the country, the green hills and stunning beaches of northern Morocco are less well-trodden ground. That's not to say these places do not have a tourist industry—in the summer, hundreds of thousands of Moroccan families descend on the towns of the Atlantic and Mediterranean coasts, massively increasing the population of towns such as Asilah—but foreign visitors are still something of a rarity in many parts of the region.

One place that is no stranger to foreign visitors is the port city of Tanger. Lying in an expansive, picturesque bay off the Strait of Gibraltar, just a few miles from the southernmost coast of Spain, Tanger has been an important trading post for centuries. With its bustling, mazelike medina, attractive modern ville nouvelle, and golden beaches, it was described by the great French artist Henri Matisse (1869–1954) as a "painter's paradise."

Tanger has a uniquely dramatic history of intrigue, art, and corruption. In 1925, the city was recognized as a key venue for diplomacy and international trade and was granted international status by colonial powers, which made the city into an essentially autonomous city-state. During the years of the international zone, the place attracted a wide variety of artistic types, wayward characters, and the very rich (American heiress Barbara Hutton and billionaire publisher Malcolm Forbes both bought palaces in Tanger, she in the 1940s and Forbes

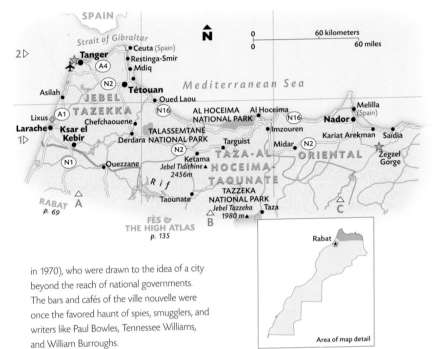

RABAT
p. 69

FÈS &
THE HIGH ATLAS
p. 135

Rabat

Area of map detail

in 1970), who were drawn to the idea of a city beyond the reach of national governments. The bars and cafés of the ville nouvelle were once the favored haunt of spies, smugglers, and writers like Paul Bowles, Tennessee Williams, and William Burroughs.

Atlantic Coast

To the south of Tanger, on the northern stretch of Morocco's long Atlantic coast, lie the picturesque towns of Asilah and Larache. These towns are a calm, relaxed contrast to the busy streets of Tanger and Tétouan, with broad, beautiful beaches, clean, well-maintained medinas, and great fortifications that speak to their turbulent history. Although some visitors to Tanger may venture as far as Asilah on a day trip, most of the coast is largely untouched by international tourism.

Mediterranean Coast

The Mediterranean coast that extends to the east of Tanger is lined with modern resorts and attractive seaside towns. The historic Spanish enclaves of Ceuta and Melilla are also along this stretch of coast, hidden by

a sea of fences, walls, and endless customs checkpoints. At Al Hoceima, Nador, and numerous other villages, visitors from across Morocco and Europe come to soak up the sun and swim in the warm blue sea.

If you venture inland, to the Rif Mountains and the towns of Tétouan and Chefchaouene, you will discover a very different Morocco from the one that you'll find at the beach resorts on the coast. Here in the high Rif Mountains, where the people did not cave in to government control until the 1950s, you will witness a more traditional way of life, where crafts such as woodcarving, weaving, and pottery are still important sources of income. Another modern commercial enterprise in this part of the world is the production of marijuana resin, which is grown and processed on an industrial scale. ■

Tanger & Around

Located in the far northern corner of the country—where the Atlantic and the Mediterranean meet—the city of Tanger seems to face outward, as if it belongs with the stateless expanses of international waters more than to Morocco. Over the centuries, it has had many masters, from Phoenician traders to French colonial bureaucrats, and each has left their mark on the cultural and physical fabric of the city.

Tanger's old town rises steeply from the shore, with the Mohamed V Mosque on the horizon.

Tanger owes its unique split personality to a complex and unusual history, during which it has rarely been united with Morocco as a whole. The city's national allegiances have shifted many times over the centuries, and even today it does not entirely feel as though it belongs to Morocco.

The modern city of Tanger has its origins in the early 20th century, when it was made into an international zone. This status was conferred on the city by European colonial powers and made Tanger into a self-governing city-state, free from trade tariffs and taxes. Expatriates and wealthy socialites from Europe and America flocked to this exotic, stateless city. Intellectuals, gamblers, artists, spies, and smugglers found a welcoming home in Tanger with its low cost of living, permissive society, and easily bribed police. Although the town prospered, its hedonistic reputation carried with it a notorious history of sex scandals, corruption, and political intrigue.

Following reunification with Morocco in 1960, the city of

Tanger suffered a long period of economic decline and neglect. King Hassan II (R. 1961–1999) disapproved of the city's seedy reputation and never visited the town. Tanger went from being an exotic, international city to an impoverished dockside town avoided by tourists.

This decline has been reversed in recent years, however, thanks to the policy of Morocco's current king, Mohamed VI, who wants to restore the city to something like its former glory, a glamorous riviera resort similar to St.-Tropez in France. When you arrive in Tanger today, you will find a city in transition—beautifully renovated hotels stand next to crumbling art deco theaters and ancient souks that have changed little in centuries.

INSIDER TIP:

Arriving at the docks in Tanger can give you a bad first impression. Try to make plans in advance so you can breeze past the hustlers and fake guides that descend on each boatload of tourists.

—CLIVE CARPENTER
National Geographic contributor

Finding Your Way

Like most Moroccan towns and cities, Tanger comprises two main areas: the old town, or medina, and the newer district known as the *ville nouvelle,* which was mostly built during the time when Morocco was a French protectorate (1912–1956).

Tanger is built on a series of steep hills that rise up from the golden beaches around the harbor. The walking can occasionally be hard work, but the views are ample reward—in Tanger even the local branch of McDonald's has a breathtaking view of the city and ocean.

Tanger's medina is located on the hill next to the ancient harbor. The highest point is occupied by the medieval **kasbah,** which formerly housed a medieval palace. To the north and east, it is bounded by the sea, while the neighborhoods of the ville nouvelle surround it to the west, south, and southeast.

The ville nouvelle is relatively easy to navigate, with broad boulevards, clear road signs, and green open spaces. The medina, however, is best described as a maze. Here hundreds of narrow streets and unnamed alleyways wind between the ancient buildings through courtyards, tunnels, and crowded, noisy marketplaces. Although confusing, the medina is quite small when compared to that of, for example, Marrakech, so if you do get lost, it doesn't usually take long to find your way back to a recognizable landmark. If you're feeling adventurous, getting lost is actually quite a good way to experience the city, if a rather bewildering one.

(continued on p. 100)

Tanger
[M] 95 A2
Visitor Information
[✉] ONMT, 29 boulevard Pasteur
[☎] (0539) 94 80 50
[⊙] Closed Sat.–Sun.

Walking in Bohemian Tanger

From Henri Matisse to William Burroughs, Tanger has a long and distinguished artistic history. Its artistic golden age came in the early 1950s, when it was an important hub for the artists and writers of the Beat Generation. Although the international zone is gone, much of the Tanger of their day remains.

Not every corner of Tanger's medina is bustling with activity—there are quiet corners, too.

Start your exploration down in the coastal streets of the *ville nouvelle*, where the writers of the Beat Generation established their informal artistic colony in the cheap-rate rooms of hotels like the Rembrandt, the Massila, and the El Muniria. Begin on the rue Magellan next to the **Hotel El Muniria** ❶, where William Burroughs lived. It was here in 1957 that Jack Kerouac and Allen Ginsberg rented rooms while they edited the thousands of pages Burroughs had scrawled in notebooks into the novel *Naked Lunch*.

If you head away from the port and turn left toward boulevard Pasteur, you will reach the **Hotel Rembrandt** ❷. This modern hotel used to host exhibitions by the likes of Brion Gysin and Paul Bowles in its bars and function rooms, while the suites above were home to Tennessee Williams and Truman Capote. The

rooms have suffered some strange redecoration efforts since the 1950s, but the bar is still worth a look.

From here, head right, along the boulevard Pasteur, past the cafés and restaurants, to the **Place de Faro** ❸, where a group of antique cannons guard a fantastic view out over the harbor and across the strait to Spain—a reminder of the qualities that have long attracted artists to this city. Head over to the **Café de France** ❹ on the northern side of

NOT TO BE MISSED:

Place de Faro • Café de
France • American
Legation Museum

the place de France, where you can enjoy a cup of coffee or a sweet mint tea in an atmospheric venue that has changed little since the days when it hosted animated discussions between the Beat writers.

From the place de France, go north along the rue de la Liberté, passing the grand buildings of the **El Minzah Hotel** ❺, where writers and musicians would gather in the glossy surroundings of Caid's Bar. After descending the hill to the busy surroundings of the Grand Socco, head through the gates and down the rue as Siaghin to **Café Central** ❻, a popular café on the Petit Socco that has changed little since it was the favorite hangout of Burroughs.

If you haven't already, take the opportunity to visit the **American Legation Museum** ❼ (see pp. 100–101) a few streets south of the Petit Socco, which houses a significant collection of art by American painters resident in Tanger, with a room devoted entirely to the

INSIDER TIP:

There's little point trying to trace locations and landmarks from *Naked Lunch*, as the "Interzone" of the book owes more to the tangled streets of Burroughs's fevered imagination than to the city of Tanger.

—CLIVE CARPENTER
National Geographic contributor

work of New York Beat Generation writer and later Tanger resident Paul Bowles.

Continue east, past the Grand Mosque, and then turn left up the rue Dar Baroud as it climbs steeply up the hill. To finish, head to the beautiful terrace café at the grand **Hotel Continental** ❽, where several scenes of the 1990 movie adaptation of Bowles's Tanger-set novel *The Sheltering Sky* were filmed.

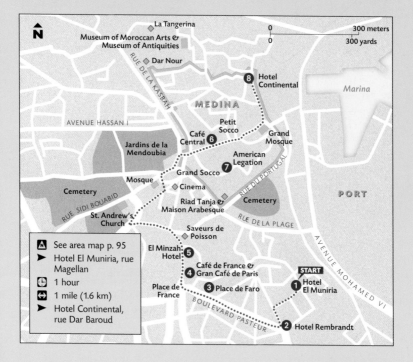

Boutique Volubilis

  15 Petit Socco, Medina

☎ (0539) 93 13 62

Boutique Majid

  66 rue les Almohades, Medina

☎ (0539) 93 88 92

www.boutiquemajid.com

Medina

The historic core of the city, with its twisting medieval streets and bustling marketplaces, is Tanger's biggest tourist attraction. Initially, many visitors are overwhelmed by the town's noisy clamor, overzealous "guides," and baffling layout. Once you've got your bearings, however, you will find that this ancient town has much to offer beyond the cheap trinkets that the street vendors off-load on European day-trippers.

The busy marketplaces and cafés that surround the **rue as Siaghin** and the **Petit Socco** form the heart of the medina. This area developed a bad reputation during the 1990s, but, with the exception of the ever present "guides" and touts, it does not deserve this today. Confident negotiators will find many excellent bargains among the tourist souvenirs. For a less hectic and pressured shopping experience, head over to the **Boutique Volubilis,** which sells fine handmade clothing, and the **Boutique Majid,** which has a dazzling array of high-quality Moroccan crafts and antiques.

While the hostels on the Petit Socco are best avoided, there are some good places to stay in the area, including the **Riad Tanja** (rue du Portugal, tel 0539/33 35 38, $$), which also has an excellent restaurant, and the **Maison Arabesque** (73 rue Naciria, place Sakaya, Medina, tel 0679/46 68 76, www.maison-arabesque.com/html /welcome.html, $$)—both within a few minutes' walk.

A short distance south from the Petit Socco, on the rue d'Amérique, lies the remarkable **American Legation Museum.** This unassuming building, constructed in the local architectural style, was the first U.S. public building outside North America when it first opened in 1821. Today the building houses a fascinating collection of documents and artifacts relating to the American community in Morocco and the history of this diplomatic outpost. Highlights include the Paul Bowles

The Musée de Kasbah is housed in part of an old palace.

EXPERIENCE: A Visit to a Tanger Hammam

Hammams, or public baths, are a common sight throughout Tanger's medina. Like their ancient Roman predecessors, hammams are an important part of civic life; they are a lively social meeting place and a practical necessity in a city where few houses have bathrooms. All public hammams are gender segregated and have several large tiled rooms containing bathing pools of varying temperatures.

Hammams can be found just about everywhere in the medina, so inquire at your hotel for directions to the nearest one. When you arrive, you will be expected to pay around 15 dirhams at the entrance and leave your clothes in an alcove—there are no lockers, so it is a good idea to leave your valuables in the hotel. In a public hammam, you should bring towels and toiletries with you,

although local olive oil soap is often sold on-site. For an additional 30–50 dirhams, you can hire an attendant, who will lead you through the various rooms in the customary order and give you a full body scrub known as *gommage*.

For women, a visit to a hammam can provide a fascinating insight into Moroccan womens' culture. In these exclusively female spaces, local women are talkative and unself-conscious, and the noise of conversation in the domed bathhouses can be deafening.

If you are daunted by the prospect of public nudity, many hotels have their own private hammams. These are usually cooler and more like Western spas than traditional hammams. Try the hammam at the **El Minzah Hotel** (*85 rue de la Liberté, tel 0539/93 58 85, www.elminzah.com/static, $$*).

INSIDER TIP:

In recent years, the American Legation Museum has become an important cultural center—ask about their recitals by traditional musicians when you visit.

—BEN HOLLINGUM
National Geographic contributor

room—containing photographs, letters, and paintings created by Bowles and the American artistic community that lived in the city during the 1950s—and historic correspondence between the legation's staff and their masters in Washington. The museum's

director, Thor Kuniholm, is a mine of useful information and entertaining anecdotes about the legation's history.

If you head up the rue des Almohades and then the rue Ben Raisouli from the Petit Socco, you will eventually reach the walls of the kasbah. Inside this medieval compound, the place de la Kasbah, perched on the high cliff-top, offers stunning views of the Strait of Gibraltar and the Spanish coast. The beautifully decorated buildings that were once the sultan's palace now house the **Museum of Moroccan Arts**—a treasure trove of Moroccan traditional art—and the **Museum of Antiquities,** whose collection includes many ancient Carthaginian and Roman artifacts. In the streets

American Legation Museum

99
✉ 8 rue d'Amérique, Medina
☎ (0539) 93 53 17
$ $
www.legation.org

Museum of Moroccan Arts/ Museum of Antiquities

99
✉ Dar el Makhzen, place de la Kasbah
☎ (0539) 93 20 97
🕐 Closed Tues.
$ $$

Dar Nour

✉ 20 rue Gourna, Kasbah

☎ (0662) 11 27 24

$ $$$

www.darnour.com/ bienvenue_eng.htm

La Tangerina

✉ 19 rue du Riad Sultan, Kasbah

☎ (0539) 94 77 31

$ $$$

www.latangerina .com/en/

Hotel Continental

(See also p. 287)

🄰 99

✉ 36 rue Dar Baroud, Medina

☎ (0539) 93 10 24

www.continental -tanger.com

that surround the former palace complex, there are several good guesthouses, the best of which are **Dar Nour** and **La Tangerina**. A short walk to the east from the kasbah brings you to the **Hotel Continental**. Although its luxury has faded slightly since the days when its guests included Winston Churchill and European royalty, its cliff-top location, good restaurant, and amazing views mean it is still popular with visitors.

Ville Nouvelle

Just as the Petit Socco is the heart of the medina, so the **Grand Socco**—located at the opposite end of the rue as Siaghines—is the heart of the ville nouvelle. This ornate public square, officially known as the **place du 9 Avril**, serves as the meeting point of old and new Tanger. To the north it is bordered by a lavishly planted green area known as the **Jardins de la Mendoubia**, and to the west by the elaborately decorated **Sidi Bou Abib Mosque**, while the southern side is occupied by cafés, offices, and the art deco facade of the **Cinémathèque de Tanger** (see sidebar). In the past the square has seen parades, festivals, and political marches. The most notable of these was the speech in support of independence that was given by King Mohamed V on April 9, 1947, for which the square is now named.

During the international zone period, the cafés and hotels of the ville nouvelle were home to two very different communities. The studded leather alcoves of the **Gran Café de Paris** (*place de France*) and the sun-drenched terrace of the **Café Hafa** (*avenue Mohamed Tazi*) once played

Cinémathèque de Tanger

Set on the south side of the Grand Socco, this elegant movie theater is a fascinating symbol of Tanger's changing fortunes. It was opened in 1938 as the Cinéma Rif, its combination of French art deco and traditional Moroccan decoration capturing the spirit of the time. During Tanger's prosperous golden age, which coincided with Hollywood's, it showed the latest films from Europe and America to an audience that comprised both locals and foreign residents. As Tanger declined, however, so did the Cinéma Rif. Its audiences dwindled and its building decayed. By the 1990s, this once grand theater was on the verge of bankruptcy and showing only Bollywood B-movies.

As with so many other Tanger institutions, it seemed destined for closure.

In 2006, however, the building was saved from demolition by a nonprofit organization led by Yto Barrada, a French-Moroccan artist who wanted to showcase and encourage filmmaking in Morocco. The organization renovated the crumbling building and transformed it into an exciting cultural center, the **Cinémathèque de Tanger** (*Cinéma Rif, 1 place du 9 Avril, Grand Socco, tel 0539/93 46 83, www.cinemathequedetanger.com/accueil-2 .html*). Today it hosts film festivals, arts exhibitions, youth programs, and, of course, nightly showings of quality films from around the world.

host to an unlikely clientele that included the writers Paul Bowles, Tennessee Williams, and William Burroughs, who came to smoke hashish and discuss literature, alongside international spies exchanging information and making deals. The remains of this era of decadent elegance can be seen everywhere in this area. Some of it has survived Tanger's years of neglect, like the eccentric Anglo-Moorish Anglican church of **St. Andrew** *(rue d'Angleterre)* and the luxurious **El Minzah Hotel,** while the fate of other landmarks, like the derelict **Grand Hotel Villa de France** *(above the Grand Socco on rue de Hollande)* and the crumbling **Teatro Cervantes** *(behind the El Minzah hotel),* hangs in the balance.

The ville nouvelle is not all European sophistication, however, and many local favorites are hidden away down the area's backstreets and alleys. For an authentic taste of fine Tanger cuisine, head to **Saveur de Poisson** *(2 Escalier Waller, tel 0539/33 63 26, closed Fri., $),* a small restaurant just off the rue de la Liberté. Just pay your 100 dirhams, take a seat at one of the communal tables, and enjoy an outstanding five-course meal that the eccentric owner, Mohamed, claims will not only fill you up but also make you more attractive to the opposite sex.

Around Tanger

Tanger is well placed for a wide variety of excursions. The attractive fortified town of **Asilah** (see pp. 104–106) is just 25 miles (45 km) along the Atlantic coast road west of Tanger. Around 7 miles (11 km) south of Tanger is **Cap Spartel,** a dramatic headland that offers stunning views of the point where the Atlantic and the Mediterranean meet. **Cap Malabalata,** on the other side of the bay, around 6 miles (10 km) from the center of Tanger, offers stunning views of the city and across the Strait of Gibraltar to southern Spain. ∎

El Minzah Hotel
(See also p. 285)
🏔 99
✉ 85 rue de la Liberté
☎ (0539) 93 58 85
www.elminzah.com/static

The spirit of Tanger: musicians in a typical restaurant

Atlantic Coast

The towns of the Atlantic coast are a refreshing and beautiful place to spend a few days—clean, calm seaside towns cooled by the breeze off the ocean and surrounded by stunning beaches. Furthermore, Asilah's vibrant cultural life and Larache's rich history mean that there is much more to do in this part of Morocco than just relax.

A mural adds a touch of color to the traditional brilliant white walls of Asilah.

Asilah
📍 95 A2

Beyond Cap Spartel, the Moroccan coast plunges abruptly away to the southwest in an uncannily straight line of beaches and cliffs that stretches all the way to the city of Rabat (see pp. 72–83). The landscape of this region is defined by low, rolling coastal hills, beautiful seaside villages, and some of the oldest historic sites in Morocco.

Asilah

Around an hour's drive, 27 miles (43 km) to the south of Tanger, lies Asilah, a friendly and colorful fishing port. Although never a great metropolis, the town has quietly prospered for thousands of years thanks to fishing, trade, and that old seafaring standby, piracy. With trade now the preserve of huge container ports and piracy no longer an option, Asilah's current well-being is largely dependent on tourism, specifically the town's enormously popular summer cultural festival, the **Asilah Arts Festival** (see sidebar opposite), and the year-round activities that have developed out of it.

Asilah doesn't have much to appeal to visitors with a checklist approach to tourism; there are few well-known historic sites or museums to draw in tour groups. Instead, the architects of Asilah's cultural renaissance have transformed its entire medina into a fantastic place to explore and relax. With its well-maintained buildings, clean streets, and sleepy atmosphere, Asilah feels worlds away from Tanger or Tétouan.

Here the dominant colors are white and blue—most houses are whitewashed, with blue doors and decorative features, while others are painted entirely in blue, like the houses of Chefchaouene (see pp. 119–121). The effect, when combined with the bright ocean sun, is dazzling (often literally; bringing sunglasses is advised) and highly photogenic. This attractive color scheme is punctuated by huge murals, a legacy of the town's annual cultural festival, during which artists from around the world are each given a wall somewhere in the medina and told to paint whatever they want. The murals are a great reward for the curious, with impressive, complex works of art lurking around every corner, transforming the whole medina into an art gallery.

One of the best ways to see the town is to take a walk around its **ramparts**. The ramparts and huge gates are still complete, and you can walk around their entire length, admiring the charming bastions (built by the Portuguese) that resemble the great fortifications of Essaouira (see pp. 216–221) in the south. To one side, the walls follow the contours of the shoreline, offering spectacular views of the Atlantic swell crashing into the rocks below.

Asilah Arts Festival

Every August, Asilah's normally relaxed atmosphere explodes into life as visitors flock to see or take part in its much celebrated international festival of culture and art. The festival was started in 1978 when Mohamed Benaïssa, then mayor of Asilah, arranged for a group of artists to come to this quiet coastal town and paint murals around the medina.

He hoped that by beautifying the streets of the crumbling medina, he could restore the residents' pride in their town and reverse the cycle of neglect and decay. The cultural festival has, by many measures, been a spectacular success, transforming Asilah from an ignored backwater to a clean picturesque city and attracting artists from around the world.

Although the festival lasts only a few weeks each summer, the beneficial effects are felt throughout the year.

Today there is much more to the festival than the mural painting competition—it has become a three-week festival of music, poetry, dance, and visual art. Typically held in July or August, the festival attracts thousands of visitors. In addition to performances and readings, there are numerous seminars and lectures, and debates are held to discuss the development of cultural expression in the Muslim world and its role in society. In recent years, the festival has attracted big-name sponsors from the Middle East, including major Arabic cultural foundations based in the United Arab Emirates.

Hotel Azayla
✉ 20 rue ibn
Rochd, Asilah
☎ (0539) 41 67 17

Hotel Patio de la Luna
✉ 12 plaza de
Zelaka, Asilah
☎ (0539) 41 60 74

San Bartolomé Church
✉ avenue de la
Liberté, Asilah

A walk along the ramparts brings you to the three-story **Palais de Raissouli,** built into the medina's ramparts in the early 20th century by Moulay Ahmed ben Mohamed er Raissouli—a notorious bandit and local governor from the Rif Mountains. When Raissouli wasn't busy kidnapping Western businessmen for huge ransoms, he enjoyed forcing convicts who had been sentenced to death to leap out of his palace onto the coastal rocks 100 feet (30 m) below. The palace now has a more benign use as a venue for cultural events.

Asilah's medina is only a small part of the present-day town, and the streets beyond the city walls are also worth exploring. The buildings of the new town, albeit not quite as well maintained, mostly conform to the medina's clean blue-and-white color scheme, with even the smallest residential buildings sporting striking paint schemes. The area around the town's main street, the boulevard Mohamed V, and its main square, place Mohamed V, is where most of the town's visitors stay. Highlights include the recently completed **Hotel Azayla** and the slightly older **Hotel Patio de la Luna.** One sight in the new town that's definitely worth a look is the church of **San Bartolomé.** Now home to an order of nuns who run a school for local children, the church is an attractive example of Spanish colonial architecture and is notable for being one of the few churches in the country that is allowed to ring its bells to announce services.

Larache

The largest town along this stretch of coast, Larache has

The ruins of the Roman city of Lixus, with Larache outlined against the sea in the background

INSIDER TIP:

Larache is the most Spanish town in Morocco. Larache was sold to Spain in 1610 and the northern part of Morocco was under Spanish control for the majority of the 20th century.

—CHRISTEL CHERQAOUI
National Geographic Books

roots going back to Roman times, when the now ruined city of Lixus (see p. 108) was built on a hill a short distance upriver from the present-day town.

Until the 20th century, Larache's economic growth was hampered by a series of treacherous sandbanks and tidal currents that made the harbor impassable to anyone but the local fishermen in their small boats. These years of obscurity are the reason why the town's medina is surprisingly small by comparison to the modern town. The drab medina doesn't have a lot to offer visitors, with neither the cultural attractions of Tanger nor the small-town charm of Asilah. The only significant sights are the town's two 18th-century fortresses (both closed to the public)—the **Château de la Cigogne** and the **Kasbah Kebibat**—which are both in a very poor state of preservation. Near the Château de la Cigogne lies the town's **Archaeological Museum,** housed in an old Spanish prison.

Its collection includes several artifacts from Lixus, although many of the more prestigious items recovered from the site reside in museums at Tétouan, Casablanca, and Marrakech.

For most visitors to Larache, including the thousands of Moroccan vacationers who come here in the summer, the main attraction is the town's stunning beach. Located just across the mouth of the Oued Loukos river, the beach can be reached two ways from Larache. The first is to drive or take the bus on a route that heads several miles upriver to the closest bridge before winding

Larache

⚑ 95 A1

Visitor Information

✉ avenue Mohamed V

☎ (0539) 91 35 32

Larache Archaeological Museum

✉ place de Makhzen, Larache

☎ (0539) 91 20 91

🕐 Closed Tues. & all March

💲 $

Msoura Stone Circle

A few miles south of Asilah lies the Msoura stone circle, a huge formation of 167 standing stones arranged in a series of concentric circles. The largest of these enigmatic monoliths stands almost 20 feet (6 m) tall. The site is thought to be around 5,000 years old and may once have contained the tomb of an ancient king at its heart. Despite its historic significance, however, the site is poorly maintained. The burial mound that stood at its center for millennia was destroyed by overzealous European archaeologists in 1935, and today the site can be reached only by a dizzyingly convoluted route that takes you down a never-ending series of unpaved roads. If you want to visit the site, it is best to inquire at your hotel for a guide or detailed local map.

Curiously, the best place to learn more about the site is not at any of the nearby towns, but at the Tétouan Musée Archéologique (see p. 112), which houses a large-scale model of the site as it looked before the excavations of 1935 as well as artifacts found during that project.

Rainbow-colored rollers can be seen near Larache.

Lixus

While not as well preserved as the monumental ruins of Chellah (see pp. 81–83) or Volubilis (see pp. 178–181), the ancient Roman settlement of Lixus is still well worth a visit. Located about a mile north of Larache, on the opposite bank of the Oued Loukos, it was a thriving metropolis between the first and fifth centuries A.D., when it was the westernmost outpost of the Roman Empire. Most of the ruins at the site date from this period, although some, like the sturdy ruin of a Christian basilica, date from the years of the city's decline, when it was competing for resources with the newly built town of Larache.

Archaeologists have discovered evidence of monoliths and burial mounds that would suggest that the town was founded by the same civilization that built the Msoura stone circle (see sidebar p. 107) to the north. The highlight of the site is the area around the ruined amphitheater, which stands on a high promontory overlooking the Oued Loukos as it winds its way to the sea at Larache.

Ksar el Kebir

Southeast and inland from Larache is the city of Ksar el Kebir. Standing at the heart of some of the best agricultural land in the region, the city has always been an important market town. Today it is best known for the Battle of the Three Kings (see sidebar opposite), the 1578 battle in which a Portuguese army was dealt a devastating

Lixus
95 A1

Ksar el Kebir
95 A1

back to the coast. The second, and much better, way to get there is to walk down to the harbor and pay a few dirhams for the five-minute rowboat trip across the river to the beach. The area around the beach will soon be home to a huge holiday resort, Port Lixus, that will include two golf courses, a marina, and a new bridge connecting Larache with the north bank of the Oued Loukos. For the moment, however, much of the land behind the beaches is a giant construction site, with vacation villas for wealthy Europeans springing up on the hills overlooking the sea.

defeat by Moroccan forces. The battle had far-reaching consequences for both Morocco and Portugal. In Morocco, the ransoms of the hundreds of Portuguese noblemen and mercenaries who were captured during the battle gave Sultan Ahmed el Mansour the funds to initiate an architectural golden age in his capital, Marrakech. In Portugal, the loss of its young king, Sebastian I, as well as the many thousands who fought with him, sent the country into a steep decline that led to it being ruled by Spain for the next 62 years.

Ksar el Kebir is mostly an agricultural market town today, with little to attract tourists. If you're passing on a Sunday, however, it's worth stopping to visit the sprawling and fantastic weekly souk. ■

The Battle of Ksar el Kebir

The Battle of Ksar el Kebir, or the Battle of the Three Kings, as it is sometimes known, was fought at Wadi al Makhazin, near Ksar el Kebir, on August 4, 1578. On one side were the 20,000 well-armed troops of King Sebastian of Portugal (R. 1557–1578) and his ally, the deposed Moroccan sultan al Mutawakkil, who had marched from Tanger. Sebastian wanted to bring Christian rule to Morocco. Opposing him were 50,000 poorly prepared infantry and cavalry under the leadership of Sultan Abd al Malik and his brother Ahmed. The invaders were forced to retreat to Larache, and casualties were heavy on both sides. Many drowned attempting to cross the Wadi al Makhazin, probably including King Sebastian and al Mutawakkil. Abd al Malik, the leader of the Moroccan forces, died the following day, and his brother became the new sultan.

The victory gave Morocco a prestige it hadn't previously enjoyed. In contrast, the body of the young king of Portugal was never positively identified, although King Philip II of Spain later claimed to have received Sebastian's remains from the Moroccans and to have buried them at a monastery at Belém, in Lisbon.

Many Portuguese and mercenaries were captured and held for ransom by the Moroccans, and this led to rumors that King Sebastian had survived and would also be ransomed. At home in Portugal, confusion reigned. There was no direct heir to the throne. Sebastian was briefly succeeded by his great-uncle, Henry, who was a Catholic cardinal. On Henry's death in 1580, Philip II of Spain intervened to prevent the succession of an illegitimate nephew of King Henry.

Portugal had lost its king and lost its independence. However, the belief that Sebastian lived was strong. Between 1580 and 1619, four different pretenders claiming to be Sebastian appeared. The last pretender, an Italian, was hanged by the Spanish in 1619, but the myth lived on.

Sebastianism, the belief that the king would return, was long-lived. He entered popular imagination as "the sleeping king," who would one day return to save Portugal. Sebastian became known as O Desejado ("the desired one") and O Encoberto ("the hidden one"). He was the subject of songs, a play, an opera (by Italian composer Donizetti), countless tales, and even a pop song as late as the 1960s. Late in the 19th century in Brazil, some peasants whose ancestors had emigrated from Portugal pinned their faith in an imminent return of Sebastian to overthrow the new Brazilian republic after the monarchy was ousted in that country in 1890.

Tétouan & Around

The chalk-white city of Tétouan, once the capital of Spanish Morocco, is one of the highlights of any visit to northern Morocco. It lies along the Mediterranean coast about 35 miles (60 km) southeast of Tanger on the lower slopes of the Jebel Dersa mountain. Its close proximity to the Mediterranean beaches, the Rif Mountains, and the Spanish enclave of Ceuta make it an ideal base for exploring the area.

The city of Tétouan is famous for its vibrant food markets.

Tétouan

▲ 95 A2

Visitor Information

✉ 30 boulevard Mohamed V

☎ (0539) 96 19 15

🕐 Closed Sat.–Sun.

Tétouan

After the dusty, earth-colored sprawl of Tanger, Tétouan's compact, chalk-white medina, standing in stark contrast to the verdant hills around it, is a refreshing change. Although little more than a stopover for many visitors—who pass it by on the way to Al Hoceima, Tanger, or Chefchaouene—Tétouan's distinctive architecture, interesting history, and traditional crafts make it worth a longer visit.

Like all the cities in the area, it is rapidly recovering and regen-

erating after a long period of administrative neglect; new hotels, restaurants, and attractions are opening every year. This regeneration, however, is being carefully managed to prevent damage to the buildings or atmosphere of the city's finely preserved medina, which was named a UNESCO World Heritage site in 2001.

Tétouan's history is defined by its centuries-old relationship with Spain. Although settlements have existed on this site since before the Romans arrived, much of the city we see today was founded

INSIDER TIP:

The bus station at Tétouan is a notorious spot for faux guides, con men, and hustlers. If you're new to Morocco, make sure to get well clear of the area before asking anyone for directions.

—CLIVE CARPENTER
National Geographic contributor

in the 15th century by Jews and Muslims fleeing persecution in Spain. As a result, Andalusian culture had a strong influence on the architecture and development of the medina. These influences were particularly strong in the *mellah*—the old Jewish quarter—whose inhabitants continued to converse in Judeo-Spanish (a mixture of Hebrew and Castilian) well into the 20th century.

In the 19th century, the city was a major garrison town for the Spanish colonial authorities. During this period, Tétouan's *ville nouvelle,* known locally as El Ensanche, was built. Its traditional Spanish architecture, itself historically influenced by Arabic design, sits more harmoniously alongside the buildings of the medina than the French art deco of Tanger's ville nouvelle.

Ville Nouvelle: The heart of Tétouan, where the ville nouvelle and medina meet, is the **place Hassan II,** a pretty public square shaded by palm trees and decorated with multicolored patterned paving. The square is surrounded by grand buildings, including the **Khalifa Palace** *(closed to the public),* a summer residence of the royal family, and the former home of the Spanish governor, which now houses Tétouan's best hotel, **El Reducto,** and its excellent

El Reducto

38 Essaid Zanqat Zawya Kadiriya, Tétouan

(0539) 96 81 20

www.elreducto.com

Tétouan's École Artisanale

As you wander around Tétouan, you get the feeling that its people are immensely proud of the city's history, and especially of its long-held traditions. Embroidery is one of the artistic crafts for which the town is famous, along with its intricately pieced-together mosaics, woven carpets, and leather fashioned into clothing. These skills are celebrated as part of the curriculum at the École Artisanale, or Craft School, where local youngsters go to be taught.

Founded in 1919, the school's aim is to preserve and develop the traditional skills that have been passed down

through the generations. Find it near the Moroccan Arts Museum (see p. 114), a few minutes' walk from the Bab Ogla. The organization that runs the school offers tours of the workshops and the rooms where the students' finest work is kept. Nothing here is for sale, but if you're thinking about getting some souvenirs, this is a good place to get an idea of the quality and range of goods that are available in the city. Opening times are variable, but the tourist office *(30 boulevard Mohamed V, tel 0539/96 19 15)* usually has details of when you can see its fascinating exhibits.

Spanish Cathedral

✉ place Moulay el Mehdi, Tétouan

Hotel Panorama Vista

✉ avenue Moulay el Abbas, Tétouan

☎ (0539) 96 49 70

www.panorama vista.com

Café Jenin

✉ 8 rue Alwehdah, Tétouan

☎ (0539) 96 22 46

Musée Archéologique

✉ 2 rue Ben Hussaien, Tétouan

☎ (0539) 96 73 03

🕐 Closed mornings & Sat.–Sun.

💲 $

Ensemble Artisanal

✉ avenue Hassan II, Tétouan

restaurant. The simple entrance to the medina stands on the western side, while the broad boulevards of the ville nouvelle radiate to the south and west.

Tétouan's ville nouvelle is small in comparison to those of many other cities and is not significantly larger than the medina. It is home to the everyday cultural life of the city—its cafés, cinemas, and restaurants. The core of this district is the place Moulay el Mehdi, a public square lined with cafés and dominated by the striking yellow-stone **Spanish Cathedral.** The ville nouvelle has several good hotels and restaurants—including the **Hotel Panorama Vista** and the **Café Jenin**—but only a few must-see sights.

Tétouan's most interesting museum, the **Musée Archéologique** (Museum of Archaeology), is located on the fringe of the medina on the rue Ben Hussaien, northwest of the place Hassan II. This museum houses an extraordinary collection of items recovered from archaeological sites across Morocco. Highlights include beautifully preserved mosaics from the ruins of the Roman city of Lixus (see p. 108), artifacts from the mysterious Msoura stone circle (see sidebar p. 107), and ornate Andalusian tombs. The museum's gardens house larger remains of ancient structures, including mosaics, pillars, and carved stonework.

Another essential stop in the ville nouvelle is the **Ensemble Artisanal,** the first of these government-sponsored stores, opened in 1970. This large store

sells a wide range of traditional crafts at fixed prices; there is no haggling here. All the products are made by a local cooperative of traditional artisans and craftspeople, who produce them in much the same way as they have for centuries. You can learn more about these local craftspeople at the **École Artisanale** (see sidebar p. 111), which is located to the west of the medina.

INSIDER TIP:

The Musée Archéologique in Tétouan is well worth a visit, if only to find out where many of the items missing from Lixus and Msoura went.

—BEN HOLLINGUM
National Geographic contributor

Medina: Most of your time in Tétouan will probably be spent in the city's stunning medina, which stretches up the side of the hill above the valley. This medina is larger than that of Tanger, and remarkably well preserved. The medina is surrounded by ramparts with seven gateways. Each gate is spectacularly sculpted and worth spending some time to admire.

Its whitewashed houses are decorated with traditional ceramics and designed in accordance with Muslim custom—the houses mostly face inward onto courtyards and enclosed gardens, providing privacy for their occupants; their outer walls are punctuated by imposing dark wooden doors, decorated with ironwork and set in elaborate tiled archways. The decorations of these old buildings often feature representations of pomegranates, which were a symbol used by the city of Granada, a great medieval Muslim stronghold.

ing area come to sell their goods. These markets are mostly concentrated in the alleyways and streets immediately behind the Khalifa Palace, off the rue Terrafin. The main square of **Souk el Houts** is dedicated to pottery pieces and rugs. Close by is the **Gherza el Kebira**, a place to purchase locally made clothing, and the

A craftworker painting fine detail onto wood in Tétouan's medina

The Jewish quarter, known as the **mellah**, in the south of the medina, can be easily identified by its distinctive architectural style; here the buildings face outward, with balconies and windows overlooking the streets.

The medina is, as it has been for centuries, an important commercial hub for the rural communities of the eastern Rif Mountains. It hosts many vibrant and busy markets, where craftspeople and farmers from the surround-

Souk el Fouki, which is always a hive of activity. All the souk areas are worth experiencing. They are lively, and often you can catch a glimpse of traditional costumes, like striped *foutas* being worn by Berbers from the Rif Mountains manning their stalls, and the white djellabas of the city folk. In the streets and squares that continue north from the Souk el Houts, there are a succession of smaller souks. Some of these are very specific—selling just leatherwork,

Moroccan Arts Museum

✉ rue Sqala, Tétouan

☎ (0539) 97 27 21

🕐 Closed Sat.–Sun.

Ceuta

▲ 95 A2

Visitor Information

✉ C/Edrossos, s/n, Baluarte de los Mallorquines, Ceuta

☎ (0034) 856 200 560

www.ceuta.es

for example—while others offer a broader range of local crafts.

If you continue farther north, you will pass the tanneries (the terrible smell means these are best avoided) and pass through the Bab Sebta into the city's vast **cemetery,** which spreads out across the hillside. As long as you are respectful, the locals are generally not bothered by visitors exploring the cemetery, although it's best to keep away on Fridays. It is worth looking at, as there are many impressive old tombs, not to mention stunning views of the city and surrounding countryside.

At the eastern end of the medina, around the ancient Bab Okla, lie two important cultural institutions. The **Moroccan Arts Museum** (Musée d'Art Marocain) houses a large collection of traditional costumes and examples of local crafts. Highlights include a beautiful Jewish wedding dress and a collection of antique jewelry. Just outside the Bab Ogla lies the **École Artisanale** (see sidebar p. 111), founded in 1928—a huge complex of workshops and class-rooms where local apprentices learn traditional crafts.

Mediterranean Coast

The city of Tétouan stands in the middle of one of the most varied and beautiful stretches of coast in northern Morocco, from the Spanish enclave of Ceuta in the north to the jagged Rif Mountain coast in the east. The coastline is characterized by attractive beaches and fishing towns, sheltered from the crash-ing ocean waves that can make

the Mediterranean coast a bit forbidding in the winter months.

Ceuta: The northernmost settlement on this stretch of coast is the Spanish enclave of Ceuta. Like its eastern counter-part Melilla (see pp. 132–133), Ceuta is a peculiar political anomaly—a tiny piece of the European Union perched on the Moroccan coastline (see sidebar p. 117). Its political status makes Ceuta a favorite transit point for those hoping to smuggle drugs—

INSIDER TIP:

The mountainous coastline around Ceuta and Tétouan is truly spectacular. If you have the time, take the small coastal roads instead of the main highways for a better perspective.

—CLIVE CARPENTER
National Geographic contributor

or just themselves—into main-land Europe. At times, Ceuta seems like a city under siege; it is surrounded by a series of walls and fences that are watched day and night by security cameras, guard towers, and army patrols. Passing through the numerous gates and checkpoints at the border can feel like entering a prison or a military base. The latter comparison is not entirely without foundation, as Ceuta is dominated by a significant mili-

EXPERIENCE: Semana Santa Celebrations

Morocco is known for its many Muslim festivals, including *moussems,* when pilgrims gather to celebrate a local saint or holy leader (see pp. 20–21). In the Spanish enclaves of Ceuta and Melilla, Christian festivals are also celebrated, especially Semana Santa, or Holy Week. It is a time of pomp and ceremony, when families come out into the streets to see Carnival-style processions depicting scenes of the Passion of Christ, and enjoy church services, family feasts, and much singing, music, and dancing.

The festival runs for several days, starting the week leading up to Easter and including Palm Sunday, Maundy Thursday, and Good Friday. The duration of the festival and its events varies between different towns and cities, but traditionally each day sees an evening candlelit procession led by a different brotherhood or church. The floats are usually decorated and carried by the men of the community, known as *costaleros,* in a gesture symbolic of the suffering of Christ. Andalusia's floats are said to be the most lavishly decorated of all the floats seen throughout Spain and its Moroccan enclaves.

The festivities are usually accompanied by music and dancing, known as a *saeta,* which always includes the extravagant flamenco. Said to have originated in Andalusia around the time of the Spanish Reconquista of the 15th century, the Andalusian-Moorish flamenco is the dance most commonly associated with Spain. The Semana Santa celebrations themselves are said to date from the 16th century, when illiteracy among the populace meant that the suffering of Christ shown through images or actions was a more effective way of relating the story than the written word.

In **Ceuta,** the celebrations tend to revolve around the main square, the Plaza de África, site of the cathedral and Nuestra Señora de África (Church of Our Lady of Africa). In **Melilla,** most of the celebrations are concentrated on the Plaza de España, which links the old part of the town with its 16th-century Medina Sidonia and the new town.

For more information on Ceuta's Holy Week celebrations, contact the **Cultural Information Point** *(Avda. Alcalde Sánchez Prados s/n, Gran Vía, opposite Palacio de la Asamblea, tel 0034/956 528 146)* in the new town. In Melilla, contact the tourist office in the Plaza de las Cuatro Culturas or at *www.melillaturismo.com.*

A float moves through Ceuta in a Semana Santa procession.

Ceuta's Royal Walls dominate the harbor entrance.

Royal Walls
✉ Avda. Martinez & Avda. González Tablas, Ceuta

Ceuta Cathedral
✉ Plaza de África, Ceuta
☎ (0034) 956 517 771

Nuestra Señora de África
✉ Plaza de África, Ceuta

Museo Municipal
✉ 30 Paseo de Revellin, Ceuta
☎ (0034) 956 517 398

tary presence in the form of the Spanish Foreign Legion, a fierce bunch who have been known to start brawls and wreck bars in the city over minor slights.

The first sight that greets you after the trip through all the gates is the towering fortress known as the **Royal Walls** (Murallas Reales). This system of fortifications is open to the public and unexpectedly contains an atmospheric modern art gallery. Beyond the walls lies Ceuta's compact downtown district, which is centered on the Plaza de África and the Paseo Colón. The **Plaza de África** is a huge square dominated by the 17th-century two-towered

Cathedral, remodeled in the mid-20th century and noted for its paintings and statues, and the 18th-century **Nuestra Señora de África** (Church of Our Lady of Africa). This lavish building with its baroque-style facades and elegant doorways was built over the ruins of a mosque destroyed when the Portuguese seized the town in 1415. Nearby is the interesting **Museo Municipal,** which contains an extensive display of coins and amphorae, pottery, tools, and pieces of armor dating back as far as Neolithic times. They were found during routine excavations in the city. A short distance away on the Paseo de Colón is the fascinating, if slightly intimidating, **Museo de la Legion**—the Museum of the Spanish Foreign Legion. Visitors might be surprised to see the prominently placed statue of legion commander and later military dictator Francisco Franco in the museum—a man the rest of Spain is trying to forget.

Ceuta is a sophisticated place, and you can find good restaurants, such as **Club Nautico** and **Gran Muralla** (see Travelwise p. 284). At its port you can catch a ferry to mainland Spain, or see the big cruise ships that arrive here after voyages across the Mediterranean or around the coastline of Morocco. A pleasing walk is up the **Monte Hacho,** a steep hill on which lies a fortress once used by the Spanish army. From this point, you can see over the border all the way to the peaks of the Rif Mountains, as well as across the strait to Gibraltar and Spain.

Beach Resort Towns & Beyond: Leaving the Ceuta enclave, the N13 highway south takes you to the beach resort towns of **Restinga-Smir, Mdiq,** and **Martil,** respectively. Although they've been heavily overtaken by European beach resorts and private compounds, there is still more than enough golden sand around these towns for everyone, even at the height of summer. Although the beaches are accommodating, it can be a challenge to find anywhere to stay at peak times, as the hotels tend to be heavily booked by Moroccan and European families on vacation. Monolithic hotel complexes like the **Barceló Marina Smir** in Restinga-Smir dominate the shoreline, and there's little of interest to nonguests other than the beaches.

As the coastline swings to the east, the Rif Mountains provide a backdrop to a narrow strip of land used for agricultural crops and small villages, which also has fabulous beaches, coves, and off-shore islands. South of Tétouan, the coast road becomes more challenging as you head for **Oued Laou.** This town is most famous for its Saturday market where Berber farmers and craftsmen from miles around come to trade their wares. For the rest of the week, the town is quiet, with little to do. If you want to go somewhere out of the way, however, then the broad empty beaches around the town can be good places to spend a relaxing day sunbathing.

If you head back to the town in the evening, there are a number of informal fish grills and small restaurants selling delicious seafood dishes that have traveled only a few hundred feet from the dock where they were landed.

From Oued Laou, follow the breathtaking **Oued Laou river gorge** inland along one of the most dramatic drives in Morocco toward the city of Chefchaouene (see pp. 119–121). ∎

Museo de la Legion

✉ Avda. Colón s/n, Ceuta

☎ (0034) 699 879 646

🕐 Closed Sat.–Sun.

Barceló Marina Smir

✉ route de Sebta, BP 768, Restinga-Smir

☎ (0539) 97 12 34

💲 $$$$

www.barcelomarina smir.com

Spanish Morocco

Although the days of the Spanish protectorate ended decades ago, Spain still holds onto a number of territories within the area Morocco claims as its own. These territories vary from the large, Spanish-speaking cities of Ceuta and Melilla to isolated military bases on the coast, and even tiny islands where the only notable feature is a flagpole (with a Spanish flag on it, of course). For such importance to be placed on these minuscule and strategically useless territories can seem a little absurd, but both sides take the issue very seriously.

In 2002, there was an incident (arguably the world's smallest war) in which a small group of Moroccan soldiers camped out on the tiny island of Leila (or Perejil, in Spanish)—a barren rock around 650 feet (200 m) from the Moroccan coast east of Ceuta. Despite the apparent insignificance of this uninhabited (and uninhabitable) island, the action caused a major diplomatic row, and the Moroccan troops were forcibly removed from the island after a few days by a Spanish force consisting of four helicopters, a team of commandos, and a navy destroyer.

Rif Mountains

The Rif is a region of spectacular natural beauty and biodiversity. Densely forested hills drop away to fast-flowing, crystal-clear mountain streams that wind their way through dramatic rocky gorges and plunge down beautiful waterfalls. This is a wild, untamed region of Morocco, and even in the towns of Chefchaouene and Ouezzane, you will find an atmosphere very different from what you'd find in the lowlands.

Farming is still a very traditional activity in the Rif Mountains.

The Rif mountain range dominates the landscape of northern Morocco, stretching 180 miles (280 km) from Cap Spartel, just west of Tanger, to the Oued Muluya, a river close to the Algerian border. Although most of the Rif's highest peaks are close to the Mediterranean coast, the range continues as far south as the town of Ouezzane, 70 miles (112 km) south of Tanger. In this lush landscape of pine forests, scrubby mountainsides, and cool highland streams live a wide variety of wild animals—look out for wild boars, foxes, and snakes on the mountainsides or at the side of the road, and eagles high above. If you are lucky, you may see a troop of Barbary macaques.

INSIDER TIP:

If you enjoy lots of outdoor activities, Chefchaouene is your ultimate destination. You can go hiking, mountain biking, horseback riding, canoeing, rafting, fishing, or even spelunking.

—SANAA AKKACH
National Geographic Books designer

The people who call this rugged region home are fiercely independent and have a long history of rebellion and resistance. Many of the towns in this area were settled in the 15th century by Jewish and Muslim refugees from Spain. They held on tightly to their traditional culture and resisted all attempts to pacify or assimilate them. Between the 1890s and the 1920s, the Berber people of the Rif Mountains fought several wars against Spanish and French colonial forces, before they were finally defeated in 1926 by a combined Spanish and French offensive. Although they were brought under the broad control of the Moroccan state in the 1950s, their way of life—in which the cultivation and processing of marijuana (see sidebar) plays a major role—means that the encroaching modernization efforts of the Moroccan government remain largely unwelcome here.

Chefchaouene

This city, 40 miles (64 km) south of Tétouan, makes a good base for trekking and exploring the high peaks of the northern Rif. The city itself has plenty to recommend it—a cool, relaxed place with plenty of fascinating historic buildings in a stunning mountain setting.

From the atmosphere of present-day Chefchaouene, you'd never guess that this city was, in the first half of the 20th century, a fearsome mountain strong-

Chefchaouene

▲ 95 A1

Visitor Information

✉ place Mohamed V, Chefchaouene

Hashish

Farmers in the Rif Mountains produce around a third of the world's hashish, a drug made from compressed marijuana resin. Although this industry has been illegal since 2004, it is still a vital part of the regional economy. Away from the towns, marijuana is cultivated on an industrial scale, with farms using tons of chemical fertilizers to produce several harvests a year. While the crop is more lucrative for the local farmers than conventional cash crops, the largest profits are made by the European criminal gangs that smuggle the compressed resin on fast boats to Spain, France, and Italy.

Despite what street touts might tell you, hashish is not legal in Morocco, and the laws on possession are enforced by the local police, especially against tourists. Police checkpoints are a common sight on the roads of the region, and if any hashish is found, the penalties are severe. Furthermore, dealers often blackmail and exploit visitors who come to them looking for hashish. Nonetheless, the region continues to attract a specific type of tourist, who can usually be seen vacantly strumming a guitar in the fields around Ketama and Chefchaouene.

Sidewalk cafés in Chefchaouene

Musée Ethnographique

✉ place Uta el Hammam, Chefchaouene

☎ (0539) 986 761

🕐 Closed Tues.

💲 $

hold—a place that few Europeans visited before 1920, and not all those who visited the city escaped unharmed. This hostility was born of the city's origins as a refugee community for Jews and Muslims fleeing the 15th-century Spanish Reconquista. For hundreds of years, it was known to Europeans as a place whose residents had a long memory for past injustices and a tendency to hand grudges, as well as traditions, down to the next generation. In the 1920s, after the Spanish finally defeated the local resistance movement, visitors to the city were amazed to find that Chefchaouene's Jewish population still spoke a dialect that strongly resembled medieval Castilian.

Although Chefchaouene is far smaller than Tanger or nearby Tétouan, there is plenty for visitors to see. Entering through the **Bâb el Aïn** at the bottom of the hill, the rue Lalla el Hora takes you on a steep climb up to the **place Outa Hammam,** a colorful

square at the very heart of the medina. Lined with cafés, the small cobbled square is a great place to relax for a while and admire the 15th-century architecture. The square is dominated by the 16th-century **Grand Mosque,** an important local landmark, notable for its unusual octagonal minaret decorated with zellij tilework.

The other notable building on the square is the town's **kasbah.** It was built by the sultans Moulay Ali el Rashid and Moulay Ismail over a period of some hundred years. It is a sturdy, unadorned building, whose appearance was dictated by defensive necessity rather than aesthetics. Nonetheless, its architecture has charm, with occasional decorative flourishes and formal gardens that betray an Andalusian influence.

Its museum, the **Musée Ethnographique,** is well worth visiting. The museum's collection tells the history of Chefchaouene in fascinating detail, focusing on everyday artifacts like Berber costumes, tools, and household items, along with photographs of the town and its people taken during the Rif War of the 1920s.

In addition to its extensive collection, the museum building itself played a small role in the region's turbulent history of rebellion and resistance. During the 1920s, it was used as a jail, and it was here that the leader of the Riffian rebels, Abd el Krim, was held after his capture in 1926. Today you can see his former jail cell and read more about this remarkable episode in Moroccan history.

The **Quartier al Andalus** lies a short walk from the place Outa Hammam and the medina and is where Muslim and Jewish refugees from Andalusia came and settled after being expelled during the 15th-century Reconquista period. It is a lively district full of pretty whitewashed houses with doors the blue color of the sky, adorned with typical Spanish architectural details like wrought iron railings and garden fountains. It is a charming area to spend some time in, and a few little cafés provide refreshment.

Close to Chefchaouene

Chefchaouene is one of the most popular starting points for hikes into the mountains. It nestles in a valley between the twin mountains of **Ech Chaoua** —meaning "the horns"—that give the city its name. A series of fast-flowing mountain streams meet on the steep hillside above the town and tumble down to the medina's walls in a series of beautiful cascades and pools. In the summer, these pools are a popular swimming spot for local youngsters, who can be seen diving from rocky waterfalls into the ice-cold pools below.

The hills and mountains around Chefchaouene make for relatively undemanding hiking and are an excellent introduction to Moroccan hiking conditions for those considering a trip to the more strenuous routes of the Atlas Mountains (see sidebar p. 150).

There any many exciting trails around Chefchaouene offering stunning views of the city and the surrounding hills, and also east of the city in Talassemtane National Park (see sidebar p. 122). The main hiking route out of the city is located to the north of the medina, reached by the main road that leads out of the Bab Majarol. Take this road up to **Camping Azilane,** a simple low-budget campsite popular with guitar-strumming Western backpackers,

Camping Azilane

✉ North of medina, Chefchaouene

☎ (0539) 98 69 79

💲 $

Chefchaouene Arts & Crafts

Chefchaouene is famous for its crafts. In fact, its largest industry is weaving, and the medina is full of tiny workshops where the striped fabrics used to make the shawl-like *foutas* and the lighter fabric that will be sewn to become the loose-fitting djellabas worn by the Riffian community are made.

Visitors will find the town's souk a wonderful place to find souvenirs. Along with the colorful fabrics, you can see leather goods, forged iron lamps, woven wool rugs, slippers, and lovely trinket boxes and items of furniture created from cedar wood. The town has a number of cooperatives, and, as well as crafts, produce from the land has become a buoyant source of income to locals.

The region's olive oil created at the olive presses—a common sight in the villages—is delicious, as are the local olives and goat cheese. Chefchaouene crafts can be seen on sale in other Moroccan towns and cities, too, and visitors have even been known to make the journey from Europe and head straight for Chefchaouene to buy authentic crafts.

INSIDER TIP:

Take a day trip to Akchour to visit the Bridge of God, a breathtaking 80-foot-high (25 m) natural arch formed by eroding red sandstone that once joined two mountains.

—SANAA AKKACH

National Geographic Books designer

where the trail begins. From this point, there is a path marked with yellow-and-white painted rocks (these are sometimes badly weathered and hard to spot) that leads to the 5,300-foot-high (1,616 m) summit of Ech Chaoua. The ascent is steep, and the path narrow, but it doesn't require any climbing or scrambling and can be easily accomplished in an hour or

two by anyone who is reasonably fit. The summit offers the best viewpoint from which to appreciate Chefchaouene's compact, brightly colored medina.

Although many choose to simply retrace their steps back down to the city, it is possible to continue north along another path to the picturesque hamlet of **El Kalaa** before turning back along a trail that skirts around the hill and back to Chefchaouene. Beyond El Kalaa, the path continues north to the **Bridge of God**—a natural bridge that arches 80 feet (25 m) above the Oued Farda. This feature is a full-day's hike away, but most of the journey can be made by car (head to the village of Akchour and follow the Oued Farda upstream) if you are short of time.

Eastern Rif

Leaving Chefchaouene, the road is a little uneven, but the secondary road fairly quickly

Talassemtane National Park

Located in the hills to the east of Chefchaouene, Talassemtane National Park (tel 0539/98 91 78, www.parc talassemtane.com) is one of the most important nature conservation areas in Morocco. Consisting of 148,000 acres (60,000 ha) of pristine mountain terrain, the park is home to a diverse range of wildlife, including the endangered Barbary macaque as well as Morocco's only remaining forest of indigenous Moroccan fir trees. The park was created in October 2004 as part of a government initiative to protect Moroccan flora and fauna from extinction. The authority

that manages the park also runs an excellent information center close the Chefchaouene entrance to the park, where a detailed profile of the area's wildlife, and the organization's efforts to safeguard it, are explained. Its website, which is currently available only in French, contains quite a bit of useful information for prospective visitors, including maps of the park's hiking trails, locations of the refuges and shelters, and a complete database of the flora and fauna of the park, complete with the areas in which they are most commonly seen.

Herding sheep through a meadow of lupins in the Rif Mountains

joins the major N2 road. This *route nationale* was built to connect the city of Tanger with the major towns of northern Morocco and the border with Algeria. Toll-free and at times with several lanes, it runs right through the Rif Mountains a few miles inland from the Mediterranean coast.

Between Chefchaouene and Ketama, the N2 winds its way through a number of small Berber villages perched high in the mountain passes. Most of them consist of a loose collection of houses and farmsteads with no obvious center or permanent marketplace. Although accommodation options here are limited to the point of practically being nonexistent, towns like **Derdara** and **Taza** are good places to stop and explore, especially if you need a break from driving. If you adore the silence of

nature and the sleepy feel of local life, then you may wish to spend a day walking in the hills around these villages. The views from the higher peaks like **Jebel Khesena** (5,500 feet/1,700 m), near Bab Taza, are lovely, although you may find yourself having to jostle your way through the ever present goats to reach them.

About a 60-mile (100 km) drive from Chefchaouene lies the town of **Ketama.** It is on the slopes of **Jebel Tidirhine**, which, at around 8,054 feet (2,450 m) high, is the Rif region's highest peak. If you've spent more than a few days in the region, or done any hiking, you'll be accustomed to seeing the calm, rural side of the Moroccan marijuana industry. Ketama, however, is home to the other, much more dangerous aspect of the business. It is here that the deals are done, where

Derdara
95 B1

Ketama
95 B1

Hotel Tidighine

✉ Ketama

☎ (0539) 81 30 16

Taza

▲ 95 B1

Visitor Information

✉ 56 avenue
Mohamed V,
Taza

European gangsters meet with their Moroccan fixers. The police presence here is small and ineffectual, and the locals don't take kindly to curious visitors. Tourists are advised to pass straight through the town, or avoid it altogether. Curiously, there is one good hotel here, the **Hotel Tidighine,** whose owners seem to be counting on the town's reputation improving dramatically in the next few years.

Taza: Roughly 114 miles (185 km) south of Ketama by road, in the southern foothills of the Rif Mountains, lies the small town of Taza. This town was once an enormously important strategic settlement, jealously guarded by the ruling dynasties of Morocco. Standing on the ramparts of the old medina, it's easy to see why this small town was so prized. With its commanding views of the Taza Pass—traditionally one of the few practical routes between the Mediterranean coast and the imperial cities of Fès and

EXPERIENCE: Hiking in the Rif Mountains

Although the tourist infrastructure is relatively underdeveloped, the Rif Mountains are still a hiker's paradise. While the range has no great peaks to compare with the High Atlas's Jebel Toubkal, it has a breathtakingly beautiful landscape of lush cedar forests, isolated villages, and cascading mountain streams. Wildlife is plentiful, ranging from elusive Barbary macaques and wild boars that can be glimpsed in the cool shadows of the forest to the hawks, booted eagles, and golden eagles that soar on thermal currents high above the valleys.

The lower altitude of the range makes the going easier than in the High Atlas, and the cooler Mediterranean climate allows trips into the wilderness even at the height of summer. There are a number of popular trails through the hills, mostly in the **Talassemtane National Park** (see sidebar p. 122) in the western Rif Mountains near Chefchaouene.

Many international adventure tourism agencies can arrange hiking tours if you book in advance before you leave for Morocco. If you're not one for planning ahead, however, your best bet is **Chaouen**

Rural (Bureau 3, rue Machichi, Qua. Administratif, Chefchaouene, tel 0539/98 72 67, www.chaouenrural.org), which can arrange gîtes (hiker's refuges), mule hire (a low-tech but effective way of taking the weight off your feet), and guides for you. Alternatively, if you don't feel like all the hassle of arranging guides, the hills are not at all a hostile environment—a good map of the area and the usual hiking supplies are generally all you need to find your way around. The locals are friendly and usually happy to point confused-looking hikers in the right direction.

The region's **tourist board** (Moroccan National Tourist Board, 30 avenue Mohamed V, Tétouan, tel 0539/96 19 15) and the **Department of Tourism, Crafts, and Social Economy** (Centre d'Affaires, Aile Sud, Lot 1 C17, avenue Ennakhil-Hay Riad, Rabat, tel 0537/57 78 00, www.tourisme .gov.ma/index_en.htm) offer suggested itineraries, too. The routes take you through the Talassemtane, the Talembote, and the Bouhachem National Parks, with each tailored to different activities, such as bird-watching or mountain climbing.

A Moussier's redstart, one of the special birds of the Rif Mountains

Meknès—whoever held this town controlled northern Morocco. Today, Taza is a quiet town, marginalized during the years of the French protectorate as a punishment for its resistance to European control.

The tense relations between the occupiers and the native inhabitants can be seen in the present-day layout of the town— the French *ville nouvelle* was built with a mile-wide buffer zone of parks and open land between it and the old medina, and although much of this area has now been built on, the two town centers stand a long way apart.

The town itself is a mix of small dwellings that are home to its 5,000 or so residents. They lie within the dried mud walls of the hilltop medina. There are several mosques facing onto the medina's main thoroughfare, which, although closed to the public, are fascinating examples of 12th-century Almohad architecture, probably some of the oldest in the

country. Near the southern end of the street, close to the impressive **Andalous Mosque** (*Mechouar, Medina*) is the town's small **museum,** which explains its role in the region's conflicts and tells the stories of its notable inhabitants. There are several reasonable hotels in the town, mostly in the ville nouvelle. While they aren't anything spectacular, they are comfortable enough, particularly the **Hotel Tour Eiffel** (*route de Fès, Taza, tel 0535/67 15 63, $$$*) and the **Grand Hotel du Dauphiné** (*Prince Héritier Sidi Mohamed, Taza, tel 0535/67 35 67, $$$*), making Taza a good base from which to explore the surrounding hills.

Tazekka National Park: To the south of Taza lies the spectacular landscape of the Jebel Tazzeka National Park. A road runs in a roughly circular route around the mountain, winding through beautiful countryside for around 110 miles (177 km) before finishing back at Taza.

The road is narrow and can be a little precarious, especially when passing oncoming traffic, but it is a great way to see the sights of this area. The cascades of the Ras el Oued, a series of waterfalls that plunges into a deep blue mountain pool, are located a few minutes' drive south of Taza. There is a small hamlet near the top of the waterfalls where you can get food from a small café before continuing, if you want, up Jebel Tazekka.

The real highlight of a trip through the park, however, is the **Gouffre du Friouato,** a massive natural cave complex located around an hour's drive from Taza. The caverns are 750 feet (230 m) deep and have been only partially explored since their discovery in 1935. To get to the main cavern, you have to climb down a lot of steps, before squeezing your way through a very narrow passage-way—it's not an excursion for the claustrophobic. If you're willing to spend a few hours down there, it's worth hiring a guide to take you to the more distant areas like the Salle de Draperies, a chamber where the rock formations look remarkably like curtains that have been turned to stone.

Past the caves, the road winds through the village of Bab Bouldir, a campsite and chalet complex that is inhabited only during the summer. A little farther on, the road passes a rough track that you can take to the summit of Jebel Tazekka (6,500 feet/1,980 m) before returning to Taza.

Ouezzane

In the western foothills of the Rif Mountains, around 50 miles (80 km) southwest of Chefcha-ouene, the town of Ouezzane is emerging from a long period of decline. Although it is still not much to look at—bulky concrete structures erected by local mining companies dominate the skyline—the town is worth stop-

An Ouezzane alley: just wide enough for a loaded donkey

ping at if you're passing through the area. Its unprepossessing architecture conceals what is, in fact, an ancient town with a rich and varied history.

In the 17th century, Ouezzane was a spiritual capital for Moroccan and North African followers of Sufi Islam (a mystical, introspective interpretation of the faith). Moulay Abdullah Cherif, a 17th-century religious figure, believed to be descended from King Idriss I (R. 788–791) created an influential religious brotherhood here, known as the Taïbia, and founded the **Zaouia Ouazzania mosque**.

The **tomb of the marabout**, in the Dar Sqaf area of the medina, is still a pilgrimage site for many Moroccan Muslims. The city has also traditionally been a place of pilgrimage for Morocco's Jewish population, who venerate Rabbi Amrane ben Diwan, a 17th-century Jewish mystic. For Muslims and Jews, this sprawling, industrial city is a place of miracles.

For the less spiritual visitor, there is more than enough to justify stopping off for a while. Ouezzane has long been associated with weaving and other crafts, and this tradition has been experiencing something of a resurgence in recent years. Several crafts **cooperatives** have been established in the town to ensure this valuable part of the town's heritage remains.

On a visit to Ouezzane, you might see wood-turners working with wood collected from the nearby forests. They are known for their finely carved *ghaitas*, a type of reed instrument that has

been used by Berber communities for centuries, and special smoking pipes known as *sebs*. You will see weavers working on looms or spinning wheels, probably making the traditional djellaba garments, known as *djellaba Ouezzania*, or carpets. All these items and more can be seen in its medina's souks and, as Ouezzane crafts are held in such high esteem throughout Morocco, are likely to be seen in shops in other cities, too.

The medina has a souk dedicated to the art of leatherwork, another craft that has been performed in Ouezzane for centuries. The **tannery** dates from the 14th century and is made up of a series of "vats" that have been dug or molded with clay to hold the various liquids needed for the tanning process. The resulting leather is used for items of clothing, such as the traditional *babouche* slippers that can be found everywhere in Morocco, and for household items like poufs, a round ottoman. ∎

Al Hoceima & Beyond

The seaside town of Al Hoceima, which was little more than a fishing village at the start of the 20th century, today commands a long stretch of the Moroccan coast, with resorts and hotels fanning out from its town center in all directions. From the fantastical island fortress of Peñón de Vélez de la Gomera to the Algerian border, this stretch of coastline is one of the finest in Morocco.

Al Hoceima, looking out toward Cap Ras-Tarf

Al Hoceima

⚠ 95 B1

Visitor Information

✉ c/o Agence de Voyage Ketama, 146 avenue Mohamed V, Al Hoceima

☎ (0539) 98 27 72

www.alhoceima.com

This stretch of the Mediterranean coast is one of the most popular vacation destinations for European and Moroccan tourists. The long beaches and relaxed Berber society that prevail in these towns make them ideal places to stop and unwind. Not all of the area is simply beaches and bars, however, and from the Beni Snassen Mountains in the east to the serene natural landscape of Al Hoceima National Park, the region has something to offer all visitors.

Al Hoceima

The attractive modern town of Al Hoceima lies on a cape near the mouth of the Oued Nekor river. By comparison with the small coastal villages and mountain towns that are dotted throughout the surrounding countryside, Al Hoceima has a very modern, cosmopolitan feel. The population is primarily drawn from the local Berber tribes, who speak their own unique language rather than Arabic, but during the peak summer months the population is augmented by tens of thousands of Moroccan and European tourists, who come to enjoy the area's golden beaches and warm weather.

The modern feel of the town is largely due to the fact that it is not, for the most part, very old. Until the mid-20th century, Al Hoceima was little more than a coastal hamlet, a few houses clustered together in the northern part of the bay. The Spanish kick-started its expansion when they landed troops and supplies here during the 1920s Rif War. Over the next few decades, the town was developed further as a garrison town and administrative center for the rebellious Rif region. In the 1950s, the calm waters were once again disturbed by landing craft, as Crown Prince Hassan landed here with several thousand Moroccan troops to suppress the Rif's short-lived independence movement. Having seen two damaging earthquakes in the last 15 years, the town has few buildings that predate the 20th century.

It is not for historic sights, however, that people visit Al Hoceima. It is rather the town's gorgeous beaches, good food, and comfortable hotels that attract visitors. If you feel the need to stop and relax for a few days, this is an excellent place to do it. While many of the hotels are large and lacking in character, the **Hotel Maghreb el Jedid** and the **Hotel Villa Florido** (formerly the Hotel Etoile du Rif) are reasonably priced and have a higher standard of cleanliness and service than many guesthouses in this part of Morocco. Days can be spent exploring **Al Hoceima National Park** (see sidebar below) or lounging around on the beach, before heading to the excellent **Club Nautique** or **Espace Miramar** restaurant for dinner with a view over the sea.

(continued on p. 132)

Hotel Maghreb el Jedid
 56 avenue Mohamed V, Al Hoceima
☎ (0539) 98 25 04

Hotel Villa Florido
✉ 40 place du Rif, Al Hoceima
☎ (0539) 84 08 47
http://florido.alhoceima.com

Club Nautique
✉ Port de Plaisance, Al Hoceima
☎ (0539) 98 16 41

Espace Miramar
✉ rue Moulay Ismail, Al Hoceima
☎ (0539) 98 42 42

EXPERIENCE: Walk in Al Hoceima National Park

Al Hoceima National Park is a huge area of pristine Mediterranean coastal land with a series of fine walks to get away from it all. Covering around 180,000 square miles (466,000 sq km) of land not far from the town of Al Hoceima, the park is operated and maintained by the local government, which encourages tourism in the area. The park's website (French and Spanish only: www.parquenacionalalhucemas.com) offers information on the culture, wildlife, and history of the area and includes several suggested walks as well as prices for the small, but clean and well-appointed, self-catering cottages located in various corners of the park. The park is an excellent place to go to escape the crowds of Al Hoceima in peak season. Hidden down various dirt tracks and side roads, there are several lovely coves and beaches largely undisturbed by vacationing families.

Drive: Zegzel Gorge

A few minutes' drive south of Saïdia, between the towns of Berkane and Taforalt, lies a 10-mile (16 km) stretch of spectacular gorge scenery.

Isolated small villages overlook the road in the Zegzel Gorge.

Lying between **Saïdia** and **Oujda** to the east of the extensive Rif mountain range is one of the country's most dramatic gorges. The Zegzel Gorge is the result of millions of years of erosion, as the waters of the Oued Zegzel river slowly sliced through the brilliant red rock of the Beni Snassen Mountains. The road that winds through this river valley is simply breathtaking. See sheer rock faces, grove upon grove of olive and citrus trees, mountains and plateaus, and the fast-flowing waters of the Oued Zegzel.

The road is worn in places and the going can be bumpy, so an off-road vehicle will make the trip easier. The route zigzags around the **Jebel Tamefout**, one of the highest peaks of the Beni Snassen range.

The best place to start this journey is in **Berkane ❶**, a nondescript inland town located around 15 miles (24 km) south of Saïdia. It is

NOT TO BE MISSED:

Grotte de Chameau • Grotte des Pigeons

here that the highway from the coast meets the main N2 highway that runs across northern Morocco from Chefchaouene to Ahfir on the Algerian border. These two roads meet at a large **traffic circle ❷** dominated by a fancy new fountain at the center. From here, take the N2 south for around a mile before turning left shortly after the road crosses the Oued Zegzel. Follow this road as it winds through some modern housing districts before curving south to run parallel with the river. After 2 miles (3 km) of villages and farmland, the road enters the **Zegzel Gorge ❸**.

After about 5 miles (8 km) of tight curves and stunning views of the valley, during which the road crosses back and forth over the river six times, you come to a turning on your left, where a side road doubles back on itself and climbs for around half a mile (0.8 km) through olive groves to the **Grotte de Chameau** ❹. This large cave complex has sadly been closed to the public for several years now as a consequence of flood damage. Even though you can't get into the caves, the site provides travelers with a nice place to stop and rest for a minute by a crystal clear river (a tributary of the Oued Zegzel) where the locals like to go bathing, and to admire the towering form of **Jebel Tafoughalt.**

A little farther along the road, the valley opens out in a broad bowl-shaped area, where the land has been carved into terraced plots by generations of local farmers. Here the road straightens out a little, forming a series of broad, sweeping curves with great views of the surrounding farmland. After a minute or two, however, it's back into the gorge for one last stretch of switchbacks before you reach the **Grotte des Pigeons** ❺, where skeletal remains of birds and humans have been found dating from the early Stone Age. This cave is currently an active archaeological site, controlled by Oxford University, so visitors can only look in rather than enter.

Another half mile (0.8 km) farther on, the road rejoins the N2 highway just north of the town of **Taforalt** ❻. Here you can either head south to Taforalt itself, where there are some good hotels and restaurants and a lively souk on Wednesdays or turn right and take the main road until it joins the N2 back to Berkane. This route, which travels about 12 miles (20 km) around the mountains back to Berkane town center, has the advantage of being mostly straight and flat.

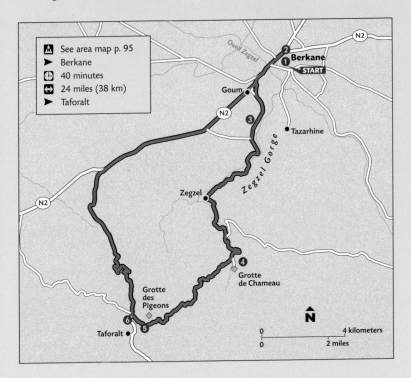

Imzouren Souk

Souks full of crafts, produce, and clothing can be found throughout Morocco, but none are quite like the souk at Imzouren. Located around 10 miles (17 km) from Al Hoceima in the city of Imzouren, it is open to Moroccan women only. It is the only souk in the country where women, most of whom are of Berber Imazighen descent, can wander freely, engage in conversation with fellow female shoppers, and make their purchases. Men are allowed entry only to assist women shoppers, and then only for a limited period of time.

Melilla

🅼 95 C1

Visitor Information

✉ Plaza de Toros, Melilla

☎ (0034) 952 675 444

www.melillaturismo .com/ingles

Museo Municipal

✉ Plaza Pedro de Estopiñán s/n, Melilla

☎ (0034) 952 681 339

🕐 Closed Mon.

Around 50 miles (80 km) west of Al Hoceima lies the spectacular fortress of **Peñón de Vélez de la Gomera**. This Spanish military outpost is one of the Plazas de Soberania, the areas within Morocco's borders that remained part of Spain after the end of the colonial period (see sidebar p. 117). The imposing military base stands on a massive rocky outcrop, which used to be an island, linked to the mainland by a small sandbank and a drawbridge. It's been more than a hundred years since the post had any military significance, but it still remains a garrisoned Spanish possession.

Melilla

Around 90 miles (145 km) east along the coast from Al Hoceima, not far from the Algerian border, lies the Spanish enclave of Melilla. Like its western counterpart Ceuta (see pp. 114–116), Melilla is an attractive if rather crowded town, surrounded on its landward side by a well-guarded border. Although

illegal trafficking, and resulting heavy security, is less of a problem here than in Ceuta, it can still take some time to make it through border control, especially if you have a car.

Melilla is dominated by the fearsome-looking fortress of the **Medina Sidonia**—a thick-walled 16th-century bastion that protected the small old town within from attacks by Moroccan armies. For much of the town's history, this fortress and the small settlement inside were all there was to Melilla. It was not until the 20th century—when it became an important cargo port for the Spanish protectorate—that the town expanded south onto the mainland away from the small peninsula.

The old town within the Medina Sidonia is well worth a look, and the notable sights and attractions are well signposted. Of particular note is the **Museo Municipal,** which houses a collection of artifacts, documents, and artwork relating to the long and varied history of this settlement and its people.

The new town outside the walls is equally enchanting, with its grand main square designed by Spaniard Enrique Nieto (1883–1954), a student of the famous architect Antoni Gaudí (1852–1926). The new town is also home to many excellent bars and restaurants; the atmosphere here is more permissive than on the other side of the border, and its varied nightlife is a refreshing change, especially for women tired of the all-male confines of

The modernist-style church of Sagrado Corazón in Melilla

most Moroccan bars. Highlights include the **Bar Alhambra, Los Salazones,** and **Casa Marta.**

Nador

Just across the border from Melilla is the sprawling modern town of Nador. This unremarkable town was just a village when Morocco gained its independence in 1957, but it grew rapidly as the trade that once passed through Melilla was rerouted here. There is nothing much to draw tourists to the town, but its reasonable selection of hotels and restaurants make it an excellent base for exploring the protected wetlands at **Kariat Arekman** and **Oued Moulouya,** a short distance to the east. The former is a salt marsh, home to a diverse population of migratory

shorebirds, while the latter is a freshwater wetland, inhabited by kingfishers, herons, and egrets.

Saïdia

The last major town on the coast before the Algerian border, Saïdia is a sprawling modern beach resort crammed with beaches, golf courses, and mid-priced hotels. It feels as if the town has been developed too fast, as it lacks an obvious core or any real cultural life. Saïdia does, however, host a popular traditional music festival every August.

Beyond Saïdia, the towns of northern Algeria look like a tempting day trip, but unfortunately the border to Algeria is closed as a result of a long-running diplomatic dispute over the Western Sahara that is unlikely to be resolved anytime soon. ■

Nador
 95 C1

Visitor Information

 Délégation du Tourisme de Nador, 80 boulevard Ibn Rochd, Nador

☎ (0256) 33 54 52

✉ Syndicat d'Initiative de du Tourisme, Hôtel Rif, Nador

☎ (0256) 60 36 37

Saïdia
▲ 95 C1

An imperial city with a medieval market and magnificent mosques, presiding over an area of majestic mountains and traditional villages

Fès & the High Atlas

Detail of Bab Boujeloud—gateway to the old town of Fès el Bali in Fès

Fès & the High Atlas

Fès, Morocco's oldest Islamic city and third largest after the capital Rabat and the commercial hub Casablanca, is a 1,200-year-old living museum of historic Hispano-Arabic culture and architecture that blends harmoniously with the cosmopolitan edge it has enjoyed for centuries. It sits on a plain overlooking the Middle and High Atlas region, which has become a haven for trekkers, winter-sports and wildlife enthusiasts, and those in search of Morocco's traditional villages and way of life.

Fès came to the fore as a major city when it was made the capital of Morocco in 809. For centuries it was home to the royal family, top politicians, and financial and commercial leaders, as well as musicians, writers, and intellectuals, many of whom were educated in its universities. Although Meknès, Marrakech, and Rabat have all since held the crown as Morocco's capital city for certain periods of time, Fès has had the longest tenure as its capital and continues to thrive as a dynamic city to this day.

Fès has three main areas, all overlooked by a necropolis and the remains of a 16th-century

palace. Fès el Bali is the oldest part of the city, characterized by a maze of lanes, courtyards, and alleyways dating from as early as the eighth century. Its *medersas* (universities), palaces, souks, mosques with soaring minarets and graceful domes, and stone dwellings (known as *fondouks*) are all fine examples of early Islamic, Moorish, and Andalusian architecture. Declared a UNESCO World Heritage site in 1983, Fès el Bali is a huge, car-free medina and an essential site for any visitor to Morocco.

Fès el Jedid, also known as Fès Jdid, is an extension to Fès el Bali. Founded in the 13th century by the Marinids, this is where the imposing Dar el Makhzen Royal Palace, the city's Jewish Quarter, and some of Fès's finest shopping areas, along the grande rue de Fès el Jedid, can be found.

The third district of Fès is the mainly residential Ville Nouvelle. Its wide boulevards, designed almost exclusively during the French protectorate, are lined by trees, plush homes, public gardens, and shady café terraces, giving it a distinctly European feel.

Fès is now the capital of the Fès-Boulemane region, which includes Fès-Dar-Dbibegh in the center and the provinces of Sefrou, Moulay Yacoub, and Boulemane. The landscape is as varied here as anywhere in Morocco. Deep valleys covered with flowers and forests of cedars contrast with mountainous terrain of foothills and peaks, gorges, palm groves, and desert. Along the way are towns made famous by their thermal springs and waterfalls, picturesque villages, and centuries-old communities.

For the traveler with time to spend in this

NOT TO BE MISSED:

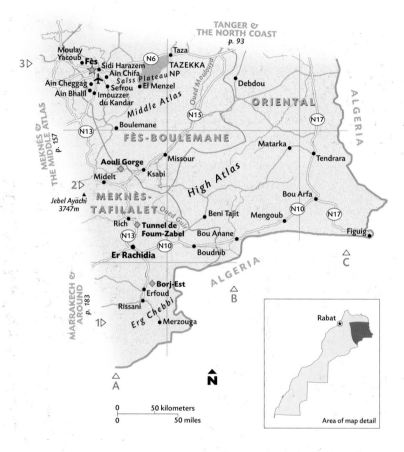

region, the towns of Moulay Yacoub, Sefrou, and Midelt are worth a visit. And there are plenty of attractive villages in dramatic landscapes. Merzouga and Rich, way to the south of Fès, are just two examples that could be included in an itinerary.

Fès lies on the Saïss Plateau on the very edge of the Middle Atlas Mountains. South of Fès, the landscape becomes hillier as it approaches the Middle Atlas, with the much higher and more extensive High Atlas range behind it. Almost due south of Fès is the mighty Jebel Ayachi, which at 12,264 feet (3,747 m) is the highest peak in the eastern section of the High Atlas, a beautiful range that is home to some of Morocco's rarest flowers, animals, and birds—and a haven for naturalists, hikers, and outdoor enthusiasts of all persuasions.

Fès and the High Atlas Mountains experience some of the most extreme temperatures of all the regions in Morocco. The summer from late June to September can be exceptionally hot with Fahrenheit temperatures in Fès reaching triple figures. Winter days are much colder, with the mountain peaks often coated with a heavy layer of snow. Winter sports are a popular pastime here, but trekkers should note that mountain passes are often closed when snowfall is at its heaviest.

From history and heritage to landscapes full of wildlife and sporting opportunities, Fès and the High Atlas region have proved key places to visit on most visitors' itineraries. ■

Central Fès

Layers of history unfold like an exotic flower in the culturally rich and complex city of Fès, from the Hispano-Arab-influenced mosques, *medersas* (universities), labyrinthine lanes, and courtyards of 8th-century Fès el Bali, to the 13th-century Marinid royal palaces and gardens surrounded by the Jewish architecture of Fès el Jedid, to the elegant, wide, tree-lined boulevards of the 20th-century French-built Ville Nouvelle.

Carpet trading shops line the cobbled streets in the Fès el Bali medina.

Fès

137 A3, 143

Visitor Information

✉ Regional Tourist Office, Immeuble Bennani, place de la Résistance, boulevard Moulay Youssef

☎ (0535) 62 34 60

✉ Syndicat d'Initiative, place Mohamed V

☎ (0535) 62 47 69

When Fès first became the capital of Morocco in 809, it was known as Madinat Fès. Idriss II built his royal palace here, along with mosques, fountains, stone houses known as *fondouks*, and a medina full of covered markets called *kissaria* in an area now known as Fès el Bali.

Morocco's first imperial city soon grew in population, size, and importance. In 817, refugees arrived from Córdoba, Andalusia, in what is now Spain, and founded the city's Andalusian district,

Adwat al Andalus, to the northeast of the city. Arab families fleeing persecution in Kairouan, today known as Tunisia, joined them in Fès a few years later and founded the district of Kairaouine, also known as Adwat al Qarawiyyin. The strong cultural heritages and architectural expertise of these two new communities were key to the development of Fès as a major Mediterranean city.

The following years saw the cityscape transform. In 857, a wealthy and highly religious

Kairouan woman commissioned the Kairaouine Mosque, one of the finest mosques in the world.

Fount of Knowledge

The mosque also became the site of Morocco's first medersa, Kairaouine University (see p. 144) in 859. Among its many scholars were the Jewish philosopher and physician Maimonides and the historian Ibn Khaldoun. Fès soon became the country's cultural, educational, and scientific center, and it remained so even when the capital shifted to Marrakech in the 12th century. In the 1250s, it regained its position as the country's capital when the Marinid dynasty made Fès the center of its empire. To house the magnificent palaces they planned to build, the Marinids created a new town, Fès el Jedid, to sit alongside the old Fès, just outside the city walls.

Fès el Jedid had its own fortifications, richly decorated palaces, Koranic schools and universities, souks, parks, and fondouks. A huge mechouar—a square for ceremonial events that would attract an audience of thousands—was incorporated into the design, along with a *mellah*, the district housing the city's Jewish population.

In the 16th century, Morocco's capital switched once again to Marrakech under a new dynasty, yet Fès continued to grow as a cultural, spiritual, and intellectual center. Its turbulent history continued in the 17th century when the Alaouite dynasty gradually took over the city. Once again declared the capital, the city became a major trading center of grain, fish, leather, and textiles.

Apart from a spell in the 17th and 18th centuries, Fès remained the capital until Morocco became a French protectorate with the Treaty of Fès in 1912. Although no longer the capital, Fès is an important commercial city and is still considered Morocco's spiritual and cultural center.

Fès el Bali

If you have only a short time to spend in Fès, the atmospheric walled old town of Fès el Bali is a must. This UNESCO World Heritage site is a labyrinth of car-free lanes, courtyards,

NOTE: Fès is a transport hub. You will find the main railway station (rue Imarate Arabia, tel 0535/93 03 33) in Ville Nouvelle. Trains leave regularly during daylight hours for Casablanca, Rabat, Meknès, Marrakech, and Tanger. The Compagnie de Transports au Maroc (CTM) bus station (place Allal al Fassi, tel 0535/73 29 92 or reservations: 0522/43 82 82) is served by relatively new and reliable state-run buses, offering services to the railway station; Fès-Saïss Airport (Imouzzer, BP A11, tel 0535/62 48 00), which is 10 miles (15 km) south of the city; all areas of Fès; and the town of Sefrou.

The Fez: A Distinctive Hat

The city of Fès is famous for its brimless, red, cylindrical hat known as a fez, fès, fèsi, or tarboosh. Until the 19th century, it was the only city in the world to manufacture this popular headgear favored by men and military personnel in the Maghreb, Greece, and the Ottoman Empire. Its origins are unclear and some stories suggest it was first conceived in ancient Greece, but the most popular account is that it came from Fès, where they can still be purchased in the medina. This hat is made of a woven fabric similar to felt and adorned with a tassel. It is generally red in color, although variations have included white and black. The red dye for the hats is produced from *kizilcik* berries that thrive on the outskirts of the city.

Bou Inania Medersa

🗺 143

✉ rue Talaa Kebira

🕐 Closed to non-Muslims Sat.–Thurs. 12 p.m.–2:30 p.m. & Fri. after 11 a.m.

💲 $

and alleyways dating back to the eighth century. It can be entered through one of four main *Babs* (gates)—**Bab Boujeloud** to the west, **Bab Guissa** to the north, **Bab Jdid** to the south, and **Bab Ftouh** to the southeast. Once inside, early Islamic and Andalusian architecture can be seen everywhere and the mosques, palaces, medersas, souks, and fondouks are beautifully adorned with carvings and other features from these periods.

Near Bab Boujeloud: Fès el Bali is perhaps best known for its massive, mesmerizing **medina** (market), ideally entered through Bab Boujeloud. Life within the medina has changed little over the centuries, and this buzzing hive of activity is filled with people making a living by selling traditional crafts, clothing, and food from stalls. Soak in the medieval atmosphere as you head up one of its two main arteries—rue Talaa Kebira to the north or rue Talaa Seghira to the south—and meander among the souks, which are arranged by theme: **Souk Nejjarine**, for example, is known for its furniture and woodwork, **Souk Tillis** for its carpets, and **Souk Attarine** for its medicines and spices. When you find your senses sated by the medina's multitude of goods, visit the area's more tranquil treasures.

Of all Fès's medersas, **Bou Inania Medersa** is the one not to miss. From Bab Boujeloud, head up rue Talaa Kebira and you'll soon see the green-tiled minaret of this elegant 14th-century

Children play around a decoratively tiled fountain in the Fès el Bali medina.

Fès Pottery

As you wander around the city's shops and souks, you will see the brilliant cobalt-blue pottery that has been made in Fès since the 11th century. Craftsmen still make it by hand in workshops off the rue Talaa Kebira, turning pots on a traditional potter's wheel as has been the practice for centuries. Water is added to the clay to make it moist and malleable before each piece is fashioned and then fired in a large kiln fueled by olive pits. Afterward, intricate geometric or floral designs are painted with delicate horsehair brushes onto the surface of the pottery, which is then sealed with a final firing. Among the pieces are jugs, vases, jars with lids, bowls, plates, and *tajines* (for cooking Morocco's famous cous cous). You can visit a pottery factory (*Cooperative des Patrons Potiers, rue de Sidi Harzeme, Ain Nokbi, tel 0535/64 92 25*) to see Fès pottery being made in the industrial quarter of Ain Nokbi, near Bab Ftouh in the Andalusian district. However, if you are looking for gifts, the best buys can be found in Fès el Bali medina's Souk el Henna, located in a square off Souk Attarine (*souk el Attarine*).

Hire a guide to navigate your way through Fès's medina. A good guide isn't expensive and will ward off pickpockets, provide stories of local flavor, and save you hours of wandering in circles.

—SUSAN STRAIGHT
National Geographic Books editor

building. Lavishly decorated with *zellij* tiles, marble, and onyx, it is considered the finest medersa built during the Marinid dynasty.

From here, go to rue Talaa Seghira, then south on rue de la Poste to reach Fès's largest museum—the **Dar Batha Museum.** Its highlights include an extensive display of traditional pottery and an interesting exhibition on the art of zellij tilework, which traces its origins back to the 14th century. Housed in the 19th-century **Batha Palace,** once the home of city dignitaries, it is surrounded by a spacious Andalusian-style garden in which to relax.

Near Bab Guissa: This entrance to Fès el Bali quickly brings you to the **Palais Jamaï** on your left. Built in the 19th century as Great Vizier Jamai's palace, its majestic Arabic architecture and lush gardens now form part of a five-star hotel offering outstanding views of the medina to the south and the atmospheric ruins of the **Marinid tombs—** where the Marinids buried their dead—on a hilltop to the north. A climb up to the tombs offers one of the best views of Fès.

If you wander southeast from here, past the lively twitter of birds for sale in the **Achebine Souk,** you come to the Tanners' Quarter known as the **Chouwara Tanneries** (see sidebar p. 145) on the banks of the Oued Fès river. A (continued on p. 144)

Dar Batha Museum
- 143
- place d'Istiqlal
- (0535) 62 34 60
- Closed Tues.
- $

Palais Jamaï
- 143
- Bab Guissa
- (0535) 63 43 31
- www.sofitel.com /gb/hotel-2141 -sofitel-fes-palais -jamai/index.shtml

A Walk Through Central Fès

This route covers Fès's most historic districts, starting with the 13th-century Marinid royal palace and Jewish architecture of Fès el Jedid, and then winds back in time through the mazelike streets of the eighth-century Arab and Andalusian Fès el Bali.

A bustling corner of the Fès el Bali medina, a winding maze of streets

If you want to take in most of the main sites of Fès by foot, a good place to start is the district of Fès el Jedid. Begin at **place des Alaouites** in the district's southwest corner and admire the entrance to the **Dar el Makhzen Royal Palace ❶** (see p. 146). The King stays here when he is in Fès, and dignitaries meet here for summits; unfortunately it is closed to the public. Stroll east along the grande rue des Merinides to see the fortified *mellah* (see sidebar p. 147), the city's Jewish Quarter, which is always busy and bursting with atmosphere. Turn north onto the grande rue de Fès el Jedid to reach the relaxing park of **Jardins de Boujeloud ❷** (see p. 146).

As you head out of the park, turn right along the avenue des Français to the place Bou Jeloud, site of one of the city's gates, the **Bab Boujeloud ❸**. This impressive structure was built in 1913 in a Moorish style with symmetri-

NOT TO BE MISSED:

Dar Batha Museum • Bou Inania Medersa • rue Cherabliyne

cal arches, extensive calligraphy, floral carvings, and blue tilework on its sides. Ahead of you is the rue Talaa Seghira, which will take you into the old city, **Fès el Bali.**

You are bound to get caught up in the addictive atmosphere of Fès el Bali, so before you do, take a short detour along the rue el Douh to your right to visit the **Dar Batha Museum ❹** (see p. 141). As you wander through the museum's themed rooms, you will see books, ceramics, woodcarvings, woven textiles, leatherwork, and colorful *zellij* tiles, with some items dating back as far as the ninth century.

After your visit to the museum, head back

toward the rue Talaa Seghira, glimpsing the minaret of the **Bou Inania Medersa** to your right (see pp. 140–141). Admire the striking Hispanic-Moorish architecture of this university's woodcarvings and zellij tiles, and don't miss the tiny rooms that were once used by scholars. If you need to stop for a break, the rue Talaa Seghira has some good restaurants and food stalls selling savory snacks like *chebakyas*, made of fried pastry with honey, and *kaab ghzahl*, known as *cornes de gazelle,* which are tasty pastry crescents filled with almonds.

Running parallel to rue Talaa Seghira is rue Talaa Kebira. If you take this route, you will come to the **rue Cherrabliyne** , one of the main thoroughfares of the Fès el Bali medina and home to numerous souks. Look for the colorful mounds of coriander, turmeric, peppers, cumin, and saffron in the spice markets, and shops selling *babouches* (slippers) and fez hats. Also notice the *fondouks*—old stone houses around courtyards where many of the medina's residents live. To your left is the Kairaouine Quarter, and on the hilltop in the distance you can see the Marinid tombs.

Continue back to rue Talaa Seghira through the medina's tiny labyrinthine streets to visit the **Zaouia of Moulay Idriss II** (see p. 145), an 18th-century mosque famous for housing the tomb of Idriss II—Morocco's most sacred shrine. Head north to souk el Attarine and turn right to reach the **Attarine Medersa** (see p. 144). Almost opposite is the spectacular ninth-century **Kairaouine Mosque** , then the **Cherratine Medersa** and the **Seffarine Medersa** (all on p. 144). At the top of the square, take the right-hand lane, Derb Mechattin, to the **Tanners' Quarter** (see sidebar p. 145), where you can enjoy the colorful spectacle of hides left to dry in the sun. From here you can cross the river to visit the **Andalusian Quarter** (see pp. 145–146), a more residential district of souks where you can peruse the locals' wares with less hassle than in the more hectic medina. As you wander through this ancient part of the city, look up to see if you can spot the nearby **Andalusian Mosque** set like a crown up on a hill.

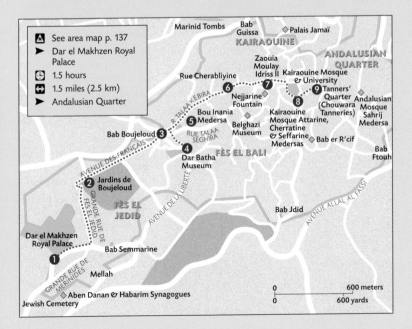

Kairaouine Mosque and University

🅰 143

✉ rue Bou Touil

☎ (0535) 64 10 16

Seffarine Medersa

🅰 143

✉ place el Seffarine

💲 $

Cherratine Medersa

🅰 143

✉ rue el Cherratine

💲 $

terrace above the vats full of colorful pigments gives a panoramic view of tanners working with the skins of goats and cows as they have for centuries at this location.

Near Bab Jdid: If you enter through Bab Jdid, follow the signs to Fès el Bali's main landmark—the ninth-century **Kairaouine Mosque and University,** named for the district surrounding it. The mosque boasts a prayer room that can accommodate up to 20,000 worshipers and an extensive inner courtyard covered in more

Ornate handle on a gilt door at the entrance to Dar el Makhzen Royal Palace

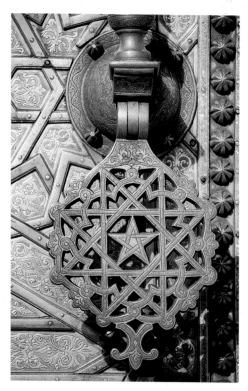

than 50,000 zellij tiles intricately laid in a geometric pattern around a marble fountain. Non-Muslims are forbidden entrance to the mosque and will have to be content with gazing through the gates—located on rue Talaa Kebira and place el Seffarine—at its imposing tiled facades, colonnaded walkways, and tall minaret. Established as a medersa as well as a place of worship, it claims to be the oldest working university in the world and today houses one of the world's leading centers of Islamic scholarship.

Three of Fès's finest medersas are located around the Kairaouine Mosque and University complex. On its southeast corner sits the 13th-century **Seffarine Medersa.** Under its magnificent carved wooden dome is a fountain surrounded by a courtyard and Fès's oldest mihrab—the niche in the wall indicating the direction of Mecca, toward which Muslims face when praying. The 17th-century **Cherratine Medersa** is located at Kairaouine Mosque's southwest corner. The only medersa in Fès built by the Alaouites, its zellij tile patterns are less ornate than those in the older medersas, but just as appealing. And on the north side of the mosque is the 14th-century **Attarine Medersa.** Reopened in 2010 after a four-year renovation, its courtyard of carved marble columns and cedarwood arches is exquisite, and its entrance hall has one of the most delicate and complex zellij tile patterns in Fès.

From here, head west on souk

INSIDER TIP:

Visit the carpenters, blacksmiths, or any type of craftspeople willing to give you behind-the-scenes access. Some of the oldest and most traditional crafts in Fès are the Moroccan slippers and the ornate and highly detailed tea service sets.

—SANAA AKKACH
National Geographic Books designer

el Attarine to see the **Zaouia of Moulay Idriss II**—the opulent mausoleum of the great sultan and founder of Fès. Non-Muslims are not allowed into the shrine room, but can peek inside to view some of its sumptuous interior.

Walk one block farther west to the **Nejjarine Fountain**—one of Fès's most beautiful and famous mosaic fountains—and **Nejjarine Museum.** Housed in a traditional fondouk—a combination of an inn and workshop, also known as a *caravanserai*—the museum's collection of Moroccan woodwork includes beautifully crafted musical instruments and friezes. Its roof terrace has an exhibition on the fondouk's renovation and a café with great views over the medina.

Due south is the **Belghazi Museum,** a 17th-century palace owned by the Belghazi family. It houses an excellent collection of weapons, carpets, and jewelry, as well as a shady courtyard café and terrace with scenic city views.

Near Bab Ftouh: If you enter Fès el Bali through Bab Ftouh, you'll find yourself in the **Andalusian Quarter.** This residential area has many souks selling items of a more practical nature, and you will be hassled

Attarine Medersa

  143

✉ souk el Attarine

☎ (0535) 62 34 60

$ $

Zaouia of Moulay Idriss II

🅰 143

✉ rue bou Touil Kairaouine

Nejjarine Museum

✉ place Nejjarine

☎ (0535) 74 05 80

$ $

Belghazi Museum

🅰 143

✉ 19 rue Derb Ghorba

☎ (0535) 74 11 78

$ $

EXPERIENCE: Chouwara Tanneries

Fès has been associated with the traditional craft of tanning since at least the Middle Ages. If you think you have the stomach for pungent odors, visit its **Tanners' Quarter**—the Chouwara Tanneries—on the riverbanks of the Oued Fès at the edge of the Andalusian Quarter.

Visitors cannot enter the tanneries, but can watch the action from balconies overlooking them. Visit one of the adjacent leather shops, climb the steps, and take in the scene. It is best to visit in the morning when the dyes are at their most brilliant. Try **Terrasse de Tannerie** (*10 Derb Chouwara, tel 0535/63 66 25, $*).

Tanning is relatively straightforward and has been practiced, almost unchanged, for centuries. Hides from cows, camels, or goats are first cleaned of flesh and hair, then soaked in a mixture made from the bark of pomegranate trees to soften them. They are next rinsed and dried; a walk around the tanneries district will discover countless hides strewn over walls and roofs to be dried in the sun.

The hides are then dyed. Although commercial dyes are more commonplace nowadays, many tanners still use dyes concocted from berries and plants, as they would generations ago.

A dye worker treats an animal hide in Fès el Bali's strong-smelling Chouwara Tanneries.

Andalusian Mosque
🅰 143
✉ rue el Nekhaline

Sahrij Medersa
🅰 143
✉ rue Sidi Bou Ghaled
☎ (0535) 63 34 60
$ $

Aben Danan Synagogue
🅰 143
✉ rue Der el Feran Teati, Mellah
$ $

Jewish Cemetery
🅰 143
✉ Mellah

far less here than in the medina. Don't miss the impressive ninth-century zellij-tiled entrance arch of the **Andalusian Mosque** and the **Sahrij Medersa**, which is one of Fès's finest medersas, despite receiving less attention than some of the others due to its more remote location.

Fès el Jedid

A newer walled extension to Fès el Bali, on its southwest side, is the district of Fès el Jedid, which means "New Fès." Built in the 13th century by the Marinid dynasty—who decided the existing walled city was too small for their grandiose architectural plans—it offers plenty of attractions for visitors today.

Running between the two districts, with its main entrance on avenue des Français just south of Bab Boujeloud, is the **Jardins de Boujeloud.** This large park is a perfect place to chill out under a shady tree on hot days or enjoy a coffee or breakfast in its café.

To reach the **Jewish Quarter** (see sidebar opposite), or *mellah,* continue west down avenue des Français, turn left onto grande rue de Fès el Jedid and through the imposing 13th-century **Bab Semmarine** to rue Sekkakine, which becomes grande rue des Merinides. Created to house the city's Jewish population in the 13th century, most of the mellah's houses, with their wood-and-wrought-iron balconies, date from the 18th or 19th century.

Halfway down grande rue de Merinides, turn left onto Derb Djaj to visit the beautiful prayer room of the 17th-century **Aben Danan Synagogue** and then continue on to the **Jewish Cemetery,** with 12,000-plus white gravestones and **Habarim Synagogue,** which houses a museum of Jewish artifacts.

An exit at the end of the cemetery leads to place des Alaouites and the magnificent entrance to **Dar el Makhzen Royal Palace,** with its gilt-bronze doors, carved arches, and marble columns. The palace, closed to the public and protected by a high level of security, is still used for government summits and as the King's residence when he is in Fès—so the nearest you will get to the palace itself is one of the striking brass doors in the wall surrounding its gardens.

The Jewish Quarter

Located in the southeast of the Fès el Jedid district is the Jewish Quarter of the city known as the *mellah*. Most major Moroccan towns and cities have a mellah, but the one in Fès is widely believed to have been the first. It dates from the 14th-century Marinid period, although the present buildings are mostly 18th and 19th century and noted for the fact that they lie unusually close together. When the mellah was created, space was limited, so families built their homes with two stories and close together. An inner courtyard provided the only outside area. As you wander around, you will see this rare form of architecture, along with many souks and workshops, where traditional crafts are being made.

INSIDER TIP:

After wandering the medina all day, retire to the roof deck of the Palais Jamaï hotel [see p. 141] for a drink. As the sun sets, the echoes of the call to prayer will begin emanating from the hundreds of mosques within the city's walls.

—JANELLE NANOS
National Geographic Traveler
magazine editor

Tourist Circuits

The chaotic, meandering streets of both Fès el Bali and Fès el Jedid make it difficult for tourists to navigate their way around these areas. The government has therefore created six thematic tourist circuits to guide tourists around, according to their particular interests. Each circuit has its own brightly color-coded signposts to follow: orange for "Walls and Ramparts," purple for "Fès el Jedid," turquoise for the "Andalusian Quarter," green for "Palaces and Andalusian Gardens," blue for "Monuments and Souks," and red for "Traditional Crafts." Maps detailing these circuits are available from the Fès Tourist Office and the Syndicat d'Initiative (see p. 138).

Ville Nouvelle

The third district of Fès, the Ville Nouvelle, lies toward the south of the city and is probably where most visitors stay. Designed in the early 20th century during the French protectorate period, the Ville Nouvelle's layout and architecture have a distinctly European feel, marked by wide boulevards such as the tree-lined avenue Hassan II and the avenue Mohamed V in its center. Top-name hotels and boutiques, chic cafés and restaurants serving cuisine to suit all tastes, and the main banks and tourist offices are all found here. And for those who find the bustle and bartering in the medina uncomfortable, the **Centre Artisanal** *(boulevard Allal Ben Abdallah, tel 0535/62 56 54)* and the shops along the avenue Mohamed V offer traditional crafts for sale at fixed prices. ■

Habarim Synagogue
🅰 143
✉ Mellah

Fès to Er Rachidia

Around Fès, many towns and rural regions deserve a traveler's time: Moulay Yacoub, to the west, with hot, therapeutic baths; Sefrou, to the south, with wonderful waterfalls and an annual Cherry Festival; the remote traditional village of Boulemane; and—heading farther south—the Middle Atlas and High Atlas Mountains and Er Rachidia.

A timeworn Atlas village looks like part of the mountainside to which it clings.

Moulay Yacoub
🅜 137 A3

Sidi Harazem
🅜 137 A3

West and southeast of Fès are two historic spa towns. The more popular, **Moulay Yacoub** (see sidebar opposite), lies 12 miles (20 km) west of the city. Moulay Yacoub developed around the region's hot sulfurous waters, which rise from nearly 5,000 feet (1,500 m) below ground and reach temperatures of 129°F (54°C). Just south of the road toward Oudja, and 10 miles (15 km) from Fès, are the thermal baths and swimming pool at **Sidi Harazem.** The town is named after one of its residents, St. Sidi Harazem, for whom a shrine was established in the 17th century by Sultan Moulay El Rashid, the son of Moulay Ali Cherif (see p. 42), founder of the Alaouite dynasty.

The best of Morocco hides from sight. Get a mule and let its owner guide you to the Berber villages of the High Atlas Mountains or of the Jebel Sarhro.

— VICTOR ENGLEBERT
National Geographic photographer

A popular *moussem* (festival) is held to honor the saint in late April *(contact Fès tourist office for details)*. Accommodation is available at the Sidi Harazem Hotel, close to the baths.

Province of Sefrou

The province of Sefrou, south of Fès, is best known for its sometimes spectacular scenery, especially its waterfalls, which attract visitors in great numbers.

The capital of the province, **Sefrou,** lies on the Oued Aggaï river and can trace its roots back to before the reign of Idriss I (d. 791), when it was a strategically placed settlement with strong links to Saharan traders and later

Jewish settlers seeking refuge from southern Algeria. Surrounded by huge 18th-century ramparts, the town is divided in two by the Oued Aggaï, with bridges linking the northern and southern sections. Enter the old medina north of the river through **Bab el Maqam** and wander downhill in a southeasterly direction. You will see the **Grand Mosque,** which dominates this part of the town, and the shrine of the town's patron saint, Sidi Lahcen Lyoussi. While the medina doesn't match the size of the one in Fès, it is just as well preserved.

The river provides a convenient landmark to keep you from getting lost as you meander about. Cross to the south over one of the bridges and you enter the Jewish *mellah.* Sefrou's culture and architecture still bear the legacy of its once large Jewish population, even though most of it has long departed, and you may notice some of the mellah's distinctive wood-galleried houses here. Just outside the southern entrance to the old town, **Bab Merba,** is a **synagogue,** though it is not open to the public. Nearby there is a covered market.

Sefrou
137 A3

EXPERIENCE: Moulay Yacoub's Spa

The hot sulfurous waters of Moulay Yacoub are claimed to ease all kinds of problems, but even people in perfect health flock here to indulge in the spa's affordable therapeutic baths, Jacuzzis, and massages—and come out feeling relaxed and refreshed. There is also a swimming pool and a hammam with separate male and female areas, showers,

and specialists to provide massages, so why not partake? A host of more upmarket spa treatments are available at a more modern spa located south of the main spa. For further information and to book well-being vacation packages, contact the **Centre Thermale de Moulay Yacoub** *(BP 120, Moulay Yacoub, tel 0535/69 40 64, www.moulayyacoub.com).*

High Atlas Mountains

The High Atlas range is the highest in Morocco, rising from the foothills east of Agadir and forming a spine running to the northeast. The highest peaks are farther east, but mighty Jebel Ayachi (12,264 feet/3,747 m) is easily accessible from Fès.

The necklace of snow-clad High Atlas peaks is a spectacular sight. From the Toubkal National Park (see p. 212) in the west to Jebel Ayachi, the mountains form a formidable barrier. Other peaks include Jebel l'Ouenkrim at 13,415 feet (4,089 m), Jebel M'Goun at 13,351 feet (4,068 m), and Jebel l'Aksoual at 12,828 feet (3,910 m). By the end of May, the plains below are already bearing the fierce heat of a North African summer, but it is still spring in the mountains. This is the best season to visit. When the snow begins to melt on the peaks, streams become rivers (*oueds*) that supply

Picking flowers in the High Atlas sunshine

the settlements to the north, south, and east of the range. Snow-topped peaks sparkle in the sun, mountain streams are in full flow, and pink, yellow, and mauve flowers bloom in lush green pastures. Indigenous Berber families migrate to the higher pastures and their summer villages with their sheep, goats, and mules.

The High Atlas range acts as a weather barrier between the harsher and more arid climate of the Sahara and the moister and—for most of the year—cooler Mediterranean temperatures to the north. Weather conditions along the range can be dramatic, and most mountain passes, like the Tizi n'Test Pass, famous for its challenging hairpin bends and spectacular views of the Saïss Plateau with the Anti Atlas range piercing the clouds, close in the winter because of heavy snowfall. Snow can be a bonus—as well as a problem—from November to April. Winter skiing is a popular activity in the High Atlas, notably in the Jebel Toubkal Massif (see sidebar p. 212).

During the spring, summer, and fall, the High Atlas also becomes a magnet for enthusiasts of hiking, rock climbing, and 4x4 excursions. For example, from Midelt there are challenging treks to the summit of Jebel Ayachi and down to Tounfite or around the classic Cirque Jaffar circuit. Note that these are not for walkers lacking in either experience or equipment: the Cirque Jaffar circuit is a challenging 50 miles (79 km).

For those seeking more relaxing mountain pleasures, the flora and fauna are wonderful. Endangered Barbary sheep can still be seen, along with unusual birdlife, including golden eagles, Moussier's redstarts, and crimson-winged finches, and there are plenty of lizards. The wildflowers are also exceptional.

If you fancy a more peaceful experience after the hustle and bustle of the medina, leave via Bab el Maqam, follow the avenue Moulay Hassan, and look for signs to **Cascades,** a small waterfall on the Oued Aggaï about 1 mile (1.5 km) west of the town. This is a popular spot for local people to picnic and swim.

Cherry Festival: Surrounded by cherry orchards, Sefrou's countryside turns a vibrant shade of pink when the trees blossom in spring. Every June the town comes alive for several days with music and dancing for the Cherry Festival, which marks the end of the cherry harvest. It culminates in a procession led by the Queen of Cherries, a title bestowed on a local girl during the run-up to the festival. This important Moroccan festival has been celebrated since 1920.

Other Sefrou Province Towns: Smaller communities within striking distance of Sefrou include the beautiful village of **Imouzzer du Kandar,** founded by the French and a popular holiday spot for Moroccans from Fès. Modeled on the French Alpine settlement of Ifrane, it wouldn't look out of place in the Alps. Its altitude—some 4,300 feet (1,300 m) above sea level—ensures that it's delightfully cool in summer. The area's temperate climate is ideal for apple, fig, and walnut trees laden with fruit, and the town hosts an Apple Festival in August.

Cascades, a popular picnic spot near Sefrou

The nearby villages of **Ain Chifa** (with a cool, refreshing pool for bathing), **Ain Cheggag,** and **El Menzel** are similarly picturesque, and in the hamlet of **Bhalil,** troglodyte (prehistoric caveman) cave dwellings have been discovered carved into the hillside. The existence of the caves proved fortuitous for the Berber tribes, who for centuries have used them to hide from invaders.

Middle & High Atlas

On the route south from Sefrou toward the High Atlas and Er Rachidia, the landscape is a heady mix of mountains, hills, and valleys. The journey has to be by road, first on the R503, then the N13. Around **Boulemane,** the route

Imouzzer du Kandar
137 A3

Ain Chifa
137 A3

Ain Cheggag
137 A3

El Menzel
137 A3

Locals chatting in the Atlas town of Midelt

Boulemane

🏔 137 A3

Midelt

🏔 137 A2

passes over the Middle Atlas Mountains, with lakes and forests, before dropping to lower altitudes and then rising again toward the northernmost terrain of the High Atlas. Along the way are Berber settlements, known as *ksours,* and the market town of Midelt, lying on the high plain between the two mountain ranges.

Midelt is nearly 5,000 feet (1,500 m) above sea level and is one of Morocco's highest communities. The plain landscape that surrounds it is similar to that of a desert, with the tall **Jebel Ayachi** mountain rising 12,264 feet (3,747 m) to provide a dramatic backdrop. Midelt has become a popular starting point for treks into the mountains, and as such, a handful

of guesthouses have sprung up, along with a souk, the **Souk Jdid** *(rue Souk Jdid),* where handmade carpets, mineral stones mined in the outskirts of the town, leather goods, and embroidered textiles are for sale.

Midelt is at the center of the region's agricultural and lead and mineral mining industries, and its population works the fields and lives in houses that echo the traditional southern squared style of architecture. Many of these were built when Midelt was transformed from a small ksour to a garrison town during the French protectorate period. Its Mediterranean climate of hot summers and cold winters is conducive to wheat, walnut, and vegetable production, along with a whole host of fruits that are used not only as food but also in the leather tanning process in Fès.

Around Midelt are gorges that attract hiking and 4x4 car enthusiasts, although most routes are passable only in the summer months. The **Aouli Gorge,** a few miles northeast of Midelt, is one such gorge where the town's lead-mining activities were once a focus. It is not used now, but evidence of its workings and machinery is still in place.

Er Rachidia & South

The road beyond Midelt follows a tortuous course as it rises higher into the High Atlas, but beyond the pass of **Tizi-n-Talrhemt** the long decline into the Ziz Valley begins. This spectacular creation of nature was formed over millions of years by the action of the Oued Ziz river as it cascaded down the High Atlas, carving gorges as it went. Its fertile valley provides agricultural land for the settlements that dot the landscape, including the small village of **Rich** and dune-swept **Merzouga.** Away from the river are lush groves of forest and date palms. In contrast, near the town of Er Rachidia the huge plain becomes drier and more desertlike.

Er Rachidia: The 20th-century French town of Er Rachidia, formerly known as Ksar es Souk, is reached by passing through the Ziz Valley's impressive **Tunnel de Foum-Zabel (Tunnel du Légionnaire),** which was built by the French in the 1920s to provide an easy route for vehicles to navigate from the north of Morocco south toward its Algerian border.

Er Rachidia is the capital of the province of the same name. Once just a small ksour, the French recognized the town's strategic placement on the edge of the Sahara desert, midway between the north and south of the country, and between the Atlantic Ocean and Morocco's border with Algeria, and developed it as a military and administrative base. Today it makes a good place to stock up with provisions if hiking into the sand dunes of Erg Chebbi (see pp. 154–155).

Having come so far, the temptation to drive (or get a bus from Er Rachidia) south along the N13 toward the desert and Erfoud is strong. If you have the chance,

do it! The road passes through an increasingly desolate and barren landscape, punctuated only by occasional oases, which were vital to the fortunes of the Berber Kingdom of Sijilmassa (see sidebar). You will pass several oases, including Sidi Abu Abdellah, Meski, Kar ej Jdid, Zrigat, and Borj-Yerdi.

Erfoud: Erfoud is a sprawling town of homes built beside the desert not far from the Algerian border. Pre-Saharan architecture characterizes Erfoud, with small, square homes built largely from red earthen bricks and set out in a gridlike fashion. Surrounded by groves of date palms—a major source of income (see sidebar p. 155)—Erfoud has the appearance of an oasis set deep

Rich
🄰 137 A2

Merzouga
🄰 137 A1

Er Rachidia
🄰 137 A2
Visitor Information
✉ Tourist Office, boulevard Moulay Ali Cherif Errachidia
☎ (0655) 57 09 41
www.errachidia.org

Erfoud
🄰 137 A1

The Sijilmassa Kingdom

The Oases du Ziz, between Er Rachidia and Erfoud, played a big part in the fortunes of the independent kingdom of Sijilmassa. Founded by Berbers in 757, this kingdom, which was centered on Rissani (see p. 155), was able to survive until late in the 14th century for two reasons. First, it controlled the wealth of produce from these fertile oases, and second, it was able to establish itself as a trading center on the Salt Road between West Africa and the north.

in the desert. Erfoud's other industry is marble, and you can visit the small workshops that create dazzling pieces of polished marble.

Erfoud does not have a long history, or at least not one that has been documented. The town was little more than a small Berber settlement until the French protectorate period from 1912 to 1956. The French set up a military lookout point in Erfoud, keen to keep a watch over the Tafilalt valley and the border areas of the country it now patrolled.

The French occupation met with some resistance from the native Berbers, who had been living in the isolated wilderness for hundreds of years and did not welcome European intruders. The Berbers were eventually won over by the French, who didn't gain control of Erfoud until 1930, making the desert town one of the last areas of Morocco to succumb to French rule. The military garrison of **Borj-Est,** built by the French and reached by a hill from the Bab el Oued Bridge, commands fabulous views of the desert.

Today, Erfoud is a bustling town with lots of amenities, including a lively souk, although there are few establishments for tourists aside from a handful of hotels and restaurants. Nonetheless, the city is a magnet for visitors who are keen to sample life deep in the heart of Morocco. Its chief attraction is the nearby **Erg Chebbi**—one of the most photographed places in the world and a popular destination for desert hikes.

Enormous sand dunes near Erfoud

Erfoud's Dates

The date harvest, held annually in October, is a time of great activity in Erfoud. Every orchard owner will have his own strategy for climbing to the top of the tall palm trees. Brandishing heavy knives or machetes for cutting through the branches, they proceed to send the bunches of yellow dates crashing to the ground. The dates will then be loaded onto carts pulled by a donkey, and the owner will head home or straight to the souk. Dates are one of the most important sources of income for the inhabitants of Erfoud. A date festival is held every year, and local tribes come to pray to Allah for a good harvest. There is dancing, feasting, and music, and the festival can last for several days.

INSIDER TIP:

One of the best desert experiences is to take a camel ride across the Erg Chebbi sand dunes as the sun goes down.

—CAROLE FRENCH
National Geographic author

Erg Chebbi: The Erg provides an iconic image of the desert. The sand dunes of this seemingly endless expanse have deep troughs and reach dazzling peaks of some 500 feet (150 m) in some places. The dunes, created by the wind, have become one of Morocco's top tourist attractions and camel treks or trips in 4x4 vehicles have become a buoyant industry.

Erfoud, the Erg Chebbi, and the tiny village of Merzouga—the last settlement before the dunes—have caught the attention not only of adventurous trekkers but of filmmakers, too. The wild location and breathtaking views of the Sahara have made Erfoud and the Erg a prized location for film shoots.

Among the films shot here are *March or Die* (1977), starring Gene Hackman, which tells the story of a team of archaeologists who discover a city buried in the sand near Erfoud, and Stephen Sommers's *The Mummy* (1999), starring Brendan Fraser and Rachel Weisz, though in that case Erfoud was masquerading as a city in Egypt.

Rissani: Head 9 miles (14 km) south of Erfoud along the Oued Ziz river to enter the town of Rissani through a large gate. This small town's history and position on the edge of the Sahara make it a fascinating place to visit. There is a lively market *(avenue Moulay Ali Cherif)* on Tuesdays, Thursdays, and Sundays. About 1 mile (2 km) southwest of the center is the large **Moulay Ali Cherif Mausoleum,** named for the founder of the ruling Alaouite dynasty, and a small **museum.** To the west, in an atmospheric desert setting, are the mud-brick ruins of the ancient Sijilmassa city. For accommodations, try the **Kasbah Ennasra** *(BP 167, Ksar Labtami, tel 0535/77 44 03, www.kasbahennasra.net).* ∎

Rissani
🗺 137 A1

Moulay Ali Cherif Mausoleum
✉ avenue Moulay Ali Cherif, Rissani

Rissani Museum
✉ avenue Moulay Ali Cherif, Rissani

An impressive range of architectural wonders, historic monuments, and busy souks set in the beautiful Atlas Mountains

Meknès & the Middle Atlas

Locals chatting in an alley of the Meknès medina

Meknès & the Middle Atlas

Known as the "Versailles of Morocco," the beautiful city of Meknès is home to extravagant palaces, terraced parks, and decorated mosques that overlook the surrounding countryside. It stands in a landscape of outstanding natural and historic beauty that includes the Middle Atlas Mountains and the Roman city of Volubilis.

Meknès was founded on the site of a small kasbah by the Miknasa Berber tribe around the tenth century. It was later, in the 17th century, that Alaouite sultan Moulay Ismail brought the town to prominence as a monumental capital city of palaces.

The once imperial city of Meknès lies around 80 miles (130 km) inland from the present capital, Rabat. A UNESCO World Heritage site, Meknès offers a wealth of visitor attractions. The city revolves around the Ville Impériale with its exquisite palace, the Dar el Makhzen, and government buildings, which are set within an extensive walled parkland. Then there is the Grand Mosque, which was built by the Almoravids in the 11th century, as well as stunning monuments such as the Koubba el Khayatine, the Agdal Pond, and the Mausoleum of Moulay Ismail. Gates surround many parts of the city. One of the most stunning is the Bab Mansour between the Imperial City and the medina, with its elaborate carvings and blue *zellij* tilework.

The city is famous for many things, not least the Haras de Meknès—a huge stable complex and national stud farm that is home to hundreds of the country's finest racehorses. Keen golfers can take in a round at the Meknès Royal Golf Club in Sultan Moulay Ismail's city grounds, while delicious olives, fine wine, and Oulmès sparkling mineral water provide the sustenance needed after a long day exploring all the attractions Meknès has to offer.

Nearby lies the site of the early Roman city of Volubilis—the capital of the Mauretania Tingitana kingdom—which was one of the most important cities in ancient Morocco, dating back to the time of the Mauretanians in the fourth and third centuries B.C. Today the site is the best preserved example of a Roman town in Morocco, and one of the best preserved in the whole of North Africa. The nearby town of Moulay Idriss is the holiest site in the country, home to the tomb of Idriss I, founder of the state of Morocco and great-grandson of the Prophet Muhammad.

The region also includes the provinces around the popular winter sports city of Ifrane, the towns of Khenifra and Er Rachidia,

NOT TO BE MISSED:

the heavily forested Tizguit Valley, home to endangered Barbary macaques, and the majestic mountains that make up the Middle Atlas range.

Its location near the Atlas Mountains gives Meknès a climate with distinct seasons. Spring sees pleasantly warm days when the forests and countryside burst into color with wildflowers and the rivers fill with crystal-clear snowmelt. This is an ideal time to explore the city center or the archaeological wonders of Volubilis. In the summer, the days are too hot, with average temperatures rising to around 91°F (33°C). As soon as the sun sets, however, the temperature drops significantly, and the evenings and nights tend to be much cooler.

In the fall, the trees change color and temperatures drop to bearable levels again, making this time of the year popular with tourists keen to explore the city's many attractions or enjoy activities in the mountainous regions. In winter, the temperature plummets to well below zero in the hills, and the heavy snowfall makes the ski slopes around Ifrane a magnet for skiers. ■

Central Meknès

Central Meknès is full of fabulous palaces and architectural marvels, reflecting a history that spans more than ten centuries. But the *ville nouvelle* (new town) district of modern hotels, residences, and open parklands blends in seamlessly with the past, making Meknès one of the imperial cities that simply has to be explored.

Built in the 18th century, the Bab Mansour is the city's most ornate town gate.

The area around Meknès has been inhabited since prehistoric times, although little evidence remains. The Phoenicians and Byzantines kept to the coastal areas of Morocco and did not venture as far inland as Meknès, while Berber tribes concentrated in the southerly Anti Atlas and High Atlas mountain ranges.

Around the eighth century A.D., Meknès was probably just a small community, whose people lived in dwellings lining the maze-like streets of a walled medina. These first inhabitants built their medina on top of a hill.

A Millennium of History

Around the late ninth or early tenth century, a Berber tribe called the Miknasa settled and is credited with founding the city of Meknès (see sidebar opposite).

Later, the Almoravids, followed by the Almohads, the Marinids, the Wattasids, and then the Saadians (see pp. 41–42), all enjoyed periods of power and continued to develop the city. Things really changed in the 17th century, when Meknès captivated the heart and soul of Ismail ibn Sharif (ca. 1645–1727), who went on to become Sultan Moulay Ismail—probably the greatest of all the rulers of the Alaouite dynasty

Tourists making their way to Fès will find Meknès the perfect introduction to its grand neighbor.

—TOM JACKSON
National Geographic contributor

(see sidebar p. 167). Meknès had entered the period when it would reach its pinnacle as one of the finest of Morocco's imperial cities. On assuming power in 1672, Moulay Ismail set about the task of ruling Morocco with an iron fist and creating a capital that he felt worthy of his power. The result was a city of such extravagance that it is often called the "Versailles of Morocco," a reference to the palace built by the sultan's contemporary, King Louis XIV of France (1638–1715).

The sultan and his thousands of construction workers—mainly slaves—built lavish palaces and mosques of breathtaking beauty, monumental gates and doors, huge squares, lakes, kasbahs, and miles of ramparts. The result was an imperial city so impressive that it, and its creator, will forever be in the history books of Morocco. Moulay Ismail died in 1727, and Meknès lost its capital city status to Marrakech in 1757, a couple of years after the city was severely damaged by an earthquake. Despite the loss of many of the grandest features from its heyday under the great sultan, Meknès nevertheless recovered into the vibrant, bustling city visitors see today.

Ville Impériale

Crossing the bridge from the ville nouvelle, you immediately get an idea of the colossal—and ultimately unachievable—scale of Moulay Ismail's ambition. The whole area is crisscrossed with huge, beautifully crafted walls—27 miles (43 km) of them, to be exact. They wrap themselves around the contours of massive palaces and sumptuous gardens that were planned, but never actually built. Even the gigantic Dar el Makhzen palace occupies only around a quarter

Mèknes

◢ 159 B3

Visitor Information

✉ 127 place Administrative, Ville Nouvelle

☎ (0535) 52 60 22

Legacy of the Miknasa Tribe

Any account of the history of Meknès tends to be dominated by the figure of Moulay Ismail, to the extent that it is easy to forget that the city was already well established when he arrived with his grand schemes and army of slaves. Meknès is named for the Miknasa tribe— a nomadic Berber community that had migrated gradually westward during the seventh and eighth centuries. It is thought that the original settlement would have looked something like the mountain town of Aït Ben Haddou (see sidebar p. 243)— a mud-brick kasbah that served as a stopping point for trade caravans and travelers. During the rule of the Almoravid and Almohad dynasties, Meknès became an important commercial center and attracted several impressive public projects, including the Almohad Grand Mosque and Sultan Bou Inania's elegant Medersa (see pp. 170–171).

Bab Mansour

🔺 165

of the total area enclosed by its great walls.

Place el Hedime: After working its way around the walled enclosures, the road from the ville nouvelle arrives at the place el Hedime. This enormous public square, reminiscent of the Djemaa el Fna in Marrakech (see p. 188), was one of the first parts of Moulay Ismail's royal city to be completed—it was built by flattening an entire neighborhood and making its citizens homeless.

During Moulay Ismail's lifetime, the place el Hedime was both public square and storage yard. Contemporary sources describe pieces of carved stone and marble—ripped from the walls of El Badi palace in Marrakech (see pp. 195–198) and pulled from the ruins at Volubilis (see pp. 178–181)—being heaped up here while Ismail decided what to do with them. Today the square is a good place to start your exploration of the imperial city, as well as a fun place to spend an evening (see sidebar below).

Bab Mansour: On the edge of the place el Hedime, between the Ville Impériale and the medina, is the Bab Mansour. This is one of the finest ornamented gates in Morocco, and it is a glorious example of 18th-century architecture. The gate features a sturdy wooden door that alone is more than 50 feet (15 m) tall.

It is sometimes called the Bab Mansour el Aleuj, meaning the "Gate of the Victorious Renegade" or the "Gate of the Renegade Mansour." The gate is named for its architect, Mansour, a Christian who converted to Islam. According to local tradition, when the gate was completed, Mansour remarked to Moulay Ismail that he could probably make something even better if he wanted. On hearing this, Moulay Ismail flew into a rage and beheaded Mansour right in the middle of the place el Hedime. Although this story is certainly plausible (Ismail was known for his murderous rages), it cannot be true, as the gate was not finished until several years after Ismail's death.

Traditional Entertainment in Place el Hedime

The place el Hedime is a large square surrounded by walls that were once the Marinid's city kasbah. This is where you are most likely to find the city's snake charmers, fire swallowers, jugglers, and storytellers. These traditional forms of entertainment have been popular in Morocco for hundreds of years, although they now are done mostly for tourists' photographs in exchange for a few dirhams. Storytelling, where listeners cluster in small circles around the narrator, dates back to the time when few Moroccans traveled beyond their immediate areas and reading a book was unheard of. Intrinsic to traditional culture, storytelling brought tales from far-off lands to the masses. Speaking in fast and strongly accented Darija (Moroccan Arabic), these storytellers are one part of the square's cultural life that is unapologetically not for the benefit of tourists.

The souk at Meknès caters to locals and visitors alike.

A masterpiece of carved friezes, intricate arches, and blue-and-cream *zellij*-covered facades, the gate was part of the unrelenting development of Meknès by Moulay Ismail and took around 150 years to complete. Its architectural detailing includes interlacing swirling motifs and loggia towers and has been the inspiration for countless other structures. Its marble columns are said to have been acquired from the nearby ancient site of Volubilis. If you are lucky, you may catch one of the temporary art and craft exhibitions that are often held here.

Around Place Lalla Aouda:

On the other side of the gate lies the place Lalla Aouda, a long rectangular public square that was once the military parade ground where Moulay Ismail's "Black Guard"—an army of African slaves—would parade for him. There is a neat little formal garden at the southern end of the square, just behind the surprisingly plain rear entrance of the Bab Mansour. During the day, horse-drawn carriages wait here for customers. For around 100 dirhams, they will take you on a tour around the major sights of the Ville Impériale. If short of time, this can be a good way to see the imperial city, although it can be a little rushed.

Southwest of the place Lalla Aouda is the **Koubba el Khayatine,** a beautifully decorated *(continued on p. 166)*

Walk: Central Meknès

The best way to soak up the sights and sounds of central Meknès is by taking a walk through the city's historic center, a compact and easily explored old town.

Meknès's place el Hedime bustles with snake charmers, fire swallowers, jugglers, and storytellers.

The starting point for this walk is the **Mausoleum of Moulay Ismail ❶** (see p. 166), the last resting place of Meknès's most enthusiastic admirer and most prolific builder. On your right as you leave the mausoleum is the **Dar el Kebira Quarter**, once the site of a grand palace, but now a pretty residential neighborhood. Continue through the gate at the end of the rue Palais to the **Koubba el Khayatine ❷** (see pp. 163–166). Although it is a relatively unassuming building compared to the city's grandiose palaces, this pavilion was where the sultan would have received ambassadors from around the world. Beneath it are the **Habs Qara** (see p. 166), many underground cells that were allegedly used to house the sultan's army of slaves.

Continue across the place Lalla Aouda to the **Bab Mansour ❸** (see pp. 162–163) on the edge of the medina. If the doors are open, head inside to look at the cavernous interior

NOT TO BE MISSED:

Bab Mansour • Dar Jamaï • Bou Inania Medersa

rooms and the exhibitions of local crafts that are often held within. Crossing the rue Dar Smen, work your way through the bustle of the **place el Hedime** (see p. 162) toward the turquoise rooftop of the **Dar Jamaï ❹** (see pp. 168–170). Although it is not particularly striking from the outside, this 19th-century mansion is a stunning example of Moroccan traditional design that perfectly complements the extensive collection of the **museum** now housed within.

After exploring the Dar Jamaï, continue north along the road that runs beside the building, take a right turn, and then follow the road as it curves north to the rue Najjarine.

Once you reach the rue Najjarine, stop to explore the souks clustered in the courtyards and alleyways that lead off it; the ones in this area specialize in *babouches* (traditional Moroccan leather slippers), which are stored in bright, colorful rows outside the stores. Continue down the street (to the east, turning right from where you joined the street), past more souks selling carpets and clothing. Soon you will reach the pretty turquoise tiled minaret of the **Grand Mosque** ❺. As always, only Muslims are permitted to enter the building, but just across the street is another historic building, equally beautiful, that is open to visitors—the **Bou Inania Medersa** ❻. This stunning building was once home to a thriving scholarly community, a satellite of the great *medersas* in Fès.

From the medersa, go north for 350 feet (105 m) before turning right onto a street that curves slightly to the left before again turning north in a stretch shaded by the leaves of a large cedar tree. Take the first significant road on the right (after about 150 feet/45 m), which will lead you to the rue Hamamouch and from there out of the medina. Cross the boulevard el Haboul and go into the **Jardin el Haboul** ❼—an attractive little park on the edge of the valley that virtually cuts Meknès in half.

Locals often come here to relax and visit the small but interesting zoological gardens. From here, you can either return to the medina or continue southeast along the rue des Moulins and from there across the bridge into the *ville nouvelle*.

⛰ See area map p. 159
▶ Mausoleum of Moulay Ismail
🕐 1.5 hours
↔ 1 mile (1.6 km)
▶ Jardin el Haboul

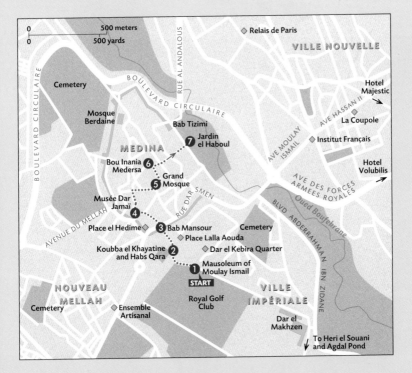

Koubba el Khayatine & Habs Qara

165

Habs Qara

$

Mausoleum of Moulay Ismail

165

rue Saraq

Closed to non-Muslims on Fri.

little building that served as an entrance hall for foreign dignitaries on visits to the city. The walls of the main room are decorated with staggeringly intricate geometric designs that weave and curve their way around the arches and windows.

Look out for the stairway that leads down from the Koubba el Khayatine to a series of underground cells, known as the **Habs Qara.** At one time, this eerie subterranean wilderness is said to have been several miles long, but an earthquake resulted in some of the roof areas caving in. This series of catacombs is reputed to be where Moulay Ismail imprisoned the army of captured Europeans and Africans that worked on his

grand projects, allowing them up into the daylight only for days of backbreaking labor. Even though most historians now agree that it was probably a grain store, not a prison, it's still an atmospheric and unnerving place, best explored with a torch and a local guide with a macabre imagination.

A short walk from the Koubba el Khayatine is the **Mausoleum of Moulay Ismail**—a funerary complex every bit as vast and ostentatious as you'd expect from such a man. The mausoleum is filled with elaborate decoration and zellij tilework and comprises a prayer hall, courtyards, and a complex of burial chambers. This is the resting place of the sultan, his wife, and their sons. Surprisingly, this tomb

The unique aquamarine tiles of the Grand Mosque's minaret

Moulay Ismail

Ismail ibn Sharif, better known as Sultan Moulay Ismail (ca 1645–1727), was a key figure in Moroccan history and the driving force behind the creation of Meknès as we see it today. He is a fascinating character, revered in Morocco as the ruler who unified the country, while at the same time widely acknowledged by historians as one of the most brutal and cruel monarchs in history.

Moulay Ismail came to power in 1672, following the unexpected death of his half brother in a riding accident. He quickly established a reputation as a skilled military commander and fearless leader, fighting off hostile forces on all fronts. Within 20 years, he had decisively repelled an attempted invasion by the Ottoman Empire in the east; recaptured the ports of Tanger, Larache, and La Mamora from European powers; and brought the Berber peoples of the Atlas Mountains under the control of an Arab-dominated Moroccan state.

Emboldened by these victories, Moulay Ismail created a new grand capital at Meknès. Ismail's terrifying power and seemingly unlimited wealth allowed him to build on an unprecedented scale, leaving his mark on Morocco forever.

Following his death, however, work on the imperial city soon dwindled away to nothing. In 1755, a massive earthquake destroyed many of Moulay Ismail's great monuments, and storms tore apart others not long after. His grandson, Mohamed III, had moved the nation's capital to Marrakech, and Ismail's great monuments were abandoned. Like the great palace of El Badi that Moulay Ismail tore apart to feed his own ambitious building project, most of his great buildings are now ruins, slowly dismantled for building materials by future generations.

is a popular place of pilgrimage for Moroccans, many of whom regard Moulay Ismail as a saintly figure.

Beyond the mausoleum lies the site of the **Dar el Kebira,** one of Moulay Ismail's finest palaces. The palace was abandoned after it was severely damaged by an earthquake in 1755. The name is now used to describe the residential neighborhood that occupies this enclosure—which is apt, considering that many of the houses in the area are made from bits of the old palace. The looming ruins of the palace jut out into the skyline throughout the area, although few of them are accessible to visitors.

Dar el Makhzen & South:

Located to the south, within its own huge, walled enclosure is the Dar el Makhzen, the only one of Moulay Ismail's palaces that is still a royal residence. The present-day palace is a much smaller affair than the sprawling behemoth built by Moulay Ismail—several wings of the old palace have been abandoned over the years and left to crumble away among the beautiful formal gardens. The entrances to this particualr compound are heavily guarded and visitors can enter the enclosure only to play a round at the **Royal Golf Club**—a compact nine-hole course constructed next to the royal palace by Hassan II in the 1970s.

Beyond the Dar el Makhzen, in the southeast corner of the Ville Impériale, stand two of the

Royal Golf Club

🅰 165

✉ Jnan al Bahraouia, Ville Impériale

☎ (0535) 53 07 53

💲 $$$$

www.royalgolf meknes.com

Houses crowd the old town area of Meknès, with the occasional minaret overlooking the cityscape.

least glamorous but arguably most impressive structures in the city. The first, the **Heri el Souani,** is a gigantic labyrinth of arches and passageways that once housed the royal stables and an important granary. Although most of the building is now a ruin, there is a section that has been restored to show the ingenuity and skill of Moulay Ismail's engineers. The ruined sections of the Heri el Souani are equally worth exploring, however.

The second attraction in this area is the impressive **Agdal Pond**—a giant stone-lined reservoir built to irrigate the royal gardens. Like the similar Menara Gardens in Marrakech (see p. 207), this artificial lake is a popular picnic spot with local families and couples, who like to come here in the evenings to watch the sun set over the water.

Medina

While few Moroccan medinas appear to have been laid out with any kind of preconceived plan, Meknès's old town looks particularly chaotic on a map. This is because the town was forced to grow around the great swaths of land that Moulay Ismail had claimed for his grand projects—bizarrely shaped corridors of densely packed houses are squeezed into the gaps between walled enclosures, while the historic core of the town has a large bite taken out of the southern corner by the place el Hedime.

On the opposite side of the place el Hedime to the Bab Mansour, positioned in symbolic opposition to the over-the-top extravagance of the Ville Impériale, lies the compact but beautiful **Dar Jamaï**—a mansion

EXPERIENCE: Thoroughbreds of Haras de Meknès

The Haras de Meknès is one of the largest and most respected stud farms in Morocco. If you adore horses, then a visit will be an absolute thrill. Get up early enough, and you will see the elegant purebred Arabs, and the Arabian and Berbers' barbs, galloping across the grounds for their morning exercise.

The Meknès region has long had a tradition of horsemanship. Indeed, Moulay Ismail himself is said to have been a keen rider and kept stables.

The **Haras de Meknès** *(Zitoune Quarter, Meknès, tel 0555/53 97 53, closed Sat.–Sun.)* was established in the early 1900s on the periphery of Moulay Ismail's Ville Impériale, when the country was a French protectorate. Its goals were to improve the bloodlines and promote the breeding of Moroccan breeds, such as the Arabs and barbs, and to create a stud farm for breeding other Thoroughbreds for racing, competitive equestrian sports, and *fantasias*.

Morocco is famous for its fantasias, which are displays of the country's horses and finest horsemanship. Meknès is known for its **Tissa Horse Fantasia** held every year in the fall. Highly decorated horses, wearing a lavish harness and embroidered saddle, are ridden by equally elaborately dressed Berber riders. During the displays, horse and rider "dance" to the sound of rhythmic music and drums. They also take part in competitions and displays for the crowd.

The Haras de Meknès stud farm covers an area of around 200 acres (80 ha), which is given over to *ménages* for training, "gallops" for exercise, and the stabling and stores for its 450 horses. You can take a guided tour of the stables and stud farm, where you can see the stallions that are loaned to around 30 elite horse owners in the Meknès area to cover their mares and thus improve their own horses' bloodlines. The breeding season runs from February to June.

Your visit to the Haras de Meknès will almost certainly include seeing some of the beautiful horses being put through their paces to maintain their fitness level. You will also learn how the stud farm's team cares for their charges. The entrance to the Haras de Meknès is just past the Royal Military Academy in the Dar el Beida palace, on the main road going out of town, past the Ville Impériale to Azrou.

Riders in the fantasia for the *moussem* of Moulay Abdallah

Arts and Crafts in Meknès

Meknès is home to a bustling arts and crafts scene. You can watch young apprentices learning the traditional craft of *zellij* tile making at the **Ensemble Artisanal** (*tel 0535/53 09 29, closed Sat.–Sun.*), located above the city bus station on avenue Zine el Abidine Riad. Head into the medina itself to browse and buy some of the extensive collection of crafts, including traditional silver damascene tableware. The French influence is very evident at the **Institut Français** (*rue Ferhat Hachad, tel 0535/51 65 00*), which has an excellent program of theater, cinema, and literary events. Students studying classical Arab-Andalusian music give occasional concerts at the Conservatoire de Musique near place Ifriquia, between avenue Mohamed V and avenue Allal Ben Abdallah.

Musée Dar Jamaï
- 🅜 165
- ✉ place el Hedime
- ☎ (0535) 53 08 63

Grand Mosque
- 🅜 165
- ✉ rue des Souks es Sebbat

Bou Inania Medersa
- 🅜 165
- ✉ rue des Souks es Sebbat
- 💲 $

built by the royal vizier (adviser) in the 1880s. The vizier in question fell out of favor only a few years later, and the palace was made into a museum in 1920. It contains an extensive collection of artistic works. Look for the colorful green-and-yellow Fassi ceramics that originated in Meknès around the 18th century. There are carpets from Meknès that have traditional geometric patterns as well as the more intricate designs from the Middle Atlas and the High Atlas, which are forerunners of the carpets made in a similar fashion today. Other works include Berber jewelry, wood carvings, and metalwork; a wonderful collection of embroidery; and a room that has been decorated and furnished as a reconstruction of the lounge of a wealthy Moroccan family.

If you head down the street that runs next to the Dar Jamaï palace, you will find yourself in the heart of the old medina. This area contains many exciting and interesting **souks,** catering to local people more than the tourists. Everything from shoes to musical instruments is on sale. As

INSIDER TIP:

Oulmès spring water may flow to the surface at temperatures of 104°F (40°C) and above, but keep it chilled and add lots of ice for a refreshing drink.

—THIERRY GOULET
Meknès restaurant owner

many tourists simply pass Meknès by on their way to Fès, these souks have a more interesting and authentic range of goods than many comparable souks in other Moroccan cities.

The area around the Grand Mosque is a good place to go whether your interest is in history or shopping. The **Grand Mosque,** a well-preserved example of traditional Almohad architecture, is worth a look, although it is closed to non-Muslims.

This area's real draw, however, is the magnificent **Bou Inania Medersa.** This elegant building comprises a cool central courtyard with a small fountain, surrounded by the cells in which the students would once have lived. The structure is decorated with intricate zellij tilework, but still manages to feel simple and restrained, especially by comparison to Meknès's other monumental buildings.

The souks in this neighborhood sell carpets and jewelry that are of a much higher quality than what you'll find in the souvenir markets of Fès or Marrakech—although they are priced accordingly, so don't expect to get a knock-down price.

Ville Nouvelle

Crossing the Oued Boufekrane valley on the rue Moulay Ismail, you find yourself in the wide open spaces of the *ville nouvelle*. This modern district houses the city's commercial center, administrative buildings, and transport connections. There are no notable landmarks or historic buildings in this part of town, so the only reason most visitors come is to eat or sleep. For this purpose, at least, the ville nouvelle is well equipped; excellent hotels such as the art deco **Hotel Volubilis** or the cool modernist **Hotel Majestic** offer respite from the dusty and chaotic streets of the medina, while restaurants like **La Coupole** and **Relais de Paris** offer a broad range of dishes. ∎

Hotel Volubilis
(See also p. 293)
- ✉ 45 avenue des FAR, Ville Nouvelle
- ☎ (0535) 52 50 82

Hotel Majestic
(See also p. 293)
- ✉ 19 avenue Mohamed V, Ville Nouvelle
- ☎ (0535) 52 20 35

La Coupole
- ✉ avenue Hassan II, Ville Nouvelle
- ☎ (0535) 52 24 83

Relais de Paris
- ✉ 46 rue Oqba, Ville Nouvelle
- ☎ (0619) 21 02 10

A devotee prays inside the Mausoleum of Moulay Ismail.

Around Meknès

Meknès is the capital of the Meknès-Tafilalet region, which stretches from just north of the city, near the ancient site of Volubilis, south and east to the border of Algeria. Surrounded by the fertile agricultural landscape of the Saïss Plateau, olive and orange groves, and vineyards, the Meknès-Tafilalet region is also bordered by the great Middle Atlas mountain range to the south.

Students at the Al Akhawayn University campus in Ifrane

El Hajeb
 159 B3

Northern Provinces

There are three main provinces around Meknès, in the north of the Meknès-Tafilalet region. The city is in the prefecture of Meknès El Menzah. To the west, the smaller Meknès-Ismaïlia province is largely rural, while El Hajeb to the south has more sites of interest, including Agourai, site of a kasbah dating from the time of Moulay Ismail; the fortified towns of Sebt Jahjouh and Boufakrane; and the provincial capital, also named El Hajeb.

The area between Boufakrane and El Hajeb is best known for its vineyards, where the grapes that produce the excellent Moroccan wine Les Celliers de Meknès are grown.

El Hajeb: El Hajeb lies in the foothills of the Middle Atlas around 18 miles (30 km) from Meknès. It is an attractive city made up of the traditional cubic homes that are a feature of the region. The area is also a popular place for adventur-

INSIDER TIP:

Don't miss the charming city of Ifrane [see pp. 174–175]. Hosting one of the biggest Moroccan universities, this ski resort has mountain architecture and is often called the Moroccan Switzerland.

—CHRISTEL CHERQAOUI
National Geographic Books

ous hikers, because the terrain features cliffs, springs, and caves carved into rock faces over thousands of years. Most of El Hajeb's population and that of its neighboring towns are from the Berber Zayane tribe of the Middle Atlas.

By the standards of the area, El Hajeb is a major town, and it's a good place to stop off if you're traveling south into the mountains. It has banks and grocery stores, a mosque, a kasbah, and a sprawling covered souk that is frequented by people from miles around. Located in the town's avenue Hassan II, the **souk** mainly sells locally harvested fruit and vegetables, along with meat and fish, bread, grains, and fragrant spices. Textiles are also sold in the souk, as well as crafts such as wooden furniture.

Southern Provinces

The mountainous south of the Meknès-Tafilalet region is divided into three provinces—Ifrane, Khenifra, and Er Rachidia—largely made up of remote towns and villages. However, there are several sites to interest visitors.

Azrou: The area around the town of Azrou is particularly popular for anglers looking to catch the region's abundant trout. The city market is also famous for selling the local Timahdite breed of sheep. If you are serious about your

Azrou
🗺 159 B3

Zayane Tribe

The Zayane are from the Berber Zayane tribe of the Middle Atlas. Although traditionally nomadic, the group forms a high percentage of the population in towns and cities such as El Hajeb and Khenifra.

The Zayane are distinct from other Berber communities, largely because they have had little influence from European or Arab cultures. They have no written alphabet and speak only Tamazight, which is a Berber language with a distinct dialect found only in the Middle Atlas and around the High Atlas region of Morocco.

Family and a love of music, dance, and horses play pivotal roles in Zayane culture. The men are skilled horsemen and are practiced riders in *fantasias,* while all Zayane take part in *ahidous*—a festival of dance and song.

The Zayane culture is deep-rooted in traditional crafts such as carpetmaking and textile weaving, which have been essential to survival. The cuisine centers around produce and grains found during their travels rather than grown as crops, supplemented by meat and poultry killed on hunting expeditions.

Friends celebrate at the marriage festival in the small town of Imilchil in Er Rachidia Province.

Midelt
159 B2

Lake Sidi Ali Aguelmam
159 B3

fishing, take the N13 south toward **Midelt** and Er Rachidia (see pp. 152–153) and visit **Lake Sidi Ali,** which is stocked with trout and pike. The rivers and streams in the hills nearby

are excellent for fishing in the spring months.

Ifrane: The province of Ifrane is a popular destination, especially for people keen on

Imilchil Marriage Festival

The small town of Imilchil in the southern Er Rachidia Province is famous for its marriage festival. As tradition goes, the festival commemorates the lives of two young people from different tribes who, having fallen in love but forbidden to see each other by their families, cried themselves to death. Such a flow of water created two lakes: Isli, meaning "his," and Tislit, "hers."

Overcome with grief, the two sets of parents reconciled their differences and decided to establish a festival, which would be held on the anniversary of their

deaths. It would bring together the two tribes and allow young people to meet and marry. The festival, the Souk Aamor Agdoud n'Oulmghenni, or Imilchil Marriage Festival, is still held today.

In an area where village communities are widely scattered and modes of transport are limited, the festival is one of the few times young people get the opportunity to meet new friends and possible life partners. The festival, held toward the end of September each year, is a time of great laughter, music, dance, and, of course, betrothals.

winter sports. The cosmopolitan capital, also named **Ifrane,** was developed by the French protectorate in the early 1900s, turning it from a small settlement to a city of flowers and a top-class ski resort. Independence brought little change to Ifrane; the new Moroccan elite flocked here as their predecessors had, and the king even built a palace in the town. Recently, however, the atmosphere of the town has been altered by the construction of Al Akhawayn University, a joint Moroccan-Saudi project.

Ifrane is one of Morocco's foremost ski centers. At nearly 5,500 feet (1,670 m) above sea level, and with a climate that gives it freezing temperatures and heavy snowfall every winter, it is a favored spot with native skiers and Europeans who want to venture beyond the usual resorts.

As you would expect, given its discerning citizens, the town is well maintained and pleasant, if expensive. If you can afford the prices (which are still considerably lower than what you'd pay in a comparable resort in Europe or North America), Ifrane is an excellent place to relax. There are many fine hotels, such as the **Hotel Perce-Neige** in the center of town, one of the most luxurious and stylish hotels in this part of Morocco. Good spots to eat and drink after a day of skiing are the **Rendezvous de Skieurs** and **Café Restaurant La Rose.**

If you actually want to go out in the cold and do some skiing, then you'll need to drive or take a taxi to nearby **Mischliffen** (see sidebar above), where there are three ski lifts and some limited equipment rental stores.

The area south of Ifrane is one of the least populated parts of Morocco. Small Berber villages dot the Middle Atlas mountain range, which runs south from the Rif Mountains in the north toward the High Atlas and the Atlantic Ocean coast. A spectacular sight, it is characterized by deep valleys and cedar forests, volcanic plateaus, tabled rock, and high peaks. Its highest mountains are **Jebel Bou Naceur** at 10,962 feet (3,340 m) and **Jebel Bou Iblane** at 10,470 feet (3,190 m). ∎

EXPERIENCE:
Skiing on the Pistes of Ifrane

Ifrane has one of the coldest climates in Morocco, with regular heavy snowfall making its slopes a magnet for skiers in the winter months. With its cosmopolitan alpine feel and relatively good facilities, the ski resort is one of Morocco's finest and trendiest.

Check in at the Mischliffen resort, take one of the ski lifts to the level that suits you, and be thrilled as you ski down the snowy pistes. You can also take part in other winter sports, such as cross-country skiing or snowboarding. It is possible to rent skis, but take your own if you are keen to use the latest equipment.

The **Ifrane Provincial Tourist Office** *(place di Syndicat, avenue Mohamed V, Ifrane, tel 0535/56 68 21, e-mail: dtifrane@menara.ma)* and the **Meknès Regional Tourist Office** *(127 place Administrative, Meknès, tel 0535/52 60 22)* both have excellent guides to skiing in the region.

Ifrane
◩ 159 B3

Hotel Perce-Neige
✉ rue des Asphodelles, Ifrane
☎ (0535) 56 64 04

Rendezvous de Skieurs
✉ avenue de la Marche Verte, Ifrane

Café Restaurant La Rose
✉ rue des Erables, Ifrane
☎ (0535) 56 62 15

Wildlife of the Middle Atlas

Along with the more common hawks, boars, and goats, the Middle Atlas Mountains are home to a shy and secretive primate species: the Barbary macaque.

The Barbary macaque is the only primate native to Morocco.

The sight of a monkey scrambling around in the trees is not one you expect to see as far north as Morocco—a country where the only animals you normally see climbing trees are the ubiquitous goats. The thick-furred Barbary macaque *(Macaca sylvanus)* is not deterred by cold winters, however, and lives happily in the forested hills as high as 6,900 feet (2,100 m) above sea level.

Although they are traditionally known as "Barbary apes," these animals are in fact distant relatives of the macaque family of primates that live in southern and eastern Asia. Over the course of their long migration, these animals have changed and adapted to their environment, gaining thick, dense fur and losing the long tail of other macaques. They are quite large animals, growing to around 30 inches (75 cm) tall and weighing somewhere in the range of 22–33 pounds (10–15 kg), but they are not

dangerous to humans. They usually live in large family groups of 15–30 individuals ruled by a matriarch (a respected older female) and spend roughly equal amounts of time in the trees and on the ground.

In recent years, the number of Barbary macaques living in the wild in Morocco has declined sharply, from around 20,000 in the 1980s to only around 10,000 today. This is primarily due to the loss of their traditional forest habitat to intensive and largely unregulated logging practices in Morocco, and they are now considered to be an endangered species. In the last ten years, the Moroccan government has made efforts to reverse this decline, establishing national parks in the Rif Mountains and High Atlas, but the population is still threatened by habitat loss.

Curiously, there is a small but stable population of Barbary macaques on the tiny British territory of Gibraltar, making them the only primate that lives wild in Europe. This particular community, which numbers around 200 individuals, has long thrived under the watchful eye of the "Officer in Charge of the Apes," a soldier whose job is to make sure that they have all the food and shelter they need.

There is a healthy population of Barbary macaques in Ifrane National Park, at the heart of the Middle Atlas. This national park comprises dense woodland of native Atlas cedar, holm oaks, and evergreens such as the

The Spanish marbled white is a beautiful addition to the Middle Atlas countryside.

INSIDER TIP:

It is advisable to hire a professional guide when exploring the mountain areas.

—FAICAL ALAOUI MEDARHRI
Moroccan National Tourist Office guide

European black pine. In the Cèdre Gouraud Forest, which lines the Azrou-to-Ifrane highway, some of the protected cedar trees are thought to be several hundred years old.

In addition to the Barbary macaques, the Middle Atlas region is also home to the elegant Barbary stag (*Cervus elaphius barbarus*). This animal has lived in Morocco since Paleolithic times, but due to its dwindling numbers, had to be reintroduced to this area from captive populations just a few years ago. The Barbary stag is found in the depths of the forest and, being a shy animal, is rarely seen. The Barbary sheep

(*Ammotragus lervia*) is another species that has been saved from extinction by a program of measures to control its territory, along with the Barbary wild boar (*Sus scrofa barbarus*) and the vagrant hedgehog (*Erinaceus algirus*). Polecats and lynxes are other endangered creatures found in this mountain range.

The mountains change with the seasons. Soft yellow buttercups are a common sight along the riverbeds or the banks of the Aguelmane Ouiouane in warmer months, and the countryside turns a subtle shade of lilac as the thorny erinacea (*Erinacea anthyllis*) carpets the mountainous slopes.

As well as being a good place to experience the stunning scenery of the Middle Atlas, the forested Ifrane National Park also becomes a popular ski resort in the winter (see p. 175).

Birdlife in the Middle Atlas

The Middle Atlas is home to an impressive range of birds, some of them found in just a few other parts of northwest Africa. One such is Levaillant's woodpecker, which haunts high-altitude conifer forests but can be very difficult to track down. More obvious are birds of prey, and the Middle Atlas supports a healthy population. Watch for booted and golden eagles and long-legged buzzards soaring high over mountainsides, and for powerful goshawks darting through forested areas in pursuit of their avian prey. Mountain streams will have dippers—so named because they swim and dive in search of food—and watch for alpine swifts and crag martins swooping and diving around cliffs.

Volubilis

The ancient city of Volubilis lies a few miles north of Meknès on a plateau in the foothills of the Zerhoun Mountains. It is one of the best preserved and extensive Roman sites in the world and the most important archaeological site in Morocco. As a result, Volubilis was declared a UNESCO World Heritage site for its historical interest in 1997.

The remains of the Basilica, abandoned by the Romans in A.D. 280, at the ancient city of Volubilis

Volubilis

⚑ 159 B3

✉ 19 miles (31 km) N of Meknès on road to Tanger

💲 $$$$

Believed to have been founded around the third century B.C. on the site of Neolithic and Carthaginian settlements, Volubilis soon became one of the wealthiest and most important cities in Morocco. Volubilis prospered over the centuries, and the Romans incorporated the city into the Kingdom of Mauretania.

Important to the power of the Roman Empire, Mauretania covered a huge area that included most of North Africa as far south as Chellah (then known as Sala Colonia) near the present-day site of Rabat. When the last king

of Mauretania died, the Roman emperor Claudius assumed power. In A.D. 40, Claudius divided the kingdom into two provinces: Mauretania Tingitana and Mauretania Caesariensis. The provinces had outposts called *colonias,* the most notable of which were Lulia Campestris Babba, Lulia Constantia Zilil, and Lulia Velantia Banasa.

Volubilis, which had continued to prosper, was declared the administrative center of Mauretania Tingitana—an important province for the Romans because of its strong trading links with the Mediterranean. Volubilis vied for attention with Tingis, which was the capital of Mauretania Tingitana on the coastal site of present-day Tanger. As the city pulling the purse strings, however, and located on the fertile plains of central north Morocco—from where it could export vast quantities of grain, fish, fruits, olive oil, and pearls to Rome and its neighboring European powers—Volubilis continued to grow in importance. The city became extraordinarily prosperous, which is evident from the archaeological remains of its infrastructure and the remains of the huge, often elaborate buildings that we see today.

Today, you can visit the site, which has been the subject of excavation works from as early as 1915 and in more recent times by the Moroccan Institut National des Sciences de l'Archéologie et du Patrimoine. New and exciting remains are still being discovered, the most recent ruins being those of a medieval town. On site is a

INSIDER TIP:

If you don't have the time to wander aimlessly around Volubilis, guides can be hired at the ticket office for around 100 dirhams.

—BEN HOLLINGUM
National Geographic contributor

small museum and café, with the route around the remains and the exhibits clearly labeled.

Touring the Site

Dominating the site is the **Basilica,** its entrance portico and sides comprising eight perfectly formed arches, which are all in remarkably good order. Inside, it is designed in a three-aisle arrangement with two apses. Nearby are the striking columns of the **Capitol ruins,** where the sacrificial altar

UNESCO & Morocco

The United Nations Educational, Scientific, and Cultural Organization, known as UNESCO, was founded in 1945 with the aim to provide a resource for the study of civilizations and cultures and to offer protection for heritage sites worldwide.

Morocco's historic city of Meknès became a UNESCO World Heritage site in 1996, and the archaeological site of Volubilis followed a year later. Other UNESCO sites in Morocco include the well-preserved medinas of Fès and Marrakech, the pre-Saharan *ksar* of Aït Ben Haddou near Ouarzazate, the former Portuguese city of Mazagan (now known as El Jadida), and the medinas of Essaouira and Tétouan. The Oudaïa Kasbah and the Chellah Necropolis in Rabat are currently being considered for World Heritage status in Morocco.

For a place to qualify as a cultural World Heritage site, a group of experts drawn from across the world must agree that it represents a unique and important example of human intelligence and creativity. Qualifying for this status boosts a site's profile enormously, and curators can access a substantial fund that allocates resources needed for the repair and maintenance of a site's buildings.

would have been located, and the **Forum.** These structures are believed to date from the second century A.D. and can be found in a section of the city where earlier craft workshops and a marketplace are believed to have been.

Temples, which were often built to the similar Greek Doric style with columns, triglyphs, and a highly sculpted metope for decoration, would have been integral to the community. Among the Volubilis ruins is the **Temple of Jupiter.**

On a visit, you can see what would have been magnificent houses, decorated with colorful mosaic floors as was the fashion of the day. You can also see the beautifully preserved remains of the **House of Orpheus,** with its mosaics depicting scenes from mythology; the **House of the Columns,** so called because of its colonnaded courtyard; and the **House of the Hercules.** There are remains of Roman *thermae,* or bathhouses, as well as **buildings for grain storage and the pressing of olives for oil**—both key features for the economy of Volubilis and for feeding its people.

One of the finest ruins of the site is the **Triumphal Arch,** which was built to commemorate the victorious achievements of Lucius Septimius Bassianus—the Roman emperor Caracalla (188–217), who reigned from 211. The arch is a monumental structure that marks the end of the city's main thoroughfare, the **Decumanus Maximus,** and is built to a classical architectural style with decorative columns and arches. Inscriptions detailing battles

The Secret Town of Moulay Idriss

Not far south of Volubilis, on a series of hills near the main road to Meknès, lies the mysterious town of Moulay Idriss. This place is the holiest pilgrimage site in Morocco, home to the tomb of Idriss I— great-grandson of the Prophet Muhammad and the first king of Morocco.

Despite its beauty and historic importance, this town is still almost completely untouched by tourism. This is because, over the years, the town has built up something of a reputation for being hostile to outsiders. While it is true that all of the town's major landmarks—ancient shrines and mosques—are off-limits to non-Muslims, the commonly held belief that the town itself is a no-go area for Westerners is incorrect. As long as you are respectful and don't try to intrude on any of the holy shrines, the locals are friendly and welcoming.

The town is a tranquil, pleasant place to spend a day or two, where the pace of life moves very slowly. The view of the town from the peak of one of its hills alone is worth making a trip here, and the simple architecture of the place is a welcome relief from the sometimes overwhelming extravagance of Meknès. The few tourists who make the trip to this town tend to leave before nightfall, and up until recently there was nowhere for them to stay. Today, however, some guesthouses are opening in the city, such as **Dar Zerhoune** *(42 Derb Zouak, Moulay Idriss, tel 0535/54 43 71, www.buttonsinn .com),* a guesthouse opened by Mike Richardson, a London restaurateur.

would have been engraved on the facades, while a statue of the emperor, possibly depicted in the stance of a warrior, would have perched on top.

After the Romans

Volubilis experienced a period of decline from around the fifth century A.D., when Morocco was invaded and conquered by the Vandals, Visigoths, and Byzantines. However, these tribes preferred Morocco's coastal areas, which was fortuitous for Volubilis, as many of its residents were able to stay unhindered by new rulers. Unlike many of Morocco's cities, Volubilis was not abandoned, and although it had fallen from grace as a major city, it continued to provide a home and a living for its people. By this time, many of the city's residents had embraced the culture of the Roman Empire and converted to Christianity.

Volubilis appears in the history books again around the same time the first Islamic settlers arrived in Morocco. It is believed that the city was then occupied by refugees from the Awraba tribe—a Berber people from the Rif Mountains. Idriss ibn Abdullah, who would become Idriss I, the founder and first ruler of the Idrisid dynasty, had fled from the Abbasids of the ruling Abbasid Caliphate of Baghdad, who had invaded his native Syria in 787.

The Awraba Berbers offered Idriss sanctuary in the city. They respected him as a descendant of the Prophet Muhammad. When Idriss declared the city

to be the capital of his dynasty, Volubilis entered another period of growth. Idriss I quickly founded Fès, which became the new capital, but the status bestowed on Volubilis, however briefly, was a source of pride. And Idriss I chose a nearby site for his mausoleum (see sidebar opposite).

INSIDER TIP:

If you plan to visit Rabat during your stay in Morocco, many of the finds from Volubilis are on display in the Musée Archéologique [see p. 80].

—LEON GRAY
National Geographic contributor

Volubilis is thought to have been inhabited during the 11th century when the Almoravids reigned, and during subsequent periods of Almohad, Marinid, and Saadian rule. Over time, the city deteriorated through neglect and was damaged by earthquakes. Its collapsed buildings were never rebuilt. It was also badly damaged in the 17th century, when Sultan Moulay Ismail had several pieces of stonework and marble columns removed from the site and used in his construction projects in Meknès. Although the extent of his plunder is not known exactly, there are a few conspicuous examples, such as the marble columns used in the construction of the Bab Mansour (see pp. 162–163). ∎

From the thronging souks of Marrakech to the jagged mountains of the High Atlas and down to the golden beaches of Essaouira

Marrakech & Around

A food stall on Djemaa el Fna, with the Koutoubia Mosque looming behind

Marrakech & Around

Marrakech is the most popular tourist destination in Morocco, a vibrant noisy city of souks and palaces. Beyond the city limits, the landscape is like Morocco in miniature, with snowcapped mountains, fertile plains, and beautiful coastlines.

Lying at the point where the coastal plains of North Africa meet the desert, with the snowcapped peaks of the High Atlas Mountains as its backdrop, this oasis city has been a market and meeting place for centuries. Once, it attracted Arab merchants from the coastal cities, Berber farmers from the surrounding hills, and even West African traders from the goldfields of Mali and Niger.

Known as the "red city" because of its massive ramparts made of dried mud (see sidebar p. 198), Marrakech was founded in 1062 under the Almoravid dynasty, which wanted a new capital for its burgeoning empire. Over the succeeding centuries, Marrakech (which means "land of God" in the Berber language) grew to become one of Morocco's greatest imperial cities, and indeed for a while was one of the wealthiest and most significant urban settlements in the entire Mediterranean region.

Today, although the city has long since given up its national capital status to Rabat, it is the administrative capital of the Marrakech-Tensift-El Haouz district, which covers an area of more than 12,000 square miles (32,000 sq km) from the foothills of the High Atlas to the beaches of Essaouira.

Marrakech is at its most appealing between autumn and spring. Summer temperatures can reach as high as 104°F (40°C) in the city. Essaouira, which is cooled by a consistent onshore breeze, stays comfortable much later into the summer, but can be cold and stormy in the winter. If you want to explore the mountains, the summer is the best time to visit, as the altitude keeps the air cool year-round, and the mountain passes are at their safest in the summer months.

Marrakech

The city is divided into two main areas: the medina, or old town, with souks, grand mosques, and fine houses hidden down its twisting streets; and the new town, Guéliz, a busy commercial hub where modern hotels sit alongside trendy restaurants, boutiques, nightclubs, banks, and offices.

Wherever you are in Marrakech, all roads seem to lead to Djemaa el Fna—a gigantic public square that is the medina's most important marketplace. The square makes a good

---

NOT TO BE MISSED:

base from which to set out in search of the other wonders of the medina, which include the 900-year-old Koutoubia Mosque with its elegant minaret, the ornately decorated 16th-century Saadian Tombs, and the Ibn Youssef Medersa, one of Morocco's oldest universities.

Other major attractions are the medina's many grand mansions and palaces. Some, like the Royal Palace, are occupied and closed to the public, but others have been opened to the public or converted into hotels and restaurants.

Should you tire of the bustle and commerce of the center, you can get some respite in a number of more peaceful attractions in the city's chic Ville Nouvelle. The imperial Menara Gardens, first established in the 12th century by the Almohads but much changed since, and the more modern Majorelle Gardens are a pair of elegant, landscaped spaces filled with blooms and long, cool reflecting pools.

High Atlas

There's also plenty to entice visitors in the rugged landscape that lies beyond the city limits, including the hikes and trails of the Toubkal National Park, site of the country's

highest peaks; the famed Saturday market at Asni; and the grand tumbling cascades of Ouzoud. Little more than an hour's travel from the center of Marrakech will take you into a mountainous wilderness, where the indigenous Berber population lives a rural lifestyle that has changed little in centuries.

Essaouira

The attractive seaside town of Essaouira is a much loved holiday spot for ordinary Moroccans, a quiet friendly town that nonetheless boasts a vibrant cultural life and excellent souks. Essaouira's impressive forti-fied medina is a fascinating place to explore, and the area's stunning beaches are popular with windsurfers and kitesurfers from around the world. ■

Central Marrakech

With its huge maze of souks, breathtaking imperial architecture, and peaceful, shaded gardens, the city of Marrakech is one of the most exciting destinations in Morocco today. If you can cope with the city's frenetic pace, even a short stay here will be time well spent.

A Marrakech storyteller entertains spectators in the Djemaa el Fna.

Marrakech

🅼 185 B2, 197

Visitor Information

✉ Moroccan National Tourist Office, 176 boulevard Mohamed V, Guéliz

☎ (0524) 43 08 86

www.marrakech -info.com

Settlements have existed in this area since before recorded history. While the coastal cities fell under the control of a succession of seafaring empires, these settlements thrived thanks to their relative stability and overland trade links.

Marrakech has its origins in the 11th century, when the Almoravid dynasty decided to construct a new capital around the springs at Marrakech. Under the Almohad dynasty, which took control of Morocco in the 12th century, the city's fortifications were enlarged,

a kasbah was built, and the city received its first hospital. The city's preeminent status was confirmed by the construction of what was to become one of the Muslim world's most spectacular places of worship, the Koutoubia Mosque.

After the fall of the Almohads in the 13th century, Marrakech lost some of its former prestige. The new ruling dynasty moved the capital to Fès. Without royal patronage, Marrakech slowly developed into a regional trade hub and educational center, eventually regaining some measure of its former glory. In 1524, it became a capital city once again under the Saadian dynasty, which ruled for a century. When the French arrived in the early 20th century, they discovered a formidable walled city with a strong sense of tradition and history.

In its entirety, the fortified medina, which encompasses several of the city's top tourist attractions—including the Saadian Tombs, the spectacular Koutoubia Mosque, and Ibn Youssef Medersa—is considered one of the finest examples of its type in Morocco and has been declared a UNESCO World Heritage site.

Today, Marrakech's medina is one of the most popular destinations in Morocco. European tour groups are a common sight in the huge maze of souks that occupy the center of town. As a result, you are less likely to suffer the kind of persistent harassment by touts and guides that is common

INSIDER TIP:

While in Marrakech, don't miss out on the food stands in the Djemaa el Fna. The roasted nuts and fresh-squeezed orange juice are a great snack.

—MARISA LARSON
National Geographic contributor

in towns where visitors are more of a novelty. Thousands of people here rely on the constant influx of Western tourists for their livelihoods—including, unfortunately, a small population of pickpockets, scam artists, and touts. While these are fewer in number than they have been in the past, it is a good idea to keep an eye on your valuables and report any serious harassment to the tourist police (who have offices on the western side of the Djemaa el

Finding Your Way Around Marrakech

Marrakech's medina is one of the largest in Morocco and, as with all medinas, its irregular shape and baffling street layout is more organic than logical. Originally the medina would have been the entire town—it's only modern developments that have expanded the city beyond its walls. The heart of the medina is the massive Djemaa el Fna square. Immediately to the north of the Djemaa el Fna, at the approximate center of the medina, lies a maze of souks selling anything from live animals to antique furniture. This busy core is surrounded by many smaller residential and commercial areas, each with their own distinct character—from

the cool, relaxed palaces in the south to the foul-smelling courtyards of the tannery district in the east.

The city's main attractions are mostly located within a few minutes' walk of the Djemaa el Fna, making it an excellent place from which to start your exploration of the city. One feature of Marrakech that you will soon come to appreciate, especially after a few days walking or cycling (see sidebar p. 206), is that the city is almost perfectly flat. You will therefore not have to contend with the stepped, near-vertical streets that you find in northern cities like Tanger and Tétouan.

Street Theater on Djemaa El Fna

As dawn breaks, Marrakech's main square is a largely deserted expanse of tarmac. It doesn't stay this way for long, however. Within hours it transforms into a cross between a giant marketplace and an open-air circus filled with various types of entertainers and craftspeople. The square offers perhaps the densest concentration of Moroccan cultural expression of any place in the country. UNESCO describes it as one of the "Masterpieces of the Oral and Intangible Heritage of Humanity."

In the heat of the midday sun, the square's entertainments can be relatively subdued, with the occasional monkey handler running his tired animal between groups of musicians and snake charmers to pose for the cameras of passing tour groups, but when the cooler evening air sweeps in, it transforms into a fantastic, dazzling spectacle. The thronging crowds are kept entertained by a constant and eclectic mix of street performers, including musicians, jugglers, dancers, acrobats, fortune-tellers, and snake charmers.

As soon as the sun goes down, the square becomes a giant alfresco food hall, with stall holders performing their own street theater as they cook. At the end of the evening, the food stalls close, leaving the square to the musicians who entertain those crowds that remain until the early hours.

Djemaa el Fna

🅰 197

Fna and farther south on the rue Moulay Ismail).

Djemaa el Fna

This massive open space was founded as a *mechouar* (parade ground) to a long since demolished Almoravid kasbah in the 11th century, which was appropriated by the city's population as a marketplace. There are several competing explanations for the name Djemaa el Fna, which means "assembly of the dead" in Arabic, but the most probable is that it is a reference to the time when this square was used as a site for public executions. Today the Djemaa el Fna offers gentler forms of entertainment, though with its open-air butchers' shops, snake handlers, and alarmingly theatrical tooth-pullers it's not relaxing by any stretch of the imagination.

Although it is best known for its street theater (see sidebar above), the square is also home to a huge outdoor market. You won't find any dazzling bargains here, but it's a good introduction to shopping in the city. During the day, you can get everything from groceries to textiles, and in the evening it becomes an open-air food hall where aromas of cooking meat and spices fill the air. Despite efforts to modernize the square, it remains a chaotic, enchanting place and a spectacle not to be missed.

Souk District

If you head north from Djemaa el Fna, through place Bab Fteuh and the Souk Qessabine, you will reach the arched entrance of rue Souk Smarine, a broad covered thoroughfare that forms the spine of the medina's souks. The northern half is called the Souk el Kebir, but it is the same street. In the many squares and streets that lead off this main artery, you will find goods arranged according to themes, with individual souks specializing in different products, such as leather, textiles, or spices. Often several souks selling the same type of product are clustered together in the same network of alleyways. The first souk you come to, the **Rabha Kedima** *(on the left, around 220 yards/ 200 m along rue Souk Smarine)* is dedicated to medicines, and is not for the squeamish. All manner of strange objects and animal parts can be seen in glass jars; they will eventually be key ingredients in dubious medicines or cosmetic products.

As you continue north, look for the **Souk des Babouches,** which sells the brightly colored leather slippers worn by locals. These beautiful and unique items are a good souvenir as they are lightweight. If you're thinking about getting something shipped back, then head to the **Souk des Tapis** (also known as the Criée Berbière; *alleyway on north side of Rabha Kedima),* where fine Moroccan carpets line the walls and lie in huge stacks on the ground. If you ask, store owners will be happy to explain the different towns and regions that each pattern or color scheme is traditionally associated with. Other, more practical examples of Moroccan crafts can be found in the **Souk el Haddadine** *(north of souk area, next to the Souk des Babouches),* where the

(continued on p. 192)

Café society in the wealthy district of Guéliz, Marrakech

Marrakech's Souks

The densely packed, colorful, and noisy souks north of the Djemaa el Fna, where shopkeepers and customers are locked in a perpetual battle over ever shifting prices, are icons of Marrakechi culture. Despite the appearance of supermarkets and boutiques on the city's outskirts, the clamor of the souks is still the place to go for both locals doing their everyday shopping and tourists scouting for souvenirs.

A souk selling ceramics in Marrakech's medina

While Marrakech's souk is not the cheapest place to shop in Morocco (the sheer volume of foreign visitors has pushed up prices considerably over the years), it certainly has the broadest range of products to choose from. The souk rambles in all directions from the north side of the Djemaa el Fna to the area around the Ibn Youssef Medersa, around half a mile (0.8 km) to the north.

Narrow alleyways lead into yet narrower alleyways, which lead into small, cavelike squares where the goods for sale—be they musical instruments, locally made textiles, or half-butchered sheep carcasses—hang from poles and rafters in great arches over your head. Throughout the area, the streets and squares are covered with wooden slats and awnings, which shield the streets from the sun

and tend to amplify whatever smells or sounds the nearby stalls are producing.

The souk is a loud, often confusing place, where the roads seem to curl around themselves. If you have no particular destination in mind or item you wish to purchase, then wandering around aimlessly can be rewarding, but those with no time to waste continually getting lost can head to the **tourist office** (176 boulevard Mohamed V, Guéliz, tel 0524/43 08 86, www.marrakech-info.com) in Guéliz, or ask at your hotel for a guide before you go.

What will also be evident as you explore the souks is that each town or city has its own traditional goods. In Fès it is the famous blue pottery, in Meknès it is wood carvings and mosaics, while Marrakech is known for its leather goods. Prices are not always displayed and, even if they are, it is expected that you will barter for a better price with the merchant (see sidebar below).

Workshops

Souks are not always just marketplaces, and the small shops out of which goods are sold are often also workshops, turning out items such as carpets, embroidery, or woodcarvings. Wealthier merchants are more likely to have their workshops away from the souk, so that the shop is simply that: a place to display goods and offer them for sale.

Souk stall owners may invite you to see a demonstration of their crafts, so you can watch as they emboss the leather or cut and sew it into shape. The craft most commonly demonstrated is the making of *babouche* slippers, which are still made with traditional methods and worn daily by Moroccans. They make a great gift or souvenir of your trip.

Cooperatives

Standing in the Marrakech souks, amid all the raucous noise and chaotically arranged products, it can seem as though this part of the city is oblivious to the changes that are sweeping through Moroccan society and is somehow resistant to the advance of time. The commercial life of this souk, however, is home to a remarkable grassroots movement. Over the last 20 years or so, numerous not-for-profit cooperatives have been established in the area. The proceeds from these fixed-price stores are used to pay the artisans a steady, reliable wage and to fund education programs that teach the artisans the literacy and numeracy skills needed to establish

INSIDER TIP:

The real struggle when browsing in the souks is to limit yourself to only what you can fit in your luggage.

—SALLY MCFALL
National Geographic contributor

their own businesses. Good examples of this movement include the **Femmes de Marrakech Coopérative Artisanale de Couture** (*67 Souk Kchachbia, tel 0524/37 83 08*) and the **Association Al-Kawtar** (*57 rue Laksour/3 rue el Mouassine, tel 0524/37 82 93, www.alkawtar.org*). By providing benefits like a high hourly wage, medical insurance, and free day care, these organizations enable local women to become socially and economically independent, no longer reliant on men for their livelihood.

EXPERIENCE: Haggling in the Souks

Haggling for a bargain may be an alarming prospect for some visitors, but it is all part of the pantomime of the souk. It is expected by the seller, and is usually conducted in good humor. You will be invited in to look at your desired purchase over a glass of mint tea, during which you may ask about the good's history and how it is made until the conversation, inevitably, turns to the price. Gentle bargaining is called for. Decide on the price you wish to pay and make your offer, or offers, with grace. Don't be surprised if the price you are offered is significantly higher than what the locals would have to pay.

The merchant will not be offended if, after haggling, you decide not to make a purchase if you cannot agree upon a price. If, however, you offer a price and the merchant agrees to it, then make the purchase (this is the merchant's livelihood remember, not a game), which should be done in cash. You can then meander along the tiny streets of the souk with your new leather item, ceramic pot, or piece of jewelry.

Koubba Ba'Adiyn

 197

✉ place Ibn
Youssef

**Ibn Youssef
Medersa**

 197

✉ place Ibn
Youssef

☎ (0524) 44 18 93

blacksmiths ply their trade, and the **Souk des Bijoutiers** *(next to Souk des Tapis)*, where you can get traditional jewelry.

Northern Medina

Only a few minutes' walk north of Souk el Kebir, on the edge of the souk district, lies one of the oldest and most prestigious neighborhoods in Marrakech,

Youssef in the 12th century. The other buildings have long since vanished—the mosque that bears his name today was built over the ruins of the original in the early 19th century—but this small ablution fountain remains as a tantalizing hint of what the lost buildings must have looked like.

Although the Almoravid mosque has been demolished,

A calèche trots past the Bab Agnaou

home to the grand Ibn Youssef Mosque and Medersa complex.

The center of this area is the place Ibn Youssef, at the northern limit of the Souk el Kebir. The southern side of this square is occupied by the exquisitely decorated **Koubba Ba'Adiyn.** This beautiful little building with its ornately carved dome is the only surviving remnant of a vast mosque and palace complex built by Almoravid ruler Ali Ibn

there is no shortage of stunning historic architecture in the area. The **Ibn Youssef Medersa,** which stands in the northeast corner of the square, is one of the most important historic buildings in the city. This Koranic college was founded in the 14th century under the Marinids and rebuilt in a new architectural style during the Saadian period. It was an important center of learning in the western Muslim world, teaching students

In the souks, it helps to carry a compass, as even with a detailed map it can be hard to orient yourself in a city where half the streets have no names, and the other half have two!

—AHMED TARIF

Tour guide

the complexities of Islamic law and scriptural interpretation. It is no longer used as a university, but you can still see the cells where the leading students of the day lived and studied, and the prayer hall where they came to worship.

Thanks to the largesse of a succession of wealthy rulers, the building provided an exceptionally beautiful learning environment for its students. An imposing bronze door leads into the *medersa* from the place Ibn Youssef, and once inside it seems that every available surface is decorated with complex stuccowork, mosaics, marble columns, carved cedarwood, and dizzying arrangements of traditional *zellij* tilework. You can purchase a ticket that allows you entry to most parts of the medersa.

While in the area, you should visit the **Souk des Fassis** that runs alongside its boundary. This street houses some of the city's finest examples of traditional inns for merchants, known as *fondouks*. Most have been sympathetically restored to show their original

beauty, and many now house artists' studios and craft workshops.

The beautifully restored late 19th-century Dar Menebhi Palace (see p. 205) now houses the **Museum of Marrakech,** and the rooms that once witnessed everyday life now display an impressive collection of Moroccan art and sculpture, coins, jewelry, ceramics, and pieces of architectural details from buildings, some of which date as far back as the time of the Idrissids. It's worth paying the price of admission just to see the fabulous building. Don't miss the glass-roofed inner courtyard, with its magnificent lamp chandelier perched above an elegant fountain, where occasional music concerts and theatrical performances are held.

Koutoubia Mosque & the Western Medina

If you head southwest from the Djemaa el Fna, beyond the place Foucauld, you will enter a much more open and calm area of the city. This area is home to Marrakech's most important landmark, its finest hotel, and some beautiful gardens.

The first thing you will see as you head away from the Djemaa el Fna is the 250-foot-tall (77 m) minaret of the **Koutoubia Mosque.** This mosque is an iconic example of Moroccan architecture, and its minaret a blueprint that influenced the design of minarets and even church towers throughout North Africa and Spain. The mosque was built in the 12th century, right next to the site where another, almost identi-

Museum of Marrakech

🗺 197

✉ place Ibn Youssef

☎ (0524) 39 09 11

🕐 Closed Mon.

💲 $

Koutoubia Mosque

🗺 197

✉ place de la Koutoubia

Mamounia Hotel
(See also p. 297)
✉ avenue Bab
Jedid
☎ (0524) 38 86 00
www.mamounia.com

cal mosque had already been built. It is thought that the first mosque, whose ruins can still be seen, was abandoned because it was found to be out of alignment with Mecca, although ironically modern measurements have found that the Koutoubia Mosque is even farther from perfect alignment than its ruined predecessor.

The **minaret** is built in the Almohad style, which paid particular attention to proportions—it is almost exactly five times taller than it is wide—and is adorned with time-worn and evocative fragments of its once-grand decoration. The interior—which, like all mosques in Morocco, is generally closed to non-Muslims—features a small courtyard and a simple, colonnaded prayer hall. The mosque's stunning wooden *minbar* (a structure similar to a pulpit in a church), which was built by Andalusian craftsmen in

the 11th century, is now kept in El Badi Palace (see pp. 195–198 & 202–204).

A short distance farther west, along the avenue Houman el Fetouki, lies the decadent luxury of the newly renovated **Mamounia Hotel.** This historic hotel was a favorite of former British prime minister Winston Churchill, and it is where he famously took U.S. President Franklin D. Roosevelt to dine and discuss strategy after the Casablanca Conference (see sidebar p. 57). While this glossy and expensive hotel may not be to everyone's taste, a reservation at its terrace restaurant will grant you access to the hotel's beautiful formal gardens. With the exception of some minor additions and alterations made by French designer Jacques Majorelle in the 1920s, the gardens predate the hotel by several hundred years and were originally the gardens of

EXPERIENCE: Traveling by Calèche

A great way to get around Marrakech, if a little touristy, is a type of horse-drawn carriage commonly referred to as a calèche. To catch one, head to place Foucauld on the west side of the Djemaa el Fna, where they usually congregate. For some common journeys, such as a trip around the ramparts of the city or to a particular district of the city, the price may be displayed, but if you have a particular request, you should expect to pay around 100 dirham an hour. If you are quoted more, haggle—that's what the driver will expect you to do.

The calèche itself is a brightly painted four-wheel carriage that originated in the 18th century. It normally has two

double seats, so that four people can sit facing each other, although some have just one double seat facing forward. The calèche driver sits in front on a high box seat to steer the horse, which, at times, can reach a fairly fast trot. Some calèches have a hood and are well worth seeking out on summer days when the Marrakech sun can be intense.

The driver will probably engage you in lively conversation about where you come from and tell you about his city, both to pass the time and, of course, to increase his chances of getting a tip—so expect plenty of compliments about your home country.

Traditional jewelry for sale at a Djemaa el Fna souk

a Saadian royal palace. If you do decide to dine here, you'll need to dress smartly, regardless of the heat, as the hotel strictly enforces its dress code.

Head north from Koutoubia, along the avenue Mohamed V, to reach the **Ensemble Artisanal**—a government-supported store where you can buy locally produced, handmade traditional crafts at fixed prices and without hassle from overzealous salesmen. The prices are typically higher than those in the souks, but it is well worth visiting, if only to have a good look at the kind of wares that are available locally in a calm, unhurried environment.

Just across the street is Marrakech's most modern public space, the **Cyber-Park Arsat Moulay Abdeslam.** This small park just inside the city walls has numerous outdoor computer terminals, and the whole area is a free Wi-Fi hotspot. In a country where Internet connections are rare and unreliable, this park is a great place to stop and check up on what's going on in the outside world, while enjoying the shade of one of the park's many olive groves (which are centuries older than the park itself).

The Kasbah & Mellah

To the south of the Djemaa el Fna, along the rue Riad Zitoun el Kedim lies the kasbah, home to the Saadian Tombs, the spectacular Bab Agnaou, and, nestled in the shadow of the area's stunning palaces (see pp. 202–205), the *mellah*—once the home of Marrakech's large Jewish population.

The monumental remains of the 16th-century **El Badi Palace**

(continued on p. 198)

Ensemble Artisanal

 197

✉ avenue Mohamed V

☎ (0524) 44 35 03

🕐 Closed Sun.

Cyber-Park Arsat Moulay Abdeslam

 197

A Walk in Central Marrakech

This walk is a way to capture the essence of Marrakech, taking you past gloriously ornate palaces and mosques, souks shimmering with life and commerce, and the great ramparts that kept them all safe over the past millennium.

A market in central Marrakech

Start your walk at the huge **Bab Agnaou** ➊. This mighty structure dates from the 12th century and at one time marked the entrance of a long since demolished Almohad palace. It is highly decorative, with geometric patterns radiating out from its arched gateway. It can be reached easily from Hivernage, Guéliz, and the medina—and as landmarks go, it's pretty hard to miss.

From here, head along the rue Oqba ibn Nafaa toward the junction of the avenue Mohamed V and the **Koutoubia Mosque** ➋ (see pp. 193–194), which has stood on this site for more than 900 years. It is not open to non-Muslims, but you can see where the faithful enter at its easternmost entrance. Next door stands the **Koubba Lalla Zohra**, a brilliant white tomb said to contain the body of a slave's daughter and local saint who, as legend would have it, magically transforms into a dove each evening and flies around the city in which she lived and died.

NOT TO BE MISSED:

Bab Agnaou • Rue Souk Smarine • Ibn Youssef Medersa • Museum of Marrakech

From here it's a few minutes' walk to the **Djemaa el Fna** ➌ (see p. 188), the city's commercial, social, and gastronomic heart where thousands come every day to entertain, be entertained, shop, and eat. One of the best views is offered from the famed rooftop terrace of the **Café de France** *(place Djemaa el Fna, Medina)* on the square's eastern side. Head north along the rue Souk Smarine to see the assorted **souks** ➍, past **Souk el Btana** (skins), **Souk des Tapis** (carpets), **Souk des Babouches** (slippers), and **Souk el Haddadine** (blacksmiths). Look for the dome of the Almoravid-built ablution fountain building, the **Koubba Ba'Adiyn** ➎ (see p. 192), poking above the rooftops by the Souk de Teinturiers where Marrakech's dyers color wool for spinning into yarn and hang it out to dry.

One of the must-see monuments in this part of the city is the **Ibn Youssef Medersa** ❻ (see pp. 192–193) on place ben Youssef, a Koranic school built during the time of the Marinids and rebuilt by the Saadians. Not only was this once the largest university in the country, but its mosque was once the main place of worship for everyone living in the medina and the surrounding countryside. Under the Almohad and Saadian dynasties, the *medersa* and the mosque were seen as exemplifying Marrakech's role as the leading provider of education in the Maghreb and as an important Islamic center.

Before you complete your walk, head across the place Ibn Youssef to spend some time in the fabulous **Museum of Marrakech** ❼ (see p. 193). Housed within the 19th-century Moorish Dar Menebhi Palace, the former home of the city's leading officials, it has displays of contemporary and Oriental arts, along with coins dating back to the time of Idriss I and Idriss II, jewelry, manuscripts, and ceramics. Just to the right is one of the city's most attractive modern mosques, the **Eloussta Mosque,** its facade adorned with intricate geometric patterns of *zellij* tilework. From here you can either backtrack to the Djemaa el Fna or continue northwest on the rue el Gza to the taxi rank just outside the Bab Moussoufa.

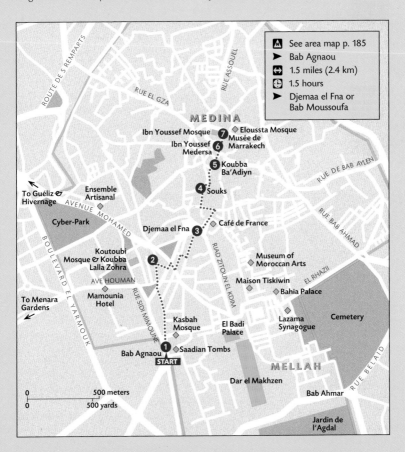

See area map p. 185
► Bab Agnaou
↔ 1.5 miles (2.4 km)
⊙ 1.5 hours
► Djemaa el Fna or Bab Moussoufa

El Badi Palace

 197

✉ rue Berrima

$ $$

Bahia Palace

 197

✉ rue Riad Zitoun
el Jedid

☎ (0524) 38 92 21

$ $$

Maison Tiskiwin

 197

✉ 8 rue de la Bahia
(off rue Riad
Zitoun el Jedid)

☎ (0524) 38 91 92

$ $$

on rue Berrima are the first port of call for many visitors. The palace was built by the Saadian ruler Ahmed el Mansour (1549–1603) as his official residence and was paid for by ransoming Portuguese noblemen captured in the Battle of the Three Kings. Its name means "the incomparable," which was apparently thoroughly deserved—contemporary accounts describe its decoration as being as fine as that of the Saadian Tombs (see p. 199), but on an epic scale. The palace was ransacked by Sultan Moulay Ismail in the 17th century, but its imposing ruins and huge sunken gardens evoke how this spectacular palace must have once looked (see pp. 202–204).

Behind El Badi Palace is the much newer **Dar el Makhzen** palace (see p. 204). This 18th-century palace is the winter residence of the Moroccan royal families, and is not open to the public. A short

distance to the northeast of El Badi Palace, on the rue Riad Zitoun el Jedid, lies a palace that is both intact and open to the public. The **Bahia Palace** (see p. 204) dates from the late 19th century, when it was the residence of Bou Ahmed, a royal adviser who effectively ruled the country between 1894 and 1900. The interior has been carefully restored, and visitors can tour the grand meeting rooms, sumptuous harem (once home to Bou Ahmed's wives and concubines), and courtyard gardens. The palace is still sometimes used for government events and is often closed to the public in the winter, when the royal family is staying at the Dar el Makhzen.

A little farther north, just off the rue Riad Zitoun el Jedid, lie two interesting museums. The first, the **Maison Tiskiwin,** is a small but fascinating place. This traditional Moroccan town house

Walls of the Medina

Marrakech's 12th-century fortifications are one of the city's most distinctive features. While many other Moroccan cities have lost most or all of their walls to erosion, invasions, and urban development, the pink mud-brick walls that surround Marrakech have survived largely complete. When you look at them, it's not hard to see why—they stand around 30 feet (9 m) high and are 7 feet (2 m) thick, increasing to as much as 32 feet (10 m) thick around the gates and towers.

Their long life would be a surprise to their creators, the Almoravids, who built them as a cheap, stop-gap defense against the encroaching Almohads. The walls

were built from mud bricks because stone was expensive and would have taken too long to import. In the end, the Almohads seized control of the city without any major fighting, and then made their own improvements to the city defenses. With the exception of the extension of the wall around the Agdal Gardens (see pp. 207–209) the walls have not been significantly altered since the 12th century.

The best way to see the city walls is by taking a ride in a calèche (see sidebar p. 194), which allows you to tour the exterior of the medina in comfort. Additionally, there are some gates that are open to the public, including the Bab Debbagh in the east and the Bab Agnaou in the south.

has been converted into an ethno-graphic museum by Dutch anthro-pologist, and resident of Morocco since 1957, Bert Flint. Its collection includes textiles, carpets, and jewelry that Flint has gathered in his many expeditions to the Atlas Mountains and Sahara desert. A little farther north lies the Dar Si Saïd (see p. 205), a former palace that now houses the **Museum of Moroccan Arts.** It doesn't have the eccentric character of the Maison Tiskiwin, but it does have a impressive collection of woodcarvings and furniture.

Saadian Tombs: A few min-utes' walk west of the palaces, behind the Kasbah Mosque, is the complex known as the Saadian Tombs. This elegant col-lection of mausoleums contains the marble tombs of around 60 leading members of the Saadian dynasty. It was built between the late 16th and early 17th centu-ries, but the entrances to it were blocked off by Sultan Moulay Ismail in the late 17th century. The complex and its gardens lay unnoticed and forgotten until 1917 when they were spotted in aerial photographs of the city and reopened.

The Saadian Tombs remain well hidden and accessible only via a small entrance next to the Kasbah Mosque. The complex consists of two **mausoleum buildings** set within a walled garden. Visitors enter the complex through the newer and more impressive of the two, built by Sultan Ahmed el Mansour in the early 17th century. The

three rooms of this mausoleum are decorated with fantastically intricate and complex carvings, which were the work of numer-ous Andalusian and Moroccan craftsmen. The marble tombs of numerous Saadian princes and sultans are placed within this building, although few get more than a simple marble slab to mark their resting place.

INSIDER TIP:

The narrow passage-ways of the Saadian Tombs can get very crowded. Visit in the early morning or late afternoon to really appreciate the calming atmosphere of this secluded site.

—FAICAL ALAOUI MEDARHRI
Moroccan National Tourist Office

The second building, which is smaller and simpler than the first, is on the other side of the lush garden, where the gravestones of royal advisers and generals line the pathways. It was originally built to house the tomb of Ahmed el Mansour's mother, but later modified to accommodate other members of the dynasty.

Bab Agnaou: Just across the street from the Saadian Tombs is the spectacular Bab Agnaou, the only surviving example of the city's original stone gatehouses. Built by the Almoravids in the

Museum of Moroccan Arts

🅰 197

✉ Derb El Bahia (off rue Riad Zitoun el Jedid)

☎ (0524) 44 24 64

🕐 Closed Tues.

💲 $

Saadian Tombs

🅰 197

✉ rue de la Kasbah

☎ (0524) 43 61 31

🕐 Closed Tues.

💲 $

Bab Agnaou

🅰 197

✉ rue de la Kasbah

Snake charmers, a monkey handler, and musicians entertain the crowds in the Djemaa el Fna.

Lazama Synagogue

✉ 6 Derb Ragrada, Mellah

🕐 Closed Sat.

Bab Debbagh

✉ rue de Bab Debbagh

Café Amandine

✉ 177 rue Mohamed el Bequal, Guéliz

☎ (0524) 44 96 12

www.amandine marrakech.com

12th century, the Bab Agnaou was originally the commoners' entrance to the kasbah, and the dazzling decorative stonework around the exterior gate was intended to impress visitors with the sultan's wealth.

Mellah: The mellah, which lies off the rue Berrima to the east of the tombs, was once the largest Jewish district in the country. Established in the 16th century, it grew apace and by the early 20th century was home to

around 16,000 residents. Most emigrated, however, following the founding of the state of Israel in 1948. Today most of the area's former synagogues have been converted into houses and shops. Only a few remain untouched, and only one, the **Lazama Synagogue,** is still in use by the area's handful of Jewish residents. The interior is plain, and usually closed to the public, but the caretaker can be persuaded to admit visitors.

Eastern Medina

The area of the medina to the east of the souks and the Djemaa el Fna doesn't have many attractions for visitors. The main draw here is the large **tannery district,** where the city's ancient leather industry can be seen operating in the same stomach-churning way that it has for centuries. If you can take the smell (and few can), a visit can be interesting, but the squeamish might find themselves put off their new *babouches,* as well as their food. Beyond the tanneries lies the **Bab Debbagh,** one of the city's oldest gates. The interior of this gatehouse is open to the public, and the view of the city from the roof is stunning.

Guéliz & Hivernage

Marrakech's new town districts of Guéliz and Hivernage lie outside the original city walls to the northwest. They were built in the early 20th century by Marrakech's French colonial rulers. The plan was to create a new residential, commercial, and financial quarter away from the disorderly confines of the medina. Wide boulevards and parklands were mapped out, mansions and administrative buildings erected, and the whole area planted with hundreds of trees and tropical shrubs.

The clean, modern streets of Marrakech's new town districts are home to few grand buildings or imposing monuments. Without the weight of history looming over them, Guéliz and Hivernage have a youthful, exciting atmosphere that is a striking contrast to the streets of the medina. It is here that you will find Marrakech's bustling café culture, its modern restaurants, and its small collection of bars (see sidebar). Highlights include the excellent, if unhealthy, **Café Amandine,** which sells traditional Moroccan sweetmeats, French pastries, and large helpings of ice cream; the outstanding **Al Fassia Guéliz** *(55 boulevard Mohamed Zerktouni, Guéliz, tel 0524/43 40 60, www.alfassia.com),* a traditional Moroccan restaurant; and the achingly modern surroundings of the **Kechmara** bar and restaurant.

The area revolves around · the **place du 16 Novembre.** Its main thoroughfares—the avenue Hassan II, avenue Mohamed V, and avenue des Nations Unies—meet there. A short walk south, on rue el Imam Ali brings you to one of the district's principal landmarks, a 1930s-built church, the **Église des Saints-Martyrs de Marrakech,** with a fine airy interior bathed during the day by red and yellow light from its stained glass.

Majorelle Gardens: The area's main attraction, however, lies not in the busy streets of Guéliz, but in a quiet residential district to the northeast. Here, among the mansions of colonial administrators, a little-known French painter built the stunning complex of botanical gardens that now bear his name. The Majorelle Gardens were originally created as a serene haven where their painter-owner, Jacques Majorelle (1886–1962), could concentrate on his work. He drew his inspiration from traditional Islamic design and combined it with European modernist ideas, creating something that has enjoyed greater and far more enduring popularity than any of *(continued on p. 206)*

Kechmara
✉ 3 rue de la Liberté, Guéliz
☎ (0524) 422 532
www.kechmara.com

Église des Saints-Martyrs de Marrakech
✉ rue el Imam Ali, Guéliz
☎ (0524) 43 05 85

Majorelle Gardens
✉ avenue Yacoub el Mansour, Guéliz
☎ (0524) 31 30 47
www.jardin majorelle.com/en

Marrakech Nightlife

Thanks to its tourism-based economy and large expatriate population, the city of Marrakech has a rather more diverse range of nightlife than most Moroccan cities. The bars can be broadly divided into two different types. The first are those frequented by local people: smoke-filled bars with an exclusively male clientele and usually no music. The second are the modern bars beloved of expatriates, tourists, and wealthy locals—these bars typically play Western music and have a mixed clientele, and are usually also very expensive. The difference between the bars and their prices—drinks in some of the modern bars cost more than most Moroccan households' weekly food bill—highlight the still large economic disparities in present-day Morocco.

Marrakech's Palaces

Marrakech boasts an impressive collection of palaces, each the work of an indulgent sultan or scheming grand vizier keen to stamp his mark on the city. They range from sumptuous urban mansions to monuments built on an astonishing, scarcely believable scale and at unimaginable expense.

The ruins of an enormous hall and an inner courtyard at El Badi Palace

Although Marrakech is just one of many Moroccan cities that have been the country's capital at one time or other, none of the other imperial cities can compete when it comes to decadent royal splendor. Not all of the palaces have survived the ravages of time—but those that remain, even as abandoned shells, are inspiring sights.

El Badi Palace

Marrakech's greatest palace, **El Badi** (see pp. 195–198), now lies in ruins, but its imposing walls and empty courtyards provide a tantalizing glimpse of its former magnificence. This extraordinary creation was commissioned by the first Saadian sultan to rule from Marrakech, Ahmed el Mansour. He became ruler of Morocco in 1578 upon the death of his brother, Sultan Abu Marwan Abd el Malik I, at the Battle of the Three

Kings, which finally put an end to Portuguese ambitions in the country. Armed with the fortune he amassed in the battle—plus wealth derived from his family's interest in Sudanese gold—he had the financial means, as well as the will, to create a palace larger and more lavish than any that had gone before.

Mansour, whose nickname was "the golden," envisaged the building as a celebration of his and the Saadis' mighty power, and a way of heightening Marrakech's imperial prestige.

Mansour was only months into his reign when he began preparing designs for his new palace, which would be known as El Badi, meaning "the marvelous." His plans called for a main building with around 360 rooms set around an inner courtyard, including several huge reception halls where the sultan would host visiting foreign officials. Anxious not to be outdone, the "courtyard" he constructed is really more of an enclosed park—the size of two football fields—with the palace stretched thinly around the edge.

Influenced by the Alhambra palace and fortress complex in Granada, Andalusia (Spain), Mansour wanted the interior of his palace richly decorated with Sudanese gold, Italian marble, and vast quantities of onyx and granite. On a less glamorous note, he also ordered the construction of an underground prison for those who disapproved of his lavish personal spending. The project took some 25 years to complete, during which time Mansour also commissioned elaborate gardens and fountains for the city and oversaw the creation of several mosques and *medersas* (universities), as well as the Saadian Tombs (see p. 199) necropolis as a place of burial for himself and members of the Saadian dynasty.

When finally complete, El Badi was considered the finest royal residence in the

INSIDER TIP:

Pay a visit to the Saadian Tombs before you go to the Badi Palace—it helps you to imagine how the ruined rooms must once have looked.

—BEN HOLLINGUM
National Geographic contributor

Muslim world. Sadly, it glittered only briefly. In the early 1600s, the Alaouite ruler Moulay Ismail, keen to enhance the prestige of his new dynasty while simultaneously undermining that of his predecessor's, had much of the palace demolished. However, it took him 12 years to destroy the enormous structure and remove many of its riches—including all the gold, marble, onyx, and granite—for use in his own new palace in Meknès.

Royals of the Saadian Dynasty

The powerful Saadians claimed descent from the Prophet Muhammad through the line of Caliph Ali ibn Abi Talib (ca 600–661) and his wife, the Prophet's daughter Fatima Zahra (ca 605–632). The dynasty conquered the country from its base in Taroudant in southern Morocco around 1554 under the leadership of Sultan Muhammad ash-Sheikh (ca 1534–1557). Soon after, Marrakech regained its former status as the country's capital city, which had been lost under the Marinids.

The first Saadian sultans to rule from Marrakech were Ahmed el Mansour, a contemporary of Queen Elizabeth I of England, and his son Zidan Abu Maali (ca 1580–1627). Both were happy to lavish their family's fortune—made largely from Sudanese gold—on Marrakech. Under their rule, the city enjoyed a period of phenomenal growth, during which the

medina, medersas, and fabulous palaces, such as El Badi, were built.

The Saadian-dynasty rulers also built a necropolis, known as the Saadian Tombs, which is today regarded as a leading landmark of the city. It comprises more than 60 royal tombs dating from the 16th to the early 17th centuries. In total, there were 16 rulers of the Saadian dynasty, of whom eight held power only in the south before the conquest of Morocco was complete.

The dynasty's rule came to an end in 1659 with the rise of the Alaouite dynasty. By 1672, the Alaouite sultan Moulay Ismail wanted to assert the authority of his dynasty in Marrakech, but could not bring himself to desecrate a burial ground. Instead, he sealed the entrances to the Saadian Tombs, which were only rediscovered and restored in 1917 by French general Hubert Lyautey.

The remains of the palace that are visible today consist of the most grand and lavish parts of the original complex, the areas meant more for grand state occasions than everyday life. Some of the rooms situated around the courtyard are still relatively complete, although they are stripped of all their original decoration. The courtyard's beautiful sunken gardens are still striking, particularly the surreal effect of having a large reflecting pool whose waters are level with the tops of the surrounding trees. A pavilion on the courtyard's southwest side houses the original *minbar* (pulpit) from the Koutoubia Mosque (see pp. 193–194)—a true masterpiece of beautifully carved and inlaid wood that was produced by some of the Muslim world's finest craftsmen in Córdoba, Spain.

Dar el Makhzen

Next to the remains of El Badi Palace is the city's current royal palace, the Dar el Makhzen, which was built by the 18th-century Alaouite sultan Sidi Muhamed ibn Abdallah, Muhamed III, to replace El Badi as the royal residence of the city. In architectural terms, the palace's design is a fine example of the period's styling, and indeed a prize example of the architect's craft, as it had to be designed and built to a precise size and shape in order to ensure it fitted the contours of the available space within the kasbah.

The palace has undergone several restorations over the decades, the most recent during the reign of King Hassan II, for whom it was a particular favorite. Today it is where the present king, Mohamed VI, stays when he is visiting Marrakech. The palace and its gardens are closed to the public, although you can glimpse the large plazas, known as *mechouars*, which are often used for parades and other special events.

Bahia Palace

Nearby is Marrakech's other main palace, the beautiful Bahia Palace (see p. 198). It was built at the end of the 19th century, not for the royal family but as a residence for the leading vizier of the city, Bou Ahmed ibn Moussa, as well as for his four wives, dozens of concubines, and various children. Its name means, appropriately enough, "palace of the

Intricate designs adorn the Bahia Palace.

INSIDER TIP:
A trip to the Bahia Palace is a fascinating reminder of how far into the modern world the country's old ways survived.

—CLIVE CARPENTER
National Geographic contributor

beautiful," in honor of its intricately carved decorations, and gardens full of fountains, courtyards and tropical plants.

Colorful *zellij* tilework and marble have been used extensively and to good effect on the exterior of the palace. Inside there are two main areas, built at different times. The apartments in the older part of the palace date from the 1890s and are laid out in a relatively simple fashion, while the later apartments are considerably more luxurious. In design and layout, the palace is regarded as a masterpiece. It took several years to build—more than was initially planned—giving rise to a local expression when something takes a long time to complete: "The Bahia is finally finished."

A white stork nests on the early 17th-century ruins of El Badi Palace in Marrakech.

Dar Si Saïd Palace

As you walk around Marrakech, several more palaces will come into view and, although none are quite as lavish as El Badi once was or the Dar el Makhzen and the Bahia still are, they are integral to the character of the city. Some now house government buildings or are private offices, but others are open to the public. The Dar Si Saïd Palace, a glorious building not far from the Bahia Palace, is today home to the **Museum of Moroccan Arts** (see p. 199). The palace was built around the same time, and by the same family, as the Bahia, and features arcades lining inner courtyards, a domed roof, and an interior decorated with zellij tiles. It holds an extensive collection of carpets, jewelry, and other craft items from around the country, displayed thematically over its three floors.

Dar Menebhi Palace

Just north of the souk district, close to the magnificent Ibn Youssef Medersa, lies the Dar Menebhi Palace (Palais Dar Menebhi), a fantastic Moorish home that once belonged to a vizier of the city. Its grand interior is now given over to the **Museum of Marrakech** (*Musée de Marrakech, Palais Dar Menebhi, place Ibn Youssef, tel 0524/44 18 93, $, www.museedemarrakech.ma*), but many of its original architectural features are still in place, despite the building having undergone a complete restoration in 1997. Classic Andalusian touches still abound in its interior, with spacious central courtyards around graceful fountains, superb zellij tilework, intricate carvings, and elegant colonnaded hallways.

Islamic Art Museum

✉ Jardin Majorelle, avenue Yacoub el Mansour, Guéliz

☎ (0524) 30 18 52

$ $

the paintings he created in the studio on the site.

Majorelle opened the gardens to the public in 1947 and managed and maintained them until his death in 1962. After his passing, the gardens fell into neglect, but were restored to their former glory in 1980 by the French fashion designer Yves Saint-Laurent and his partner, philanthropist Pierre Bergé. They kept the gardens open to the public and converted Majorelle's villa into their winter residence.

Today the studio houses the city's **Islamic Art Museum** (Musée d'Art Islamique), which displays a collection of jewelry, old photographs, and manuscripts. The villa (still a private residence and closed to the public) and studio stand in the heart of the gardens where walkways of zellij tilework weave their way around ponds, beds of succulent shrubs and palms, a forest of bamboo, tall cypress trees, colorful displays of

INSIDER TIP:

If you only have time to visit one of the city's gardens, head to the beautiful Menara Gardens. Here the sultan's engineers created a verdant paradise where before there was only dust.

— AHMED TARIF
Tour guide

oleander and bougainvillaea, and hundreds of cactus plants.

Marrakech's Gardens

Beyond the built-up center are a number of formal gardens and large areas of parkland, which offer respite from the often hectic pace of city life. These beautiful public spaces are larger and quieter than their urban counterparts in the medina and

---

EXPERIENCE: Exploring Beyond the Medina on Two Wheels

Outside Marrakech's city walls, the baking heat and relative remoteness of many attractions make walking an undesirable way of getting around. If you want to explore the shady groves of La Palmeraie (see p. 209) or head over to the relaxing Majorelle Gardens (see pp. 201–206), there are few better ways of getting around than by bicycle or scooter.

Bikes can be hired by the day from many locations in Marrakech, but the most reliable companies are **Loc 2 Roues** (212 boulevard Mohamed V, Guéliz, tel

0524/43 02 94, www.loc2roues.com) and **Marrakech Motos** (31 avenue Abdelkarim el Khattabi, Guéliz, tel 0524/44 83 59), whose offices are in the heart of Guéliz. Loc 2 Roues even allows customers to book their scooters or motorbikes online before they arrive in the country. Typical prices are around 100 dirhams a day for bicycles, and between 200 and 400 dirhams a day for scooters. Make sure that you test the brakes and tires of your bicycle or scooter before you set off, and always agree on a price in advance.

Guéliz. Perhaps the best known is La Palmeraie (see p. 209), on the road from Marrakech to Casablanca. The following parks are farther from the city center than most would be willing to walk, so it is advisable to hire a grand taxi or a calèche (see sidebar p. 194) for the day to visit them. Or, you could rent a bicycle or scooter (see sidebar opposite) and explore them at your own, unhurried pace.

Menara Gardens: The oldest of these public spaces is the Menara Gardens (Jardins Menara), built by the city's Almohad rulers in the mid-12th century. These gardens consist of several acres of olive groves, orchards, and winding pathways surrounding a large artificial lake. The **reservoir,** which is as old as the gardens, is a masterpiece of medieval engineering. It was built entirely above ground from stone and is fed by an underground aqueduct that carries cool, clear water several miles from the Atlas Mountains. The serene, flat water reflects stunning views of the nearby mountains and is home to a shoal of enormous carp.

A network of underground channels radiates out from the reservoir to irrigate the gardens' orchards and olive groves, keeping them lush and green in all seasons. The gardens were more than just a retreat for the ruling family, however—the orchards and olive groves have always had a practical purpose, providing produce and income for the city's inhabitants.

Gathering the fruit of argan trees south of Marrakech

Today the gardens are loved by locals and visitors alike. Their lawns appeal to picnicking families, courting couples, and others looking to relax. To reach the Menara Gardens, head west from Djemaa el Fna, through the Bab Jdid, and continue along rue Menara for about a mile (1.6 km).

Agdal Gardens: Stretching south of the medina, the Agdal Gardens (Jardins de l'Agdal) were also created in the 12th century, but little, if anything, of the original layout remains. What you see today

Menara Gardens
✉ avenue de la Menara, Marrakech

Agdal Gardens
✉ rue Bâb Irhil/ rue Bâb Ahmar, Marrakech

Marrakech's Architecture

While most visitors come to see Marrakech's grand palaces, there is much more to the city's architecture than monuments and mosques. From its dusty pink city walls to its unassuming courtyard houses, the city of Marrakech has a unique architectural style that is well worth exploring.

Marrakech's distinctive dusty pink hue comes from the fact that most of its older buildings are made from a mixture of dried mud and straw known as *pisé*. The red earth of southern Morocco, when compressed and baked dry, forms an exceptionally strong building material, much cheaper than stone and easier to shape. This construction method has given the city a distinctive appearance that successive local administrations have sought to protect.

When walking around the medina, there is one particular feature of the local architecture that you cannot fail to notice: Almost none of the houses have windows or balconies

Marrakech airport's daring modernist design

facing onto the street. This is because Islamic architecture places a strong emphasis on privacy, especially for women. A house may be a sumptuous mansion, but from the outside all you see is a blank wall with an ornately carved doorway. The only exception to this rule is the *mellah*, whose Jewish citizens had no problem with balconies and windows facing the street.

Outside the medina, in the French protectorate-era districts of Guéliz and Hivernage, the architecture is much more Western, with some older buildings looking thoroughly out of place in a Moroccan city. The more recent building projects in the area, however, are more sympathetic to the traditional style. The Jnane housing district to the east of Agdal Gardens, built in the mid-1990s, is a good example of this new style. A far grander example of this Moroccan modernism is the new terminal building at Marrakech airport, which uses traditional design but updates it with modern high-tech engineering and materials.

In the past, the architectural contrast between medinas and *villes nouvelles* (new cities) was mirrored by social and economic divides: The buildings of the medina were inhabited by the poor and allowed to decay, while all new construction took place in the wealthy, Westernized ville nouvelle. Today, however, more affluent Moroccans are moving back into the inner cities. Many of the medina's old buildings are being renovated, and those beyond help are being replaced by sympathetic designs that blend traditional and modern features. And many of the medina's *riads* (traditional Moroccan houses with interior gardens) and hotels have been renovated in the last 10 or 20 years.

The reservoir of the 12th-century Menara Gardens is a masterpiece of medieval engineering.

was constructed during the 19th century. The gardens are known for their lavish plants, with numerous orchards, olive groves, citrus groves, and vineyards that in centuries past supplied the city with many of its staple foods. Today the gardens have a slightly neglected look, and many areas have become rather overgrown.

Despite successive sultans' fondness for the gardens, the royals have not always had the best of times here. Indeed, two sultans met their demise in Agdal Gardens. Moulay el Rashid was knocked from his horse by a falling branch in 1672, and Mohamed IV drowned while boating on the lake with his son in 1873.

La Palmeraie: Outside the city's confines is one of the icons of Marrakech, La Palmeraie, a 5-mile-long (8 km) grove of palm trees that helped shape the city's character as an oasis at the foot of the High Atlas Mountains. La Palmeraie lies on the city's far northern edge and covers an area of around 54 square miles (140 sq km). During the Almoravid period, it was planted with more than 100,000 date palms, interspersed with olive and fruit trees and irrigated by an innovative network of *khettaras*—interlinked underground wells and pipes that use gravity to draw water from aquifers. The area offers visitors a taste of the rural delights outside the city. ■

Around Marrakech

From practically the moment that Marrakech's minarets and rooftops drop out of view, you'll feel you've entered another world. The familiar streets of the city give way to the organic, otherworldly architecture of Berber villages and the dramatic scenery of the High Atlas, with snowcapped peaks and crystal-clear mountain streams.

The Atlas Mountains rise above groves of date palms outside Marrakech.

From the city of Marrakech, the High Atlas Mountains appear almost as a sheer wall of rock and snow, dominating the skyline to the south and east. In keeping with its appearance, the region has been remarkably resistant to the winds of change—kings, royal dynasties, even entire civilizations have come and gone without making any significant impact on life in the mountains. The Berbers were here first, and no invading army—from the Arabs in the 12th century to the French in the 20th—has had much success in assimilating them or driving them out. Even today, life in Berber villages feels a very long way removed from the national government in Rabat.

When planning trips through the region around Marrakech, it is worth remembering that much of the area is impassable to vehicles. The main roads follow established routes that wind through valleys and high mountain passes, and very rarely connect with each other. To go from one area of the High Atlas to another often requires backtracking all the way to the lowlands around Marrakech before heading back out again. Most of the roads in the area are well maintained, although even the newest stretches of road can seem precarious at times. Between November and March, check the conditions before you travel; many of the high mountain roads become blocked with snow in the winter.

South to Jebel Toubkal

Probably the busiest tourist route out of Marrakech is the R203, which takes you directly south into the mountains. Every year, this road carries thousands of hikers heading for the peak of Jebel Toubkal, which at 13,671 feet (4,167 m) is the highest mountain in Morocco. The road goes from Marrakech to Taroudant and climbs through a succession of high mountain passes and dramatic valleys, culminating in the spectacular Tizi n'Test pass, where the road reaches an altitude of 6,864 feet (2,092 m).

Although this mountain route has been used for centuries, the present-day road was built in the early 20th century by the French, who had to blast their way through the rocky terrain, creating a navigable road where previously there were only mule trails and precarious steep, boulder-strewn paths (see sidebar).

INSIDER TIP:

Try to witness a traditional mud house being built in a small local town in the Ourika Valley, in the foothills of the High Atlas.

—SANAA AKKACH
National Geographic Books designer

The first section of the road, which goes from Marrakech to the town of Tahanaout in the foothills of the Atlas, is relatively straightforward. The road is well maintained, and the only challenge is negotiating the typically Moroccan traffic of overloaded trucks, aging buses, and unpredictable taxis. Passing through **Tahanaout,** you will notice how different the village looks from

Jebel Toubkal

⛰ 185 C2

Tahanaout

⛰ 185 B2

Lords of the Atlas

Before the French bulldozed their way through this landscape, it was the domain of a small group of Berber families known as the Lords of the Atlas, who extracted a high fee from anyone who wished to travel through the routes they controlled. In the high mountain passes to the south, you can still see their fortified villages and kasbahs perched high above the road in strategic places.

Asni
⚠ 185 B2

Imlil
⚠ 185 B1

the towns around Marrakech. The small earth-colored houses cling to the sides of the steep valleys, and the women walk unveiled through the streets. Try to visit on a Tuesday, when the village hosts a large and interesting market.

Beyond Tahanaout, the road climbs more quickly, traveling up the route carved through the mountains by the Oued Reraia—a shallow, boulder-strewn river that becomes a raging torrent during the spring snowmelt. After around 6 miles (10 km) of hairpin bends, the pilgrimage town of **Moulay Brahim,** set on a dramatic cliff-top, comes into view. Although the main road passes just below the town, the almost vertical slopes that surround it require you to continue for another 4 miles (6 km) before doubling back along a vertiginous access road. The town offers amazing views of the **Oued Reraia Valley** and the plains beyond it to the north. It is popular with locals and religious pilgrims, who come to pray at the shrine to the local saint, for whom the town is named.

The roadside village of **Asni** is where mountain climbers leave the R203 and head up the narrow road to **Imlil** and **Jebel Toubkal** (see sidebar), the crown of Toubkal National Park. For those with their eyes on the peaks, Asni holds little interest, as it is a little too far north to be a practical base for exploring the mountains. However, with the exception of a few hustlers gathered around the stores and bus station, it is a quiet and peaceful place—more a collection of villages than a single settlement—shaded by date palms and cooled by the fast-flowing waters of the Oued Reraia.

It is this reputation that draws comfort seekers. Those who prefer luxury to adventure can stay in the **Kasbah Tamadot** *(Asni, tel 0524/36 82 00, www.kasbah tamadot.virgin.com, $$$$$),* the eccentric creation of an Italian artist that was recently converted into an exclusive resort by British billionaire Richard Branson, or the recently completed **Dar Tassa** *(Ouirgane, near Asni, tel 0524/48 43 12, www.dartassa.com, $$$$$),* a

EXPERIENCE: Climbing Jebel Toubkal

During the summer months, when the snow has melted from even the highest peaks, the summit of Jebel Toubkal draws hikers and climbers from all over the world. Although it is a long and tiring ascent, you don't need to do any rock climbing or serious scrambling to reach the summit. Information on the best route to take can be obtained in the village of Imlil, which has an exciting base camp feel to it—it is often filled with

windswept climbers carrying huge packs and climbing gear. Equipment can be rented from the trekking shop run by the **Dar Adrar** *(Imlil, tel 0668/76 01 65, www .daradrar.com),* which is also the town's most comfortable *riad.* A typical route to the summit involves climbing to the well-staffed and surprisingly comfortable refuges at Toubkal or Les Mouflons on the first day, and then ascending the mountain on the second.

A typical Berber mountain village scene south of Marrakech

short distance farther south on the R203 road.

South of Asni, the main road climbs through a succession of high mountain passes and dramatic valleys. Away from the well-trodden route to Jebel Toubkal, the road takes on a rougher, even less forgiving character; straight sections become less and less frequent as the road twists and turns through the increasingly difficult terrain. Surprisingly, even in this high and remote landscape, there are still plenty of people around—the villages of Ouirgane and Ijoujak are friendly and pleasant places to stop and are largely untouched by tourism. Around 27 miles (44 km) south of Asni, not far from the village of Ijoujak, lies the beautiful and spectacular **Tin Mal Mosque,** the base from

which Mohamed Ibn Toumart (ca 1080–ca 1130), a firebrand Islamic preacher, founded the Almohad dynasty in the 12th century. The mosque is a well-preserved example of Almohad architecture and, importantly, is open to the public.

Ourika Valley

The Ourika Valley in the foothills of the High Atlas is a beautiful region lying some 18 miles (30 km) south of the city. The valley is thick with luxuriant countryside that provides a home to both the local Berber people, who enjoy a traditional way of life, and numerous species of native wildlife. Small villages dot the landscape, including **Jardin du Safran,** around which, as the name suggests, saffron crocuses

Tin Mal Mosque
- 185 B1
- Tin Mal
- Closed Fri.
- $

Splash White Water Rafting Morocco

✉ Riad Splash, 7 Derb Gnaoua, Ben Saleh, Medina, Marrakech

☎ (0618) 96 42 52

www.morocco adventurestours .com

grow in abundance. The village supplies much of the region with this very valuable spice (still more expensive than gold by weight), which gives dishes a distinctive yellow coloring. Look for the small saffron farm right in the center of the village, which is often open for visitors to explore.

dirhams for a half-day trip.

To the south of the Ourika Valley is the Toubkal National Park, with Jebel Toubkal as its centerpiece, where you can enjoy challenging mountain hikes in summer (see sidebar p. 212) and skiing in the winter months from the resort town of **Oukaïmeden.** This attractive town lies on the

A Berber villager and his mule ascend into the High Atlas Mountains.

Oukaïmeden

▲ 185 C2

The valley is also known for its fabulous waterfalls and fast-flowing river, along which **white-water rafting trips** are offered. Although the upper and middle sections of the river are steep and require a high degree of technical ability, the lower region is less challenging. The Marrakech-based **Splash White Water Rafting Morocco** organizes rafting trips for both novice and more experienced rafters. Expect to pay around 600

slopes of Jebel Attar, almost 8,530 feet (2,600 m) above sea level. The town is reached by a good, if winding, road that can become a little treacherous in winter—do not attempt this route unless you have some experience driving on mountain roads.

If you're used to European ski resorts, the amenities at Oukaïmeden can seem a little primitive, but the exhilarating descent from the top of the ski lift (which takes

INSIDER TIP:

To escape the heat of Marrakech during summer, go to Oukaïmeden. Located just an hour's drive south and 10,700 feet (3,260 m) above sea level, this is Morocco's best ski resort.

—CHRISTEL CHERQAOUI
National Geographic Books

you up to 10,690 feet/3,258 m) makes you forget all about the vaguely defined pistes and 1970s rental equipment. Many of the skiers here are on day trips from Marrakech, but if you decide to stay here for a day or two, there are several good hotels in the town, including the cosy **Chez Juju** and the **Kenzi Louka.**

Ouzoud Cascades

Some 95 miles (150 km) east of Marrakech is the picturesque village of **Ouzoud.** Its name derives from the Berber word for olive, a reference to the many olive groves that surround the community. Though the village has its charms, it is best known as the home of the Ouzoud Cascades (Cascades d'Ouzoud), a series of spectacular waterfalls that have become one of the most popular visitor destinations in the region.

The waterfalls comprise three tiers of rock from which water tumbles down from a height of around 360 feet (110 m) into a lake, sending up a fine spray that fills the air and creates a near-permanent rainbow effect.

It's a short walk from the village to the foot of the falls along a pleasantly shaded grove of olive trees. The trek to the top of the falls is, however, slightly more challenging, although you will be rewarded with sweeping panoramic views, and possibly even a sighting of one of the rare Barbary macaques that live locally. From here you can also follow the river's banks to the enchanting **Gorge of Oued el Abid.** ■

Hotel Chez Juju
✉ Oukaïmeden
☎ (0524) 31 90 05
www.hotelchezjuju .com

Hotel Kenzi Louka
✉ Oukaïmeden
☎ (0524) 31 90 80

Ouzoud Cascades
⚠ 185 C2

EXPERIENCE: Water Sports at Bin el Ouidane

If you adore sailing on tranquil waters, Jet Skiing, kayaking, or fishing, then you will love Bin el Ouidane reservoir, near Ouzoud. A dammed artificial lake created to provide irrigation for the surrounding land and a source of hydroelectricity for Morocco's population, it lies between the Middle and High Atlas ranges.

Hire a boat from one of the hotels that have sprung up around the reservoir and head off to fish for carp, pike, perch, or bass in the lake's deep waters. You can also take trips out to view the coast, the nearby dam, rivers, and coves or notch up the speed on a kayak or Jet Ski.

One of the hotels offering these activities is the **Hotel Bin el Ouidane** *(tel 0523/44 26 00, www.hotelbinelouidane .com)*, while specialist company **Morocco Carp Fishing** *(www.moroccocarpfishing .com)* will completely outfit you for fishing excursions.

Essaouira

The compact seaside town of Essaouira, with its relaxed atmosphere and cool sea breeze, seems worlds away from the dust and crowds of Marrakech. Despite its diminutive size, however, the town has much to offer—including stunning beaches, a beautifully preserved medina, and impressive 18th-century ramparts and fortifications.

A cannon atop Essaouira's ramparts

Essaouira is a charming, colorful fishing town about three hours' travel west of Marrakech. It consists of a heavily fortified 18th-century medina surrounded by a very modern, but compact, new town. For thousands of years, Essaouira's harbor attracted traders and invaders from across Europe. During the first century A.D., ships came from across the Roman world to trade gold and other valuables for the most prestigious commodity in the Roman world at the time—imperial purple dye. This dye was made from a type of sea snail, which lived around the rocks of Essaouira's Ile de Mogador (see sidebar opposite).

The town continued as a quiet fishing and trading port until it caught the attention of the Portuguese, who captured the port in the 16th century. Over the next hundred years, the town was fiercely contested between Morocco and the seafaring nations of Europe. After a number of close calls, the Alaouite sultan Mohamed III decided to take action. He saw Essaouira as a key part of his empire's valuable trade with Europe, and thought it would make a suitable base for Morocco's navy. As such, it needed protection.

The man who was commissioned to realize the sultan's vision was the French engineer Theodore Cornut, captured by the Moroccans from a French ship. Cornut's design included more than just enclosing the city with walls. He also drove a number of wide, straight boulevards through the center of the medina. His designs form the core of the Essaouira we see today, a well-ordered place laid out around its port, with a more open and less cluttered atmosphere than neighboring Marrakech.

The Medina

The pedestrian-only medina is where most of the town's permanent residents live. It is also home to the majority of Essaouira's markets, restaurants, and hotels. It is divided roughly into quarters by two main thoroughfares, the avenue Mohamed Zerktouni, which runs southwest from the Bab Doukala to the harbor, and the rue Mohamed el Qory (also known as the rue Abdelaziz el Fechtaly), which runs from the Bab Marrakech to the seawall. Where the roads meet at the center of the town are the main

INSIDER TIP:

For a delicious and inexpensive lunch, go to the port in Essaouira. At the fish stands, choose your own seafood from that morning's catch, and they grill it right on the spot.

—MARISA LARSON
National Geographic contributor

souks, which sell craft goods and the town's main export, freshly caught fish.

While the souks lie at the center of the town, the commercial hub of this fishing port is the **place Moulay Hassan,** down by the harbor. This square is divided into halves that are linked by a narrow walkway. Lined with cafés and shops, it is where locals and visitors gather to relax and enjoy the atmosphere. The eateries range from the informal **Patisserie Chez Driss,** to the fabulous **Taros** restaurant (see p. 295), which serves traditional Moroccan cuisine and *(continued on p. 220)*

Essaouira

 185 A2, 219

Visitor Information

✉ 54 boulevard de la Princesse Lalla Amina

☎ (0524) 78 35 30

Tyrian Purple Dye

The Tyrian purple dye, which is made from sea snails, was first harvested in Tyre (giving the dye its name) in southern Lebanon during the time of the Phoenicians (1500–300 B.C.). It reached its height of use during the glory years of the Roman empire, when it was used to color the clothes of emperors and wealthy aristocrats. Essaouira became a second source of the dye when these small sea snails were also found living on the rocks around the Ile de Mogador. The dye was produced by grinding up the snail shells, a time-consuming process that required many shells to produce even a small amount of dye, hence its high price.

A Walk in Essaouira

With a fascinating medina full of narrow, winding streets, some first-rate architecture, and long stretches of sweeping sand fronting the Atlantic, Essaouira offers a microcosm of Morocco's charms.

Local women chat next to a shop in Essaouira.

From the port known as the **Porte de la Marine ❶**, you can see the long sweep of beaches to your right, which are considered among Morocco's finest. The port has none of their tranquility, however, and is a cluttered, chaotic maze of nets, boats, and multicolored ropes. As you leave, admire the huge **arched gateway** linking the port with the town. Built by Sultan Sidi Muhammad ibn Abdallah in the late 18th century, it is flanked by two columns topped by a trian-

NOT TO BE MISSED:

The colorful boats in the Porte de la Marine • The ramparts of the Sqala de Ville • The woodcarvers' souks

gular pediment and a series of towers.

Continue along the boulevard Mohamed V and turn left on avenue Lalla Aicha; then make a right along the rue el Moukaouama. The Catholic church, the **Église Notre Dame ❷** *(avenue El Moukaouama, tel 0524/47 58 95),* is directly ahead of you, just outside the medina area proper on a road heading toward the beaches.

Retrace your steps along the avenue Mohamed V, past the place Orson Welles, named after the legendary filmmaker who shot his version of *Othello* in Essaouira in the 1940s, and its **Othello Gardens** where locals love to sit, until you reach the **avenue Oqba ibn Nafia ❸**. This is one of Essaouira's main thoroughfares linking the port with the medina and is the location of the city's main square, the **place Moulay Hassan,** where festivals and special events are held. The rectangular square is the focal point of the city and is usually buzzing with activity.

You are now within the kasbah and heading toward the former *mellah* district. Look out for the **Damgaard Gallery ❹** (see p. 220). Founded by Frederic Damgaard in the 1980s, it is an influential art gallery where local artists exhibit their works, along with the many visiting painters who, captivated by the beauty of Essaouira, come here to paint. The Damgaard was the first of many art galleries to open in the city, which is now home to a thriving artistic community.

Continue along avenue Oqba ibn Nafia and make a left into the rue el Attarin, which leads into the rue Darb Laalouj, where you will find a small but fascinating ethnographic museum, the **Museum of Sidi Mohamed ibn Abdallah** ❺ (see p. 220).

Just in front is the **Sqala de la Ville** ❻ on rue de la Sqala, a formidable sea fortification that at one time helped to protect the city from invaders. The great tower bastion at the northern end provides stunning views across the town and out to sea. A walkway leads from the *sqala* to its twin, the **Sqala du Port,** which once shielded the harbor from invaders from the north and now offers a chance for a refreshing stroll away from the bustle of the city center.

From the Sqala de la Ville, make your way into the heart of the medina to your right, where you will find numerous souks dotted among the labyrinth of narrow streets and alleyways, including ones selling the woodcarvings for which the city is famous. The largest of these is the **Souk Lazghal** ❼—it is well worth a visit. Daily markets also set up shop in this area, where everything from freshly caught fish from the nearby port to local crafts is sold. Continue north to reach the former mellah where the city's Jewish population once lived. The walk finishes at the mighty gatehouse, the **Bab Doukkala** ❽, where several sets of gates once protected the town from land-based attackers.

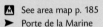

- ⓜ See area map p. 185
- ► Porte de la Marine
- 🕓 40 minutes
- ↔ 1.8 miles (2.9 km)
- ► Bab Doukkala

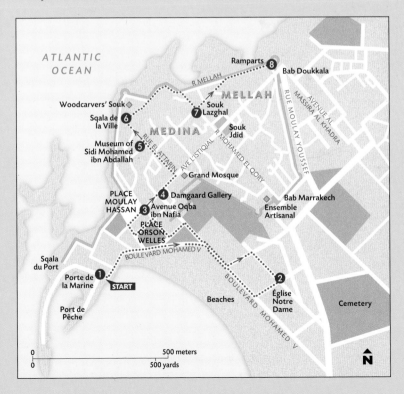

Seagulls soar above the old city walls of Essaouira.

Damgaard Gallery

✉ avenue Oqba ibn Nafia, Medina

☎ (0524) 78 44 46

www.galerie damgaard.com

Museum of Sidi Mohamed ibn Abdallah

✉ rue Darb Laalouj

☎ (0524) 47 53 00

🕐 Closed Tues.

💲 $

has a roof terrace that overlooks the harbor and the bay beyond.

A short walk from the square along the rue Darb Laalouj is the **Museum of Sidi Mohamed ibn Abdallah** (Musée Sidi Mohamed ben Abdallah). Housed in a building dating from the French protectorate period, it has been laid out like a local resident's dwelling from the 1800s. There are examples of regional crafts, such as basketry and weaving, on display, along with Moorish instruments and weapons discovered in the countryside around the city.

Located a short distance north of the avenue Oqba ibn Nafia are the **Grand Mosque** and the town's preeminent art gallery, the **Damgaard Gallery** (Galerie Damgaard). Essaouira's beautiful coastal views, bustling town scenes, and clear natural light

have long caught the eye of artists, prompting a Danish resident of the city, Frederic Damgaard, to found a gallery in the 1980s where local artists could showcase their work. Today it is regarded as a highly influential gallery and has provided a platform for many artists whose work might otherwise have gone unseen. Like its northern counterpart, Asilah (see pp. 104–106), Essaouira is keen to encourage this aspect of its cultural life, and you will find many more small informal art galleries in your travels around the town.

In the far northwest of the medina lies the **Sqala de la Ville,** a huge gun battery built during the town's 18th-century reconstruction. From these ramparts, you can get an excellent view of the islands around Essaouira. These islands are dotted with ruined fortresses, which once guarded the harbor against attack. Enticing though they are, the islands are now a nature reserve, closed to visitors. With a good pair of binoculars, however, the ramparts are a good place to watch for the island's most celebrated inhabitants, the Eleonora's falcons that breed on the islands in the summer.

The vaulted ammunition stores below the ramparts are now home to a bustling **woodcarvers' souk.** Here artisans carve and shape the beautiful thuya wood that grows in the area around Essaouira, making boxes, ornaments, and furniture. Other good places to buy thuya wood include the **Ensemble Artisanal** *(inside Bab Marrakech on rue Mohamed el Qory),* a government-sponsored fixed-price boutique, and the **Cooperative Tamoute,** where all the goods sold, from the wooden boxes to the bottles of Argan oil, are made by local artisans who are paid a fair price.

Outside the Walls

Over the years, Essaouira has outgrown its original confines, and today there are areas of parkland and housing outside the city walls. One of the prettiest parts of the city lies immediately beyond the ramparts near the port and beach.

The **place Orson Welles** and the **Othello Gardens** are named after the filmmaker who shot his version of *Othello* here in the 1940s. The garden looks out over the **beaches** for which Essaouira is famed. These long, wide stretches of sand are considered some of the best in Morocco and attract visitors throughout the year. ■

EXPERIENCE: Windsurfing off Essaouira

Essaouira is blessed with some of the finest beaches in Morocco, but strong winds off the Atlantic Ocean can make sunbathing a tad uncomfortable. Conditions for windsurfing, however, are ideal.

The main windsurfing areas are the **bay at Essaouira** itself and **Sidi Kaouki** to the south, which are suitable for all levels and abilities, with generally favorable winds from the northwest—although periodic strong gusts can make conditions more difficult. **Cap Sim,** also to the south, offers similar conditions, but with a prevailing southerly wind and occasionally powerful sea swells. The conditions at **Moulay Bouzerktoun** beach are more challenging and suitable only for intermediate and advanced windsurfers, as wind speeds can reach 25–30 miles per hour (40–48 kmh).

Several companies offer surfing packages and equipment rental for experienced surfers and tuition for beginners, as well as changing and shower facilities. Good choices include **Ocean Vagabond** *(boulevard Mohamed V, Essaouira, tel 0524/78 39 34, www.oceanvagabond.com)* and **Essaouira Kitesurf** *(tel 0672/06 37 25, www.essaouirakitesurf.com),* but the most popular is **Explora** *(2 place Chrib Atay, Rue Laalouj, Essaouira, tel 0611/ 47 51 88, www.exploramorocco.com),* which is run by a group of friendly and knowledgeable locals who have been surfing in Essaouira for decades. Some places offer kite surfing and water surfing courses, too. It's worth making sure that your travel insurance covers water sports before you surf.

Around Essaouira

Essaouira's bay is dotted with little islands poking their heads out of the water. The Ile de Mogador, which gave Essaouira its former name, provides shelter to the city's busy harbor from the strong winds coming off the Atlantic Ocean. It was this shelter that probably led to the early colonization of the area.

Colorful Moroccan glasses for serving tea

Diabat

🗺 185 A2

Cap Hadid & Cap Sim

🗺 185 A2

Diabat

A short distance along the main road south of Essaouira, there is a fork in the road; the main road veers off to the left, heading inland, while another unpaved road continues along the coast toward the Oued Ksob and the small village of Diabat. This road was the main route south from Essaouira until a storm washed away the bridge and the road was diverted farther inland.

Today you can cross the river (except at high tide) on a raised causeway made from the rubble of the collapsed bridge. The shallow, wide mouth of the **Oued Ksob** river beyond the bridge is home to a wide variety of wading birds and seabirds, including terns, egrets, herons, and cormorants. In the summer, the breeding colony of Eleonora's falcons from the Ile de Mogador come here to eat the large insects that fly over the river.

Just on the other side of the river is the fascinating ruin of a **royal pavilion** occupied by the 18th-century sultan Sidi Muhammad ibn Abdallah. Little is known about this site, but it's a fascinating place to scramble around.

A little farther out, half-submerged at the mouth of the river, lies a ruined fortress, the **Borj el Baroud.** The remnants of its once formidable ramparts are now settled at strange angles and worn into smooth, organic shapes by the sea. The locals will tell you that this evocative sight inspired Diabat's most famous visitor, Jimi Hendrix, to write the song "Castles Made of Sand" (but the truth is that he wrote the song over a year before he visited the area).

Cap Hadid & Cap Sim

The coastline around Essaouira is lined with deep indented coves interspersed by long, wide sandy beaches. The farther you go from Essaouira, the emptier

INSIDER TIP:

Bring a soccer ball to the beach and in five minutes you'll have a full-on pickup game. It's a great way to meet the locals and enjoy the gorgeous ocean views.

—JANELLE NANOS
National Geographic Traveler
magazine editor

the beaches become. A particularly pleasant stretch lies to the north at Cap Hadid, where the Oued Tensift flows into the sea, having made its long meandering journey from the hills around Marrakech.

To the south of Essaouira is Cap Sim, a somewhat desolate place where the beaches are battered by strong winds. Farther along the coast, heading toward Tamanar, are the little hamlets of **Smimou,** which has a super little souk every Sunday, and **Tafelney,** most famous for its huge horseshoe-shaped bay created by the crashing of the strong Atlantic waves on its shores. Like many of the beaches along the coast around Essaouira, the beach at Tafelney is popular with both nature and windsurfing enthusiasts alike.

Tamanar

Tamanar may be a small town, but it is the largest urban settlement on this stretch of coastline. Surrounded by olive groves and small forests of the argan tree, which are classified as UNESCO biosphere reserves, it has remained unchanged for centuries and is a great place to head to if you really fancy getting away from the bustle of city life.

The village is also one of the best places in Morocco to buy bottles of the oil extracted from the nuts of the argan tree. Endemic to the semidesert of the Sous Valley, this exceptionally hard, gnarled, and thorny tree has been put to many uses by the people of the region. The process of extracting the oil is a time-consuming and complicated one that has changed little since the time of the Phoenicians and Romans. Today, production of oil is the major economic activity in the village (see sidebar below). ∎

Argan Tree Cooperatives

As you approach the town of Tamanar, you will be greeted by the sight of trees filled with strange dark shapes. The dark shapes, you'll soon realize, are goats—they perch implausibly on the highest and most delicate-looking branches to get at the fruit of the argan tree. This oddity represents the first stage in a process that powers the economy of Tamanar. After they pass through the goats, the fruits are reduced to a hard, indigestible core. This hard nut is then cracked, crushed, and roasted to extract argan oil, which can be used for everything from cooking to beauty treatments. For the women of Tamanar, this oil has become a tool of economic empowerment; at the **Cooperative Amal** *(Village de l'Arganier, Tamanar)* dozens of women work to produce oils that are sold throughout Morocco and beyond.

Long sandy beaches lapped by the Atlantic, age-old towns guarded by giant red ramparts, plus Morocco's filmmaking capital

Agadir, the Drâa Valley, & the South

The deep pink walls and towers of Aït Ben Haddou, one of Morocco's best preserved *ksars*

Agadir, the Drâa Valley, & the South

Located in a huge, horseshoe-shaped bay of golden sands that stretch for miles alongside the crystal blue waters of the Atlantic Ocean, and boasting a temperate climate with warm sunshine almost every day of the year, the modern city of Agadir is Morocco's foremost seaside resort. Here you can enjoy everything from jet skiing and sailing to a round of golf or horse riding on the beach.

Agadir has a fresh, dynamic feel unlike any other Moroccan city. There are no imposing red *pisé* ramparts, huge fortresses, or chaotic medinas here, and no ancient kasbahs or souks to explore. Instead, its wide boulevards are lined with contemporary buildings, neatly sculpted parklands, and European-style sidewalk cafés where you can sit with a coffee watching the world go by.

Seeing its shiny new buildings and smartly laid-out streets, you could be forgiven for thinking Agadir is a new town, but it has a long, if now largely invisible, history. It was one

of the wealthiest strongholds in the country, with a bustling kasbah and several palatial buildings, when a devastating earthquake struck on February 29, 1960, burying most of the city beneath a pile of rubble. The disaster prompted Morocco's then ruler, King Mohamed V, to declare that a new Agadir would be erected near the site of the old.

Deliberately designed in imitation of—and in answer to—European-style resorts, the new Agadir has grown to become the country's main package holiday destination, attracting hordes of visitors throughout the year, mainly from Morocco and Europe. True, it has a slightly more international, slightly less Moroccan feel to it than many of the country's other holiday hot spots—much of its architecture conforms to the standard Mediterranean resort template—but it does what it does well, with a good collection of hotels and restaurants, and some of Morocco's finest beaches.

Sun, sand, and sea are by no means Agadir's only charms, however. It is also the cultural and economic hub of the region, and the country's largest fishing port, which adds a bit of real-life grit to all that holiday sheen.

Just a few miles south of the city, at the foot of the Anti Atlas Mountains where the Oued Sous flows into the ocean, lies the start of the Souss-Massa National Park, a huge protected environment of reed beds and sandbars. This magnificent landscape attracts birds and wildlife in even greater numbers than the city does vacationers. Apart from boasting the world's largest colony of critically rare northern bald ibises, the park also has flamingos, spoonbills, rare marbled ducks, and thick-billed larks.

Farther inland are mountains, river valleys, huge plains, and, to the south, great sweeps of pre-Saharan desert, where an equally diverse range of flora and fauna exists.

Agadir has often been described as the gateway to the Drâa Valley and the south, and it is ideally located for excursions to places such as the ancient cities of Tafraout and Tiznit, set in breathtaking scenery near the Kerdous Pass, or Taroudant, known as the "Little Marrakech" because of its mighty red pisé fortifications. You can also head farther inland to the centuries-old city of Ouarzazate, which comprises a series of kasbahs dotted over the desert plateau landscape and is today a major center of film-making, or to the astonishing brilliant red town

of Zagora in the very heart of the Drâa Valley.

Agadir also makes a good base for exploring the Tifrit Valley, widely considered one of the most beautiful in Morocco, or heading farther south to the epic scenery of the Sahara, passing through several fascinating towns and cities on the way. These include Goulimine, which is famous for its camel souk; the thriving fishing ports of Tan-Tan and Tarfaya; busy Laâyoune, which enjoys a beautiful desert setting; and Dakhla, which nestles in a pretty bay less than 200 miles (320 km) from the northern border of Mauritania.

From the modernity of Agadir and the rich greenery of the Drâa Valley to the sand dunes and rock terrain of the Sahara, this is one of the most awe-inspiring and diverse regions of Morocco. ■

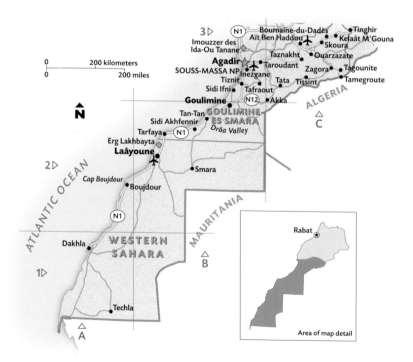

Agadir & Around

Agadir, which means "walled fortress town" in Berber, is the capital of Morocco's Souss-Massa-Drâa region. It is best known as a vacation hot spot where sprawling hotels, chic restaurants, and a suntan-guaranteeing climate ensure it is always bustling with visitors. But the city is also an important fishing port, which employs many of the local people and provides the country with much of its supply of sardines, one of the staple foods.

A flotilla of fishing boats, small and large, in Agadir's fishing harbor

Agadir

◪ 227 B3

Visitor Information

✉ ONMT, avenue
du Prince
Heritier Sid
Mohamed,
Immeuble A

☎ (0528) 84 63 77

◷ Closed Sat.–Sun.

✉ Syndicat
d'Initiative,
avenue
Mohamed V

☎ (0528) 84 03 07

A Little History

Scholars believe that the very first settlement at Agadir was probably founded by the Phoenicians, who arrived in Morocco around 1000 B.C. and began creating trading posts all along the coast. Early Agadir was by no means a large town like its contemporaries Chellah (near present-day Rabat), Lixus (now Larache), or Mogador (now Essaouira). Rather, the records suggest that it remained little more than a small fishing community until its fortunes

changed with the arrival of Portuguese colonizers in 1505. They built a kasbah on a hill overlooking the bay, within which they laid out narrow streets lined with homes and souks. Under King Manuel I of Portugal, this tiny settlement was soon turned into an important port of call on the then thriving trading route between Africa and Europe.

The Portuguese did not get long to enjoy Agadir, however. They were evicted from the town in 1551 by the Wattasid dynasty, and indeed from the entire country following the Battle of the Three Kings in 1578 (see sidebar p. 109) under the Wattasids' successors, the Saadians, who conquered the country from their base at Tagmadert in the Drâa Valley.

In 1731, a mighty earthquake all but flattened the town, leaving its walls in ruins and its infrastructure weakened. Agadir fell into decline for a long period.

Agadir Today

The Agadir we see today is almost entirely modern, having been constructed in the wake of the another earthquake, the worst in Morocco's history, which leveled almost the entire city in 1960 (see sidebar). Agadir is like no other Moroccan city. There is no ancient medina to explore and no *ville nouvelle* (new town) created during the French protectorate period. Most of the architecture dates from the 1960s or later. The seafront is a made up of a line of bright white buildings, many housing hotels, that stretches for miles alongside golden sandy beaches. The only

INSIDER TIP:

Moroccans go out for walks at sunset. In Agadir, the most popular place to walk is along the boardwalk on the beach. You can see a beautiful sunset while taking part in this tradition.

—MARISA LARSON
National Geographic contributor

Bus Companies

✉ CTM, rue Yacoub Mansour, Agadir

☎ (0528) 43 82 82

✉ Supratours, 10 rue des Orangiers, Agadir

☎ (0528) 84 12 07

Agadir Al Massia Airport

✉ BP 2000, Aéroport Agadir Al-Massira

☎ (0528) 83 9112

www.agadir-airport .com

Agadir's Earthquake of 1960

On February 29, 1960, Agadir suffered the most devastating earthquake in its history. Measuring 5.7 on the Richter scale, the earthquake's epicenter was very close to the city center and also very shallow, so the intensity of the shaking unleashed unprecedented destruction.

The quake started at 11:40 p.m., when most of the city's 45,000 inhabitants were in their homes and tourists were in their hotels. It killed at least 12,000 people, injured many more, and left thousands homeless. Even the ancient kasbah, which had survived the great quake of 1731 virtually unscathed, was flattened.

Rescue teams were drafted in from around the world as attempts were made to recover those trapped beneath the debris. Thankfully the city's airport,

located away from the center, was undamaged, allowing rescue teams and emergency supplies to be flown in. The airport was also used as a temporary hospital in the weeks following the quake. Two days after the earthquake, the Moroccan authorities ordered an evacuation of the city amid fears that diseases might begin to spread.

The late King Mohamed V visited Agadir a week after the quake and, though understandably shocked and horrified by the destruction, made the bold declaration: "If Agadir is doomed to be destroyed, then its rebuilding depends on our will." He also vowed that the city would be rebuilt within a year. The new city was constructed 1 mile (1.6 km) from the quake's epicenter.

tangible reminder of the city's pre-earthquake past is a single wall of the 16th-century **Oufella Kasbah,** which can still be seen on a hill 4 miles (7 km) to the northwest. Although it's a little way out of town, and there's not much to see of the fortress itself, the views of the bay, the city skyscape, and the lively port make it well worth the journey.

Agadir has more than 6 miles (10 km) of beaches. Most of these stretches of sand are exceptionally wide and rarely crowded. Where there are no hotels, they sit in front of a backdrop of pine, eucalyptus, and tamarisk forest, which scents the air. Among the best beaches are Agadir Bay itself, which looks out over the deep harbor, as well as Taghazout, Timzguida, and Imouran, which lie just north of the city. The Atlantic Ocean is generally calm here, and sailors, jet skiers, and windsurfers can often be seen enjoying themselves in the waters.

Most of the city's neighborhoods are largely residential. The main tourist area, however, the **Secteur Touristique,** has been purpose-designed for visitors to the city. It's spread out alongside the Corniche d'Agadir, the main seafront road running next to the beaches. This great sweeping road takes you from the marina and the city's two ports—one specializing in vegetables and fruit, especially citrus fruits, the other in fish—to the other side of the bay.

Be sure to visit the **Port d'Agadir** during your stay to see the fascinating and chaotic auction that takes place every morning when the fishing boats are unloaded and the fresh fish

Fishermen repairing their nets in the fishing port of Agadir

are sold. The selling starts around 8 a.m., but if you get there earlier, you can secure a prime viewing spot to see the fishermen unloading their often exotic catches—everything from hammerhead sharks to giant tuna. The auction is fast and at times bewildering as fish are quickly displayed one after another, with buyers shouting out their bids. By noon, the action is complete. Most fish will have been bought by local hotels and restaurants, including the port's very own **Restaurant du Port** (Port d'Agadir, tel 0528/84 37 08), where they will be prepared for that evening's dinner.

Marina d'Agadir: The city's yacht marina, to the east of the fishing ports, is a relatively recent addition to the seafront and was designed to enhance the leisure amenities of the city. It was completed in 2007 and can accommodate up to 320 vessels in a harbor protected from onshore winds. It has all the usual facilities for visiting yachtsmen, and also has some restaurants, including **La Madrague** (Résidence 6, M3/M4, Marina d'Agadir, tel 0528/84 24 24; see also p. 300) and a clubhouse where non-yachties can go. The marina has a real buzz to it after dark and makes a particularly pleasant place to go for an evening stroll.

This seafront district is where many of the city's best hotels and resorts can be found, most of them standing in richly planted gardens full of colorful bougainvillea and palm trees. These establishments tend to offer guests a whole host of amenities, including buffet restaurants, nightclubs, health suites, hammams, swimming pools, tennis courts, and sometimes even sailing yachts and golf courses. Some welcome nonresident guests, so it's worth inquiring if you wish to use any of their facilities.

Marina d'Agadir
✉ La Corniche d'Agadir
☎ (0528) 84 63 77

Agadir Crisis

In 1911, as France and Germany looked to expand their overseas territories, Morocco was coming under increasing pressure. French troops were massing, ready to take control, prompting the Germans to deploy a gunboat, the *Panther*, to protect a community of Germans in Agadir. In what came to be known as the Agadir Crisis, the tension between France and Germany ratcheted up, prompting Britain to send its own battleships to the region in case war broke out. After a series of negotiations, France achieved full protectorate over Morocco in 1912, which it retained until the country's independence in 1956.

Nouveau Talborjt: Agadir's throbbing heart is the Nouveau Talborjt district, known affectionately as Agadir's ville nouvelle by locals. It can be found a short walk inland from the **Corniche d'Agadir,** the beachside promenade. In Nouveau Talborjt, you can shop endlessly, stopping only to refresh yourself in any one of the dozens of European bistro-style sidewalk cafés that line the little squares of the area. In the evening, many of these same, seemingly

(continued on p. 234)

Walk: Central Agadir

Although its miles of sandy beach are Agadir's premier attraction, the city also offers plenty of opportunities for walks around its cosmopolitan center, taking in its extensive parkland areas, its modern medina, and museums dedicated to its fascinating history.

Locals chat over a meal in Agadir's port.

With the port and beach behind you, and the Corniche d'Agadir in front, head along the **rue de la Plage** ❶ until it meets boulevard Mohamed V. A short walk will take you to the **Vallée des Oiseaux** ❷ (see p. 235), an animal park dedicated, as the name suggests, mostly to birds—with enclosures full of colorful and exotic species, including parrots and ostriches. Flamingos roam the grounds around ponds bordered by oleanders and bougainvillea.

From here, walk along the boulevard Hassan II and turn right onto boulevard des Forces Armées Royales to the modern heart of the city, **Nouveau Talborjt** ❸. This district is made up mainly of modern office complexes, banks, and shops and is known locally as the *ville nouvelle*. Nouveau Talborjt is particularly worth visiting for the small

NOT TO BE MISSED:

Vallée des Oiseaux • Musée de la Memoire • Musée du Patrimoine Amazighe • Palais Royal

Musée de la Memoire ❹ (see p. 234) on boulevard du Président Kennedy. This gem of a museum, which stands in a picturesque garden, **Jardin de Olhão,** tells the story of the city's defining moment, the 1960 earthquake. Displays document the extent of the destruction and tell how the city rose again from the ashes. It provides a glimpse into the soul of Agadir.

Now head along the rue Chinguit and the boulevard du Sidi Mohamed, past the

Grand Market ⑤ before turning left onto the boulevard Hassan II. Continue along this road for around 500 yards (460 m) before turning right onto the pedestrianized Passage Aït Souss, site of Agadir's main museum, the **Musée du Patrimoine Amazighe** ⑥ (see p. 235). This small museum holds a fascinating exhibition on the life of the Berber communities that have lived in the Sous plains around Agadir for centuries, and has an extensive collection of ancient silver jewelry. There are also many household items, textiles, ceramics, tools, and furniture. The museum's collection includes a display of antiques and artwork amassed by the Dutch art historian Bert Flint, who has lived in Morocco for much of his life. More of his amazing collection can be seen in the Maison Tiskiwin (see p. 198) in Marrakech.

A little farther along from the museum, as you approach boulevard Mohamed V, is the **Théâtre de Plein-Air** ⑦ (see pp. 234–235), where plays and concerts are staged in the summer. After passing through the bowl-shaped Place Aït Souss, turn left onto boulevard Mohamed V, and head for the parkland surrounding the **Palais Royal** ⑧ on the right-hand (ocean) side of the road. This is an especially attractive part of the city where King Muhamad VI stays when he is visiting.

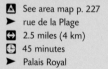

▲	See area map p. 227
▶	rue de la Plage
↔	2.5 miles (4 km)
⏱	45 minutes
▶	Palais Royal

EXPERIENCE: Learn to Speak Tamazight

Tamazight is the most common Berber language spoken by the communities living around Agadir and in the Drâa Valley. It is based on a phonemic three-vowel system that is very similar to Arabic and utilizes a standard sentence arrangement of a verb followed by the subject, and then the object.

For much of its existence, Tamazight was an unwritten language used only for verbal communication, but in recent times a written version has been developed, based largely on the Latin alphabet.

It is now taught in some local schools, and courses for adults to learn Tamazight have also become available. If you are interested in learning the basics, you can purchase a course from **Talk Now Tamazight** (www.eurotalk.com), which you can tackle in the comfort of your home.

Jardin de Olhão
 233
✉ boulevard du Président Kennedy

Musée de la Memoire
 233
✉ boulevard du Président Kennedy

Théâtre de Plein-Air
🅰 233
✉ boulevard Mohamed V
☎ (0528) 84 07 84

humble eateries transform into some of the city's chicest dining places. Three worth trying are **Via Veneto** (boulevard Hassan II, tel 0528/84 14 67), **La Tour de Paris** (boulevard Hassan II, tel 0528/84 09 06), and **Restaurant Daffy** (rue des Oranges, tel 0528/82 00 68).

The district's **Jardin de Olhão** is an enchanting garden set amid office buildings where visitors mingle with city folk on work breaks. On the grounds is a small museum, the **Musée de la Memoire** (Museum of Memory), which is both a memorial to the many people who perished in the earthquake of 1960 and an exhibition telling the story of how the city rose again from the rubble. It's a fascinating place divided into three main areas. The first has a collection of photographs that show what Agadir looked like before 1960, with its ancient kasbah and medina reminiscent of so many other Moroccan cities. These are juxtaposed with modern images of Agadir, which is almost unrecognizable from its former incarnation.

INSIDER TIP:

Visit Mirleft in Tiznit [see p. 238] and its beautiful beaches with some of the most renowned and dazzling surfing spots in all of Morocco.

—SANAA AKKACH
National Geographic Books designer

The most moving section has newspaper cuttings showing the devastation of the city and detailing the tragedy its people suffered. There are reports on how people were rescued from the rubble, and how the city coped during the days and months after the quake. The museum also explores how the city gradually started to come to terms with the disaster and rebuild itself.

Boulevard Mohamed V:
Running almost parallel with the Corniche d'Agadir is the boulevard Mohamed V, a wide thoroughfare. Here you will

find trendy restaurants, pubs, and clubs, as well as a few other attractions, including the **Théâtre de Plein-Air** (Open-Air Theater), where shows, theatrical performances, and musical events are put on regularly in the summer months.

Just to the north of the theater is the **Vallée des Oiseaux** parrots; lakes provide a home for swans, ducks, and flamingos; and there are pens with mountain goats, sheep, ostriches, and llamas.

Also on the boulevard Mohamed V, to the south of the park, is the **Musée du Patrimoine Amazighe** (Amazigh Heritage Museum). It was opened on February 29, 2000, to commemo-

Vallée des Oiseaux

🅰 233
✉ boulevard du 20 Août
☎ (0548) 84 63 77
🕐 Closed Mon.
💲 $

A game of football on Agadir beach—the sign on the mountain in the background proclaims "Allah, el-Watan, el-Malik—God, Homeland, King."

(Valley of Birds), which provides a welcome breath of fresh air in what can at times be a busy, bustling, and congested city. The park and zoo are crammed into a long strip of land running from the boulevard du 20 Août, near the seafront, up to the avenue Hassan II, not far from the city's Grand Mosque. Set among palm trees, banana trees, and tropical shrubs, the zoo is popular with local families. Aviaries hold exotic

rate the devastating earthquake that struck exactly 40 years earlier and to celebrate the subsequent rebuilding of the city. Inside, its displays examine Agadir's Berber communities who have lived in the Sous and pre-Saharan regions for centuries. Exhibits tell the story of their lives, and you can see examples of the elaborate silver jewelry—like necklaces, brooches, and rings—that have long been prized by the Berber people.

Musée du Patrimoine Amazighe

🅰 233
✉ boulevard Mohamed V
☎ (0528) 82 16 32
🕐 Closed Sun.
💲 $

Palais Royal

🅐 233

✉ boulevard
Mohamed V

Souk al Had

✉ rue Chai-
al Hamna
Mohamed ben
Brahim

🕐 Closed Mon.

Polizzi Medina

✉ Ben-Sergaou

☎ (0528) 28 02 53

💲 $

www.medinapolizzi
.com

Palais Royal: If you continue south along the boulevard Mohamed V, you eventually reach the Palais Royal (Royal Palace), where King Mohamed VI and his family stay when in Agadir. Although the house is not open to the public, you can explore the attractive landscaped grounds.

If you fancy something a little more lively, take a detour along the boulevard Abdullahim to the **Souk al Had** (also known as the Grand Souk), a vast market area where produce from all over the region is sold. It's a feast of colors and aromas, with great banks of peaches, pears, oranges, lemons, and kiwis interspersed with mounds of herbs and spices.

About 2.5 miles (4 km) south of the city center, on the road to Inezgane, is the site of Agadir's modern medina. Known either as **Polizzi Medina** or **La Médina d'Agadir,** it was conceived after the 1960 earthquake flattened much of the town's architectural heritage. Designed by Coco Polizzi, an Italian architect, it was built to look like a traditional medina, with red *pisé*-style walls surrounding a tight-knit labyrinth of small cobbled streets lined with homes and souks. The project was heralded a success, and today it houses craft workshops, an exhibition dedicated to Morocco's craft traditions, a jewelry souk, and a Moorish-style café.

Around Agadir

There are many places to explore close by, and almost all will be reached by heading off along roads lined with argan trees. Endemic to the region, this somewhat unattractive tree of thornlike branches produces nuts from which is extracted a gold-colored oil that is used in Moroccan cuisine, in beauty products, and in massage oil (see sidebar p. 223). You will pass through a landscape dotted with tiny villages and covered with olive trees, citrus groves, and almond trees that in spring sprout pink-hued blossoms.

EXPERIENCE: Timitar Music Festival

A celebration of Berber music that brings together performers from around the world, the Timitar Festival is the largest musical event in Agadir. Although it began as a niche festival, dedicated solely to the traditional folk music of the Sous region, it has over the years adopted a more multicultural approach to the performance of Berber music. Today the organizers actively welcome the participation of musicians from other genres, encouraging them to take traditional folk songs and rework them in jazz, reggae, or rock styles to give them a more contemporary sound.

The festival is usually held over four or five days in early summer, providing dozens of free concerts at various venues across the city, including the Théâtre de Plein-Air. Musicians can apply to take part in the festival by contacting the organizers (*tel 528/82 03 38, www.festivaltimitar .ma*). As a spectator, you can simply go along to a venue to watch. You do not need a ticket. Check the website and local posters for details of forthcoming shows.

Horse riding at sunset along Agadir's sandy beach

About 8 miles (13 km) south of the center of Agadir is **Inezgane,** a "real" Moroccan town rather than a tourist destination. This active district has grown from being a relatively small Berber town into a bustling mix of homes, mosques, and souks. Try to visit on a Tuesday, when it seems every resident of Inezgane and the surrounding communities takes to the streets to buy and sell at the souks. The atmosphere is electric, and mingling with the locals here is a great way to soak up the local culture.

The town is especially well known for its silver jewelry, in the form of necklaces, bracelets, anklets, and, in particular, brooches, which most Berber women tend to wear in pairs. They are sold in the souks alongside pottery and ceramics adorned with geometric patterns that are typical of this region, spices such as saffron and turmeric, textiles, wood, and leather, as well as fruits and vegetables that grow in abundance along this fertile stretch of coastal plain. You will also see lots of fish. The Atlantic coast towns' souks are known for their freshly caught seafood, including sardines, shrimps, and sole.

North of Agadir

The twisting, turning road from the coastal town of Tamrhakht through the Paradise Valley gorge and into the foothills of the High Atlas eventually snakes its way to **Imouzzer des Ida-Ou Tanane,** 3,900 feet (1,200 m) above sea level. This popular hiking destination is renowned for its beautiful waterfalls (which slow to a trickle in summer) and its almond blossoms in spring. The village is very small, though

Inezgane
🅰 227 B3
✉ avenue du
   Prince Moulay
   Abdullah

**Imouzzer des
Ida-Ou Tanane**
🅰 227 B3

EXPERIENCE:
Golf in Agadir

You may not be surprised that golf is a serious business in Agadir. You can choose among no fewer than four high-quality courses within close proximity of the bay. These are the **Soleil Golf Club** (*route Bensergaou, chemin des Dunes, BP 901, Agadir, tel 0528/83 45 59, www.golfdusoleil .com*), which has a 9-hole, par-36 course located right near the beaches; the **Ocean Golf Club** (*Atlantic Palace Resort, chemin de l'Oued Sous, Benserga, tel 0528/82 41 46*), which boasts three 9-hole courses in the suburb of Inezgane; the **Agadir Royal Golf Club** (*Km 12, route Aït Melloul, tel 0528/24 85 51*) in the district of Aït Melloul, which has a 9-hole, par-36 course; and the **Dunes Golf Club** (*chemin de l'Oued Sous, Benserga, tel 0528/83 45 59*), which enjoys perhaps the most spectacular setting, with its course overlooking the Oued Sous river.

Souss-Massa National Park
🏔 227 B3
☎ (0528) 33 38 80

Tiznit
🏔 227 B3

Taroudant
🏔 227 B3

it does have a souk every Thursday. **Hôtel des Cascades** (*Immouzer des Ida-Ou Tanane, tel 0528/21 88 08, www.cascades-hotel.net, $$$$$*) makes an ideal base for hiking or simply relaxing. Day visitors can get sustenance at the **Café du Miel** near the waterfall parking lot or in the village.

South of Agadir

Nature lovers should make time to explore the great expanse of coastal wilderness of the **Souss-Massa National Park** (*Parc National de Souss-Massa*), south of Agadir. Covering a huge area between the rivers Oued Sous and Oued Massa, the park's varied habitats—wetlands, cliffs, sand dunes, forest, and farmland—are home to a vast array of flora and fauna. Hundreds of species of birds have been seen here, but Souss-Massa's biggest claim to fame is its breeding northern bald ibises (see sidebar p. 31). The majority of the world's population of this ugly and endangered species—about 400 birds—lives here, and the park has instigated a program to monitor and aid their conservation. Other types of wildlife include the mhorr gazelle, Barbary deer, and Barbary striped grass mouse.

Continue south on the N1 to reach **Tiznit**, which has a desert feel cooled by the breeze of the Atlantic Ocean 13 miles (20 km) away. It is famed for its thick walls, with 29 towers and nine gates, a mosque with a minaret reminiscent of those found in Mali, and its Thursday market. If you want something more energetic, head northwest to hit the coast at **Aglou Plage**, where the surf can be good.

A beautiful winding road running east from Tiznit into the Anti Atlas brings you to the village of **Tafraout**, with its stunning collection of ancient homes in varying shades of pink. In late February or early March the villages in this area celebrate the almond harvest with all-night dancing and singing.

Taroudant

The ancient town of Taroudant lies around 45 miles (70 km) east of Agadir on the road to Ouarzazate. Its high and exceptionally thick crenellated rampart walls topped by mighty watchtowers make an imposing sight as you approach. The walls run for about 3 miles (5 km). If this is too far to walk, but you feel like investigating, there are several places where bikes can be rented.

Once the capital of the Saadian dynasty, before the royal seat was moved to Marrakech, Taroudant is no longer one of Morocco's top-ranking cities, although it is still a major market town for the region. Farmers and merchants come here from miles around to buy and sell their wares. The town has two souks, one on either side of place Talmoklate ("square of the little pot")—officially place en Nasr. **Souk Arab Artisanal,** to the northwest, specializes in traditional crafts, such as pottery, carpets, and artifacts fashioned from the local stone. **Marché Berbère,** to the south, is Berber and has a

much stronger emphasis on produce. There is a good selection of basic, inexpensive cafés between place Talmoklate and Taroudant's other main square, place Assarag (officially place Alaouine).

In the east of the walled town is the old **kasbah.** This was once a winter palace complex for the Saadians (see p. 42), and it contains the ruins of a fortress built by Moulay Ismail. It is easy enough to walk there from place Talmoklate and the souks. Just follow avenue Bir Zaran, then avenue Moulay Rachid, where you will find another, slightly pricier eaterie, **Chez Nada** (Moulay Rachid, tel 0528/85 17 26). The **Hôtel Palais Salam** (avenue Moulay Ismail, tel 0528/85 23 12) that's nestled within the kasbah's walls is probably the best in town. For a small fee ($) nonresidents can use its swimming pool. Taroudant is also home to a new facility for the Zohr University of Agadir. ■

Souk Arab Artisanal
- place Assarag, Taroudant
- Closed Sun.

Marché Berbère
- place Talmoklate, Taroudant

To get the best impression of Taroudant's long and imposing walls, rent a bike and cycle them.

Ouarzazate & Around

Overlooked in the north by some of the highest peaks of the High Atlas and sitting astride the meeting place of two great valleys—those of the Drâa and Dadès Rivers—Ouarzazate is a delightful provincial city, packed with red-pink buildings. The predominantly Berber population is joined by visitors drawn to the region's dramatic mountain and desert landscapes, and to its famous film studios.

Berber men and women singing at Aït Ben Haddou, a World Heritage site near Ouarzazate

Ouarzazate

 227 C3

Visitor Information

✉ ONMT,
boulevard
Mohamed
V, Kasbah
de Taourirt,
Ouarzazate

☎ (0524) 88 24 85

**www.visitmorocco
.com**

Bus Station

✉ CTM, boulevard
Mohamed V

☎ (0524) 88 24 27

Ouarzazate

Ouarzazate lies at the cross-roads of Morocco's traditional north–south trading links, which at one time saw camel caravans passing by from pre-Saharan Africa to the major trading centers of Marrakech and Fès. The city sits surrounded by simply stunning landscapes, marking the point where the mountains meet the desert, giving rise to a series of oases that have provided the region with precious water over the millennia.

Until the 20th century, Ouarzazate was a small and largely undeveloped place that saw one kasbah after another built by the local Berber communities in the countryside surrounding it. These little fortified villages of stone houses were home to the famous Glaoua tribe (see p. 243), a Berber people from the mountains, who were attracted to the Ouarzazate region by its natural resources.

Built of dried red mud and sur-rounded by palm trees and fields of crops irrigated by the rivers, the kasbahs blended in complete har-

INSIDER TIP:

If you can, visit the Handicapped Project Horizon in Ouarzazate, which helps rehabilitate patients. Many have been taught to make traditional handicrafts.

—JANELLE NANOS
National Geographic Traveler
magazine editor

mony with the landscape. Today they form part of the modern city laid out by the French during the protectorate period. This led to Ouarzazate being dubbed the "city of a thousand kasbahs." The most notable include the 18th-century Taourirt Kasbah in the city center,

while just outside the city, near the road out to the west, is the towering 17th-century Tiffoultout Kasbah, which commands impressive views of the Atlas Mountains.

When Morocco came under the control of the French in the early 20th century, Ouarzazate's fortunes changed dramatically. Attracted by its strategic location at the head of the Drâa Valley, the French Foreign Legion established a garrison town here. During the 1920s and 1930s, it was developed further, its infrastructure was improved, and Ouarzazate became an important administrative and customs center for the surrounding area.

Today, Ouarzazate is a beautiful, quiet place, as befits its name, which means "without noise" in the local Berber language. It is not a big tourist center, but it is

Handicapped Project Horizon

✉ The Intrepid Foundation, BP 181, avenue de la Victoire

www.cph-ouarzazate.com

EXPERIENCE: Run the Marathon des Sables

If, by some strange chance, you fancy jogging your way through mile after mile of hot, scorching desert, then the Marathon des Sables is the competition for you. This six-day ultra event held every spring around Ouarzazate brings together hundreds of runners from across the world for a run of approximately 142 miles (230 km) across the southern Moroccan Sahara desert. It is considered the most demanding race of its kind in the world.

Potential participants need to register with the organizers *(www.darbaroud.com/index)* and meet all the necessary entry conditions, before being assessed for ranking according to age and sex. Once accepted, runners must prepare intensively to ensure they can achieve the necessary level of fitness.

One of the main conditions of the marathon is that all runners must carry with them a backpack containing the resources they'll need for the race. This includes food, but not water, which is supplied by the organizers. Winners receive the celebrated Marathon des Sables trophy and prize money.

Of course, most runners take part in this ultimate energy-sapping competition not so much for the glory, but for sponsorship, to raise money for their chosen charities. The Marathon des Sables itself attracts a good deal of sponsorship, which has been used to found the Solidarité Marathon des Sables, an organization dedicated to helping and improving the lives of Morocco's many underprivileged children.

Ouarzazate Arts & Crafts Center

✉ boulevard Mohamed V, Ouarzazate

Taourirt Kasbah

✉ boulevard Mohamed V, Ouarzazate

becoming more popular and there is a small selection of luxury hotels and resorts, as well as budget options. Ouarzazate even has its own airport *(Taourirt Airport, BP 30, Ouarzazate, tel 0524/88 23 83)*, a little over a mile (2 km) north of town, with regular—though not daily—flights to Casablanca and Paris.

Visitors come to the town throughout the year to experience Berber life and to explore the rugged terrain of the Drâa Valley and the extreme wilderness of the desert and its dunes.

Ouarzazate lies at an altitude of about 3,800 feet (1,160 m), south of the High Atlas Mountains and facing the pre-Saharan desert, on a large plateau nestled in groves of palm trees. The best times to visit are in spring or fall. Supremely hot temperatures—104°F (40°C) is not rare—can make it uncomfortable (nigh unbearable) in summer, while perhaps surprisingly the icy winds from the snow-covered mountains send temperatures plummeting in winter.

It's a compact place with just one main thoroughfare, the boulevard Mohamed V. From here, you can easily get to the town's hotels, its handful of restaurants, the new **Ouarzazate Arts & Crafts Center**—where you can see artisans at work on copper items, silver jewelry, and stone sculptures—and its most historic attraction, the quite magnificent Taourirt Kasbah.

Taourirt Kasbah: Dating from the 18th century and remodeled in the 19th century, the Taourirt Kasbah is one of the city's oldest

Textiles for sale in Ouarzazate's Taourirt Kasbah

Aït Ben Haddou—a World Heritage Site

A fortified city, or *ksar*, Aït Ben Haddou (see p. 244) lies around 19 miles (31 km) northwest of Ouarzazate on the banks of the Oued Mellah, overlooking the Ounila Valley. Founded in the 11th century, though many of its buildings are younger, it was once an important place for merchants to rest and trade on the caravan route between the Sahara and Marrakech.

Aït Ben Haddou is recognized as one of the most complete examples of ancient pre-Saharan architecture in the world, leading UNESCO to declare it a World Heritage site in 1987. The ksar is a stunning sight, with its great defensive walls, angled towers, and red-earth houses set against the steep mountainside. It is laid out in the traditional fashion: courtyards, homes, mosques, and *medersa* (university) buildings are set around a central marketplace. There are sweeping panoramas from the fortress's upper levels.

Immortalized in films such as the 1962 classic *Lawrence of Arabia* and 1977's *Jesus of Nazareth*, Aït Ben Haddou is now a tourist attraction and film location rather than a place for people to live. A new village has been built for its former occupants on the opposite side of the river, and film revenues have helped pay for the fortress's upkeep.

buildings and was built in a style typical of the pre-Saharan architecture of the period. Its facade is striking. The high walls are smooth, with a series of arches, geometric patterns, and motifs indented in negative relief. The windows are covered by decorative *mashrabiyya* screens that allowed the kasbah's inhabitants to look out without being seen, and its roof is topped by crenellated towers. Inside, the decoration is a mix of lavishly decorated stucco walls and carved cedar ceilings.

It was once the home of Thami el Glaoui (1879–1956) and his extended family and servants. As the chief of the Glaoua tribe and a pasha of Marrakech, el Glaoui was a powerful feudal lord. His family had helped depose Sultan Abdel Aziz in 1908, and he worked with the new colonial rulers to develop this part of the country. Decades later, he engineered the exile of Mohamed V in 1953, only to have it backfire with a nationalist uprising. Despite siding with the enemy, following independence in 1956, el Glaoui was forgiven by the new Moroccan king, Mohamed VI.

Today the Taourirt Kasbah has been renovated and is listed as a national heritage building. It houses an art gallery where an eclectic collection of works by local artists is displayed, an exhibition hall, a library, and an amphitheater where musical events and festivals are held. It is easy to find, right opposite the city's much signposted arts and crafts center. Next to the kasbah is a small residential area that was built around the same time and gives an interesting insight into traditional local life.

Souks: Nearby are Ouarzazate's souks. Here you can buy original Ouazguita carpets, famed throughout Morocco. Made of wool, the carpets are character-

Aït Ben Haddou
🄰 227 C3

ized by their intense geometric patterns and the use of bold colors, usually red or orange, on a black background. They are made only in Ouarzazate. You may also find Taznakht carpets on sale, which have been made in the High Atlas for centuries, and can be instantly recognized by their use of dark green, white, and red wool woven into neat, symmetrical patterns.

Around Ouarzazate: A few miles out of town on the road signposted to Marrakech is **Aït Ben Haddou,** one of the oldest and finest examples of a fortified city in the world (see sidebar p. 243). Standing dramatically on a steep

INSIDER TIP:

Do have mint tea with a rug seller. Do take a bus ride to a small town with some locals. Do sample olives in the market. Don't use your left hand.

—HEATHER PERRY
National Geographic contributor

hillside overlooking the Ounila Valley, it attracts thousands of visitors—and large numbers of filmmakers. In fact, the site has appeared in more than a dozen Hollywood movies.

Nearby lie Ouarzazate's

Moviemaking in Ouarzazate

Even if you've never been to Ouarzazate, you've probably seen it in a film. The city's dramatic landscape and kasbahs have provided the locations for dozens of movies over the decades, including numerous Hollywood productions.

Early movies filmed in the area include the 1962 epic *Lawrence of Arabia*, considered one of the greatest films ever made. Starring Peter O'Toole and Omar Sharif, the movie won seven Oscars at the 35th Academy Awards in 1963, including best picture, best director, and best sound.

Other famous movies made here include *The Man Who Would be King* (1975), starring Sean Connery and Michael Caine; *The Message* (1976), which recounts the life of the Prophet Muhammad (though, in accordance with Muslim beliefs, the Prophet is never shown); and the 1977 classic *Jesus of Nazareth*, which stars Robert Powell.

In the 1980s, Ouarzazate made appearances in the fantasy film *Time Bandits*, directed by Terry Gilliam; *The Jewel of the Nile*, starring Michael Douglas, Kathleen Turner, and Danny DeVito; the 15th James Bond movie, *The Living Daylights*, starring Timothy Dalton as 007; and Martin Scorsese's controversial *The Last Temptation of Christ*, starring Willem Dafoe as Jesus.

The filming of American writer Paul Bowles' most famous novel, *The Sheltering Sky*, in 1990 was slightly unusual in that, unlike most movies shot here, the story was actually set in Morocco. There seem to be very few places that Ouarzazate has not stood in for at one time or another. In recent years, it's been Tibet in *Kundun* (1997); ancient Egypt in *The Mummy* (1999); and a province of the Roman Empire in director Ridley Scott's 2000 classic, *Gladiator,* which starred Russell Crowe and Joaquin Phoenix.

famous **Atlas Film Corporation Studios.** This is one of three studios to have opened here in recent decades, as Ouarzazate has developed into perhaps North Africa's prime filming location (see sidebar opposite). You can visit the studios when filming is not taking place, when you may be able to see a set resembling ancient Rome or find yourself in a replica of a 3,000-year-old Egyptian temple. All the studios have workshops where the sets are made, and tours can also be arranged around these.

Ouarzazate has its own little museum celebrating its links with Hollywood. Run by Atlas Studios, the **Cinema Museum** (Musée du Cinema) holds items from sets, as well as photographs and film posters from some of the movies filmed in the city. As the opening times of both the Atlas Studios and the museum vary depending on whether a movie is being filmed, it is best to contact the tourist office in Ouarzazate, where the staff will be happy to assist you in arranging a visit.

The film industry provides jobs for most of the population of the city, be it making sets, providing support services, or as extras. Ouarzazate even has its own film school where locals can learn all there is to know about the movie industry, from how to create special effects and apply makeup to evaluating props for their authenticity and, of course, how to be a "background artist." If you are visiting when the latest blockbuster is being filmed, you never know—you might even find

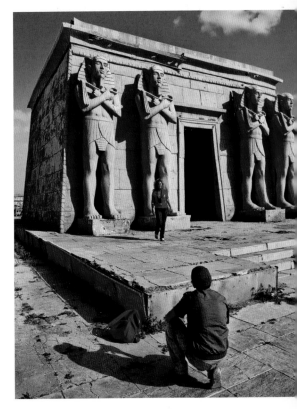

Ouarzazate's Atlas Studios is one of the area's three studios that represent a thriving filmmaking industry.

yourself on the set next to a big Hollywood star.

Ouarzazate is surrounded by breathtaking valleys, gorges, and some of the most picturesque towns and villages in Morocco.

Much of the landscape has been carved by the Oued Drâa, which at over 680 miles (1,000 km) is the longest river in Morocco. It rises somewhere deep in the High Atlas Mountains and follows a meandering course south, flowing into the Atlantic Ocean not far from Tan-Tan. Stretches of the river form the

Atlas Film Corporation Studios

✉ Off route N9 to Marrakech

☎ (0524) 88 22 12

🕐 Studios closed during filming

www.atlastudios .com

Cinema Museum

✉ boulevard Mohamed V

☎ (0524) 88 24 85

🕐 Studios closed during filming

💲 $

Traders wait for customers at a date market near Ouarzazate.

Skoura
◭ 227 C3

Kalaât M'Gouna
◭ 227 C3

country's border with Algeria.

Beyond Aït Ben Haddou is the 19th-century **Tamdakht Kasbah,** which stands an impressive five stories high and has nine towers built into its formidable walls.

Dadès Valley

The broad valley running east from Ouarzazate is blessed with dozens of palm-tree-filled oases, rich agricultural fields, and an astonishing number of kasbahs. In fact, the road east (the N10 toward Boumalne-du-Dadès and Tinghir) is known as the **Route des Kasbahs.** There are several just west of the town of **Skoura,** which makes a great base from which to explore them—and also the mountains to the north and south of the valley. Near the town center, the 18th-century

Kasbah Aït ben Moro has been restored and is now a hotel *(Douar Taskoukamte, Skoura, tel 0524/85 21 16, closed July, $$$$$),* and nearby is **Kasbah Amerdihl,** where figs and lemons grow around a fountain and a small donation to the caretaker will grant you admission. There are plenty of accommodation options, including, about 5 miles (7 km) west of Skoura, **Chez Talout** *(Oulad Aarbiya, Skoura, tel 0662/49 82 83, www.talout.com, $$$),* which is inexpensive and has some great views.

Thirty miles (50 km) east of Skoura is **Kalaât M'Gouna,** where Morocco's most celebrated roses—used for making rosewater—grow in huge numbers. Each May, 3,000–4,000 tons of roses may be gathered in a single week.

When the harvest is over, the town hosts the Rose Moussem festival. There is music, dancing, and exhibitions of local crafts. And women are only too happy to demonstrate how they distill the rosewater.

Not far beyond Kalaât M'Gouna, the Route des Kasbahs divides: go left and you enter the amazingly dramatic **Dadès Gorge;** take the other road and you are in the friendly town of **Boumalne-du-Dadès,** where there is a market on Wednesday and where you can rent bikes from **Chez Youssef** (avenue Mohamed V, tel 0667/69 02 14, $$$) to explore the valley at a more relaxed pace.

One of the largest communities in the Dadès Valley is **Tinghir,** several villages clustered around an oasis on the banks of the Oued Todra river. In January 2009, King Mohamed VI granted approval to upgrade Tinghir from a town to a prefecture city, which has really helped to put this enchanting place on the map.

There are no words to describe just how beautiful the landscape around Tinghir is. It is a stunning place built on terraces that follow the lines of the landscape. The homes, all made from bright red *pisé* in the traditional pre-Saharan style, blend almost seamlessly into a backdrop of foothills of the same color. The area around Tinghir is best known for its deep gorges carved out of the limestone over millennia by the region's rivers, and not surprisingly it's a popular spot for mountain and valley hiking. The **Todra**

Gorge has some particularly spectacular terrain, with sheer rock faces reaching 1,000 feet (300 m) high in places.

Taznakht & Zagora

If, instead of traveling east from Ouarzazate, you drive west, then south toward Agadir, you will arrive at the small town of **Taznakht,** which is famous

Date Festival
The towns and villages around Ouarzazate are known for their delicious dates. In October every year, as the fruit becomes ripe, the region's Berber tribes gather to celebrate the harvest at the Date Festival. During the event, people enjoy a feast of traditional foods (including, of course, plenty of dates), perform music, dance, and, perhaps more unexpectedly, take part in camel races through the sand dunes.

for its green, red, and white geometric-patterned carpets, which have been woven here since ancient times.

Visitors who make the 75-mile (100 km) journey southeast from Ouarzazate through the Drâa Valley to **Zagora** will be rewarded with one of the prettiest towns in southern Morocco. Full of bright cerise bougainvilleas, pink oleander bushes, and palm trees, Zagora is home mainly to Berbers. From the time of the Almoravids in the 11th century, they lived in desert kasbahs, and only moved to the town when it was developed in the early 1900s under the French.

A few of the local Berber people still live in the fortified villages around Zagora but come together on market days and for the town's major festival of the year, the **Moussem of Moulay Abd el Kader Jilali.** The *moussem*, which honors a Sufi saint, is held in the summer months, when communities gather to dance, feast on local produce, and play the intense, rhythmic music of the region.

Zagora's houses, like those in many towns of the pre-Saharan region, are built from the red earth that forms the surrounding landscape. In days gone by, the earth would have been collected,

INSIDER TIP:

Don't miss out on Morocco's corner of the Sahara. Experiencing the dunes at sunrise or sunset is awe-inspiring.

—MARISA LARSON
National Geographic contributor

mixed with gravel, water, and a little animal blood (to help cement the mixture), and then gradually formed into walls. Each layer would need to dry before the next was laid. Sometimes pre-formed bricks of dried mud were used instead. Once hard, the walls would then be adorned with patterns.

Famously, Zagora was the last oasis on the ancient caravan route used by camel trains before they set out across the depths of the desert to the trading outpost of Tombouctou in Mali. Berber, Arab, and Jewish traders would have stopped in the town to refresh and rest in preparation for the long, arduous journey ahead. Even on camels, it would have taken nearly two months to cross the desert. A sign in the center of Zagora declares, rather ominously, "*Tombouctou 52 jours*—Tombouctou 52 days."

Jebel Zagora, the peak that rises precipitously above the town, is topped by the remains of an Almoravid fortress, and the area around Zagora is rich with kasbahs constructed in the traditional fashion. Among those worth seeking out are **Tinzouline** and **Igdaoun.** Also check out the villages of Taz-

---

EXPERIENCE: Making Pottery in Tamegroute

Tamegroute is known throughout Morocco for its pottery. It was first made here in the 17th century by the Nasiriyya Brotherhood, which saw it as a way of raising money to establish a medina. Taking their inspiration from the craftspeople of Fès (see pp. 138–147), a city also famed for its pottery, the brothers created a distinctive swirling style. The main colors used were, and still are, green and ocher.

Stop at one of the open-air workshops in Tamegroute and you will almost certainly be rewarded with an invitation from the potter to help create a pot, jar, or pitcher. The workshops are equipped with ovens and wheels, and they use the local clay. Try **Ma Bonne Etoile Poterie** (*avenue Mohamed V, Tamegroute*).

Nature-trekking by camel in the Drâa Valley near Tazzarine

zarine; **Amazraou,** known for its intricately fashioned silver jewelry; and **Agdz,** where the 400-year-old **Tamnougalt Kasbah** has sculpted stucco walls and carved wood ceilings.

Tamegroute: From as early as the 11th century, Tamegroute has been an important religious and educational center near Zagora. Unlike the surrounding villages, it boasts several centuries-old mosques with distinctive blue earthenware tiled roofs and brilliant white minarets that dominate the skyline. The town became famous when its Sufi *medersa* (university) was established in the 17th century, attracting students from great distances to study.

Tamegroute became the seat of the Sufi Brotherhood of the Nasiriyya, an order that was respected in many parts of southern Morocco. It was founded by the religious leader Sidi Mohamed ibn Nasir (1603–1675), who was instrumental in establishing the famous **Zaouïa Naciria Library** in Tamegroute, one of the most important in Morocco. The holy man's tomb lies near the medersa's courtyard and forms the centerpiece of the annual Moussem of Sidi Mohamed ibn Nasir, held in his honor.

Tamegroute and its neighboring village of **Tagounite** sit close to the **Dunes de Tinfou.** A wonderful spectacle of nature, the dunes comprise a huge "wall" of sand on a ridge rising from the desert. It is pure *Lawrence of Arabia* country, and over the decades has tempted numerous directors looking for that perfect desert shot. ■

Tamegroute
🅰 227 C3

Zaouïa Naciria Library
✉ Le Ksah, Tamegroute

Goulimine & Around

The huge region of Morocco south of the Anti Atlas Mountains, sandwiched between the Atlantic Ocean, the Algerian border, and Western Sahara, is short on people and big on desert. It is a region of vast arid plains, rolling foothills, dry river valleys, and dunes that stretch as far as the eye can see. And to the south and east, it is virtually uninhabited.

Bargaining at a camel souk near Goulimine

Goulimine

   227 B2

Visitor Information

✉   3 residence Sahara, route d'Agadir

☎   (0528) 87 29 11

🕐   Closed Sat.–Sun.

Goulimine

A generally sleepy town of red *pisé* houses with blue-painted doors and window shutters, Goulimine is sometimes called the "gateway to the Sahara." A welcoming place on the N1 south of Agadir, the coast is within striking distance at **Sidi Ifni** and **Foum-Assaka.** The former, with its decaying art deco buildings, was once a base for Spanish slave-trading operations. It is now popular with surfers and paragliders.

Goulimine itself was once an important market center and

stopping-off point for camel trains moving from the Sahara along the coastal plains to the cities of Marrakech and Fès. Nowadays, travelers reach the town by bus from Agadir (two hours), Marrakech (seven hours), or Laâyoune (seven hours) or by car.

Goulimine is principally known for its souk, a short way out of town on the road to Tan-Tan, and its camel fair in July or August. The fair is attended by Tuareg camel traders, known as the "blue men of the desert" because of their traditional blue djellabas, who arrive from all

INSIDER TIP:

Make sure to eat a traditional Berber *tagine* that has been cooked for at least six hours; its succulent and nuanced flavors make for a hearty yet sophisticated meal.

—SANAA AKKACH
National Geographic Books designer

over the region to buy and sell desert-ready dromedaries. The ruins of the **Palace of Caid Dahman** *(behind Hôtel de la Jeunesse, boulevard Mohamed V)* are thought to be about a hundred years old. In recent times, Goulimine has also become associated with the production and sale of a type of jewelry known as Goulimine beads, fashionable accessories during Morocco's 1960s hippie era.

For a real desert adventure, drive east from Goulimine, then take the N12 from Bou-Izakarn, and you will end up tracking the southern slopes of the Anti Atlas, with nothing but desert between you, the Algerian border, and the mighty Sahara. This was once the trade route between Zagora (see pp. 247–248) and Tan-Tan. When you reach the **Akka oasis,** stop for a rest and find a guide to take you to the ancient rock engravings at **Oum el Alek Herbil.**

The next town, **Tata,** is a great base for mountain hiking and desert camping. Check at the tourist office for information. If you want overnight accommodation in the town, try the **Hôtel Renaissance** *(avenue Mohamed V, tel 0528/80 22 25, $$$)* or **Les Relais des Sables** *(avenue Mohamed V, tel 0528/80 23 01, $$$$)*. On the plain nearby are several smaller communities, including Fam el Hisn, Akka, and Foum Zguid, all traditional villages where life revolves around the agricultural fields, the olive and fruit groves, and the central marketplace.

Beyond Tata, the road runs along the north of the ridge of Jebel Bani, eventually reaching the remote outpost of **Tissint,** where there is a kasbah.

Tan-Tan

For travelers determined to explore the very far south, including Western Sahara, there

Tata

⚠ 227 C3

Visitor Information

✉ Maison du Patrimoine Tatoul, avenue Mohamed V

☎ (0572) 13 03 95

✉ Delégation de Tourisme, avenue Mohamed V

☎ (0528) 80 20 76

Tan-Tan

⚠ 227 B2

Sahrawi Tribe

Meaning "desert" in Arabic (it's the same word from which "Sahara" is derived), the Sahrawi tribe of Arab-Berber-Moorish descent has lived in the region now known as Goulimin-Es Semara for centuries. Historically part of the Sanhaja, one of the largest tribal communities of the Maghreb, the Sahrawi are a largely nomadic people and have traditions that reflect their multicultural origins, including some that derive from French and Spanish colonial times. They follow the Sunni form of Islam and speak a variety of languages, including French, Spanish, and Hassaniya, the Arabic dialect spoken by Berber tribes in Mauritania.

The Venus of Tan-Tan

In 1999, German archaeologist Lutz Fiedler was taking part in an archaeological dig in river deposits of the Oued Drâa when he discovered a small, strangely shaped quartzite rock. After much examination, Fiedler declared the rock to be one of the world's oldest sculptures, a representation of the human female form made between 300,000 and 500,000 years ago, which has since become known as the Venus of Tan-Tan.

However, there has been considerable debate about whether the Venus was truly created by human hands or, as several experts contend, has merely been weathered to resemble a human form.

Unfortunately, the Venus is now in private ownership and cannot currently be viewed by members of the public.

of a pilgrimage, the **Tan-Tan moussem** simply celebrates all things Berber. This is the biggest gathering of nomadic tribes in North Africa and has been described by UNESCO as a "masterpiece of the oral and intangible heritage of humanity." The tribes bring with them their own dances telling stories of life in the desert, accompanied by music that can be both energetic and haunting. They bring crafts, too—everything from robes and jewelry, for which southern Berber tribes are famous, to ceramics, hats, and spices. The tribespeople, particularly the women and children, dress up in bright clothing and wear elaborate headgear and beads. They also paint their hands and feet with intricate patterns. Men tend their camels and join in with the music and dancing, and all enjoy a feast with friends and family. If you get a chance to witness the spectacle, make sure you do: You will feel honored to be there.

Tarfaya

Tarfaya

🅰 227 B2

Visitor Information

✉ ONMT, avenue de l'Islam

☎ (0528) 89 16 94

🕐 Closed Sat.–Sun.

is only one road—and it leads to Tan-Tan across 78 miles (125 km) of flat, stony desert. For the nomadic Berber tribes of southern Morocco, Tan-Tan is where everyone congregates once a year for a major festival. But for historians it is probably best known for another reason: this is where—in the opinion of some experts—one of the oldest known pieces of sculpture, the Venus of Tan-Tan, was discovered (see sidebar).

On arrival, you could be forgiven for thinking this is a one-camel town. That all changes for one week every September, though, when the town hosts one of the liveliest *moussems* in the whole of Morocco. The event began in the 1960s and is unusual in that, while most moussems honor a saint or take the form

Tarfaya

South again, the road runs close to the Atlantic most of the way to Tarfaya, just 60 miles (100 km) or so east of the Spanish archipelago of the Canary Islands. Along the road, you will see fishers' huts, and they sell their catch roadside. You may also wish to stop at the only settlement of note between Tan-Tan and Tarfaya, **Sidi Akhfennir**, where rooms are available at the **Auberge Pêche et Loisirs** *(Sidi Akhfennir, tel 0561/21 19 83, $$$)*. Nearby,

INSIDER TIP:

About 31 miles (50 km) from Tan-Tan is Oued Chbika, where the flat, rocky desert landscape meets the ocean. The whole area is unbelievably breathtaking.

—SANAA AKKACH
National Geographic Books designer

watch flamingos and shorebirds at the nature reserve at **Laïla lagoon.**

Lying by the headland of Cape Juby, Tarfaya is a small but attractive fishing village set on a harbor surrounded by beaches. The scenery in this area—the Tarfaya Strip—is magnificent, with golden dunes that stretch to the horizon. The coastline is littered with shipwrecks, the result of a combination strong onshore winds and regular thick fog in the days before modern navigation technology.

The village has a mixed history. It was part of the Spanish-controlled zone and was then called Cape Juby or Villa Bens. Indeed, the Spanish once issued postage stationery and stamps for the town, overprinted (from 1934–1948) with the words "Cape Juby." And the legacy of Spanish control still remains in a stronghold that can be seen offshore: the **Casa Mar,** or "house in the sea."

When Morocco gained independence in 1956, the Spanish were asked to leave, but there was considerable resistance. In battles that saw fighting in Sidi Ifni, along the coast north of Tarfaya, and in Tan-Tan, the Spanish and local Berber Sahrawi vied for control. The Ifni War, as this conflict became known, culminated in the town returning to Moroccan rule—and being renamed Tarfaya.

Today Tarfaya has a prosperous fishing industry and is popular with sailors and windsurfers. One of its main annual events is the **Dash,** an endurance competition across the ocean from Lanzarote in the Canary Islands. ■

Berber women weaving traditional carpets for a *moussem*

Western Sahara

Western Sahara has been populated, albeit sparsely, by tribes of Arab-Berber-Moorish descent for centuries. Until the 1970s under Spanish control, its sovereignty today is still in dispute, contested by Morocco and the Algeria-based Polisario Front, which wants the region to become an independent state.

Tourists ride their camels across the mighty dunes of Western Sahara.

Western Sahara
 227 A1–B2

Erg Lakhbayta
227 B2

South of Tarfaya, the N1 highway crosses the old border of Spanish Sahara at Tah and traverses a huge area of sandy desert, the **Erg Lakhbayta.** Every so often, the desert is broken up by enormous salt flats whose waters were prevented from draining into the ocean and evaporated to leave a salty crust (Sebkha Tah and Sebkha Oum Dba are two of the largest of these).

A Disputed Region

The recent history of Western Sahara is a complex and troubled one. Having long enjoyed good trading links with its neighbors, Algeria to the northeast and Mauritania to the south, this strategically placed region became increasingly coveted by European powers in the 19th century. The well-worn camel caravan routes that linked the Atlantic coast to the central trading post of Tombouctou in Mali further increased the region's appeal.

Both the Portuguese and the Spanish recognized its usefulness as a key trans-Saharan route and sought to add it to their empires. It was the Spanish who won out in the 19th century, founding the new colony of Spanish Sahara, which was made up of two provinces: Río de Oro and Saguia el Hamra.

For decades, Western Sahara remained a Spanish territory, but when Spain came under pressure to withdraw in 1975, a power struggle ensued over the future of the area. King Hassan II claimed the region for Morocco, citing historical ties. To the south, Mauritania also sought to annex it. The Sahrawis themselves had founded their own independence movement, the Polisario Front, in 1973, and had begun a guerrilla war against the Spanish occupation. Although the International Court of Justice only partially vindicated some of Morocco's claims, King Hassan II organized a historic

INSIDER TIP:

The French Foreign Legion used to train soldiers by making them climb Saharan dunes. Give it a try if you're feeling hearty. You'll get breathless, but the views will seem even more spectacular.

—JANELLE NANOS
National Geographic Traveler
magazine editor

march to demonstrate Moroccan commitment. In November 1975, around 350,000 unarmed civilians converged on the southern Moroccan city of Tarfaya, before

Wildlife in the Sahara

The Western Sahara may appear desolate and lifeless, with its great rolling expanses of sand punctuated by the odd isolated community clinging tightly to the edge of an oasis, but it is actually home to a surprising abundance of wildlife. Around 40 species of mammals and more than 100 species of birds—notably larks, sandgrouse, and some warblers—thrive, seemingly against all the odds, in the harsh terrain.

Most of the mammals are small, so as to best cope with the limited food available. Rodents are the most numerous group and include the Barbary ground squirrel and Chudeau's spiny mouse, which are both well adapted to life amid the slim pickings of the tropical dry scrub-land. There are bats, hares, shrews, and hedgehogs, too. Among the latter, the tiny desert hedgehog grows to no

more than a few inches in length.

These small mammals are preyed upon by a number of larger desert carnivores, such as the sand cat and the Saharan striped polecat. Other larger desert mammals include the threatened dorcas gazelle and the Barbary sheep.

Most desert mammals are extremely wary of humans, which means that the animals you are most likely to encounter are birds. Many of Western Sahara's bird species are temporary visitors, stopping by briefly to feed or breed. Among the more permanent residents are rare houbara bustards, desert sparrows, cream-colored coursers, and thick-billed larks. Coastal lagoons attract cormorants, storks, spoonbills, pelicans, herons, and shorebirds. And hawks, harriers, falcons, and eagles are found wherever there are other animals to hunt.

Laâyoune

⚑ 227 B2

Visitor Information

✉ ONMT, avenue de l'Islam

☎ (0528) 89 16 94

⏲ Closed Sat.–Sun.

crossing over into Western Sahara. It was dubbed the "Green March" after the holy color of Islam. When Mauritania withdrew its sovereignty claim, Morocco took control of the territory, although the Polisario Front, with Algeria's backing, still seeks a referendum on independence.

Laâyoune

For travelers from the north, Laâyoune is the first settlement of any size that will be encountered, sitting on the coastal plain 65 miles (110 km) south of Tarfaya, and just inland from the Atlantic coast. With more than 200,000 inhabitants, it is easily the biggest in the region.

For visitors, Laâyoune—also known as El Ayun, meaning "the springs" in Arabic—appears like an oasis as you approach through the sands from the main N1 highway that runs from Agadir. Since 1976, when Laâyoune passed from Spanish to Moroccan control, the city has attracted considerable investment, transforming it into one of southern Morocco's most modern communities.

The city is not especially beautiful, but it does have an unusual atmosphere, which has been described by some visitors as seeming like a town under occupation. This probably has a lot to do with the hundreds of United Nations peacekeeping troops stationed here. Its old Spanish quarter has a timeless, historical feel to it, despite being less than a hundred years old, while the new district that has grown up since 1976 offers a fresh-looking counterpoint, perched on a hill and packed with neat, modern

---

EXPERIENCE: A Camel Trek in Western Sahara

Travelers wishing to sample camel rides in the desert are attracted to the coastal region of Western Sahara where the cool Canary Current in the adjacent Atlantic Ocean reduces the temperature. As a result, the heat is less intense, particularly in the morning.

Riding a camel is an unforgettable experience. The exotic surroundings, the wide-stretching sandy desert, and the wonderful scenery add to the sensation, but the greatest factor is the animal itself. Forget everything you know about horse riding. On a camel, you are much higher off the ground, your posture is totally different, and a camel's rolling gait, almost a waddle, is quite unlike anything else. Getting on and off a camel, even though it is lying down for you, is an acquired skill,

so follow the instructions of your guide exactly. What you wear is also important. The sun will be hot, so a hat is essential, but also remember to wear socks—to avoid chafing—and long pants; otherwise, your trip could become uncomfortable. And don't worry: Despite their reputation, camels are gentle animals.

Some hotels in Laâyoune and Dakhla are able to arrange a camel ride for you. This could be either a short journey for a couple of hours or a longer adventure, spending a night ot two under the perfect starry skies of the Sahara and living in a tent. Hotel Dakhla (*www.hotel-dakhla-sahara.com*) organizes desert safaris and camel treks, including spending a night in the desert, but shop around for the deal that suits you.

Sahrawi women meet in Laâyoune.

architecture. The main industry around here is phosphate production, which has brought a good deal of wealth to the town, reflected in the high standard of its homes and amenities and many of its hotels and restaurants.

The original Spanish town lies close to the Oued Saquia el Hamra riverbed, north of the modern admistrative center, and it is here that you should wander first. Bustling **Souk Djemal** is the liveliest part of Laâyoune, and this is where you'll find the best food stalls and the most interesting street life. Nearby, the (now closed) **Spanish cathedral,** with its curved walls, tall tower, and large domed roof, provides a welcome splash of white among all the rich red-and-ocher lines of Spanish-style buildings, interspersed with palm trees. And if you want accommodation in this part of town, check out the **Hôtel Lakouara** *(avenue Hassan II, tel 0528/89 33 78, $$$$).*

Uphill, the newer town has less character. The **place du Méchouar,** site of the modern Palais de Congrès, is the city's focal point where all the main festivals and any special events are held. Off to one side is the modern **Grand Mosquée Moulay Abdel Aziz,** a pretty whitewashed structure with an imposing minaret. Non-Muslims are not allowed to enter.

A short walk to the southwest, along boulevard de Mekka, takes the visitor to the third area of town, around **place Dchira,**

(continued on p. 260)

Spanish Cathedral

✉ Off place Méchouar, Laâyoune

Atlantic Fishing Industry

The busy commercial harbors of Laâyoune and Dakhla throng with brightly colored fishing boats. As well as local craft, owned and run by Moroccans who have settled in the Western Sahara, some 160,000 fishing boats sail along the coast from northern Morocco in summer and the early fall. Larger Spanish boats add to the cosmopolitan atmosphere of these ports.

Laâyoune's fishing port is a constant frenzy of activity.

The waters off Western Sahara are among the richest and most bountiful in the North Atlantic. When the region was a Spanish colony, fishing was a small-scale local industry. Family-owned boats fished close to the shore for shrimp, mackerel, sardines, and tuna, while Spanish vessels operated farther out.

Since the annexation of the region by Morocco in 1976, commercial fishing has been encouraged. Both Laâyoune and Dakhla have been developed, the former employing some 8,000 fishers in the port. Quays have been expanded, and fish-processing facilities established. The Moroccan authorities plan greater development, and already more than $100 million of fish pass through Laâyoune alone every year. Today, despite controversy over fishing along this coast, the fishing harbors of Laâyoune and Dakhla are thriving hubs of activity. Many workers are employed and growing numbers of travelers visit. The ports are lined by small fishing boats, called dories, as well as by larger commercial boats crewed by up to 20 people.

Small boats catch nearshore fish as well as taking shrimp and octopus. Lobster traps are laid, and hooked lines, often more than 1 mile (1.6 km) long, are used to take fish from migrating schools. Typically smaller boats leave port in the early morning and return later in the day, drawing their craft onto the beach and stretching out their nets to dry.

Larger boats often set sail in the afternoon or early evening. Their crews fish all night, coming back to port the following morning.

These modern boats are better equipped and most use trawler nets. Onboard freezers allow them to bring their catch back to port fresh. Sardines account for more than three-fourths of the catch, with mackerel making up another one-sixth. Foreign boats land a greater quantity of fish than Moroccan vessels, but Morocco's fishing industry has modernized, with the ports of Laâyoune and Dakhla at the forefront of progress.

International Aspect

The status of the Western Sahara region is still disputed, although it is effectively part of Morocco. The native Sahrawis raised camels and had little involvement with the sea. A 15-year war for possession of the region began in 1975, when Spain withdrew, and ended with the annexation of all of Western Sahara by Morocco (see p. 255) and the flight of more than half of the Sahrawis into exile in Algeria. The settlement of the region by people from northern Morocco changed the population structure of Western Sahara and began the generously funded redevelopment of Laâyoune and Dakhla. A prosperous commercial fishing industry was a direct result of Moroccan investment. Now Sahrawis are outnumbered by Moroccans by more than two to one, and the fishing and other industries are controlled by Moroccans.

In 2005, Morocco signed a fisheries agreement with the nations of the European Union (EU). One of the less publicized clauses was a concession to EU fishers to operate along the coast of Western Sahara. Some argue that this agreement effectively gives EU recognition to Morocco's annexation of Western Sahara. Spain, the former colonial power and one of the EU's major fishing nations, was influential in drawing up the pact. Since the fishing treaty came into force, the overwhelming majority of EU fishing boats in these waters have been Spanish. Some Europeans have protested the agreement, and a number of international observers and bodies have declared it to be illegal.

EXPERIENCE: Fishing at Dakhla

Fishing is the main commercial activity of the port of Dakhla, but it is also a popular leisure pursuit for visitors. As well as growing numbers of foreign travelers, Moroccan fishing enthusiasts journey to the city from all over the country.

Some hotels offer fishing opportunities. **Hotel Riad Dakhla** (tel 0661/19 13 34, www.hotel-dakhla-sahara.com), for example, has its own fishing boat for visitors, who are able to enjoy an entire day fishing at sea.

The waters off Dakhla are a great rough-sea fishing environment. Meanwhile, Dakhla Bay is a sheltered nursery for many types of fish. The species-rich waters around Dakhla are home to sharks, sea bream, eagle and guitar rays, leerfish, croakers, catfish, and wolf fish.

Dakhla provides an unusual fishing experience between the wide open ocean and the desert. The port is not yet a developed center for package vacations, but some companies do organize fishing vacations. **JMO Aventures** (www.jmo-aventures-4x4.com) offers seven-day vacations in Dakhla, with professional guides accompanying tourists on different fishing excursions. The company provides equipment, bait, and instruction.

Surf casting provides good sport, too. Companies such as **Auberge Rio Aguila Aventure** (www.rioaguilaaventure.com) transport clients by jeep to beaches near the city for a day's fishing as well as offering dinghy trips. The price includes equipment and an appetizing meal of fish, freshly caught and cooked on the beach.

Boujdour
⚑ 227 A2

first passing the budget **Hotel Jodesa** *(223 boulevard de Mekka, tel 0528/99 20 64, $$)* then the bus station *(CTM, boulevard de Mekka)* and **Au Palais des Glaces** *(boulevard de Mekka, tel 0528/98 04 76),* which is supposed to serve the best ice cream in Laâyoune.

If you've had enough of desert roads and want to fly the next step of your journey, Laâyoune does have an airport with flights to Agadir and Casablanca, and even to the Spanish Canary Islands. If you plan to move on to Dakhla and Mauritania, you may wish to give this serious consideration—because the border is a very long way south.

Beyond Laâyoune

The intrepid traveler who wants to get off the beaten track might want to visit the Saharan oasis of Smara, about 150 miles (230 km) east of Laâyoune. The town was a stopover for traders moving north or south across the desert, and unlike the coastal towns of Western Sahara, it lacks Spanish architectural influences. The ruins of the palace and mosque of the Blue Sultan in the center of town are worth a visit, as is the area around the souk, which becomes lively in the evening. However, most visitors head south from Laâyoune. The road is well maintained and easy to navigate, although it is unwise to do any impromptu off-road exploring, as the area around the city is reported to have land mines still left over from the previous decades' battles.

The city is surrounded by sand dunes, but every now and then you may come across a lake or a pool of water fed by the Oued Saquia el Hamra. Here, amid the arid tranquility, you might catch sight of a flock of flamingos or some other migratory birds, which can provide relief from the dust and bustle of central Laâyoune.

INSIDER TIP:

Discover Dakhla's casual attitude and atmosphere at the beach, where you can see the mesmerizing Duna Blanca and enjoy kite surfing while savoring fresh seafood fare.

—SANAA AKKACH
National Geographic Books designer

Boujdour is on a promontory, **Cape Boujdour,** which lies along a desolate stretch of rocky and sandy coastline lapped by the Atlantic Ocean. The promontory has a notorious reputation among sailors because of a hidden underwater reef that follows the contours of the coastline and is believed to have been the cause of many shipwrecks here over the centuries. From the 15th century onward, the waters off Boujdour's coast formed part of the important Portuguese international trade route between Europe, Africa, and later, India.

Today, this former Spanish protectorate town has a buoyant

population mainly made up of native and displaced Sahrawis. Its whitewashed buildings dot the landscape and are adorned with features such as colonnades, elaborate windows, and balconies that hint at Andalusian architecture. It has a handful of public buildings and a small fishing harbor with a lighthouse and a long beach. There are few amenities here, only basic hotel accommodation and a few cafés, but it can be a welcome base for visitors exploring this stretch of coastline as they head south to Dakhla.

Dakhla

Dakhla is perched at the end of a narrow peninsula 30 miles (50 km) long and some 340 miles (550 km) south of Laâyoune. In the days of Spanish rule, Villa Cisneros, as it was then known, was out of bounds for all but the colonists and those working for them. The Sahrawi nomads living in the nearby desert were excluded. Set by one of the

The Music of Western Sahara

The haunting music of Western Sahara, played at *moussems* and other festivals, lies at the very heart of Sahrawi culture. It is performed using a lute-like instrument, known locally as a *xalam*, consisting of a wooden neck and body (covered in hide) and five nylon strings that are plucked to produce the distinctive sound.

Dakhla

🔺 227 A1

Visitor Information

✉ 1 rue Tiris

☎ (0528) 89 82 28

🕐 Closed Sat.–Sun.

A Tuareg man in a traditional djellaba plays the flute near Boujdour.

Grand Mosque

✉ avenue Mohamed V, Dakhla

prettiest bays along Morocco's entire Atlantic coastline, Dakhla's low-rise whitewashed buildings stretch along the shoreline with the endless sand dunes of the Sahara disappearing across the horizon behind it.

The town was founded in 1502 when a shipload of Spanish settlers came ashore, liked what they saw, and decided to colonize the area to expand Spain's overseas territories. As homes were built and its population grew, Dakhla became increasingly powerful; in the 19th century, it was made the capital of one of Spanish Sahara's two provinces, Río de Oro. In more recent times, it became the capital of Tiris al Gharbiyya, a province created when Western Sahara was under Mauritanian rule in the late 1970s.

Today, as one of the very few places to visit and refresh along the Saharan coastline, Dakhla regularly attracts visitors making

the drive down from Laâyoune or arriving by plane from one of Morocco's other cities. The country's national carrier, Royal Air Maroc, operates almost daily flights from Casablanca, Agadir, Fès, Rabat, and Ouarzazate, plus Tanger and Oujda in the north. Dakhla's airport, which is used by the Royal Moroccan Air Force as well as for civilian flights, is impressive, with a modern passenger terminal and a runway capable of receiving Boeing 737s.

Dakhla is a popular stopover with visitors wishing to cross the border into Mauritania. Although the paperwork is relatively straightforward, there is the possibility that once you have gone across the border, the Moroccan authorities may not let you cross back again because of their strict exit regulations. Make sure you check before you cross, as regulations can change.

EXPERIENCE: Enjoy Water Sports at Dakhla

Once a colonial frontier town, Dakhla has become one of the most hip resorts in North Africa for action vacations. Morocco has invested heavily in the city, but its geography is what makes Dakhla a destination for water sports enthusiasts.

Conditions for surfing are almost perfect. The water temperature is a near constant 77°F (25°C) and the ocean topography gives a long right-breaking wave. The wind is also consistent. As a result, Dakhla is the dream environment for surfing and kite surfing.

Dakhla lies along a long narrow peninsula. Surrounded by dunes, the sheltered lagoon to the east is ideal for beginners;

its calm, flat waters make it the perfect, safe place for the less experienced. By contrast, the breakers of the open Atlantic Ocean to the west are enough to test more seasoned surfers.

Dakhla is primarily a kite surfing destination. Offshore and in the 15-mile-long (25 km) lagoon, young people can be seen riding and jumping the waves and gliding the water, sometimes accompanied by shining silver darts of flying fish.

As yet, not too many people have discovered Dakhla. It remains largely unspoiled, and its waves are free from the crowds of surfers that flock to some other surfers' paradises.

Center & Beaches: Dominating Dakhla's skyline is the **Grand Mosque,** an ocher and red structure that stands alongside a large *méchouar* (square) used for the city's *moussems* (festivals) and special parades. Its streets and buildings show all the characteristics of its Spanish heritage. Market day in the souks is when the city's inhabitants come out and engage in animated conversations and commerce.

From the city center, it's an easy walk to the beaches. Usually deserted and offering miles of soft sand, they have a handful of small eateries where you can enjoy a fresh fish meal, which if served in the traditional way—grilled and sprinkled with local herbs and spices, or as part of a *tajine*—is sure to be delicious. Try **Café Restaurant Samarkand** *(avenue Mohamed V, tel 0528/89 83 16, $$)* or **Casa Luis** *(14 avenue Mohamed V, tel 0528/89 81 93, $$).* As fishing is the big industry in Dakhla, the fish you'll be eating will have come from the huge new port built to serve Morocco's biggest fishing fleet.

The beaches provide endless opportunities for quiet walks and for active water sports (see sidebar opposite). The stroll up to the old **Spanish lighthouse** is especially pleasant, although it is unwise to venture too far inland on foot. Not only is the terrain harsh, but it is also believed that there may still be some land mines here, a legacy of the still unresolved Western Saharan conflict.

Dakhla's small **harbor,** set back in a deep bay, is both picturesque

Windsurfing off the coast of Dakhla, within sight of the endless sand dunes of the Sahara desert

and practical. Here you can listen to the waves while you enjoy a drink or a meal, and watch as fishing boats arrive with their daily catches of huge tuna, mullet, sea bream, and swordfish. Fishing is Dakhla's main industry, and it has brought prosperity to this otherwise isolated city. ∎

TRAVELWISE

Locals chug by Marrakech's grand walls on the city's ubiquitous scooters and bicycles.

PLANNING YOUR TRIP

When to Go

With its varied climate, vibrant cultural calendar, and bustling, exciting cities, there will be plenty for you to do and see whenever you choose to visit Morocco. If you have a specific destination or outdoor activity in mind, however, it's best to time your visit to coincide with the ideal conditions.

Although it is known as a hot, arid country, Morocco's climate and landscape are actually tremendously varied, so there is no universally applicable advice on when it is best to go. In a country a little larger than the state of California, visitors can bask on glorious sun-soaked beaches, explore the twisting streets of ancient cities, ski in the High Atlas Mountains, or trek across the scorching Sahara desert.

In the winter, most of Morocco stays reasonably warm, with temperatures almost never dropping below around 40°F (4°C) near the coast. In the mountain regions, however, temperatures fall much further. Higher peaks become covered in deep snow, attracting skiers from across Europe and North Africa. There is even the possibility of such heavy snowfall that mountain passes, like the Tizi n'Test Pass in the High Atlas, have to be closed to traffic. Winter is also a popular season for desert trekking, as daytime temperatures drop down to comfortable levels.

After the cooler, wetter, and often snowy winter months, spring brings pleasingly warm temperatures that help turn much of the countryside to a colorful blanket of flowers with a backdrop of snow-tipped mountains, while the southern desert regions are already bathed in hot sunshine. This is a good time to explore the foothills and peaks of the Atlas Mountains and their beautiful cedar forests. Be aware that the sudden rise in water levels can lead to flooding and landslides in mountain regions, which can block minor roads for weeks at a time.

The summer months see searing heat in most parts of Morocco. Only the mountain peaks and the coastal plains, cooled by winds coming off the sea, remain comfortable. Places like the Ifrane Valley and the Atlas Mountains, famous for their skiing in winter and fresh temperatures in the summer, are great places to go hiking and hill climbing from June through to September, while the inland cities of Fès and Marrakech are best avoided due to the heat.

Fall is when visitors flock to the cities, as the heat is less intense but the weather is more reliable than it is in spring. Late summer and fall constitute the peak season for the Moroccan tourist industry, and accommodation is at its most expensive then.

When planning your visit, you should also consider the timing of Morocco's many religious and secular festivals. Exciting public events take place in Morocco throughout the year, including highlights such as Salé's Candle Festival, which takes place in May, or the Marrakech National Festival of Popular Arts, which takes place in June. Religious festivals, such as Ramadan and Aïd, begin on different dates each year in accordance with the Islamic lunar calendar. It is worth checking to see if these festivals will occur during your visit, as the opening times of businesses and attractions will be affected.

What to Take

Be sure to pack clothing that is suitable for the nature of your stay. Evenings on the coast and higher altitudes can get quite cold, so you will need a sweater or light jacket for warmth.

Sunscreen and a hat are essential. Although such precautions are obvious during the summer months, it is important not to underestimate the strength of the sun even in winter. This is especially true if you are hiking in the clear air of the High Atlas. In the cities, you may not need layers specifically for warmth, but you will need them for etiquette. Morocco is an Islamic country and, while attitudes toward Western dress are becoming increasingly relaxed,

religious customs still hold sway for many, particularly outside the tourist resorts and cities of the north. Some Moroccan women wear head scarves according to tradition, but many prefer not to.

It is not necessary for women visiting the country to wear head scarves. Nonetheless, visitors should be mindful that they will be treated more respectfully by the locals if they wear appropriate clothing. Shoulders should always be covered, women should not wear shorts or miniskirts, and men should wear pants and a long-sleeved shirt. Dressy or smart casual clothing is required in the more expensive restaurants. Items such as hiking gear can be bought in the major cities, but for the challenging trails of the Atlas Mountains, you would be better off bringing your own worn-in boots and other equipment.

It is a good idea to pack enough prescribed medicines to last the full length of your stay. It is also advisable to pack them in your hand luggage and to take a doctor's note explaining what the pills are in case you are questioned at airport security. You might consider bringing a first-aid kit and water purification tablets if you are planning trips to isolated areas.

Those who are traveling with babies are advised to bring any formula milk or food they might need with them because, although these items are readily available in supermarkets, the brands will almost certainly be different than those your child is used to.

Make photocopies of your visa, insurance documents, and passport, and carry them separately in case you lose the originals.

Insurance

Taking out adequate travel insurance before you leave for Morocco is strongly advised. If you need to seek medical or dental care during

your stay, you will almost certainly be expected to pay the full amount for your treatment at the time and then claim the amount back from your insurers. Be sure to tell your insurance company of any problems as soon as possible, not when you return home, and make sure you have sufficient cash, traveler's checks, or credit cards with you to cover your stay and any unforeseen expenses. To make an insurance claim, you will need to supply a receipt from your medical or dental provider.

Be aware that some insurance policies exclude what they term "dangerous" activities, like white-water rafting, skiing, and mountaineering, and you may need to make provision for this should you be planning to engage in these activities. One thing to consider is the cost of getting home in the event of an accident, which can be especially expensive.

Similarly, if you are the victim of theft and report it to your hotel or the police, always keep a copy of any documentation for your insurance company.

HOW TO GET TO MOROCCO
Entry Formalities
Passports & Visas

For most visitors to Morocco, all that is required is a full passport valid for a minimum of six months after the day of entry into Morocco. Your passport should always be stamped with the day you entered the country at passport control. Check that this has been done before leaving the airport, as visitors have experienced problems trying to leave Morocco without this stamp.

Lone parents traveling with children should take documentary evidence of their parental status to avoid running the risk of being refused entry or, if already in the country, refused permission to leave Morocco with the children. These measures are in place to combat human trafficking, which has been a problem for Morocco in the past.

No visa is required for visitors from any of the European Union member states, the United States, or Canada. People from almost any country, in fact, can stay for up to three months with just a valid passport. As visa requirements can change at short notice, however, do check before departure. Anyone wishing to stay longer than 90 days must make an application for an extension to the police. You must always enter the country through an officially recognized entry point, such as an airport or seaport. You may not enter across Morocco's border with Algeria.

Moroccan Embassies
United States
Embassy of the Kingdom of Morocco
1601 21st Street, N.W.
Washington, D.C. 20009
United States
Tel (202) 462-7979
http://dcusa.themoroccan embassy.com

Canada
Embassy of the Kingdom of Morocco
38 Range Road
Ottawa, Ontario
K1N 8J4
Canada
Tel (613) 236-7391
www.ambamaroc.ca

United Kingdom
Embassy of the Kingdom of Morocco
49 Queen's Gate Garden
London
SW7 5NE
United Kingdom
Tel (020) 7581 5001
www.moroccanembassy london.org.uk

Customs
Customs formalities are relatively straightforward. Providing you have the correct documentation, you will only need to complete a short declaration form on arrival at passport control. The form should be handed to you on your flight if arriving by air, or be available on board if arriving by sea. Otherwise, it will be available for you to fill out at passport control.

Visitors may bring in one 750 ml (25 fl oz) bottle of spirits and a bottle of wine, 200 cigarettes, and 50 cigars or 250 grams (8 oz) of tobacco. (The official individual allowances for these goods are only in metric units, but are shown here with approximate imperial equivalents for reference purposes.) You may also bring in sufficient money for the length of your stay, which will need to be exchanged for the local currency, the dirham. Importing or exporting dirhams is strictly prohibited. You will need special permission to bring in a vehicle. As customs rules can change, be sure to check with your embassy before you depart for your visit.

Airplane Arrivals & Departures
Airports & Airlines
Morocco has several international airports that are well served by European, Asian, and African airlines. Many Moroccan cities have airports that carry regional and internal flights, but the majority of international airline traffic is handled by the airports at Casablanca, Rabat, Marrakech, and Tanger.

Royal Air Maroc is the national carrier and, together with its budget subsidiary Atlas Blue, serves Casablanca, Marrakech, Tanger, and Fès, with connections to other cities. For example, from London's Heathrow Airport, there are daily flights to Casablanca. From Casablanca, it is then possible to fly to Essaouira, Nador, Oujda, Ouarzazate, Laâyoune, or Dakhla. From its hub in Casablanca, Royal Air Maroc flies to two airports in North America (New York–JFK and Montreal–Trudeau) and has connections via New York to Washington, Tampa, San Francisco, Seattle, and Los Angeles. Royal Air Maroc plans to open a service between Casablanca and Washington–Dulles Airport in late 2010.

Although it is possible to fly direct to Morocco from North America, it is typically cheaper and more convenient to fly via one of the major European hubs, such as Paris–Charles de Gaulle or London–Heathrow. During the peak season, many European airlines operate regular flights to airports near popular tourist destinations such as Agadir, Al Hoceima, and Nador and increase the frequency of flights to the major cities.

The country's largest airport is Casablanca's **Mohamed V International Airport** (CMN, *tel 0522/53 90 40, www.onda.ma*). This busy airport handles more than 6 million passengers a year and serves as Royal Air Maroc's transatlantic hub. The airport has hotels, car rental facilities, and regular bus and train services to the heart of the city. The capital city is served by **Rabat–Salé International Airport** (RBA, *tel 0537/80 80 90, www.onda .ma*), located in the Salé district of Rabat, a short distance from the center of the city. Rabat–Salé sees flights arrive daily from Europe, Africa, and the Middle East. Marrakech's **Menara Airport** (RAK, *tel 0524/44 79 10, www.onda.ma*) is located around 4 miles (6 km) from the city. It experiences a significant increase in traffic during peak season and is a common port of entry for tourists arriving from Europe. Tanger's **Ibn Battouta International Airport** (TNG, *tel 0539/39 37 20, www.onda.ma*) is being extensively modernized and expanded, but is currently little used.

Boat Arrivals

At the Strait of Gibraltar's narrowest point, only 8.8 miles (14.2 km) of water separates Morocco from Spain. For visitors arriving from Europe, the many ferries that ply this narrow channel are an excellent way to arrive in the country. Most visitors traveling by boat will arrive at the port of Tanger on the Strait of Gibraltar, the Spanish enclave of Ceuta, or along the coast at Melilla or Nador. You can hop on board a fast boat that takes around an hour or a slower ferry with a sailing time of a little over two hours from such ports as Algeciras, Málaga, and Almería (all in southern Spain) to Morocco. Departures from the ports' modern terminals are frequent, especially on the Algeciras-to-Tanger route, and usually several times a day.

Several ferry companies run services on this route. Among them are **Acciona Trasmediterránea** (*www.trasmediterranea.es*), which operates regular fast ferries, **Comarit Espana** (*www.comarit.com*), and **Balearia** (*www.balearia.com*). There's no need to book your crossing in advance, although the facility is there for you to book online if you prefer. When returning, booking in advance allows you to avoid the hassles of Tanger's port, which can be a stressful place. You can simply purchase your ticket at the terminal's ticket offices when you arrive. It is likely there will be a queue and you will need to complete an exit form before boarding, so allow time for this in your schedule. On your return, you will need to complete an embarkation form and have your passport stamped before you board the boat and leave Morocco.

Some holiday companies offer packages whereby you can travel from, for example, London or

Paris to Morocco via train services combined with a ferry crossing. Eurostar runs between London and Paris, and a fast TGV rail service operated by SNCF links the French capital with Algeciras. Visitors also arrive by cruise ships that regularly pull into ports along the Atlantic Ocean coast, such as Casablanca. Morocco has around 30 ports receiving visitors by cruise ship or ferry daily.

GETTING AROUND
By Airplane

Getting around Morocco by airplane is relatively straightforward, and most of the regions' larger towns have their own airports. The Cherif Al Idrissi Airport serves Al Hoceima on the Mediterranean coast, while Nador International Airport serves Nador a few miles away. Mogador Airport serves Essaouira on the Atlantic coast. There are other airports, too. Angads Airport serves Oujda; Ouarzazate has its own airport; and the smaller airports like Hassan I Airport in Laâyoune and Dakhla Airport in Dakhla in the south all have services from the main cities.

Services are provided by the national carrier **Royal Air Maroc** (*www.royalairmaroc.com*), its budget offshoot, **Atlas Blue,** or smaller private companies like **Regional Air Lines,** which is based in Casablanca and runs routes from the city to Spain and the regional airports. Many of the country's smaller airports run on a seasonal basis, among them Tan-Tan Airport in Western Sahara, Tétouan's Sania Ramel Airport, and Goulimine (Guelmin) Airport serving the southern city of Goulimine.

By Car

A great way to see Morocco is by car. There are many companies offering car rental in Morocco. International names like **Avis**

(*www.avis.ma*) and **Hertz** (*www .hertz.com*) are complemented by Moroccan firms with networks around the country. Among the companies offering car rental are **4x4 Driver** in Marrakech (*tel 0524/43 31 80*), **Caf Car** in Rabat (*tel 0537/77 54 88*), **Abid Rent a Car** in Agadir (*tel 0528/ 84 70 30*), **Allo Auto** in Casablanca (*tel 0522/25 25 87*), and **KB Car** in Laâyoune (*tel 0528/89 24 24*). A comprehensive list of car hire companies can be found on the Moroccan National Tourist Office's website (*www.visitmorocco.com*). Renting a car is expensive, but as there is so much competition, it is possible to negotiate a better deal. Be sure you have adequate insurance coverage.

The rules of the road are based on the French system, with vehicles driving on the right and giving way to vehicles on the right. This rule applies to traffic circles, too; you must give way to any vehicles already on the traffic circle. In terms of speed limits, be sure to keep to 40 kph (25 mph) in built-up areas unless directed otherwise, 100 kph (60 mph) on open roads, and 120 kph (74 mph) on highways; be aware that fines are hefty if you are caught exceeding these limits.

Even if you do not exceed the limits, you may find yourself being stopped and fined anyway by the rare, but extremely annoying, policemen who collect fines for their back pocket rather than for the state. No matter what the circumstances, however, the easiest and simplest option is to pay the fine immediately. These fines are rarely more than around 200 dirhams (around $25).

If you are planning to drive in urban areas, be prepared for lengthy delays caused by the sheer volume of vehicles, trucks, and bicycles. You can drive around most areas of cities, and even some medinas, but some streets may be extremely narrow and mazelike, so it is best to have a good local map with you. Highways and main roads are generally in good repair and well signposted, especially in the north. They can take you long distances with some stunning views to enjoy. If you intend to explore more isolated areas, you will find that many roads are little more than dirt tracks. It is best to have a four-wheel-drive vehicle and ensure that someone knows where and when you will be going. Driving in the desert is not advisable without the supervision of a guide.

When parking in most larger towns and cities, don't be surprised if you catch the attention of a parking attendant patrolling the area. He (probably not she) will be wearing a badge issued by the local authority and will help you park, watch your vehicle while you are away, and then help you when you leave. It is generally expected that you will wish to offer a few dirhams for his services, depending on the length he has looked after your vehicle. As a rough guide, allow around two dirhams per hour. This practice makes the theft of cars or personal items left inside rare in Morocco, so it is a small price to pay for peace of mind when you leave your car to explore a town.

You will find all types of fuel are readily available in towns and cities, but less so in rural areas, so be sure to fill up your tank before starting out on your journey. If you are involved in an accident, always call the police and wait for them to arrive. They will take control, assess the situation, and provide you with a written statement for your insurers, as well as help you return to your hotel or car rental company.

By Taxi

Taxis tend to take two forms. The first type is the larger vehicles,

usually old Mercedes saloons, seen outside hotels and airports. These vehicles, known as *grand taxis,* can accommodate groups of up to seven individuals (this sounds implausible, but it's common practice). Rather than ferrying you to where you ask to go, grand taxis usually run between towns and cities. They can be hired for pre-planned excursions, but they do not have a meter, so you should agree on a fare before you travel. Allow around 250 dirhams for a half day's hire, although if the driver has been especially helpful, you might like to add a little more at the end of the hire period. On routine trips between towns, you may be asked to share the taxi, and its cost, with others wishing to make the trip at the same time as you. This is common practice and helps reduce the cost of travel dramatically.

The other form of taxi is the *petit taxi*. These are smaller and cheaper, and by far the best option to get around town easily. They are identified by a sign on their roof that reads "petit taxi," and should be fitted with a meter. Check that the meter is switched on when you start your journey. A straightforward trip across town should cost no more than 10 dirhams, but the driver will expect you to pay in cash, so have plenty of coins handy. You may also find that the driver stops en route to pick up other passengers, but this should lower the fare you are charged.

Petit taxis can be hailed in the street or found in taxi ranks. It is not usually necessary to telephone for a taxi, but your hotel reception will assist should you need a taxi to, for example, take you from the hotel to the airport at a specific time to catch a flight.

By Bus

Buses operate in the main towns and cities and are an inexpensive

way to get from one side of a city to the other, or from one major town to another. Short trips will be just a few dirhams, so have plenty of small change with you to pay the driver as you step on board. Its destination is almost always written in Arabic, so finding the right one to board may be difficult. Traveling by bus is not the most comfortable mode of transport; buses are, however, very cheap, and they can be a great way to mingle with the locals.

Bus stations can be found in all the main cities and towns, and even in most smaller towns. They tend to be signposted and easy to find, and staff are generally helpful with advice. Here you can get timetables and tickets. Be aware that bus stations are also favorite haunts of touts and thieves, so make sure that you give money only to uniformed workers—preferably those behind desks or in kiosks. Bus services are operated by a number of companies, including the CTM group of companies (*www.ctm.ma*), Supratours' agencies, Gare Routiere, and Pullman du Sud.

By Train

Morocco has a good railroad network linking Tanger in the north with the cities of Rabat and Casablanca along the coast, and from there to the inland cities of Fès and Marrakech. Trains used for longer journeys are generally modern, clean, and air-conditioned, while commuter trains and short-distance services tend to be none of these things. The system is fast, efficient, and run to a tight schedule. On the most popular routes—such as Casablanca to Tanger, which takes around three hours, or Casablanca to Marrakech, which takes two hours—the trains depart several times a day.

There are classes of seats, and for longer journeys it is possible to purchase a ticket allowing you access to the compartments where seats convert to beds or couchettes. The operator ONCF *(tel 0890/20 30 40, www.oncf.ma)* has offices and rail stations in the major towns and cities where timetables and tickets can be purchased, or you can buy tickets from the railway station on the day of travel or in advance of your journey. Tickets are relatively inexpensive (although this depends on the class of travel you prefer) and concessionary tickets are available for families and groups.

You should ensure you travel in your chosen class of compartment, and have your ticket with you for your journey, as it will be inspected. If you cannot show your ticket, you will be required to purchase another. If, in fact, you had not purchased one, perhaps because of boarding a train as it was about to leave a station, then it is acceptable to buy tickets on board, but they will always be more expensive.

Railway stations are typically located in the downtown areas of a city's *ville nouvelle* (new town) district. While some of the bigger cities have a limited suburban rail system, most towns have only one station, so they're not hard to find.

PRACTICAL ADVICE
Communication
Internet Access
Morocco has one of the most advanced telecom networks on the African continent and a rapidly growing base of Internet users. Hotels, cafés, and restaurants may have wireless networks, although this is less common outside urban areas. Because the cost of an Internet connection is still too high for many households, Internet cafés are common. Charges based on the length of time the computer is connected to the Internet can vary, as can the quality of the connection. Check the rate before you connect and make a note of the time so you can calculate how long

you have used the computer.

Maroc Telecom launched a 3G service in 2008, providing high-speed data connections for smart phones and 3G-enabled laptops. Méditel offers a rival service, which uses a different transmission method that is incompatible with Maroc Telecom's network. At the moment, the 3G network is only available in urban areas and tends to slow down on weekends and evenings. Although both Maroc Telecom and Méditel have arrangements that allow visitors to use their 3G network, it is not advisable to do so, as phone companies typically levy extremely high rates for overseas 3G use. For just 200 dirhams ($23), however, you can buy a Maroc Telecom SIM card that provides unlimited 3G access for one month. These cards can be bought from Téléboutiques and other shops that sell phone cards.

The Internet is censored to an extent in Morocco. Access to major websites, such as YouTube, is occasionally blocked for short periods, often with no publicly stated reason. Websites relating to the Polisario Front and the conflict in Western Sahara are the most commonly censored, as well as those that advocate militant Islam or criticize the monarchy. For everyday use, however, it is unlikely you will notice any difference.

Post Offices
You can buy stamps, send telegrams and faxes, and mail letters and parcels at all post offices. All major towns and cities, and many villages, have post offices that are generally open from 8:30 a.m. to 6 p.m. or 6:30 p.m. Smaller post offices may be open mornings only. Stamps can also be purchased at tobacconists, newspaper kiosks, and most hotel receptions. It is better to post your letter at a main postbox adjoining a post office rather than in one of the yellow boxes found in the street,

where collections can be unreliable. Urgent or important packages can be sent by courier companies, such as FedEx or DHL Express.

Telephones
In the towns and cities, public telephone boxes are usually found outside bus stations, post offices, and railway stations, and outside similar public buildings in rural villages. The national operator Maroc Telecom has embraced the concept of telephone cafés, charmingly known as Téléboutiques, where there are many telephone booths, with an attendant who sells phone cards. Here you can also send faxes. Although they are quite popular, they are generally found only in city centers.

Public telephones have traditionally only been coin operated, but the use of phone cards is fast becoming the preferred and most practical way to make calls, especially long-distance or international calls. Phone cards can be purchased at post offices or any outlets showing the phone card sign.

Morocco's cell phone network is well developed and fairly reliable, although phone reception can be harder to get in rural areas. The two operators—Maroc Telecom and Méditel—provide reliable service. The two have arrangements with most major operators around the world so that visitors wishing to use their own mobile or cell phone should find their service is supported. Calls made and received using supported non-Moroccan networks are likely to be expensive, however. An alternative is to buy a SIM card from either operator, which will give you a local number and can be placed in your own phone to make as many local or international calls as you wish until you have reached the credit limit of your card. There are different credit levels available.

To telephone Morocco, use the

country code of 212 followed by the area code without the leading 0 and the six digit local number. If phoning a Moroccan number from within Morocco, the leading 0 should be dialed. To dial internationally from Morocco, dial 00 followed by the country code and the local telephone number.

The system for area codes has recently been updated from three to four digits, making Moroccan phone numbers 10 digits long. You may encounter numbers written in the previous format on signs, stationery, and listings that have not been updated. Numbers that previously started with the digits 02 or 03 now start with 052 or 053. Similarly numbers that started with the digits 08 or 09 now start with 080 and 089, respectively. For area codes that start with other numbers, (e.g., 05 or 07), the number 6 is added, making 065 or 067.

Conversions
1 kilogram = 2.2 pounds
1 liter = 0.2 U.S. gallon
1 meter = 1.1 yards (3.3 feet)
1 kilometer = 0.6 mile

Electricity
Electricity: 220 volts. The plugs used in Morocco are the same round two-pin type used in most of Europe. Adaptors are required, but relatively easy to find.

Etiquette & Local Customs
Most Moroccans are Muslims, and their customs and traditions should be treated with respect. The most important event in the Muslim calendar is Ramadan, a holy month during which Muslims fast during daylight hours. Non-Muslims are not expected to fast, but should be aware that during Ramadan cafés and restaurants may open at different times.

If you are invited to dine in a person's home, always dress smartly, arrive promptly, take a small gift of fruits, pastries, or nuts—never alcohol unless you know whether your host drinks or not—and be prepared to remove your shoes. Do not offer anyone a gift or money for a purchase with your left hand, which is considered the height of bad manners.

Guides
If you are engaging the services of a guide, ask to see their permit. They should also be wearing a badge. Guides as well as drivers and their vehicles are checked by their local authority to ensure their knowledge and service is up to standard, and a permit given for the year. Each city or district is responsible for issuing permits, so if, for instance, you hire a guide to show you around Fès, check that his or her permit was issued by the Fès authority. That way, your guide should be knowledgeable on the sights. Spontaneous checks are made by the police, but assuming your guide has all his or her paperwork in order, there is no need to worry if your party is stopped.

Health
One of the most common health problems you are likely to experience in Morocco is a stomach upset, resulting from a change of diet or from contaminated food. Avoid fruit, salads, and vegetables unless they have been washed with purified water, and do not drink tap water, even in the cities. Consume only bottled water, and always check that the bottle was sealed and is opened in front of you. Avoid ice cubes and any fruit drinks that are made with water. Take water purification tablets with you on treks to ensure you are always drinking water that is safe.

Holidays
Moroccans enjoy a number of public holidays. On these days, many businesses and some restaurants will be closed, roads may be more congested, and the beaches will be busier. The most important of these holidays is the Feast of the Throne, a day of national celebration on the anniversary of Mohamed VI's accession to the throne.

January 1—New Year's Day
January 11—Anniversary of the Declaration of Independence
May 1—Labor Day
July 30—Feast of the Throne
August 14—Fête Oued Eddahab (Oued Eddahab Allegiance Day)
August 20—Révolution du Roi et du Peuple (Anniversary of the King and the People's Revolution)
August 21—King Mohamed VI's Birthday
November 6—Marche Verte (Anniversary of the Green March)
November 18—Fête de l'Indépendance (Independence Day)

In addition, there are several religious public holidays each year. These are Mouloud, a festival to mark the Prophet's birthday; Aïd al-Adha, the Feast of the Sacrifice; Fatih Moharam, the Muslim New Year; and Aïd al-Fitr, which marks the end of Ramadan, a month of fasting. Because the months of the Islamic lunar calendar drift in relation to the seasons, dates of these holidays vary. For the next few years, Mouloud will fall in February, Aïd al Adha in November or October, Fatih Moharam in November, and Aïd al-Fitr in August.

Liquor Laws
The consumption of alcohol is acceptable, and it can be purchased at supermarkets, hotels, and

restaurants. If you are dining with a local family, be sure to respect their wishes if they choose not to drink wine or spirits.

During Ramadan, many liquor stores close, and some restaurants stop serving alcohol. It should also be noted that some visitors who look like they might be locals (particularly those of North African or Middle Eastern descent) may be refused alcohol during Ramadan if they cannot prove their nationality. This is because many local authorities prohibit the sale of alcohol to Moroccan Muslims during the month of Ramadan.

Media

There are two main television companies: the government-owned Radio Télévision Marocaine (RTM), which operates Television Marocaine TVM and broadcasts in Arabic and French, and 2M, which is partially state owned and broadcasts predominantly in French. These two companies operate a satellite channel aimed at Moroccans who live abroad, called Al Maghribiya. Morocco has embraced satellite television, with dishes seen on hotels, restaurants, and many private homes. Viewers can pick up a vast choice of international channels, along with the privately owned Moroccan satellite channels that are springing up, such as Medi 1 Sat based in Tanger.

Morocco has several national radio stations, broadcasting everything from political debate to popular music. Their programs are in Arabic, French, or Berber, with some stations broadcasting in a mixture of languages. Typically radio stations operate on different frequencies in different towns, so it can be hard to keep track of a single station while traveling. Most stations have detailed broadcast information on their websites. Popular stations include Atlantic Radio (*www.atlanticradio.ma*), Medi1

(*www.medi1.com*), and Chada (*www.chadafm.net*).

Newspapers are numerous and varied, with the government-owned *Al Anbaa* and the French-language *Le Matin* being among the most popular dailies. There are a few privately owned dailies, too, including the Arabic-language *Al Massae* and *Assabah* and the French-language *Libération, Le Journal,* and *Telquel. L'Economiste* is the business daily.

Money Matters

The currency of Morocco is the dirham (MAD), which is divided into 100 centimes (sometimes referred to as santimat or francs). It comes in bills of 20, 50, 100, and 200 dirhams, and coins of 1, 2, 5, and 10 dirhams. There are also coins for 1, 5, 10, and 20 centimes.

There is no limit on the amount of foreign currency that can be imported into the country, but the importation or exportation of the Moroccan dirham is strictly prohibited. *Bureaux de change* and ATMs can be found in the airports, as well as most cities, banks, and some hotels. When changing money, you will almost certainly be expected to show your passport. Remember to change your money back again at the end of your stay. If you have more than 50 percent of the original amount exchanged to change back, it may be confiscated by customs officials. Credit cards are not widely used in Morocco, with only large tourist-oriented businesses accepting them.

Opening Times

In the larger towns and cities, most shops selling such items as clothes or household goods open from 9 a.m. to around 7 p.m. or 8 p.m. with an extended break of a few hours for lunch. Food shops tend to keep similar hours, except during Ramadan when they are likely to

open early, close for much of the day, and open again after dark. The larger supermarket-style shops that are appearing in some cities usually keep long hours. Most open from 9 a.m. to around 9 p.m. in the evening, seven days a week.

Souks and fruit markets operate from early morning to around midday, while post offices are usually open 8:30 a.m. to 6 p.m. or 6:30 p.m., with smaller post offices opening in the mornings only. Banks typically open from 8:30 a.m. to midday and again in the afternoon until around 4 p.m., Monday to Thursday. On Friday and during Ramadan, times are variable. Traditional trading days are Monday to Thursday, with selected shops open Friday to Sunday. Friday is a day of rest for Muslims, Saturday is the Sabbath observed by Morocco's Jewish population, and Sunday is the day most businesses are closed.

Religion

Morocco is an Islamic country, and the vast majority of its people are Muslim. Muslims pray five times a day, and you may be woken by the call to prayer. Ramadan is the most important time of the year. It lasts a month, and its timing varies from one year to the next based on the Islamic lunar calendar. Followers fast from sunrise to sunset, and you may find that some restaurants are closed during the day.

Rest Rooms

Finding a public rest room can be a bit hit and miss, and if you do manage to find one, it often can be rather primitive. It is by far the best option to use your hotel's more modern amenities before you leave, and then visit restaurants and cafés during the day. A good idea is to have some toilet paper with you, and a water-free hand sterilizer or wet wipes to wash your hands.

Time Differences

Morocco is on Greenwich mean time (five hours ahead of eastern standard time), with the exception of the Spanish enclaves of Melilla and Ceuta which are on Spanish time (six hours ahead of eastern standard time).

Tipping

A service charge is not automatically included in restaurant bills, although you may find in cities like Agadir that it is. It is best to leave change on the table so that it reaches the person for whom you intended it. The easiest way to show gratitude to a taxi driver is to round up the fare, while for chambermaids or porters 10 dirhams or so should do the trick. Tipping is, however, entirely discretionary.

Travelers with Disabilities

Travelers with disabilities may find Morocco a challenge. Uneven and often broken pathways, tiny entrances to buildings in its medinas, and palaces and mausoleums with steep steps rather than ramps are some of the hazards. Moroccans are helpful, though, and will assist anyone needing help. The country is changing. Brand new resorts and hotels are now introducing amenities like wheelchair-friendly entrances and specially designed rest rooms. Restaurant owners, too, are making their establishments easier for visitors with limited movement. Provision of facilities for visitors with limited sight and hearing, however, is still in its infancy.

Visitor Information

There are tourist information offices to be found in all the major cities in Morocco and overseas. They can assist with accommodations, tours, and information.

Visit the country's official tourism website (www.visitmorocco.com) for more details.

Canada

1800 Avenue McGill College
Suite 2450
Montreal, Quebec H3A 3JG
Canada
Tel (514) 842-8111
Fax (514) 842-5316
info@tourismemarocain.ca
www.tourismemarocain.ca

United Kingdom

205 Regent Street
London W1B 4HB0
UK
Tel (020) 7437 0073
Fax (020) 7734 8172
mnto@morocco-tourism.org.uk
www.visitmorocco.org

United States of America

104 W. 40th Street
Suite 1820
New York, NY 10018
USA
Tel (0212) 221-1583
Fax (0212) 221-1887
rachid.maaninou@mnto-usa.org
www.visitmorocco.com

EMERGENCIES

Crime & Police

Morocco is by and large a safe country, with crime usually involving petty theft rather than violent behavior. It relies heavily on tourism, and the safety of visitors is considered a priority. Great strides have been made to ensure visitors' trips are as carefree as possible. For example, tourist police are stationed in every city with the aim of keeping an unobtrusive watch and acting on any incidences that may cause alarm to visitors. One such issue is likely to be street sellers who often target tourists thinking they'll be an easy sale, but they are really more of a nuisance than a threat. Simply walk away

with a polite no. Anyone caught committing a serious crime is severely reprimanded, which in itself is a deterrent. Morocco has seen terrorist activity in the past, but is generally considered a politically stable country.

Embassies & Consulates in Morocco

Most of the major countries of the world have an embassy in Morocco. Be sure to find out where your embassy is before you travel and keep a note of its telephone number in case you run into problems during your stay. Embassies can assist you should you lose your passport or visa or encounter any serious problems during your stay. Among them are:

Canada

Embassy of Canada
13 Bis Jaafar As-Sadik
Agdal, Rabat
Tel (0537) 68 74 00
Fax (0537) 68 74 30
rabat@international.gc.ca

United Kingdom

British Embassy in Rabat
28 Avenue SAR Sidi Mohamed
Soussi, Rabat
Tel (0537) 63 33 33
Email: rabat.consular@fco.gov.uk

British Consulate-General in Casablanca
Villa Les Sallurges
36 Rue de la Loire Polo
Casablanca
Tel (0522) 85 74 00
british.consulate2@menara.ma

British Consulate in Tanger
Trafalgar House
9 rue de l'Amerique du Sud Tanger
Tel (0539) 93 69 39
uktanger2@menara.ma

British Honorary Consulate in Marrakech

Résidence Taib
55 boulevard Zerktouni, Guéliz
Marrakech
Tel (0524) 42 08 46
Fax (0524) 43 52 76
matthew.virr@fco.gov.uk

United States of America
U.S. Embassy in Rabat
2 Avenue de Mohamed el Fassi
Rabat
Tel (0537) 76 22 65
ircrabat@usembassy.ma

American Consulate in Casablanca
8 boulevard Moulay Youssef
Casablanca
Tel (0522) 20 41 27
acscasablanca@state.gov

Emergency Telephone Numbers
Police 19
Fire Department 150
Directory Inquiries 160
Road Safety Services 177

FURTHER READING
Morocco has been widely written
about over the years, and there
are many books to choose from.
Here are a few suggested titles.

Nonfiction
History & Culture
*Allah's Garden: A True Story of a
Forgotten War in the Sahara
Desert of Morocco* by Thomas
Hollowell (2009)
The Conquest of Morocco by
Douglas Porch (2005)
*Dreams of Trespass: Tales of
a Harem Girlhood* by Fatima
Mernissi (1995)
In Morocco by Edith Wharton
(1920)
Morocco That Was by Walter
Harris (1921)
Popular Culture in the Arab World by
Andrew Hammond (2007)
*Return to Childhood: The Memoir
of a Modern Moroccan Woman*
by Leila Abouzeid (1993)

*Skeletons on the Zahara: A True
Story of Survival* by Dean King
(2004)

Nature
*Morocco Fauna and Wide Open
Spaces* by Joudia Hassar-
Benslimane (2010)
*Prion Birdwatchers' Guide to
Morocco* by Patrick Bergier and
Fedora Bergier (2003)
Sahara: A Natural History by
Marq de Villiers and Sheila
Hirtle (2002)

Outdoors
*Climbing in the Moroccan Anti-Atlas:
Tafroute and Jebel el Kest* by
Claude Davies (2004)
*Morocco Overland: 45 Routes from
the Atlas to the Sahara* by
Chris Scott (2009)
*The Mountains of the Mediterranean
World* by John Robert McNeill
(2003)
Rock Climbing Atlas by Wynard
Groenewegen Marloes van
den Berg and Daniel Jaeggi
(2007)
Trekking in the Atlas Mountains by
Karl Smith (2004)

Travel
*The Caliph's House: A Year in
Casablanca* by Tahir Shah
(2006)
*Glory in a Camel's Eye: A Perilous
Trek Through the Greatest
African Desert* by Jeffrey Tayler
(2005)
*A House in Fez: Building a Life in
the Ancient Heart of Morocco* by
Suzanna Clarke (2008)
*In Arabian Nights: A Caravan of
Moroccan Dreams* by Tahir
Shar (2009)
Quest for the Kasbah by Richard
Bangs (2009)
Sahara by Michael Palin (2005)
Stealing Fatima's Hand by
Carolyn A. Theriault (2010)
Taming the Sahara by Andrew
Borowiec (2003)

Fiction
Folk Tales from Morocco by Raja
Sharma (2010)
*Hope and Other Dangerous
Pursuits* by Laila Lalami (2005)
Leaving Tangier: A Novel by
Tahar Ben Jelloun (2009)
The Sheltering Sky by Paul
Bowles (1949)
The Spider's House by Paul
Bowles (1955)
Year of the Elephant by Leila
Abouzeid (1983)

Online Resources
There are many active Moroccan
bloggers online today, writing on
a wide range of subjects from
cinema to postcolonial politics.
The vast majority of these bloggers, however, write in either
French or Arabic. If you're curious
about Moroccan politics, culture,
or society as seen by these uncen-
sored young writers, go to **Global
Voices Morocco** *(www.globalvoices
online.org/-/world/middle-east
-north-africa/morocco)* where trans-
lations of discussions and articles
are frequently published from the
Moroccan online world.

Hotels & Restaurants

Morocco has a wide range of places to stay or eat, and the selection given in this book is limited to some of the best or most interesting choices in varied price ranges. There are many other places that are just as good, and lack of a listing here does not mean you should not stay or eat there.

Hotels

Accommodation in Morocco comes in a variety of different forms, each suited to individual budgets or tastes. The cheapest options in most towns are pensions—small hostel-like hotels with shared bathrooms and sometimes no hot water for showers. While often pretty grim places to stay, these establishments are usually positioned right in the center of town and are often cheaper than a plot in a campsite. En suite rooms in more conventional hotels range in price from just a little more than a pension to prices that wouldn't be out of place in a European city.

In many towns and cities you will find small, family-run establishments known as *riads*. Riads are guesthouses in historic properties located in medinas. Most will have a small courtyard garden, which provides a great place to relax. In the past, a riad might have been the home of a government official or a wealthy merchant. These guesthouses have typically been tastefully renovated to incorporate modern amenities while retaining original decorative and architectural features.

Away from major urban centers or coastal resorts, more informal guesthouses, known as *gîtes d'étape* and *auberges*, are common. These places are often self-catering and are used most by hikers traveling cross-country.

The star rating system used in Morocco reflects what functioning amenities a hotel has, and as such is not necessarily an indicator of the quality of the service or the state of the rooms. A hotel with a restaurant or a swimming pool will always receive a higher star rating than one without, regardless of the hotel's overall condition. The star ratings are checked fairly regularly by the Moroccan National Tourist Office.

Restaurants

Morocco's choice of restaurants can be varied in the larger towns and cities, with local cuisine complementing dishes from around the world. You will find French, Italian, and Asian restaurants, along with an increasing number of American-style fast-food eateries. Vegetarians are unlikely to find a restaurant serving only nonmeat dishes, but most venues will happily cater for vegetarian diners, although not so much vegan or other diets.

Street stalls are a common sight in the cities and market towns. Here you will find kebabs of skewered meat and *bocadillos,* a Spanish sandwich filled with salad and meat. There are also sweet snacks like almond-flavored biscuits called *faqqas, sfenj* dough balls covered in sugar and honey, and *halwa shebakia,* a cake made with honey.

The choice of restaurants and informal eateries in tourist areas can be plentiful, but the cuisine tends to be more European with just a hint of Moroccan. Most hotels have a café or restaurant on site, as do some riads. Some smaller riads can also provide meals for guests if booked in advance, even if they do not have a restaurant as such.

Finding somewhere for breakfast can be a bit of a problem, as most restaurants open mid-morning for the lunch period of noon to 3 p.m., or later for evening dining only. Dinner is usually from around 7 p.m. to 10:30 p.m.

Organization & Abbreviations

Hotels and restaurants are organized by chapter, then by price and then in alphabetical order, with hotels first followed by restaurants. Few businesses other than hotel and restaurant chains accept credit cards.

Abbreviations used: AE (American Express), DC (Diner's Club), MC (MasterCard), V (Visa).

PRICES

HOTELS
The cost of a double room with private bath and hot water in the peak season is given by **$** signs. Low season rates can be considerably lower.

$$$$$	over $200
$$$$	$100–$200
$$$	$50–$100
$$	$25–$50
$	Under $25

RESTAURANTS
The average cost of a two-course meal for one person, without tax, tip, or drinks, is given by **$** signs.

$$$$$	over $50
$$$$	$40–$50
$$$	$25–$40
$$	$15–$25
$	Under $15

CASABLANCA & THE COAST

BENISLIMANE

🍽 LE RYAD DU VIGNERON
$$$
DOMAINE DES OULED THALED
TEL (0523) 29 84 66
This elegant country house restaurant, surrounded by vineyards, lies only a short journey from Casablanca. The chic restaurant is famous for its fine wines and local Moroccan dishes served with a French twist. It has great views from its poolside terrace to the verdant countryside beyond. A wonderfully relaxing place to spend an evening away from the bustle of the city. Reservations essential for lunch and dinner.

🪑 60 🅿 💲 🔏 All major cards

CASABLANCA

HOTELS

🏨 HYATT REGENCY CASABLANCA
$$$$$
PLACE DES NATIONS UNIES
TEL (0522) 43 12 34
FAX (0522) 43 13 34
casablanca.regency
.hyatt.com
This branch of the international Hyatt chain is located in the heart of Casablanca, not far from the city's ancient medina. The Regency is not somewhere to go if you're looking for something authentically Moroccan, but the cool, well-maintained rooms, polite staff, and excellent amenities will be much appreciated by those recovering from a stressful airplane journey or a hot day walking around the town.

🛈 255 🅿 💲 🔏 ⛵ 🌡
🔏 All major cards

🏨 ROYAL MANSOUR MÉRIDIEN
$$$$$
27 AVENUE DEL ARMÉE ROYALE
TEL (0522) 31 30 11
FAX (0522) 54 07 84
www.leroyalmansour
meridien.com
With their impressive views of Casablanca's busy harbor and the towering minaret of the Hassan II Mosque, the rooms in this luxurious hotel really make you appreciate the hotel's position in the heart of the city. In addition to the views, the rooms are pleasant and well maintained, with spacious bathrooms and comfortable beds. The hotel has many excellent amenities, but it should be noted that access to some of these costs extra.

🛈 186 🅿 💲 🔏 🕸 🌡
🔏 All major cards

🏨 BEST WESTERN HOTEL TOUBKAL
$$$$
9 RUE SIDI BELYOUT
TEL (0522) 31 14 14
FAX (0522) 31 11 46
www.bestwestern.com
Located within walking distance of the ancient medina. The decor is modern with decorative touches from art deco and traditional Moroccan design. All the rooms are fully air-conditioned, with Wi-Fi, satellite television, and well maintained en suite bathrooms. The hotel has four nonsmoking floors, which is a welcome touch in Casablanca.

🛈 67 🅿 💲 🔏 🔏 All major cards

🏨 HOTEL LES SAISONS
$$$$
19 RUE ORAIBI JILALI
TEL (0522) 49 09 01
FAX (0522) 48 16 97
www.hotellessaisons
maroc.ma
Located only a few minutes' walk from the medina, this hotel provides luxurious accommodation with a little more charm and character than its corporate rivals. The staff is friendly and attentive, and the prices are very competitive. The rooms come in three different types: standard, superior, and deluxe. The standard rooms are comfortable, well equipped, and clean, but the size and quality of decoration increases dramatically if you go for one of the more expensive rooms.

🛈 48 🅿 💲 🔏 🌡 🔏 All major cards

🏨 JNANE SHERAZADE
$$$$
8 RUE DE BELGRADE
TEL (0522) 29 45 51
www.jnanecasablanca.com
Housed in an attractive modernist villa in Casablanca's eastern suburbs, the Jnane Sherazade is decorated with a pleasing mixture of modern and traditional styles. The rooms are comfortable and spacious, and all have en suite bathrooms. The junior suite, which looks onto the garden, is wheelchair accessible—something of a rarity in small Moroccan hotels even today.

🛈 8 💲 🔏 Cash only

🏨 RAMADA LES ALMOHADES CASABLANCA
$$$$
AVENUE MOULAY HASSAN II
TEL (0522) 82 17 65
FAX (0522) 26 02 42
Another pleasant hotel that caters to Casablanca's international business travelers. Inside the unassuming building, the rooms are clean and spacious, the staff professional and efficient. Discounted rates can be found if you book during the quiet times of the year.

🛈 138 🅿 💲 🔏 🔏 All major cards

🏨 DAR ITRIT
$$$
9 RUE RESTINGA
TEL (0522) 36 02 58
FAX (0522) 36 03 40
www.daritrit.ma
Positioned in the quiet, leafy suburbs not far from the city's international airport, this small friendly guesthouse has the feel of a private home. Dar Itrit was converted from a 1940s colonial villa in 2004. Guests are greeted with cold drinks (sometimes even beer and wine) and helpful advice on how to best experience the city from the multilingual owners. The rooms are comfortable and charmingly decorated, and if you choose to dine in, the home-cooked food is excellent. Wi-Fi is available in the communal areas, and there is an on-site public computer.
🛈 3 🎴 🗟 Cash only

🏨 HOTEL TRANSATLANTIQUE CASABLANCA
$$$
79 RUE CHAOUIA
TEL (0522) 29 45 51
FAX (0522) 29 47 92
www.transatcasa.com
Housed in a splendid art deco building in the heart of the city, the Transatlantique has been a Casablanca institution since 1922, housing famous guests like the French chanteuse Edith Piaf. On arrival you are greeted by a spectacular entrance hall complete with art deco lighting, onyx statues, and acres of gold and silver leaf. The rooms are less grand, but comfortable nonetheless. If you're a light sleeper, it's a good idea to get a room on one of the upper floors, away from the bars of this fairly noisy area.
🛈 75 🎴 🗟 MC, V

🏨 HOTEL GUYNEMER
$$
2 RUE MOHAMED BELLOUL
TEL (0522) 27 57 64
FAX (0522) 47 39 99
www.guynemerhotel.com
A reliable and friendly hotel with good service and comfortable rooms. For the price, the Guynemer's rooms are probably the best deal in the city. The hotel's small but well-managed restaurant serves a variety of traditional Moroccan dishes, and features live music by a Moroccan *oud* player on most nights. Be aware, however, that when the hotel is heavily booked, there is a chance you might get one of the hotel's smaller, stuffier rooms, so if possible, book in advance.
🛈 29 🎴 🅿 🗟 MC, V

RESTAURANTS

🍴 A MA BRETAGNE
$$$$$
BOULEVARD DE L'OCÉAN ATLANTIQUE, SIDI ABDERRAHMAN
TEL (0522) 39 79 79
A high-quality restaurant that recently celebrated its 50th anniversary, this eatery specializes in fish and seafood with mouthwatering sauces. The cuisine is almost entirely French, with a few more exotic dishes, such as those made with the house specialty, ostrich meat. For a special occasion, this restaurant is one of the best options in Casablanca. The interiors are beautifully decorated and attractively lit, and the staff discreet and helpful. The kitchens are run by the esteemed French chef André Halbert, who also presides over the well-stocked wine cellar.
🕒 Closed Sun. 🅿 🎴
🗟 All major cards

🍴 LA BAVAROISE
$$$$$
131/139 RUE ALLAL IDN ABDELLAH
TEL (0522) 31 17 60
www.bavaroise.ma
Popular with businesspeople and couples, this elegant restaurant is right in the city center near the commercial district. The brasserie-style menu and superb wine list reflect the tastes of its discerning owners, maitre'd Mehdi Touhami and French chef Bernard Bremond. Even in Casablanca, where the morning's catch makes its way to the city's plates within a few hours, the Bavaroise is known for the exceptional quality and freshness of its fish and seafood. Smart dress only. Reservations essential.
🕒 Closed Sun. 🎴 🗟 MC, V

🍴 LE PILOTIS
$$$$$
BOULEVARD DE LA CORNICHE
TEL (0522) 79 84 27
Located right in the center of the beachfront Corniche district, within the rambling buildings of the Tahiti Beach Club complex, this restaurant is famous for its original take on Mediterranean cuisine. Dance the calories off in its music lounge next door, which is open every day until late.
🎴 120 🅿 🗟 All major cards

🍴 LA MAISON DU GOURMET
$$$$
159 RUE TAHA HOUCINE, QUARTIER GAUTHIER
TEL (0522) 48 48 46
FAX (0522) 48 48 45
www.lamaisondugourmet.ma
With its minimalist, modern interiors and artfully presented contemporary cuisine, this restaurant has established itself as the place to be seen in Casablanca since its opening in 2006. The young head

chef and co-owner, Meryem Cherkaoui, is a native of nearby Rabat who learned her trade in France.

🕐 Closed Sun. 💳 🏧 All major cards

SOMETHING SPECIAL

🍽 OSTRÉA

$$$$

PORT DE PÊCHE

TEL (0522) 44 13 90

With its colorful decor that mixes navy blue and red with gold detailing, this upscale restaurant is as famous for its style as it is for its fine fish dishes. Here you can choose your fish before it's cooked. As you'd expect for a restaurant that places such pride on the freshness of its fish, it is located harborside.

🔢 40 💳 🏧 All major cards

🍽 LE QUAI DU JAZZ

$$$$

25 RUE AHMED EL MOKRI

TEL (0522) 94 25 37

This pricey bar/restaurant, with its bohemian styling and live music, is emblematic of the surprisingly harmonious coexistence of Casablanca's artistic and business communities. Like most restaurants in this city, the menu is dominated by French dishes and specializes in seafood and fish. The live jazz and trendy crowd make this an exciting and atmospheric place to spend an evening.

🕐 Closed Sun. 💳 🏧 All major cards

🍽 RICK'S CAFÉ

$$$$

248 BOULEVARD SOUR JDID

PLACE DU JARDIN PUBLIC

TEL (0522) 27 42 07

FAX (0522) 27 42 08

As a modern re-creation of the movie *Casablanca*'s principal setting, you'd be forgiven for thinking that Rick's Café is nothing more than a tacky tourist trap. While there is something a little weird about this painstaking reconstruction of a place that never existed (the inspiration for the movie's setting was actually a bar in the south of France, and the closest real-world equivalent was probably Dean's Bar in Tanger), the café is undoubtedly a work of love, filled with art deco decoration and period-correct details. The food is an eclectic mix of Moroccan, European, and American cuisine and the bar is well stocked with spirits, wines, and beers. And yes, there is a resident pianist (but his name isn't Sam).

💳 🏧 All major cards

🍽 LA BASMANE

$$$

BOULEVARD DE L'OCEAN ATLANTIQUE, AÏN DIAB

TEL (0522) 79 70 70

www.basmane -restaurant.com

La Basmane oozes North African character. The interior is decorated with traditional Moroccan features and resembles the beautiful courtyards and hallways of Marrakech's historic riads. Diners sit comfortably at large round tables, while traditional musicians and dancers perform. The menu is an award-winning selection of authentic Moroccan dishes, made with the finest, freshest local ingredients. As a result, it is no surprise that La Basmane is a favorite of locals and is popular with businesspeople at lunch time. Reservations are recommended. Smoking and nonsmoking sections are effectively divided.

💳 🏧 All major cards

🍽 LA SQALA

$$$

AVENUE DES ALMOHADS

TEL (0522) 26 09 60

If you're fresh off the plane and looking for an authentically Moroccan dish on your first night in the country, then La Sqala is a good choice. This delightful Moroccan restaurant is located within an old fortification, or *sqala*, built into Casablanca's old city walls alongside a craft boutique and a small art gallery. The menu features a mixture of international cuisine and more interesting Moroccan dishes, such as an excellent fish *tagine*. Meals are served in a beautiful garden area complete with Andalusian water fountains and a great view of the harbor.

🕐 Closed Mon. 🅿

🏧 All major cards

🍽 LA TOSCANA

$$$

7 RUE YAALA ALIFRANI RACINE

TEL (0522) 36 95 92

La Toscana is a popular, busy Italian restaurant. Light and airy, the stylish decor is modern. It offers a range of classic Italian dishes, including more simple pasta dishes and pizzas. There is also a tempting choice of desserts and a good wine list. The service is friendly and informed. Booking is advisable, particularly for dinner.

🏧 Cash only

🍽 KIOTORI

$$

8 RUE DU COMMISSAIRE LADEUIL

TEL (0522) 47 16 68

FAX (0522) 22 66 84

www.kiotori.com

Opened in late 2006, the Kiotori is rapidly building an excellent reputation in Casablanca for its authentic Japanese cuisine, particularly its excellent sushi lunches and artfully prepared seafood. The red-and-black minimalist decor befits the theme, and the service is impeccable.

🔌 40 🕐 🌀 All major cards

🍴 LA TAVERNE DU DAUPHIN
$$

115 BOULEVARD HOUPHOUET BOIGNY, EL HANSALI
TEL (0522) 27 79 79
FAX (0522) 22 15 51
www.taverne-du-dauphin.ma
This restaurant has been owned by the same French family since 1958. The interiors are a fascinating snapshot of chic vintage French design, little changed since the restaurant's opening. The menu is distinctively French, with few nods to local cuisine, and includes an excellent selection of fish and seafood dishes. Reservations are recommended, as this popular restaurant is often packed by the early evening.

🕐 🌀 MC, V

EL JADIDA (MAZAGAN)

🏨 LE PALAIS ANDALOU
$$

BOULEVARD PASTEUR
TEL (0523) 34 37 45
Housed in a beautiful turn-of-the-century palace, this hotel is a fascinating place to spend the night. While the palace doesn't receive the maintenance and care that it deserves, it's still a beautiful building. The rooms have a traditional Moroccan feel, although the furnishings are all a little dated. Well-cooked meals are served in the courtyard garden.

🛈 28 🅿 ⬇ 🕐 🌀 All major cards

MOHAMMEDIA

🏨 HOTEL JNANE FEDALA
$$$

6 RUE ABDERRHMANE SERGHINI
TEL (0523) 32 69 00
www.jnane-fedala.com
This modern hotel does a good impression of the style you'll see in the authentic riads of Marrakech, Fès, and Tanger. The simple, clean rooms are enlivened with brightly colored fabrics and densely patterned wall hangings. Located on the Atlantic coast about halfway between Rabat and Casablanca, the hotel is well situated for excursions to either city.

🛈 70 🅿 ⬇ 🌀 MC, V

🏨 HOTEL HAGER
$$

AVENUE FERHAT HACHARD
TEL (0523) 32 59 21
FAX (0523) 32 59 29
www.hotelhager.ma
This simple and plain little hotel provides uncomplicated and comfortable modern rooms, all with en suite bathrooms. The interiors are modern, but do have occasional distinctively Moroccan touches. The hotel is located close to the center of town and only a few minutes' walk from the beach at Mohammedia. Its rooftop restaurant is well known for its great views out over the sea.

🛈 18 🅿 🕐 🌀 MC, V

🍴 RESTAURANT DU PORT
$$$$

1 RUE DU PORT
TEL (0523) 32 24 66
Recognized as one of the best gastronomy restaurants on the periphery of Casablanca, and the best in Mohammedia, this stylish eatery is right near the harbor. It specializes in fresh fish dishes and seafood that Moroccans travel far to enjoy. Taking advantage of their coastal location, the staff create an enticing range of dishes using locally sourced meat and fish.

Diners are often treated to performances by excellent local musicians on selected evenings.

🕐 Closed Mon. 🅿 🌀 All major cards

◼ RABAT

MOULAY BOUSSELHAM

🏨 LA MAISON DES OISEAUX
$$

BP 66, MOULAY BOUSSELHAM
TEL (0537) 43 25 43
This unique guesthouse is owned and operated by a French artist, Gentiane Dartigue, whose artwork decorates many of the rooms. Set within a lovely garden and boasting stunning sea views, the Maison des Oiseaux

is an ideal base for those heading across the water to the Merdja Zerga nature reserve. Although there is no formal restaurant, the staff are happy to prepare traditional dishes for the guests, made with locally caught fish and seafood.

🚹 8 🅿 🏧 Cash only

🏨 VILLA NORA
$$
MOULAY BOUSSELHAM
TEL (0537) 43 20 71
Standing close to the serene waters of the Merdja Zerga nature reserve, this British-owned guesthouse is a relaxing and isolated place to spend a few days. The manager, Mustapha, can organize boat trips on the nearby lagoon for those who wish to go bird-watching.

🚹 6 🅿 🏧 Cash only

RABAT

HOTELS

🏨 DAR AL BATOUL
$$$$$
7 DERB JIRARI LAALOU, MEDINA
TEL (0537) 72 72 50
FAX (0537) 72 73 16
www.riadbatoul.com
This fine 18th-century mansion has been lovingly restored and made into a small luxury hotel. The one suite and eight rooms are all decorated in the traditional Moroccan style, and all have en suite bathrooms. The staff is attentive and the building well maintained (although the plumbing can be a little temperamental). The public spaces are sumptuously decorated and the hotel has its own hammam.

🚹 9 🎽 🏧 Cash only

🏨 LA TOUR HASSAN
$$$$$
26 RUE CHELLAH
TEL (0537) 23 90 00
FAX (0537) 72 54 08
www.latourhassan.com
This expensive hotel does a good job of reconciling authenticity with luxury. Some of the rooms are a little small for the price, but they're comfortable and interestingly decorated. The on-site facilities (including a gym and private hammam) are well maintained and have been recently renovated. The interiors manage to incorporate elements of Moroccan design and decoration without ever becoming fussy or cluttered.

🚹 140 🅿 🏧 🏊 🎽 🏧 All major cards

🏨 VILLA MANDARINE
$$$$$
19 RUE OULED BOUSBBA, SOUISSI
TEL (0537) 75 20 77
FAX (0537) 63 23 09
www.villamandarine.com
This exclusive boutique hotel is located about 20 minutes' drive outside of Rabat, not far from the prestigious Dar es Salaam golf club. The hotel is set within more than 3 acres of lush gardens and orchards, with public terraces, living rooms, and a well-equipped gym and spa. Each of the rooms and suites is individually decorated using a color palette derived from a work of art and has a private terrace screened off from the public spaces by dense vegetation. The hotel's lovely restaurant is run by Michelin-starred chef Wolfgang Grobauer and serves a menu of inventive modern dishes, cooked using fresh local meat and seafood.

🚹 36 rooms 🅿 🏧 🎽 🏧 All major cards

SOMETHING SPECIAL

🏨 ART RIAD
$$$$
16 RUE ESSAM, MEDINA
TEL (0537) 20 20 28
FAX (0537) 26 21 35
www.artriad.com
Located in the heart of the ancient medina, this recently opened riad is pack with cool, contemporary charm. The owner, Sebastian Manni, has chosen to decorate the rooms in a clean, modern style that manages to combine minimalist chic with the cozy comforts of Moroccan design. Although the rooms are rather small, the beds are comfortable and the decor thoughtfully personalized to the conditions of each room. The Art Riad is run in partnership with the slightly more expensive Riad Kalaa (see p. 280), just down the road, and guests at the Art Riad may use Kalaa's swimming pool, hammam, and restaurant if they wish.

🚹 5 🅿 🏧 MC, V

🏨 DAR ZAHOUR
$$$$
4 IMPASSE RUE D'BARGACH, MEDINA
TEL (0537) 70 68 97
FAX (0537) 70 10 02
www.darzahour.com
Located in the north of Rabat's medina, this lovingly restored riad offers a comfortable and relaxing place to stay within a few minutes' walk of all the major sights. The rooms are a little small, but all have en suite bathrooms and manage to feel cozy rather than cramped. Each of the rooms has its own unique decor, and a similar amount of care has been lavished on the interiors of the communal spaces. The riad also has a lovely roof terrace, a small hammam, and a beautiful courtyard.

🚹 5 🎽 🏧 Cash only

🚭 Nonsmoking ❄ Air-conditioning 🏊 Indoor Pool 🏊 Outdoor Pool 🎽 Health Club 🏧 Credit Cards

🏨 GOLDEN TULIP FARAH
$$$$

26 PLACE SIDI MAKHLOUF
TEL (0537) 23 74 00
www.goldentulipfarah
rabat.com

While expensive, this hotel provides a reliably high standard of service and accommodation. Part of a large international chain that also operates hotels in Marrakech and Casablanca, the Farah is an opulent resort, with a swimming pool, several restaurants, and a gym. The rooms are extremely comfortable if not terribly memorable, with neutral decor and generic furnishings. The world-class facilities mean that few people will want spend much time in the rooms.

🛏 192 P 🛗 🔲 🏊 📺
🔲 All major cards

🏨 HELNAN CHELLAH
$$$$

2 RUE D'IFNI
TEL (0537) 70 02 09
FAX (0537) 70 63 54
www.helnan.com

Owned and operated by Helnan, a Dutch company, this large hotel is housed in an unprepossessing modern building near the center of town. The rooms are clean, and the food served in the restaurant is a good balance of Moroccan and international cuisine. Popular with tour groups and short-stay tourists, this hotel provides an agreeable base from which to explore the city.

🛏 117 P 🛗 🔲 📺 🔲 MC, V

🏨 RIAD KALAA
$$$$

3–5 RUE ZEBDI, MEDINA
TEL (0537) 20 20 28
FAX (0537) 26 21 35
www.riadkalaa.com

This 200-year-old mansion in the heart of the medina was built by the Emir Ben Tachfine, an important figure in Rabat's history. It has been recently restored, using only local craftsmen and materials, to create a guesthouse on a par with anything Marrakech or Fès has to offer. Although some of the guest rooms are rather small, all are beautifully decorated and comfortable. Meals are served in the lovely courtyards and roof terraces, and the menu includes a wide variety of traditional Moroccan dishes. The Kalaa boasts several features that are unusual in a riad, such as a hammam, several large communal spaces, and even a rooftop swimming pool.

🛏 11 🔲 🏊 📺 🔲 MC, V

🏨 RIAD OUDAYA
$$$$

46 RUE SIDI FATEH
TEL (0537) 70 23 92
www.riadrabat.com

Located in the heart of Rabat's ancient medina, the Riad Oudaya is a beautifully restored old building with four comfortable and brightly decorated rooms. For the price, however, the rooms are a little small, and the lack of modern amenities such as air-conditioning can be a little unpleasant on warmer nights. Nonetheless, it is an authentic and romantic place to stay in a fantastic location.

🛏 4 🔲 Cash only

🏨 MAJLISS
$$$

6 RUE ZAHLA
TEL (0537) 73 37 26
FAX (0537) 73 37 31
www.majlisshotel.ma

This hotel is located in the center of the new town, very close to the train station and Moroccan government offices. The rooms, with their bulky furniture and slightly gloomy decor, are not going to win any design awards, but they are extremely comfortable and well kept. The chunky double-glazed windows keep out most of the sounds of this noisy city, making it one of the few places where you're almost guaranteed a decent night's sleep.

🛏 98 P 🛗 🔲 📺 🔲 MC, V

🏨 RIAD KASBAH
$$$

49 RUE ZIRARA, KASBAH DES OUDAÏAS
TEL (0537) 70 23 92
www.riadrabat.com

Run by the owners of the Riad Oudaya (see this page) in the southern medina, this small riad is located right in the heart of the medieval kasbah at the mouth of the Oued Bou Regreg. The rooms are clean and brightly decorated, but they are a little small and none are en suite. Despite its prime location, this riad's smaller rooms and less luxurious facilities mean that the rooms are significantly cheaper than its sister, the Oudaya.

🛏 4 🔲 Cash only

SOMETHING SPECIAL

🏨 RIAD MARHABA
$$$

3 RUE ES ÇAM, MEDINA
TEL (0537) 70 65 54
riadmarhaba.blogspot.com

Although it has only been open for a few years, this beautiful and charming little riad has quickly established a reputation as one of the best places to stay in Rabat. It has one fairly small guest room and three spacious suites, each with en suite bathrooms, Wi-Fi, and stunning traditional decor. The riad is arranged around a central courtyard, surrounded by balconies and ornately carved stonework. Meals are served either in the courtyard or on the lovely roof terrace, which has comfortable furnishings, a great view, and plenty of cool places to sit in the shade. The owners, Fred and Cécile, as well as their staff, provide attentive service and are happy to help arrange airport transfers, excursions, and the like.

ⓘ 4 🚭 🅜 Cash only

🏨 SOUNDOUSS
$$$
10 PLACE TALHAH AGDAL
TEL (0537) 67 59 59
FAX (0537) 67 58 68
www.soundousshotel.ma
Due to its location on the fringes of the city, not far from the offices and factories of the business district, this hotel sees few guests interested in sightseeing. If you're looking for somewhere to stop off for the night, perhaps on the way to the nearby airport, this is a reasonable choice. It has interesting, palace-like decor and well-furnished, very comfortable rooms with air-conditioning and Wi-Fi.

ⓘ 60 🅿 🚭 🎽 🅜 MC

🏨 LE PIETRI
$$
4 RUE DE TOBROUK
TEL (0537) 70 78 20
FAX (0537) 70 82 35
www.lepietri.com
This small hotel manages to achieve a high standard of comfort, cleanliness, and service without the high prices and self-conscious five-star luxury of the city's larger hotels. Located in a relatively quiet area near to the center of the ville nouvelle, Le Pietri is a good choice for those who want to explore the city properly. The unpretentious restaurant on the ground floor serves excellent tagines in the evenings, as well as hearty breakfasts for guests.

ⓘ 35 🚭 🅜 All major cards

RESTAURANTS

SOMETHING SPECIAL

🍴 DINARJAT
$$$$$
6 RUE BELGNAOUI, MEDINA
TEL (0537) 70 42 39
www.dinarjat.com
Housed in a jaw-droppingly pretty 400-year-old mansion in the medina, Dinarjat is one of the most atmospheric restaurants in Rabat. The menu consists of Moroccan standards and a selection of international dishes. It's arguably a little overpriced, and the dishes are not always prepared in the most authentic or traditional manner, but for a special night out, this romantic restaurant is hard to beat. Reservations are advised, as it fills up fast in the evenings.

🍽 60 🅜 MC, V

🍴 LE ZIRYAB
$$$$$
10 IMPASSE ENNAJAR, RUE DES CONSULS
TEL (0537) 73 36 36
FAX (0537) 73 44 66
www.restaurantleziryab.com
Like the similarly inviting Dinarjat, Le Ziryab is an expensive restaurant where you're paying for the ambience as much as you are for the food. There's not a huge amount of choice here; you're pretty much restricted to a five-course set menu (make sure you're hungry before you go) of traditional Moroccan dishes. While the food is good, the presentation can make the whole experience feel like it has been Westernized for the benefit of tourists (meals are served on china plates rather than in tagines, for example). The terrace that overlooks the medina is a wonderful venue for predinner drinks, however.

🍽 40 🚭 🅜 MC, V

🍴 LE GRAND COMPTOIR
$$$$
279 AVENUE MOHAMED V
TEL (0537) 20 15 14
Located in the heart of the ville nouvelle, this traditional French brasserie manages to capture an atmosphere of colonial-era luxury—complete with art deco furnishings and decor—despite only being a few years old. Popular with French expats and well-heeled Moroccan couples, Le Grand Comptoir serves delicious French cuisine with an emphasis on traditional meat and fish dishes.

🍽 80 🚭 🅜 MC, V

🍴 L'ENTRECOTE
$$$
74 AVENUE EL AMIR FAL OULD OUMIER
TEL (0537) 67 11 08
One of the longest established restaurants in Rabat, this unpretentious French eatery is justly renowned for its delicious meat and fish dishes, indulgent desserts, and excellent wine list. The slightly somber atmosphere of the place is typically enlivened by performances by local jazz bands and traditional musicians.

🍽 60 🚭 🅜 MC, V

🍴 LE MAMMA
$$$
6 RUE TANATA
TEL (0537) 70 73 29
This lively family-run eatery has been serving its authentic Italian pasta dishes, grilled meats, and crispy, stone-baked pizza for more than two generations. Its bright decor and attentive staff add to the cozy ambience. The prices are reasonable, and the portions extremely generous.

🍽 100 🚭 🅜 MC, V

🍽 MATSURI

$$$

155 AVENUE JOHN KENNEDY,
ROUTE DES ZAERS
TEL (0537) 75 75 72
The sight of dozens of little plates of sushi slowly revolving around a restaurant on a conveyor belt is an unusual one in Morocco. This unexpected outpost of stylish Japanese modernity serves a tasty range of sushi dishes, and the chef can make many others to order. While it is fairly expensive for Morocco, it can make a welcome change from the more commonly available cuisine.
🔢 40 🅂 🅂 MC, V

🍽 PICOLO'S

$$$

149 AVENUE JOHN KENNEDY,
ROUTE DES ZAERS
TEL (0537) 63 69 69
FAX (0537) 63 86 86
Established a few years ago by its French owner and renowned chef, Philippe Bonnet, Picolo's serves inventive international cuisine with a distinctive French flair. In addition to the fine food, the restaurant boasts a lush garden dining area, shaded by parasols and lemon trees—ideal for warm fall evenings.
🔢 60 🅂 MC, V

🍽 SORMANI

$$

ANGLE AVENUE DE FRANCE ET
RUE OUARGHA
TEL (0537) 68 05 68
Perhaps the best value eatery in town, Sormani has a diverse menu of delicious Mediterranean dishes and a great wine list. The interior has a striking red-and-black decor and is popular with the city's young and trendy set.
🔢 60 🅂 🅂 MC, V

SALÉ

🏨 RIAD À LA BELLE ÉTOILE

$$$

14 RUE SANIAT SABOUNJI, BÂB
LAMRISSA, MEDINA
TEL (0537) 88 58 58
FAX (0537) 88 34 12
www.riad-alabelle-etoile.com
Just across the Oued Bou Regreg from Rabat, in the quieter medina of neighboring Salé, lies this lovely small riad. Each of its unique and traditionally decorated guest rooms has air-conditioning, Wi-Fi, and an en suite bathroom. In terms of comfort and service, La Belle Étoile is the equal of any of Rabat's newly opened riads; its lower prices are a consequence of its location. However, while the location is an inconvenience for anyone who wants to explore Rabat, it's not a major one, and it makes for a more interesting trip into town than you could expect if you stayed in a ville nouvelle hotel.
ℹ 5 🅂 🅂 Cash only

TÉMARA

🏨 HOTEL LA FELOUQUE

$$

GOLDEN SANDS BEACH, ROUTE
DE RABAT
TEL (0537) 74 43 88
FAX (0537) 74 45 65
www.lafelouque.com
This pleasant beachfront hotel is located about a 20-minute drive south of Rabat, in the town of Témara. The rooms are simple, but comfortable and well kept, while the location makes it an ideal place to relax by the beach, while still being relatively close to the bustling streets of the capital. The grounds of the hotel contain a swimming pool, tennis courts, and lush gardens.
ℹ 24 🅿 🅂 🅂 🅂 All major cards

PRICES

HOTELS
The cost of a double room with private bath and hot water in the peak season is given by **$** signs. Low season rates can be considerably lower.

$$$$$	over $200
$$$$	$100–$200
$$$	$50–$100
$$	$25–$50
$	Under $25

RESTAURANTS
The average cost of a two-course meal for one person, without tax, tip, or drinks, is given by **$** signs.

$$$$$	over $50
$$$$	$40–$50
$$$	$25–$40
$$	$15–$25
$	Under $15

◼ TANGER & THE NORTH COAST

AL HOCEIMA

🏨 HOTEL MAGHREB EL JADID

$$$

56 AVENUE MOHAMED V
TEL (0539) 98 25 04
This hotel is comfortable enough, with spacious en suite rooms and air-conditioning, but its interiors don't seem to have been updated or cared for since the 1980s. During the summer, there is a lively bar and restaurant on the top floor overlooking the sea, but during the low season this place can feel rather dead.
ℹ 40 🅂 🅂 Cash only

HOTEL VILLA FLORIDO
$$$

40 PLACE DU RIF

TEL (0539) 84 08 47

florido.alhoceima.com

Formerly known as the Hotel Étoile du Rif, this glamorous art deco hotel has recently been extensively refurbished and reopened in autumn 2010. The old Étoile du Rif had a reputation as a high-quality, if faded, place to stay—it's too early to say whether the new management and refurbished interiors will improve on this, but it has the potential to be one of the best hotels in town.

① 50 🅿 🔄 🚭 🔥 MC, V

HOTEL AMIR PLAGE
$$

1 PLAGE DU MATADERO

TEL (0539) 98 32 90

FAX (0539) 98 48 53

This modern hotel is located a few hundred feet from the waves of the Mediterranean Sea on the beautiful Plage du Matadero. The rooms are clean and comfortable. All have en suite bathrooms, air-conditioning, and, of course, lovely sea views. Downtown Al Hoceima is only a few minutes' drive away along the coast. Ideal for those looking to spend a few days lounging on the beach.

① 30 🅿 🚭 🔥 All major cards

CLUB NAUTIQUE
$$

THE FISHING PORT

TEL (0539) 98 16 41

This small seafood restaurant is a local institution, with a reputation for serving the finest and freshest fish and seafood in town. The menu's principal ingredients come off the boats that land their catches only a few yards from the restaurant's kitchens. Club Nautique's popularity is certainly helped by the fact

that it's also one of the few restaurants in Al Hoceima that is licensed to serve alcoholic drinks.

🅿 🔥 Cash only

ESPACE MIRAMAR
$$

RUE MOULAY ISMAIL

TEL (0539) 98 42 42

This lively open-air eatery offers a wide range of dishes, from Moroccan tagines to pizzas and other European standards. The service is prompt and professional, and the food is surprisingly good for a place with such a diverse menu. The outdoor areas are a great place to spend an evening in Al Hoceima.

🅿 🔥 Cash only

ASILAH

HOTEL PATIO DE LA LUNA
$$$

12 PLAZA DE ZELAKA

TEL (0539) 41 60 74

This hotel, recently converted from a private residence, is a pleasant and reasonably priced place to stay in the center of Asilah. The rooms are attractively decorated in a simple traditional style and very comfortable, but can get a little cold in the winter.

① 8 🔥 Cash only

HOTEL AZAYLA
$$

20 RUE IBN ROCHD

TEL (0539) 41 67 17

This cheap but welcoming hotel isn't exactly the most characterful place, but it is centrally located and clean. The staff is friendly and helpful, although few of them speak much English.

① 20 🚭 🔥 Cash only

CEUTA

PARADOR DE CEUTA
$$$$

15 PLAZA DE AFRICA

TEL (0956) 51 49 40

www.paradores.com

This four-star hotel is probably the most luxurious option for those looking to spend a few nights in Ceuta. Like the nearby Hostal Central (see below) the rooms are a little plain, but clean, spacious, and well furnished.

① 106 🅿 🔄 🚭 🔥 All major cards

ULISES HOTEL
$$$$

5 CALLE CAMOENS

TEL (0956) 51 45 40

FAX (0956) 51 45 46

www.hoteluloses.com

This recently renovated hotel right in the heart of Ceuta offers stylish modern accommodation and excellent facilities, such as an indoor swimming pool, restaurants and bars, and free Wi-Fi. It's worth spending a little extra and getting one of the more spacious rooms, as the entry-level accommodation can be a little spartan. It should be noted that the lack of on-site parking means that those with cars have to spend about €10 a day on municipal parking.

① 124 🚭 🏊 🔥 All major cards

HOSTAL CENTRAL
$$

15 PASEO DE REBELLIN

TEL (0956) 51 67 16

www.hostalesceuta.com

This clean and comfortable hotel, while nothing fancy, is a good choice for those on a budget. It has air-conditioning, en suite rooms, Wi-Fi, and bright, modern interiors. Its almost identical sister hotel, the Hostal Plaza Ruiz, stands around 110 yards (100 m) down the road. Both are located right in the center of Ceuta.

[i] 18 [P] [⚙] [♿] All major cards

🍴 CLUB NAUTICO
$$$

CALLE EDRISIS
TEL (0956) 51 44 00
With its prime location overlooking the marina, Club Nautico has long been a favorite destination with both locals and tourists. The menu has something for every budget and a good selection of locally caught fish and seafood dishes.

[♿] Cash only

🍴 GRAN MURALLA
$$$

PLAZA DE CONSTITUTION
TEL (0956) 51 76 25
In this case, "Gran Muralla" refers to the Great Wall of China, rather than the walls of Ceuta. This popular Chinese restaurant is much loved by weary travelers who have grown tired of tagines and couscous.

[⚙] [♿] All major cards

CHEFCHAOUENE

🏨 CASA HASSAN
$$$$

22 RUE TARGUI
TEL (0539) 98 81 96
www.casahassan.com
Casa Hassan has traditional Moroccan decor with carved wooden doors, colorful local carpets, and stylish bedrooms. This family-run small hotel is set in a former villa and, although the guesthouse is in the medina, has two parts: a charming older building and a more modern section, which has larger rooms. There is pleasant terrace and a large patio where guests can relax.

[i] 22 (8 in Casa Hassan, 14 in the Dar Baibou annex)
[♿] Cash only

🏨 DAR MEZIANA
$$$$

7 RUE ZAGDUD
TEL (0539) 98 78 07
www.darmezianahotel.com
This delightful little riad is located a few minutes' walk from the center of Chefchaouene. The hotel's handful of rooms are beautifully decorated, if a little small, and the staff is friendly. The views from the terrace are stunning.

[i] 7 [♿] Cash only

🏨 ATLAS CHAOUEN
$$$

BP 13, RUE SIDI ABDELHAMID
TEL (0539) 98 60 02
FAX (0539) 98 71 58
www.hotelsatlas.com
This striking white hotel stands on a hillside high above the city of Chefchaouene. It has been open for only a few years, so it hasn't had a chance to establish much of a reputation. The rooms are well furnished and comfortable, if a little plain, while the hotel's facilities (including a pool, spa, and restaurant) are excellent. Although it provides astounding views, the hotel's commanding location has a downside in the form of the extremely steep and tiring walk down to, and up from, the medina.

[i] 63 [P] [⚙] [♨] [♿] MC, V

SOMETHING SPECIAL

🏨 DAR ECHCHAOUEN
$$$

RAS EL MAA
TEL (0539) 98 78 24
www.darechchaouen.ma
Situated close to the historic medina, this attractive small hotel manages to combine the atmosphere of a riad with the facilities of a modern hotel. In order to capture the distinctive feel of the town, the hotel has been decorated using the skills of local artisans and designers.

The rooms are comfortable and attractively decorated, the staff attentive, and the swimming pool a welcome bonus, unusual in a hotel this size.

[i] 18 [⚙] [♨] [♿] MC, V

🏨 HOTEL PARADOR
$$$

PLACE EL MAKHAZEN
TEL (0539) 98 61 36
FAX (0539) 98 63 24
www.hotel-parador.com
The Parador is only a few minutes' walk from Chefchaouene's ancient medina and the kasbah, making it a good choice for sightseeing and experiencing local life. It has a modern feel with cozy guest rooms and a restaurant serving local and international dishes.

[i] 55 [P] [⚙] [♨] [♿] MC, V

🏨 CAMPING AZILANE
$

RUE SIDI ABDELHAMID
TEL (0539) 98 69 79
www.camping chefchaouen.com
This well-maintained campground stands on a hill above the town and is a popular base for those heading out into the hills. There is also a small and very spartan youth hostel on-site for nights when the wind is howling through the valley.

[i] 144 campsites [P] [♿] Cash only

LARACHE

🏨 LA MAISON HAUTE
$$

6 DERB IBN THAMI
www.lamaisonhaute.com
Meaning "the tall house," La Maison Haute is housed in a traditional Arab-Andalusian building that is about a floor taller than most of those around it. Its rooms are comfortable and lovingly decorated, and most have en

suite bathrooms. The hotel has a wonderful roof garden that looks right out over the bay.

[i] 7 [cash] Cash only

HOTEL ESPAÑA
$

6 AVENUE HASSAN II

TEL (0539) 91 56 29

The guest rooms in this two-star hotel come equipped with a private bathroom and satellite television, with many looking out over Larache's lively main square. It has its own restaurant where the cuisine is authentic Moroccan.

[i] 36 [P] [cash] Cash only

TANGER

HOTELS

EL MINZAH
$$$$$

85 RUE DE LA LIBERTÉ, VILLE NOUVELLE

TEL (0539) 93 58 85

FAX (0539) 93 45 46

www.elminzah.com

This grand 1920s hotel, with its fine guest rooms, pool, and spa, is the only one of Tanger's great international zone hotels to survive undiminished to the present day. The hotel's luxurious grounds and attentive staff make this one of the finest places to stay in Tanger.

[i] 140 [P] [icons] All major cards

HOTEL NORD-PINUS
$$$$$

11 RUE RIAD SULTAN, KASBAH

TEL (0661) 22 81 40

FAX (0539) 33 63 63

www.nord-pinus-tanger.com

This unique guesthouse straddles the rue Riad Sultan, in the highest reaches of the kasbah. With its lavish decoration, adjoining hammam, and professional service, the Hotel Nord-Pinus is a cut above the kasbah's other riads. The views from the roof terrace are simply stunning.

[i] 5 [P] [icons] MC, V

SOMETHING SPECIAL

DAR NOUR
$$$$

20 RUE GOURNA, KASBAH

TEL (0662) 11 27 24

www.darnour.com

Located in a quiet street at the rear of the kasbah, Dar Nour is a beautifully renovated traditional Moroccan home. The rooms are colorful and bright, with en suite bathrooms in most, and some of the suites and larger rooms have private terraces overlooking the sea. The French owners and their friendly staff are more than happy to help you plan and navigate your days in the medina. There is no air-conditioning, but the well-ventilated traditional design keeps the temperature down, even in summer.

[i] 11 [P] [icons] MC, V

DAR SULTAN
$$$$

49 RUE TOUILA, KASBAH

TEL (0539) 33 60 61

www.darsultan.com

Perched high above Tanger's medina, this recently renovated riad is located at the heart of the kasbah. This commanding position gives guests stunning views across the town, especially when eating breakfast on the roof terrace. The rooms are tastefully decorated with locally made furniture and Moroccan antiques, and the staff has a reputation for being extremely helpful and friendly.

[i] 6 [P] [icons] MC, V

MAISON ARABESQUE
$$$$

73 RUE NACIRIA, MEDINA

TEL (0679) 46 68 76

www.maison-arabesque.com

This recently refurbished riad, located very close to the American Legation Museum, has five tastefully decorated guest rooms, each with its own distinctive style. Breakfast is served on the roof terrace, which has a sea view. The riad's Dutch owner, Peter Van der Drift, is happy to arrange excursions to sites around Tanger in addition to trips around the medina.

[i] 5 [P] [icons] MC, V

HOTEL CONTINENTAL
$$$

36 RUE DAR EL BAROUD

TEL (0539) 93 10 24

www.continental-tanger.com

This grand old hotel has been a Tanger landmark since the late 19th century. Standing high above the docks on a sublime hillside site, the four-story building is clearly visible from the ferry long before you reach Tanger. The hotel's sumptuously decorated, if somewhat faded, public spaces are redolent of Tanger's exciting and varied history and the hotel's own glorious past. The owners are currently working their way through the guest rooms, renovating and redecorating, so if you can, try and get one of the newer, fresher rooms.

[i] 56 [icons] All major cards

LA TANGERINA
$$$

19 RUE RIAD SULTAN, KASBAH

TEL (0539) 94 77 31

FAX (0539) 94 77 33

www.latangerina.com

La Tangerina is the result of its owners' passion to transform what was once an ordinary medina house into a hotel with a distinctive European colonial feel. The ten or so rooms are decorated in a variety of styles and boast stunning views of the straits and beyond to Spain. An elegant dining hall and hammam are provided for guests.

(i) 10 🛏 🗝 All major cards

🏨 LE DAWLIZ
$$$
42 RUE DE HOLLANDE
TEL (0539) 33 33 77
FAX (0539) 37 06 61
www.ledawliz.com
Le Dawliz is minutes from the medina and beach, with its restaurant and most of its guest rooms affording views of the bay. Family oriented, the hotel offers a babysitting service and a pool especially for children.

(i) 36 **P** 🗝 🗝 🛏
🗝 All major cards

🏨 RIAD TANJA
$$$
RUE DU PORTUGAL, ESCALIERS AMÉRICAINS
TEL (0539) 33 35 38
FAX (0539) 33 30 54
www.riadtanja.com
Located amid the tiny streets of the medina not far from the American Legation Museum, this historic property has been converted into tasteful suites with an Arab-Andalusian decor. It has its own restaurant (see this page), which serves Moroccan dishes to a nouvelle cuisine style.

(i) 6 🗝 MC, V

🏨 EL GOLLA
$
SIDI ABOU ABDELLAH
TEL (0535) 57 40 05
www.elgolla.com
This two-star stone-built complex lies in the countryside a few miles outside Tanger city. Be sure to have breakfast on its terrace and take in the views. The hotel's guest rooms are cozy, and all are equipped

with a private bathroom and satellite television.

(i) 22 **P** 🗝 Cash only

RESTAURANTS

🍴 EL MINZAH KORSAN
$$$$$
HOTEL EL MINZAH, 85 RUE DE LA LIBERTÉ
TEL (0539) 33 34 44
This elegant restaurant within the historic hotel El Minzah (see p. 285) offers classic Moroccan dishes in addition to a varied range of international cuisine. The service is discreet and attentive. The only downside is the rather high price and slightly uninspiring atmosphere. In the evenings, however, meals are accompanied by performances by excellent local musicians who enliven things considerably.

🔲 40 🗝 🗝 All major cards

🍴 LE MIRAGE
$$$$$
HOTEL CLUB LE MIRAGE, LES GROTTES D'HERCULE
TEL (0539) 33 33 32
www.lemirage-tanger.com
Located within the spectacular cliff-top grounds of the Mirage hotel complex, the Mirage's restaurant is spread out over a series of terraces and rooms with amazing views over the Strait of Gibraltar. The restaurant has two menus: one offers contemporary international dishes, while the other consists of traditional Moroccan dishes. All are made with fresh, locally sourced ingredients and prepared with care and skill.

🔲 60 **P** 🗝 🗝 All major cards

🍴 LE RELAIS DE PARIS
$$$$
42 RUE DE HOLLANDE
TEL (0539) 33 18 19

PRICES

HOTELS
The cost of a double room with private bath and hot water in the peak season is given by **$** signs. Low season rates can be considerably lower.

$$$$$	over $200
$$$$	$100–$200
$$$	$50–$100
$$	$25–$50
$	Under $25

RESTAURANTS
The average cost of a two-course meal for one person, without tax, tip, or drinks, is given by **$** signs.

$$$$$	over $50
$$$$	$40–$50
$$$	$25–$40
$$	$15–$25
$	Under $15

This classic Parisian-style restaurant offers sophisticated French cuisine prepared using the finest local seafood and produce. The restaurant's stylish interiors are matched by an equally lovely garden terrace, where diners can enjoy the warmth of Tanger summer evenings and the views across the town.

🔲 80 🗝 🗝 All major cards

SOMETHING SPECIAL

🍴 RIAD TANJA
$$$$
RUE DU PORTUGAL, ESCALIERS AMÉRICAINS
TEL (0539) 33 35 38
This beautifully presented inn-style restaurant is not far from the seafront. Celebrity chef and proprietor Moha

---

🏨 Hotel 🍴 Restaurant **(i)** No. of Guest Rooms 🔲 No. of Seats **P** Parking 🕐 Closed 🗝 Elevator

Fedal presents a cuisine that is Moroccan with a modern, innovative twist. It's a good idea to reserve in advance, particularly in the peak season, when Moha is often cooking for a full house of guests.

🛏 40 🚭 🅰 All major cards

🍴 CAFÉ DE PARIS
$$

1 PLACE DE FRANCE, VILLE NOUVELLE

TEL (0539) 93 84 44

This gloomy but atmospheric café/bar has been serving drinks and snacks in its leather-clad lounge since the 1930s and has changed little since the days when it was filled with writers, refugees, and spies. In the evening it's not the most woman-friendly place around, but during the day it's a friendly, cool place to take the weight off your feet.

🅰 Cash only

🍴 HAFA CAFÉ
$$

AVENUE MOHAMED VI, MARSHAN

This café is an old Tanger institution—a cliff-top hangout with a steeply terraced garden that overlooks the sea. The café is located in the Marshan district to the west of the kasbah. It was once a favorite meeting place for Tanger's bohemian artistic colony, and it retains some of the relaxed attitude that drew them there. It is the best place in Tanger to drink sweet mint tea and look out over the sea.

🅰 Cash only

SOMETHING SPECIAL

🍴 SAVEUR DE POISSON
$

2 ESCALIER WALLER, VILLE NOUVELLE

TEL (0539) 93 63 26

This unique little restaurant,

with its hand-painted sign and eccentric interior decor, is a favorite with locals. It is located on a steep staircase that climbs from the rue du Portugal to the rue de la Liberté near the hotel El Minzah. Guests pay their 100 dirham, and sit at one of the communal tables, where they are served a delicious five-course traditional seafood meal by the owner and chef, Mohamed.

🅰 Cash only

TÉTOUAN

HOTELS

🏨 BLANCO RIAD HOTEL
$$$$

25 ZANKAT ZAWIYA KADIRIA

TEL (0539) 70 42 02

www.blancoriad.com

This exciting newcomer to Tétouan opened in spring 2010 but has already established a stellar reputation for the quality of its accommodations, its restaurant, and its friendly, welcoming staff. Housed in a former palace in the center of the medina, the interiors of the building are simply breathtaking, and the rooms are comfortable and well maintained. While the building is centuries old, the hotel's facilities are not—all rooms are en suite, and there is artfully integrated air-conditioning throughout.

ⓘ 8 🚭 🅰 MC, V

SOMETHING SPECIAL

🏨 HOTEL EL REDUCTO
$$$$

38 ZANKAT ZAWIYA KADIRIA

TEL (0539) 96 81 20

www.riadtetouan.com

This riad is housed in a grand mansion that was once the home of the Spanish governor of Tétouan. Today it has been

tastefully renovated to offer some of the best accommodation options in the Tétouan area. The traditionally decorated rooms are stunning, and they are surprisingly cheap considering how much work has clearly been put into making them look as good as they do.

ⓘ 5 🚭 🅰 MC, V

🏨 SOFITEL THALASSA MARINA CLUB MED SMIR
$$$$

ROUTE DE SABTA, SMIR

TEL (0539) 97 12 34

FAX (0539) 97 12 35

www.sofitel.com

A large complex built around its swimming pool and lush gardens, the resort has every amenity, from a business suite to a health center, sports, and restaurants. Guest rooms are stylish and modern.

ⓘ 334 🅿 🔄 🚭 🏊 🏊 🍷
🅰 All major cards

🏨 HOTEL PANORAMA VISTA
$$$

RUE MOULAY ABBAS, VILLE NOUVELLE

TEL (0539) 96 49 70

FAX (0539) 96 49 69

www.panoramavista.com

This well-kept and modern hotel is a reliably good choice in the center of Tétouan. The rooms are clean and spacious, and many of them boast stunning views over the town to the Rif Mountains beyond. The hotel's café is popular with Tétouan's affluent young population.

ⓘ 63 🅿 🔄 🚭 🅰 MC, V

🏨 RIAD DALIA
$–$$$

25 PLACE EL OUESSA

TEL (0539) 96 43 18

www.riad-dalia.com

A stunningly decorated old mansion located in the heart of Tétouan's historic medina, the Riad Dalia offers a range of rooms, from well-appointed grand suites to single-occupancy rooms with shared bathrooms that cost little more than a night in a campsite.

[1] 7 🅢 Cash only

RESTAURANTS

🍴 RESTAURANT PALACE BOUHLAL
$$$$
48 JAMAA KEBIR, MEDINA
TEL (0539) 99 87 97
This impressive restaurant is housed in a converted 19th-century palace, and its sumptuous interiors are exactly what you'd expect given its history. The food is traditional, but fairly inventive. This restaurant is one of the favorite places for tour guides to take their charges for lunch, so it can be quite crowded at times—the tour guides are also about the only people who can reliably find it in the winding streets of Tétouan's medina.

🅢 Cash only

SOMETHING SPECIAL

🍴 BLANCO RIAD
$$$
BLANCO RIAD, 25 ZANKAT ZAWIYA KADIRIA
TEL (0539) 70 42 02
www.blancoriad.com
This recently opened restaurant offers a sophisticated menu created in partnership with a Michelin-starred cookery school. Only the freshest ingredients are used by the restaurant's talented chef. The menu features many local seafood dishes and traditional meat dishes, alongside contemporary European cuisine.

🅢 🅢 MC, V

🍴 EL REDUCTO RESTAURANT
$$$
38 ZANKAT ZAWIYA KADIRIA
TEL (0539) 96 81 20
www.riadtetouan.com
The restaurant of Tétouan's finest riad (Hotel El Reducto, see p. 287) is open to non-residents in the evenings and serves excellent traditional fare, along with some European dishes, in the hotel's tastefully decorated dining rooms.

🅢 🅢 MC, V

🍴 RESTAURANT RESTINGA
$$$
21 AVE MOHAMED V
VILLE NOUVELLE
TEL (0539) 96 35 76
This popular restaurant has almost no indoor seating, so make sure the weather's going to be good (it usually is) before reserving a table. The menu is dominated by locally caught seafood and fish, but there are other options. The restaurant also has the distinction of being one of the few places in the area that is licensed to sell alcohol.

🅢 Cash only

🍴 SALON DE THÉ, HOTEL PANORAMA VISTA
$$$
HOTEL PANORAMA VISTA, RUE MOULAY ABBAS, VILLE NOUVELLE
TEL (0539) 96 49 70
FAX (0539) 96 49 69
www.panoramavista.com
This café is a clean, modern affair, popular with young locals more than it is with tourists. While the decor is unremarkable, the views are impressive and the food is excellent.

🅢 🅢 Cash only

◼ FÈS & THE HIGH ATLAS

FÈS

HOTELS

🏨 HOTEL LES MERINIDES
$$$$$
AVENUE BORJ DU NORD
TEL (0535) 64 52 26
FAX (0535) 64 52 25
www.lesmerinides.com
Overlooking Fès from its outstanding hillside location, this large, modern hotel offers some stunning views of the city. The hotel's rooms and facilities are clean and comfortable, although not particularly distinctive. While the hotel is luxurious, the area around its grounds has seen better days, and guests are discouraged from leaving the hotel on foot. The hotel is located several miles from the center of town. If you don't mind paying for the daily taxi ride to and from the medina, this is a pleasant and mostly quiet place to stay away from the crowds of the old town.

[1] 106 P 🅢 🅢 🅢 🅢 All major cards

🏨 MAISON BLEUE
$$$$$
2 PLACE DE L'ISTIQAL, QUARTIER BATHA
TEL (0353) 63 60 52
www.maisonbleue.com
Three courtyards connect the rooms of this luxurious riad. Once the home of a famous Moroccan writer and scientist, it still has a wonderful library of rare books. The authentic feel of a Moroccan palace is not compromised by the use of fine European furniture, including some four-poster beds, alongside the best in local design. A welcoming pool in one of the courtyards is popular with guests. The romantic atmosphere is

enhanced by traditional music to accompany dinner.

🛈 6 🅂 🕾 🛡 🅶 MC, V

🏨 RIAD EL AMINE
$$$$$
94–96 BOUAJJARA, BÂB JDID, MEDINA
TEL (0535) 74 07 49
www.riadelaminefes.com
This luxurious riad has spacious rooms and suites, furnished with great style, mixing traditional Moroccan and Western tastes. All rooms have Internet access and satellite television. A spa and a small pool are among the facilities. The restaurant, which seats up to 70 in two comfortable, opulent salons, serves gourmet food on the finest china and glass.

🛈 8 🅂 🕾 🛡 🅶 All major cards

🏨 RIAD LAAROUSSA
$$$$$
3 DERB BECHARA, MEDINA
TEL (0674) 18 76 39
www.riad-laaroussa.com
Riad Laaroussa is a converted 17th-century palace with a grand courtyard. An ambience of splendor makes this a special place. The furnishings are a mix of traditional Moroccan and elegant antique and modern European styles. Each of the suites and rooms has been tastefully restored, and guest accommodations are air-conditioned and surprisingly spacious. The riad also boasts a hammam and spa, a rooftop terrace, and a shady garden patio. The restaurant serves traditional local dishes from a set menu.

🛈 9 🅂 🛡 🅶 MC, V

🏨 RIAD SHEHERAZADE
$$$$$
23 ARSAT BENNIS, DOUH
TEL (0555) 74 16 42
FAX (0555) 74 16 45
www.sheheraz.com
This former palace has been transformed into a luxurious riad-style hotel. Most of the hotel's accommodation comes in the form of large, opulent suites—the largest of which, the royal suites, boast massive four-poster beds, private patios, and access to the swimming pool. Each of its rooms and suites is unique, with a distinctive decorative theme. The views over the city from its terrace are enchanting.

🛈 13 🅿 🅂 🕾 🛡 🅶 All major cards

🏨 SOFITEL PALAIS JAMAÏ
$$$$$
BÂB GUISSA
TEL (0535) 63 43 31
FAX (0535) 63 50 96
www.sofitel.com
Housed in a late 19th-century palace built by the powerful Jamaï family, this luxury hotel is one of the most spectacular hotels in Morocco. Like the Mamounia (see p. 297) in Marrakech, this refurbished palace provides attentive service and luxurious facilities in a dramatic historic location. The rooms are comfortable and spacious, although they lack the fabulous decor of the medina's riads. Set among lush gardens, the hotel boasts a spa, a gym, and several swimming pools, as well as a variety of restaurants and bars.

🛈 142 🅿 🅂 🅂 🕾 🚤 🛡 🅶 All major cards

SOMETHING SPECIAL

🏨 DAR ROUMANA
$$$$
ZKAK ROUMANE
TEL (0535) 74 16 37
FAX (0535) 63 55 24
www.darroumana.com
Founded in 2006 by American Cordon Bleu chef Jennifer Smith, the Dar Roumana is a sumptuously decorated oasis in the heart of Fès's medina. With only five individually styled suites, the hotel is intimate and comfortable. The service is impeccable, and the food (cooked by the owner) is fantastic—you'll never want to leave (see p. 291).

🛈 5 🅂 🅶 MC, V

🏨 DAR SEFFARINE
$$$$
14 DERB SBAA LOUYATE, SEFFARINE
TEL (0671) 11 35 28
FAX (0535) 63 52 05
www.darseffarine.com
This delighful riad is located right in the center of the old medina, in a quiet street behind the Keraouine *medersa*. Housed in an ancient palace, the riad's interiors are traditional, but not cluttered, and its handful of well-appointed rooms are spacious and quiet.

🛈 6 🅂 🅶 Cash only

🏨 PALAIS DE FÈS DAR TAZI
$$$$
15 RUE MAKHFIA ER'CIF
TEL (0535) 76 15 90
www.palaisdefes.com
On the edge of the medina, this riad is next to a public square that is full of life. The riad itself is peaceful, however. The rooms are furnished with fine traditional decor and fittings, while the public spaces are elegant. Spacious patios add to a real air of opulence, and the covered terrace is a gem. The restaurant serves Moroccan cuisine, and the staff is helpful and friendly.

🛈 8 🅂 🅶 All major cards

🏨 RIAD BARTAL
$$$$
21 RUE SOURNAS, QUARTIER ZIAT
TEL (0535) 63 70 53
www.riadalbartal.com
Lush vegetation welcomes guests to a cool, arcaded central courtyard. Stylish decor gives the riad great character,

while air-conditioning in all rooms and a helpful, friendly staff ensure a pleasant and relaxing stay. Despite its small size, the riad offers guests Wi-Fi and Internet access. The restaurant serves authentic, tasty Moroccan cuisine.

🛏 5 🍴 ⚙ MC, V

🏨 RIAD DAR CHRIFA
$$$$
20 ARSAT EL HAMMOUMI ZIAT, MEDINA
TEL (0535) 63 78 50
www.riaddarchrifa.com
Riad Dar Chrifa offers an authentic Moroccan experience in a beautiful house. Quality Western furniture and fittings, including some four-poster beds, seamlessly marry with traditional decor. Breakfast may be served in the delightful central courtyard. Rooms are well equipped, with some on the ground floor, and the bathrooms are spacious. A terrace offers a wide view across the city, which is enhanced by the building's hilltop location.

🛏 7 🍴 ⚙ MC, V

🏨 RIAD FÈS
$$$$
5 DERB BEN SLIMANE, ZERBTANA
TEL (0535) 74 10 12
www.riadfes.com
A boutique hotel, Riad Fès oozes character. The courtyard-patio is quaint and, although the building is old, the rooms are comfortable. The riad has gained a reputation for one of the best restaurants in the medina. Although the menu is limited, both Western and Moroccan options are available. The outer courtyard set around a water feature is magical.

🛏 17 🍴 ⚙ MC, V

🏨 RIAD LUNE ET SOLEIL
$$$$
3 DERB SKALLIA, DOUH, BATHA,

MEDINA
TEL (0535) 63 45 23
www.luneetsoleil.com
Within the medieval city walls, this riad offers luxury accommodations and a peaceful setting. Orange and lemon trees grow in the courtyard, at the center of which is a fountain. The ground-floor rooms open onto this leafy central space. The rooms and public areas are furnished with the owners' collection of antiques and craft items. Some rooms have a Jacuzzi, and there is Wi-Fi access. The largely traditional Moroccan menu is of high quality.

🛏 6 🍴 ⚙ MC, V

🏨 RIAD SARA
$$$$
17 DERB EL GABASSE DOUH, MEDINA
TEL (0535) 63 68 20
www.riad-sara.com
A large house, dating from the 17th century, Riad Sara is a comfortable, elegant guesthouse offering luxurious accommodations. Ornately carved pillars and clever planting make the courtyard a charming place to sit. The location is handy, just off one of the main routes through the medina but close to the souks. The rooms are large and well furnished, and the rooftop terrace offers a wide view across Fès.

🛏 7 🍴 ⚙ MC, V

🏨 RYAD MABROUKA
$$$$
TALAA KBIRA DERB EL MITER
TEL (0535) 63 63 45
FAX (0535) 63 63 10
www.ryadmabrouka.com
In a city where there is no shortage of riads, this large converted mansion offers a distinctive and luxurious experience. Each of the rooms and suites has its own unique decor, with stunning tradi-

tional features such as *zellij* tilework, sculpted stonework, and ornately carved cedarwood furniture. In the unusually large courtyard garden, there is a small but very pleasant swimming pool for guests. The staff is very knowledgeable about the area and happy to arrange excursions and activities for guests.

🛏 8 🍴 🏊 ⚙ MC, V

🏨 ZALAGH PARC PALACE
$$$$
OUED LOTISSEMENT
TEL (0535) 75 54 54
FAX (0535) 75 54 91
www.zalagh-palace.ma
A luxurious five-star hotel with individually designed rooms and suites, all located around lavish gardens and a swimming pool. Among its facilities are

---

🏨 Hotel 🍴 Restaurant 🛏 No. of Guest Rooms 🪑 No. of Seats 🅿 Parking 🕐 Closed 🛗 Elevator

a beauty salon and its own bowling alley.

ℹ 488 P ⬌ 🅿 🛋 🏊 📺
🅒 All major cards

🏨 DAR EL GHALIA
$$$
13–15 RAS JNANE, MEDINA
TEL (0535) 63 41 67
The black-and-white tiled central courtyard of this historic riad is magical, a wonderful place to relax or eat away from the bustle of the city's medina outside the gate. Dar el Ghalia dates from the 17th century, is part of a former royal palace, and has been in the family of the present owner for 300 years. The romantic atmosphere is enhanced by the traditional costume worn by the staff. All rooms are beautifully furnished and air-conditioned.

ℹ 11 ⬌ 🅒 🅒 All major cards

🏨 RIAD HALA
$$$
156 DERB LAKRAM, TALÂA KEBIRA
TEL (0535) 63 86 87
FAX (0535) 63 86 84
www.riad-fes-hala.com
A small but comfortable riad in the historic medina. While it lacks some of the flair of the Dar Roumana or the Dar Seffarine (see p. 289), it is still an excellent choice for those who want an authentic personalized experience of the historic city.

ℹ 8 🅒 🅒 All major cards

🏨 RIAD NUMÉRO 9
$$$
9 DERB EL MASID, KAK EL MAA, TALÂA KABIRA
TEL (0535) 63 40 45
www.riad9.com
Restored over three years using only traditional materials, Riad Numéro 9 is a delight. A mix of North African, French, and English antique furniture gives this riad an

air of opulent comfort. The Moroccan tiles, carpets, and carved woodwork are exquisite. The management has made this a place to "escape" to, a haven of peace in the medina of Fès. The personal service makes staying at the riad like staying in the owners' home. The sunken dining area in the courtyard is ingenious. Guests also enjoy fine dining on the terrace, which has panoramic views.

ℹ 3 🅒 Cash only

🏨 HOTEL DE LA PAIX
$$
44 AVENUE HASSAN II
TEL (0535) 62 50 72
FAX (0535) 62 68 80
One of the better low-cost options in Fès's ville nouvelle, this smartly presented hotel offers spacious air-conditioned guest rooms with en suite bathrooms, televisions, and comfortable beds.

ℹ 42 P ⬌ 🅒 🅒 MC, V

RESTAURANTS

🍽 DAR EL GHALIA
$$$$$
15 ROSS RHI
Authentic Moroccan à la carte cuisine is served in this converted riad in the Fès el Bali district. Its traditional decor adds plenty of atmosphere. Be sure to try its tagines.

➕ 60 P 🅒 🅒 MC, V

🍽 MAISON BLUE
$$$$$
2 PLACE DE BATHA
TEL (0535) 74 18 43
In this magnificent restaurant within the walls of the Fès el Bali, chef Lalla Khadija serves gourmet à la carte Moroccan cuisine. It has a huge following with locals. Outside dining available.

➕ 100 P 🅒 🅒 MC, V

🍽 RIAD FÈS
$$$$$
5 DERB IBN SLIMANE
TEL (0535) 94 76 10
Presented with a modern decor of terra-cotta blended with beige and browns, this contemporary restaurant specializes in classic Moroccan cuisine. It can be found near the Musée Dar Batha.

➕ 60 P 🅒 🅒 MC, V

🍽 DAR ROUMANA
$$$$
DAR ROUMANA, ZKAK ROUMANE
TEL (0535) 74 16 37
FAX (0535) 63 55 24
www.darroumana.com
Serving a mixture of traditional Moroccan fare and more adventurous dishes, the restaurant in the fantastic Dar Roumana (see p. 289) is open to nonresidents for evening meals and drinks. Reservations are essential, as there isn't space for many when their guesthouse is fully booked.

P 🅒 🅒 MC, V

🍽 PALAIS JAMAÏ
$$$$
BÂB GUISSA
TEL (0535) 63 43 31
A top-quality restaurant housed in a centuries-old palace building, the Palais Jamaï serves gastronomic-style Moroccan dishes. It has a wine list to match, and local music plays in the background.

➕ 40 P 🅒 All major cards

🍽 MEZZANINE
$$$
17 KASBAT CHAMS
TEL (0535) 63 86 68
www.restaurantfez.com
On three floors and with an outside terrace, Mezzanine is one of the most fashionable spots in Fès. The lounge bar has minimalist modern decor.

🅒 Nonsmoking 🅒 Air-conditioning 🅒 Indoor Pool 🅿 Outdoor Pool 📺 Health Club 🅒 Credit Cards

The popular lunchtime restaurant becomes a chic dining and social hub in the evening. Guests relax on the terrace to admire the city walls and the huge palms in neighboring Jnan Sbil Gardens. From traditional Moroccan tagines and European-style cooking to tapas, the restaurant caters to all tastes. Reservations recommended.

🔌 🔼 All major cards

SOMETHING SPECIAL

🍴 CAFÉ CLOCK
$$
7 DERB EL MAGANA,
TALÂA KBIRA
TEL (0535) 63 78 55
www.cafeclock.com
Café Clock is named for the nearby historic water clock. It has dining areas on several floors, on the roof terrace, and in the courtyard of a carefully restored 18th-century building. Popular for lunch, tea, and dinner, the café is known for its delicious homemade cakes. Local art hangs on the walls. Café Clock runs courses in Moroccan cooking.

🔼 Cash only

🍴 FÈS ET GESTES
$$
39 ARSAT EL HAMOUMI
TEL (0535) 63 85 32
www.fes-et-gestes.ma
In this teahouse and restaurant, patrons may enjoy tea or a set-menu lunch or dinner. Choose to sit by the fountain in the elegant courtyard or in the library or the salon. Fès et Gestes is an oasis and, like a real oasis, is not easy to find, but it is a haven where guests can enjoy a memorable meal of Moroccan cuisine in a beautiful setting.

🔼 Cash only

🍴 YANG TSE
$$
23 RUE ERYTHERIA
TEL (0535) 62 14 85
A city-center Chinese restaurant, the Yang Tse is an attractive little place that serves meat, fish, and seafood dishes that draw inspiration from Chinese and Vietnamese cuisine. If you're in town for a few days, you'll want to go for something more distinctively Moroccan, but if you've been on the road for a while, this place can be a welcome break from all the tagines.

🍽 60 🔌 🔼 MC, V

◼ MEKNÈS & THE MIDDLE ATLAS

IFRANE

🏨 MICHLIFEN IFRANE
$$$$$
AVENUE HASSAN II BP 18
TEL (0535) 86 40 00
FAX (0535) 86 41 41
www.michlifenifrane.com
Located in the ski resort of Ifrane, this hotel is dedicated to leisure and well-being. It has a spa with a hammam, sauna, and treatment rooms, along with a pool and gourmet restaurants. Accommodation is in alpine-style lodges and suites.

🛏 40 🅿 🔌 🔼 🎦 🔼 All major cards

🏨 LE GITE LAC DAYET AOUA
$$
KM 7, IMMOUZER–IFRANE ROAD
TEL (0535) 60 48 80
FAX (0535) 60 48 52
This small modern guesthouse is situated on the edge of a beautiful mountain lake a few miles northeast of Ifrane. The rooms are simple, but spacious and comfortable. There is a large, if slightly rustic, outdoor pool for guests in the summer months. The owner, Abdelha-

mid Gandhi, and his staff are friendly and happy to arrange a variety of excursions and activities in the surrounding mountains.

🛏 18 🅿 🔼 🔼 Cash only

MEKNÈS

HOTELS

🏨 PALAIS DIDI
$$$$
30 DERB HAMMAM MOULAY ISMAIL, MEDINA
TEL (0535) 55 85 90
www.palaisdidi.com
A stunning black-and-white courtyard, with a cooling fountain, lies at the center of this fine example of Moroccan architecture and decorative art. From the terrace, there is a good view of the medina and Royal Golf Meknès is within reach. Rooms are decorated in a mix of North African and European styles, and some feature carved niches with opulent cushions, inviting guests to relax.

🛏 9 🔌 🔼 MC, V

🏨 RIAD FELLOUSSIA
$$$$
23 DERB HAMMAM JDID, BÂB AISSI
TEL (0535) 53 08 40
www.riadfelloussia.com
This traditional riad in the heart of the city offers fine views of the main square and the Bâb Mansour gate. The central patio has cedar beams and a fountain. Four rooms open onto the courtyard. They are decorated with Moroccan craft items, rugs, and furniture, but none of this distracts from the cool white walls of each tastefully furnished suite. Guests may dine on the terrace and watch the bustle of the square below.

🛏 4 Cash only

🏨 Hotel 🍴 Restaurant 🛏 No. of Guest Rooms 🍽 No. of Seats 🅿 Parking 🕐 Closed 🛗 Elevator

🏨 RIAD YACOUT
$$$$
22 LALLA AOUDA
TEL (0535) 53 31 20
www.riad-yacout
-meknes.com
Close to the main gate to the medina, Riad Yacout is a luxurious guesthouse. The courtyard has a charming patio garden with a central fountain and two terraces provide quiet places to unwind. The decor is both traditional North African, with carved cedar doors and ornate plasterwork, and modern European, resulting in comfort and style. The menu is Moroccan, with ingredients sourced from local producers. Other facilities include a pool and hammam.
🛈 9 🏊 🏧 Cash only

🏨 HOTEL MAJESTIC
$$$
19 AVENUE MOHAMED V, VILLE NOUVELLE
TEL (0535) 52 20 35
Like the nearby Hotel Volubilis (see below), this stylish hotel is a relic of the French colonial period. Time has been a little kinder to the Majestic, however, and the management is enthusiastic about updating and improving the place. Some of the rooms have en suite bathrooms and balconies, which provide excellent views over the town.
🛈 23 🏧 Cash only

🏨 HOTEL VOLUBILIS
$$$
45 AVENUE DES FAR, VILLE NOUVELLE
TEL (0535) 52 50 82
This grand old 1930s hotel is probably a little past its prime, but still pleasant enough, if a little noisy. The art deco styling of the public areas is impressive. It is located close to the center of town and the rates are reasonable.
🛈 58 🍴 🏊 🏧 All major cards

🏨 RIAD LAHBOUL
$$$
6 DERB AIN SEFLI, ROUAMZINE
TEL (0535) 55 98 78
www.riadlahboul.com
The three-tier terrace overlooking the garden and the city is just one charming feature of this small guesthouse. Rooms are compact and tastefully furnished and two have a fine view as far as the Atlas Mountains. Walls and ceilings have ornate carving, and the decor is local. This is a family-run riad and guests can be sure of a warm welcome.
🛈 9 🍴 🏧 MC, V

🏨 RIAD ZAHRAA
$$$
5 DERB ABDELLAH EL KASRI, MEDINA
TEL (0535) 53 20 12
www.riad-zahraa.com
Furnished with antiques as well as Moroccan craft items and modern fittings, Riad Zahraa is centrally located in the medina. The owners, lecturers at the university, have restored the riad with great taste. The carved cedar doors and the peaceful inner courtyard are two particularly nice features. The staff is welcoming and helpful.
🛈 8 🍴 🏧 Cash only

🏨 RYAD BAHIA
$$$
TIBERBARINE, MEDINA
TEL (0535) 55 45 41
www.ryad-bahia.com
Visitors to Ryad Bahia can relax in the charming central courtyard, where mint tea is served. A lovingly restored riad, this small guesthouse is comfortable and friendly. Rooms are simply furnished and comfortable. Traditional Moroccan food, including memorable tagines, is served. Although in the medina, this riad is easily accessible and peaceful.
🛈 8 🍴 🏧 MC, V

🏨 HOTEL AKOUAS
$$
27 RUE AMIR ABDELKADER
TEL (0535) 51 59 69
FAX (0535) 51 59 94
www.hotelakouas.com
Decorated in an interesting art deco style, this ville nouvelle hotel offers reasonably spacious guest rooms with en suite bathrooms, air-conditioning, and well-soundproofed windows (a feature you'll appreciate when the call to prayer starts blaring out of nearby mosque loudspeakers at 5 a.m.).
🛈 50 🍴 🏊 🏧 MC, V

🏨 HOTEL DE NICE
$$
10 RUE D'ACCRA AND RUE ANTISIRABÉ
TEL (0535) 52 03 08
FAX (0535) 40 21 04
www.hoteldenice
-meknes.com
One of the better cheap options in Meknès, the Hotel de Nice is located right in the center of the ville nouvelle, around a 5-minute walk from the railway station, and 20 minutes from the medina. Away from the reception areas, the interiors are rather spartan; the rooms have only simple, utilitarian furnishings and plain white walls. With air-conditioning, comfortable beds, and en suite bathrooms, however, the rooms are a good enough deal to overlook the simple decor.
🛈 45 🍴 🏧 MC, V

RESTAURANTS

🍴 A CASA
$$$$
8 BOULEVARD MOULAY YOUSSEF
TEL (0535) 52 40 19
A favorite of the well-heeled Meknés elite, this elegant Parisian-style restaurant serves

a wide range of Moroccan and French dishes with an inventive modern twist. The wine list is superb, and the service discreet and attentive.

⊞ 80 ⊕ Closed Sun. ☒ ☒ MC, V

🍴 RIAD ARABESQUE

$$$$

20 DERB EL MITER

TEL (0535) 63 53 21

Housed in an atmospheric 19th-century riad, this restaurant is renowned for its unpretentious traditional cooking. The riad has two separate restaurant areas, the first, Le Jinan, is located in the courtyard, while the second, Al Manzah, is up on the rooftop terrace. The menu here is authentically Moroccan, based on traditional family recipes that are generations old.

⊞ 40 ☒ ☒ MC, V

🍴 LE DAUPHIN

$$$

5 AVENUE MOHAMED V

TEL (0535) 52 34 23

This restaurant in the city's busiest avenue specializes in fish and seafood dishes. Its large size and traditional cuisine make it a popular choice with tour groups, so reservations are recommended. Be sure to try the lobster in herb butter sauce.

⊞ 100 ☒ MC, V

MOULAY IDRISS

🏨 DAR ZERHOUNE

$$$

42 DERB ZOUAK

TEL (0535) 54 43 71

www.buttonsinn.com

This recently opened riad is the only real accomodation option for those who opt to stay in Moulay Idriss. Luckily, the riad is clean and well kept, with attractive interiors and en suite rooms. The view from the roof terrace is impressive,

and the serene atmosphere makes this a great place to stop and relax away from the big cities.

① 4 ☒ Cash only

VOLUBILIS

🍴 LA CORBEILLE FLEURIE

$$

ENTRANCE TO VOLUBILIS

Serving light snacks and tagines, this restaurant is popular due largely to its location at the entrance of the Volubilis ruins. You can sit outside and enjoy great views across the valley.

⊞ 100 🅿 ☒ Cash only

◾ MARRAKECH & AROUND

ESSAOUIRA

HOTELS

🏨 HEURE BLEUE PALAIS

$$$$$

2 RUE IBN BATOUTA

TEL (0524) 78 34 34

www.heure-bleue.com

An elegant hotel, Heure Bleue Palais has spacious public areas. There are even palm trees in the luxurious main hall, which is also lined by arches. Throughout the hotel, the decor is a mix of European and North African tastes. First-story rooms are clustered around a patio and have showers rather than bathtubs. Second-story suites have marble bathrooms. All of the guest rooms have Internet access and a DVD player. A gourmet restaurant offers a menu of European and Moroccan cuisine. Lunch is also served beside the pool on the rooftop terrace.

① 35 ☒ ☒ ☒ All major cards

🏨 RYAD WATIER

$$$$$

16 RUE CEUTA

TEL (0524) 08 18 33

www.ryad-watier-maroc.com

Ryad Watier is in the medina, but it is a quiet place to stay. The hotel has a delightful garden and terraces and also offers a hammam and an extensive library. The building, which is on four levels, has been carefully renovated in a traditional style. The decor features the highest levels of craftmanship. The hotel is set around a central courtyard with comfortable suites off cool, beautifully furnished passageways. The beach and the ocean stretch out in the breathtaking view from the rooftop terrace.

① 10 ☒ Cash only

🏨 Hotel 🍴 Restaurant ① No. of Guest Rooms ⊞ No. of Seats 🅿 Parking ⊕ Closed ⊟ Elevator

SOMETHING SPECIAL

🏨 VILLA DE L'O
$$$$$
3 RUE MOHAMED BEN MESSAOUD
TEL (0524) 47 63 75
www.villadelo.com
Beside the medina walls, Villa de l'O is an 18th-century riad. The hotel is close to the beach and the souks. While the interior has a seductive Moroccan design, the facilities are modern. The setting is romantic, while the rooms and suites are luxurious. Some rooms have a fine ocean view, which can also be enjoyed from the rooftop terrace. Villa de l'O treats guests to impeccable but friendly service and attention to detail.
🛏 12 🗝 MC, V

🏨 RIAD AL MADINA
$$$
9 RUE ATTARINE
TEL (0524) 47 59 07
www.riadalmadina.com
Riad al Madina is a restored riad in the shade of the city's medieval walls. The peaceful courtyard is just the spot to rest on a hot day, while the large roof terrace is another pleasant place to unwind. The decor is an artistic modern interpretation of traditional North African design, and the main public areas are spacious. The restaurant serves Moroccan and Western dishes. The staff is friendly, and the hotel has many charming features.
🛏 54 ❄ 🗝 All major cards

🏨 RIAD LE GRAND LARGE
$$
2 RUE OUM-RABIA
TEL (0524) 47 28 66
www.riadlegrandlarge.com
The plant-filled courtyard of this compact riad is a haven in the busy city. The understated decor of the rooms reflects both traditional Moroccan tastes and minimalist simplicity. Decor is more ornate in the public areas, but the whole riad oozes charm. The terrace has a stunning view over the medina. The beach is only a short walk away.
🛏 10 🗝 MC, V

RESTAURANTS

🍴 LE CHALET DE LA PLAGE
$$$$
BOULEVARD MOHAMED V
TEL (0524) 47 59 42
The specialty of Le Chalet de la Plage is seafood, and the ambience is chic. This seafront restaurant has photos of movie stars and other famous international figures who have dined there. The restaurant has a veranda that faces onto the beach. It is busy and popular and, while the fish and shellfish menu is justly renowned, it offers a rather limited choice of nonfish dishes for the main course. Reservations recommended.
🗝 MC, V

🍴 TAROS
$$$
2 RUE SKALA, OFF PLACE MOULAY HASSAN
TEL (0524) 47 64 07
FAX (0524) 47 64 08
www.taroscafe.com
A relaxed café, bar lounge, and restaurant, Taros is one of the places to be seen in Essaouira, particularly in the bar lounge, which is known for its cocktails. The tasteful decor marries traditional and modern styles. Taros is famous for its seafood, tagines, and refined French cuisine. Locally sourced ingredients are used as much as possible. The attractive terrace, with an ocean view, is a relaxing place to have lunch.
🕐 Closed Sun. 🗝 MC, V

🍴 VILLA MAROC
$$$
10 RUE ABDELLAH BEN YASSINE
TEL (0524) 47 31 47
www.villamaroc.com
Villa Maroc was one of the first riads in Essaouira to be converted into a hotel. It has been lovingly restored by a Swiss-Moroccan couple. Comfort and personal service characterize Villa Maroc, which has small intimate salons, where couples may dine in romantic snug surroundings, rather than a large dining room. The cuisine is both traditional and innovative, using locally sourced ingredients.
🗝 Cash only

🍴 DAR LOUBANE
$$
24 RUE DE RIF
TEL (0524) 47 62 96
Set in the medina, Dar Loubane serves a traditional Moroccan menu. The restaurant is in the courtyard of an old riad and is popular with locals. The set menu is inexpensive, but diners can also choose from a more extensive à la carte menu. The atmosphere is friendly, traditional, and authentic, while the cuisine attracts many visitors to come again and again.
🕐 Closed Wed. 🗝 Cash only

MARRAKECH

HOTELS

🏨 DAR LES CIGOGNES
$$$$$
108 RUE DE BERRIMA
TEL (0524) 38 27 40
FAX (0524) 38 47 67
www.lescigognes.com
Housed in a revovated mansion in the heart of the historic medina, the Dar les Cigognes is a luxurious boutique hotel with its own hammam. There are seven "deluxe" double rooms, three slightly smaller

"superior" rooms, and one suite, all clustered around a large central courtyard with a roof terrace above. Excellent meals are served in a spectacular dining area.

[i] 11 [S] [icon] MC, V

🏨 DELLAROSA HOTEL AND SUITES

$$$$$

5 AVENUE MOULAY EL HASSAN

TEL (0524) 42 22 27

FAX (0524) 44 89 09

www.dellarosa-marrakech.com

A tasteful hotel presented in bold colors with a modernist vibe, the Dellarosa is popular with both leisure travelers and businesspeople. It is near the commercial district and minutes from the Djemaa el Fna square. Amenities include a spa and à la carte restaurant.

[i] 74 [icons] All major cards

🏨 LA MAISON ARABE

$$$$$

1 DERB ASSEBBE, BÂB DOUKKALA

TEL (0524) 38 70 10

FAX (0524) 38 72 21

www.lamaisonarabe.com

An impressive 19th-century mansion converted into a hotel in the 1940s, the Maison Arabe is one of the finest hotels in Marrakech. The hotel, along with its sister country club (15 minutes away on a complimentary shuttle bus out of town) manages to fit in all the amenities and luxuries of a grand hotel like the Mamounia (see p. 297), while maintaining the atmosphere of a small riad or boutique hotel.

[i] 52 [icons] AE, MC, V

🏨 MAISON MK

$$$$$

14 DERB SEBBAI, QUARTIER KSOUR

TEL (0524) 37 61 73

www.maisonMK.com

Maison MK offers guests an indulgent vacation in a boutique hotel. The rooms are decorated with rich fabrics and have luxurious bathrooms with deep tubs and a shower. MK has the facilities you would expect in a larger hotel, including 24-hour service, a spa, a small gym, and a hammam. The view from the terrace toward the Atlas Mountains is stunning, while the lounge, with its central copper firepit, is an ideal spot to relax in the evening. A seven-course gourmet set menu is just one of the options in the restaurant.

[i] 6 [icons] All major cards

🏨 LA MAMOUNIA

$$$$$

BÂB JEDID

TEL (0524) 38 86 00

FAX (0524) 44 40 44

www.mamounia.com

Built as a royal palace in the late 19th century, this fabulous hotel has lost none of its glamour or opulence over the years. Sir Winston Churchill and a host of Hollywood stars have stayed at this legendary hotel, located just a few minutes' walk from the Koutoubia Mosque and the Djemaa el Fna. The interiors are traditionally decorated, with lots of elaborate zellij tilework and ornately carved wood. The rooms are spacious and the service discreet and attentive. Guests are also treated to acres of gardens, swimming pools, a spa, and several restaurants serving the finest gourmet cuisine.

[i] 210 [P] [icons] All major cards

SOMETHING SPECIAL

🏨 NOIR D'IVOIRE

$$$$$

31 DERB JEDID, BÂB DOUKKALA

TEL (0524) 38 16 53

www.noir-d-ivoire.com

The creation of British interior designer Jill Fechtmann, this riad is a stunningly beautiful oasis of quiet and comfort only a few minutes from the Djemaa el Fna. The more expensive suites boast features like private roof terraces, hot tubs, and astoundingly comfortable beds. The public spaces, including a small but well-appointed gym, a restaurant, and a library, are all immaculately maintained. The staff provides a personalized service that includes helpful touches like the mobile phones (programmed with the contact numbers of the staff) they lend to newcomers in case they get lost in the medina.

[icon] 9 [icons] All major cards

🏨 RIAD ANAYELA

$$$$$

28 DERB ZERWAL

www.anayela.com

This luxurious riad is decorated to the highest standards with modern interpretations of Moroccan furnishings. The rooms are large and have airconditioning and beautifully appointed bathrooms. The central arcaded courtyard, with its inviting heated pool, is palatial. Opulently furnished with drapes and rugs, the "Flying Carpet" is a tower on the terrace where meals may be taken in a romantic Arabian Nights setting. Impeccable service and fine traditional cuisine complete a memorable experience.

[i] 5 [S] [icon] Cash only

🏨 VILLA DES ORANGERS

$$$$$

6 RUE SIDI MIMOUN

TEL (0524) 38 46 38

FAX (0524) 38 51 23

www.villadesorangers.com

Like the Maison Arabe (see this page), this luxury hotel manages to capture the

---

🏨 Hotel 🍴 Restaurant [i] No. of Guest Rooms [icon] No. of Seats [P] Parking [icon] Closed [icon] Elevator intimacy of a small riad or private home, while at the same time having all the facilities you'd expect from a grand hotel. This hotel boasts three swimming pools, its own hammam, and a gym. The rooms and suites are all spacious and beautifully decorated, with more expensive ones offering features like access to private terraces, swimming pools, and fireplaces (a romantic detail that is surprisingly useful in the winter).

🛏 27 P 🔄 🅢 ♨ 🍸
🅢 AE, MC, V

🏨 KSAR CATALINA

$$$$

MEDINA

TEL (0524) 33 54 99

www.ksarcatalina.com

With its luxury spa complete with a hammam, this traditional palace-style riad is in the center of Marrakech. Its guest rooms are sumptuous and well equipped, and its restaurant serves local and international gourmet cuisine.

🛏 10 P 🅢 ♨ 🍸 🅢 All major cards

🏨 RIAD ARIHA

$$$$

90 DERB AHMED EL BORJ

TEL (0524) 37 58 50

www.riadariha.com

With its clean, minimalist interiors, this riad is a far cry from the densely packed Moroccan decor of most riads. The pure white rooms still manage to feel authentically Moroccan, however, and the centuries-old mansion that houses the riad is a refreshing, cool, and quiet place.

🛏 5 🅢 🍸 🅢 MC, V

🏨 RIAD DAR SBIHI

$$$$

25 DERB TAHT EL KHOCHBA, ZAOUIA EL ABBASSIA, MEDINA

TEL (0524) 38 59 58

www.riaddarsbihi.com

A typical riad, Dar Sbihi has a romantic garden patio with a beautifully tiled cooling fountain at the center. Arcades surround this courtyard, with rooms opening off under the arches. The property has been restored by two generations of a family that still runs the riad as a stylish guesthouse. It is decorated in the traditional local style with colorful lanterns and fabrics. Guests will enjoy good food and the attentive service offered by the staff. A rooftop terrace has fine views over the city.

🛏 10 🅢 🅢 ♨ 🅢 All major cards

🏨 DAR IHSSANE

$$$

14 DERB CHORFAA EL KEBIR, NEAR MOUSSAINE MOSQUE

TEL (0524) 38 78 26

www.darihssane.com

With its excellent location and surprisingly quiet premises, this mid-priced riad is a good choice for those who want to spend their days exploring the nearby souks. The rooms can be a little stuffy, and there is no air-conditioning, so it's not the best place if you're planning to lie in every day.

🛏 5 🅢 Cash only

🏨 DAR SALAM

$$$

162 DERB BEN FAYDA, NEAR BÃB DOUKKALA, MEDINA

TEL (0524) 32 93 09

FAX (0524) 38 31 10

www.dar-salam.com

The rooms in this riad are rather small, and the decor a little garish, but it offers a more interesting experience than most other accomodations in this price range—the location in the medina, within walking distance of the city's great sights, is also a plus. If you're looking for somewhere cheap and interesting to stay, ask about the Berber tents they erect on the rooftop in

the summer.

🛏 8 🅢 🅢 Cash only

🏨 JNANE MOGADOR

$$$

116 RIAD ZITOUNE KEDIM

TEL (0524) 42 63 24

FAX (0524) 42 63 23

www.jnanemogador.com

A recently opened riad in the historic medina, close to the Djemaa el Fna. While the location is convenient for sightseeing, it also means that the hotel tends to be rather noisy. The public areas, including a roof terrace and restaurant, are pleasant, but the rooms can be a little cramped and stuffy.

🛏 7 🅢 🅢 MC, V

🏨 RIAD BELDI

$$$

3 DERB LALLA AOUICH, ASSOUEL

TEL (0661) 20 50 47

www.riadbeldi.com

This riad, while not spectacularly situated or decorated, is known for its friendly staff and good traditional food. The owners also specialize in organizing treks to the mountains, the desert, and other places of interest.

🛏 5 🅢 Cash only

RESTAURANTS

🍴 BÔ-ZIN

$$$$$

DOUAR LAHNA, ROUTE DE L'OURIKA

TEL (0524) 38 80 12

FAX (0524) 38 80 14

www.bo-zin.com

If you want to get away from Marrakech's narrow streets, then this restaurant, located on the road south to Asni, is a good choice. The food here is a fusion of high-class international cuisine and traditional Moroccan, resulting in dishes like lobster tagine or Mechoui lamb with truffle oil. Similarly, the interiors are decorated in a

---

🅢 Nonsmoking   🅢 Air-conditioning   🅢 Indoor Pool   ♨ Outdoor Pool   🍸 Health Club   🅢 Credit Cards

contemporary style with strong Moroccan influences. Although the food here is slightly overpriced, the modern, exciting atmosphere and well-stocked bar make it a popular spot with locals and tourists alike. The restaurant doesn't open until 8 p.m., but stays open late.

🛏 275 🅿 🔲 ⬛ AE, DC, V

🍴 RESTAURANT STYLIA
$$$$$
34 RUE EL KSOUR
TEL (0524) 44 35 87
www.restaurant-stylia.com
Restaurant Stylia offers the opportunity to dine in ornate surroundings in one of three salons, each decorated in luxurious modern renditions of Moroccan design. Bouquets of flowers, wafts of incense, and soothing traditional music from a lute and tambour add to a romantic atmosphere. Set in a converted palace, diners enjoy refined gourmet dishes from an extensive menu. Stylia has been awarded the highest grade in restaurant classification in Morocco; the quality of the food and impeccable service make the restaurant among the most famous in the country.

🔲 ⬛ AE, MC, V

🍴 AL FASSIA GUÉLIZ
$$$$
BOULEVARD MOHAMED ZERK-TOUNI, GUÉLIZ
TEL (0524) 43 40 60
www.alfassia.com
Located just a short walk outside the medina, Al Fassia is a popular restaurant known for the quality of its traditional Moroccan dishes. The staff (both in the kitchen and out on the floor) are almost all women. Make sure you make reservations a few days in advance, as the place is usually fully booked in the peak tourist season.

🔲 ⬛ AE, MC, V

SOMETHING SPECIAL

🍴 GRAND CAFÉ DE LA POSTE
$$$$
CORNER OF BOULEVARD EL MANSOUR EDDAHBI AND AVENUE IMAM MALIK, GUÉLIZ
TEL (0524) 43 30 38
FAX (0524) 43 42 24
www.grandcafedelaposte.com
Located in what was once a French colonial sorting office, this Marrakech institution has been a popular restaurant since the 1920s. While the interiors have been updated and modern amenities like air-conditioning installed, the place still has a glamorous colonial-era atmosphere to it. The food served includes dishes from all over the world, with an emphasis on French and Moroccan cuisine. The food is rather expensive, however, so visitors may just want to stop in here for a drink in their well-stocked and fashionable bar.

🛏 350 🅿 🔲 ⬛ AE, DC, V

🍴 KECHMARA
$$$$
3 RUE DE LA LIBERTÉ, GUÉLIZ
TEL (0524) 42 25 32
www.kechmara.com
This trendy and modern bar/restaurant is the most fashionable place to be seen in Marrakech. With its good, if unremarkable, French and Italian cuisine and minimalist decor, there's nothing here to draw visitors looking for a distinctively Moroccan experience. But if you're looking for a cool, quiet place to get lunch, or a fun place to go in the evening, Kechmara—with its live music and club nights—is the best option in town.

🔲 ⬛ MC, V

PRICES

HOTELS
The cost of a double room with private bath and hot water in the peak season is given by $ signs. Low season rates can be considerably lower.

$$$$$	over $200
$$$$	$100–$200
$$$	$50–$100
$$	$25–$50
$	Under $25

RESTAURANTS
The average cost of a two-course meal for one person, without tax, tip, or drinks, is given by $ signs.

$$$$$	over $50
$$$$	$40–$50
$$$	$25–$40
$$	$15–$25
$	Under $15

🍴 DAR MOHA
$$$
81 RUE DAR EL BACHA
TEL (0524) 38 64 00
FAX (0544) 38 69 98
www.darmoha.ma
Housed in a palace built in the early 20th century for an adviser to the notorious warlord El Glaoui, this restaurant offers a unique fusion of traditional Moroccan and modern European cuisine. It is a good idea to reserve a day or two in advance if you want to get one of the tables by the reflecting pool in the lovely courtyard.

🕐 Closed Mon. ⬛ MC, V

🍴 LE FOUNDOUK
$$$
55 SOUK HAL FASSI, KAT BENNAHÏD
TEL (0524) 37 81 90

FAX (0524) 37 81 76
www.foundouk.com
Tucked away behind a nondescript doorway in the north
of the medina, this beautifully
decorated restaurant is well
worth the considerable effort
it takes to find it. Rather than
attempting to fuse the traditional and colonial influences
that compete for attention
in Moroccan cooking, this
restaurant simply has two
menus—one Moroccan and
one French. If you reserve a
table in advance, you will be
met at the nearest taxi rank
by a waiter and stand a good
chance of getting a table on
the wonderful roof terrace.
🏧 MC, V

🍴 KSAR EL HAMRA
$$$
28 RIAD ZITOUN LAKDIM
SABT IDN DAOUD
TEL (0544) 42 76 07
FAX (0544) 42 77 42
www.restaurant-ksar
elhamra.com
A few minutes' walk from the
Djemaa el Fna square, this
traditional restaurant housed
in a former palace is right
in the heart of the medina.
Elegant and lavishly decorated,
it serves authentic Moroccan
dishes that include tagines,
grilled fish, and a selection of
pastries as desserts.
🔲 100 🔳 🏧 MC, V

🍴 AMANDINE
$$
177 RUE MOHAMED EL BEQUAL
TEL (0524) 44 95 88
FAX (0524) 44 60 42
www.amandine
marrakech.com
This delightful little café is
divided into two halves: one
specializes in ice cream, while
the other sells French and
Moroccan pastries. Both sides
of the café are wonderful.
The Moroccan pastries, in
particular, are amazing. Pick up
a platter of honey-and-almond

briouates with a friend and sit
down at one of the pavement
tables with a cup of coffee.
🏧 Cash only

THE HIGH ATLAS

🏨 KASBAH TAMADOT
$$$$$
ASNI
TEL (0524) 36 82 00
www.kasbahtamadot
.virgin.com
This exclusive resort, owned
by British entrepeneur Richard
Branson, is located in the hills
just ouside Asni. For those
who can afford it (which
isn't many), it offers a serene
getaway from the world that
is still within a hour's travel of
Marrakech.
🔲 24 🅿 🔳 🕳 🎽 📺 🏧 All
major cards

SOMETHING SPECIAL

🏨 DAR TASSA
$$$$
OUIRGANE, NEAR ASNI
TEL (0524) 48 43 12
www.dartassa.com
About a 90-minute drive from
the bustle of Marrakech, this
immaculately kept and lovingly
decorated riad offers a peaceful hideaway with stunning
mountain views. The attentive
staff is happy to organize
excursions and hikes into the
surrounding hills, as well as
trips to the city of Marrakech.
🔲 10 🅿 🔳 🏧 Cash only

🏨 KENZI LOUKA
$$$$
OUKAÏMEDEN
TEL (0524) 31 90 80
This whimsical brown-and-
beige pyramid-shaped hotel
looks like it would have been
the height of jet-set fashion
around 1974. Although the
interiors are a little dated, the
rooms are clean and well maintained, and the facilities excellent. The pool with a retractable

roof is an unusual feature.
🔲 101 🅿 🔳 🏧 All major
cards

🏨 CHEZ JUJU
$$
OUKAÏMEDEN
TEL (0528) 31 90 05
FAX (0528) 84 43 79
This cheap but pleasant guest-
house is popular with skiiers
in the winter and hikers in the
summer. Although this slightly
utilitarian hotel doesn't have
much in the way of facilities or
luxury features, the beds are
comfortable and the rooms
clean.
🔲 18 🅿 🏧 Cash only

■ AGADIR, THE DRAÂ VALLEY, & THE SOUTH

AGADIR

HOTELS

🏨 DORINT ATLANTIC PALACE
$$$$$
SECTEUR BALNEAIRE AND
TOURISTIQUE
TEL (0528) 82 41 46
FAX; (0528) 82 41 70
www.atlanticpalace
-agadir.com
The five-star Dorint Atlantic
is a pretty standard beachside
resort, complete with a large
outdoor pool, comfortable
guest rooms with balconies,
and a selection of bars and
restaurants. The clientele is
primarily European families
who spend their days around
the pool.
🔲 280 🅿 🕳 🔳 🕳 🎽 📺
🏧 All major cards

🏨 RIAD AIN KHADRA
$$$$$
ROUTE D'AGADIR, TAROUDANT
TEL (0528) 85 41 42

🏧 Nonsmoking 🔳 Air-conditioning 🕳 Indoor Pool 🕳 Outdoor Pool 🎽 Health Club 🏧 Credit Cards

Located about halfway between Agadir and the inland town of Taroudant, this delightful riad offers a relaxing hideaway with an authentically Moroccan feel. Although it is advertised as a riad, the Ain Khadra, with its swimming pool and large rooms, has more in common with boutique hotels than traditional riads. The food is excellent.

🏨 8 🅿 🔁 ⛱ Cash only

🏨 ROYAL MIRAGE HOTEL
$$$$$
BOULEVARD MOHAMED V
TEL (0528) 84 32 32
FAX (0528) 84 43 79
www.royalmiragehotels.com
With its dramatic decor of bold colors and lavish furnishings inspired by Moroccan designs yet with a modern twist, this luxury hotel is one of the best in Agadir. Enjoy its poolside à la carte restaurant and fitness suite.

🏨 183 🅿 🔁 🚭 ⛱ 🛗
🔁 All major cards

SOMETHING SPECIAL

🏨 VILLA RIADANA
$$$$
DOMAINE DE RIADES
BENSERGAO
TEL (0528) 28 32 00
www.agadir-riadana.com
This family-run riad offers a number of lovingly decorated, spacious rooms and suites. Although it is much smaller than many of the other options in town, the Riadana still manages to fit in a well-appointed spa and a pool. The service is attentive and the staff friendly. It should be noted, however, that it is not particularly close to the center of town, and taxis can be hard to come by, so it is a good idea to rent your own transport.

🏨 11 🅿 🔁 🔁 MC, V

🏨 ARGANA HOTEL
$$$
BOULEVARD MOHAMED V
TEL (0528) 84 83 04
www.argana-hotel.com
One of the better options within Agadir itself, this large modern hotel offers all the usual amenities, such as a pool, a bar, and air-conditioning. Like many of the hotels in Agadir, the prices for food and drinks are very high in the hotel itself—because many of its European guests remain on-site for the duration of their stay—and the surrounding beaches can be a little crowded. It has several family-friendly features, such as a children's pool and plenty of no-smoking areas.

🏨 234 🅿 🔁 🚭 ⛱ 🛗
🔁 All major cards

RESTAURANTS

🍽 LA MADRAGUE
$$$$
RÉSIDENCE 6 M3, MARINA
TEL (0528) 84 24 24
FAX (0528) 82 01 30
This restaurant is a relatively new addition to Agadir's small collection of quality eateries, but it has already established a good reputation. The menu includes both French and Moroccan dishes, with an emphasis on fish and seafood. The wine list is extensive and well selected, and the staff is happy to advise on what would go best with your meal. There is a large outside seating area, which is particularly popular in the evenings.

🍽 120 🅿 🔁 🔁 All major cards

🍽 L'ORANGE BLEUE
$$
ON THE CORNER OF BOULEVARD DU 20 AOUT AND CHEMIN DE OUED SOUSS
TEL (0528) 84 69 30

Located in the center of town, this popular restaurant offers authentic Moroccan cuisine. The menu includes well-known fare, like tagines, but also a number of more exotic local dishes like saffron chicken. The interiors are attractively decorated and furnished, and there is a pleasant outdoor dining area on the terrace.

🅿 🔁 🔁 MC, V

DAKHLA

🏨 HOTEL RIAD DAKHLA
$$$$
THE BAY OF DAKHLA
TEL (0661) 19 13 39
www.hotel-dakhla
-sahara.com
This exclusive beachside resort is an unexpected outpost of Moroccan charm a long way from the cities of the north. The interiors are decorated in a simple style that uses modern furnishings but a traditional color palette. All the rooms are en suite bathrooms, and many have features like private access, access to the hotel pool, and stunning sea views.

🏨 43 🅿 🔁 ⛱ 🔁 All major cards

🍽 CAFÉ RESTAURANT SAMARKAND
$$
AVENUE MOHAMED V
TEL (0528) 89 83 16
The list of available ingredients starts to look distinctly thin once you get this far south, but the cooks at this restaurant do amazing things with what they have. The best options are, of course, the dishes made with locally caught fish and seafood.

🔁 Cash only

🍽 CASA LUIS
$$
14 AVENUE MOHAMED V

🏨 Hotel   🍽 Restaurant   🏨 No. of Guest Rooms   🍽 No. of Seats   🅿 Parking   🔁 Closed   🔁 Elevator

TEL (0528) 89 81 93
A small Spanish restaurant selling excellent omelettes and a range of seafood dishes that includes a very fine paella.
🅢 Cash only

LAÂYOUNE

🏨 HOTEL LAKOURA
$$$$
AVENUE HASSAN II
TEL (0528) 89 33 78
This comfortable and reasonably priced hotel is located in the modern half of the town. The rooms are simple, but have en suite bathrooms and good views across the town. It should be noted that this hotel is sometimes entirely booked by UN officials, so it's worth making a reservation early.
🅿 🅢 Cash only

🏨 HOTEL JODESA
$$
233 BOULEVARD DU MEKKA
TEL (0528) 99 20 64
This budget hotel offers comfortable, clean rooms, with shared bathrooms and free Wi-Fi. It doesn't have much in the way of facilities, but is a good choice for the price.
🅿 🅢 Cash only

🍽 AU PALAIS DES GLACES
$$
BOULEVARD DU MEKKA
TEL (0528) 98 04 76
The idea of ice cream in the desert is a slightly surreal one, but there is no doubting their assertion that they serve the best desserts and ice creams in Western Sahara. It's also a good place to get some early-morning coffee before heading on to your next destination.
🅢 Cash only

OUARZAZATE

🏨 LE BERBERE PALACE
$$$$

QUARTIER MANSOUR EDDAHBI
TEL (0544) 88 31 05
FAX (0544) 88 30 71
While it has been a long time since this place had a face-lift, the luxurious interiors, comfortable rooms, and excellent service mean that this hotel is still one of the best options in town. Guests can relax in the shade of the palm trees around the pool or eat in its excellent restaurant.
🛈 222 🅿 🅢 🏊 🅥
🅢 MC, V

🏨 IBIS MOUSSAFIR
$$$$
AVENUE MOULAY RACHID
TEL (0524) 89 91 10
www.ibishotel.com
This chain hotel makes more effort with its interior decoration than you'd expect. The rooms are comfortable and modern, but not without some Moroccan decorative details. It is an ideal place to stop over if you're traveling from the southern desert to Marrakech and beyond.
🛈 104 🅿 ⬌ 🏊 🅢 All major cards

🏨 DAR RITA
$$$
39 RUE DE LA MOSQUÉE, HAY TASSOUMATE
TEL (0654) 16 47 26
www.darrita.com
This recently opened riad is situated in the heart of Ouarzazate's ancient medina. It hasn't had an opportunity to establish much of a reputation as yet, but its British owners have grand plans for their project. Despite the age of the building, all the rooms have en suite bathrooms, air-conditioning, and Wi-Fi. Meals are served either in the cozy dining room or up on the roof terrace.
🛈 7 🅢 🅢 Cash only

🏨 LE PETIT RIAD
$$$
1582 HAY AL WAHDA
TEL (0524) 88 59 50
Although it is really more a small hotel than a riad, the Petit Riad is not lacking in local character or charm. The hotel is located a fair distance from the center of the town, so it's probably better suited to those with their own transport. This distance from the town does ensure peace and quiet, however, especially on the lovely terraces and around the small pool.
🛈 7 🅢 🏊 🅢 Cash only

🍽 RESTAURANT LE OUARZAZATE
$$$
QUARTIER SIDI DAOUD
TEL (0544) 88 31 10
FAX (0544) 88 44 06
A lively restaurant where only Moroccan cuisine is served, including huge tagines of meat and locally grown vegetables that are brought to your table with considerable flair, this is one of the most popular eateries in Ouarzazate. Music and dancing are a specialty.
🍴 100 🅿 🅢 Cash only

Shopping

Morocco is a country known for its shopping. Visitors come for the vibrant life of the big-city souks (where you can get anything from a pair of handmade shoes to a live chicken) and the authentic simplicity of small-town craft stalls. For those less comfortable with crowds and haggling, Morocco's *ville nouvelles* (new towns) are also home to numerous modern cosmopolitan boutiques.

Haggling

The aspect of shopping in Morocco that elicits the most surprise and confusion from Western visitors is the ubiquitous negotiation over prices between shopkeepers and customers. While ville nouvelle boutiques and other Western imports typically stick to their fixed prices, out in the world of the souks and stalls, the value of everything from food to furniture is a far more fluid concept. A lot of people come to Morocco thinking that this haggling culture will allow them to pick up astonishing bargains, and many do, but it should be remembered that no matter how far you've talked down a shopkeeper, he (or sometimes she) wouldn't be selling anything to you if he weren't making a profit on it.

The most important thing is to decide how much you think an item is worth before you begin negotiating over it. Have a look at the quality of goods on sale in other parts of town, watch to see what the locals think of each shopkeeper's wares, and, if you have time, visit an Ensemble Artisanal (most towns have one) to see what sort of prices particular items fetch if sold at fixed prices. Once you've begun haggling, don't be put off by the protests and furious faces the shopkeeper might make—the theatrics of the negotiation are all good-natured. Remember your price range and stick with it, until the shopkeeper either relents or sincerely tells you to look somewhere else. If he doesn't lower his price to your level, then politely refuse his offer and walk away—this act alone may be enough to bring one final reduction in the price.

Once you've reached an agreement, you will be expected to pay in cash. Be sure to promptly pay the agreed price—this is their livelihood, after all, not a game; to back out after formally agreeing on a price is seen as rude and insulting.

Precautions

In Morocco, all sales are final. Once you've handed over your cash, the item is yours. Even if it falls apart in your hands as you walk out of the store (which is improbably, admittedly), the shopkeeper is extremely unlikely to give you a refund or offer a replacement. There are also a wide variety of scams to catch tourists looking for unreasonably low prices. These range from vendors passing off cheap, mass-produced items as handcrafted goods, to sales of artfully forged historic artifacts. Any antique items with a claimed connection to Morocco's largely vanished Jewish population are suspicious, as are items that appear to have been removed from historic buildings. It is not uncommon for criminal gangs to severely damage neglected historic buildings in order to salvage items they can sell. Don't encourage this practice by giving them your custom.

Where to Shop

There are several different types of stores in Morocco, each with its own etiquette and distinctive features. The term "souk" is often used to describe any kind of old-town shopping area, particularly covered markets specializing in a particular type of product. Typically souks take the form of broad streets with stores on their sides. The stores in souks are open at the front, and it is not always clear where the store begins and the street ends. The objects in souks, particularly in tourist cities like Fès and Marrakech, are rarely made on site, or even locally. In souks, customers are expected to haggle, often loudly and assertively. Outside of the big cities, souks tend to be more mundane affairs, filled with women buying groceries and clothes, and men lounging around smoking or drinking mint tea. Craft goods sold in these places are likely to have been made by the person selling them, or at least someone nearby.

The more conventional stores of Morocco's ville nouvelles are more reserved places. Bargaining with the owner will likely earn you an angry reprimand or at the very least a dirty look. For the most part, the goods on sale here are imported, high-status items for the Moroccan middle class that would likely seem pretty unremarkable to tourists.

Workshops and cooperatives are increasingly common sights in Morocco's towns and cities, their growth driven by a developing interest among both tourists and locals in high-quality Moroccan craftsmanship, rather than just souvenir trinkets. In these places, the store often does double duty as the owner's workshop and home. Cooperatives are often relatively large organizations, employing large groups or even whole communities. Cooperatives allow craftsmen and women to sell their wares directly to customers, without middlemen taking their share. They are often allied with social projects or charitable institutions—

providing an independent source of income for Moroccan women, for example.

What to Buy

No matter how tempted you are by the beautifully carved and inlaid furniture or the sumptuously woven carpets, for the most part visitors to Morocco restrict their purchases to what will fit in their luggage. The craftsmen and women of Morocco are just as good at making things small as they are at making them big and heavy, however, so those looking for a beautiful and uniquely Moroccan reminder of their trip don't have to be restricted to tourist trinkets.

As a lightweight alternative to the heavy and expensive knotted carpets that every hustler and guide will try to foist on you, look for Berber rugs and blankets, known as *foutas*. These are bright and colorful, woven with imaginative and interesting abstract patterns. Expect to pay up to $100 for more complex and well-made examples, much less for smaller and simpler ones. The more drab ones are often made entirely with natural dyes, while the more garish examples are typically made using industrially manufactured dye.

One of the most distinctive sights in any souk is the storefronts laden with rack upon rack of multicolored *babouche* slippers. Comfortable, small, and very pretty, these pointed shoes make an ideal gift. They can cost anywhere from around $10 to as much as $50 for the highest quality examples. Most are made from the soft, traditionally tanned leather (often goatskin) that can be found across Morocco. If you're really curious (or just have no sense of smell), then head to the tanneries in Fès, Marrakech, or Tétouan to see how this leather is made. A quick warning for those very fond of their newly purchased

babouches, though: It's hard to describe the process without using the word "rotting" at least once.

Although large items of furniture are not an option for most travelers, even the smallest piece of Moroccan wood carving is often exceptionally beautiful. The most common choices for visitors are the ornate inlaid boxes sold in souks across the country. These range in price from around $50 to several hundred dollars. Traditionally the most sought after have been those made from the local *thuyya* wood, although tourists are now advised to avoid products made from this fragrant, dense wood, as some of the last remaining thuyya forests are being cut away to create souvenirs for Western tourists.

Lastly, Morocco has a long tradition of jewelry making, crafting attractive decorative bracelets, necklaces, and earrings. Although the local style tends to be a little overworked, the simpler items made from silver and semiprecious stones make for lovely and distinctive souvenirs.

Payment

Credit cards are still a fairly rare sight in Moroccan stores, and the vast majority of transactions are still done in cash. The larger stores of the ville nouvelle often take cards, and every now and then you might come across a prosperous, tourist-oriented store in the medina that accepts them, but this is very much the exception. If you want to shop in Morocco, you have to carry cash. Despite the dense crowds you find in medinas, theft from tourists is rare, and as long as you take reasonable precautions, you shouldn't have to walk around tightly clutching your bag and staring down anyone who comes near you.

Sales Tax

Morocco has one of the highest rates of sales tax of any North African country, standing at around 20 percent. This can mean that prices in restaurants and stores may rise rather alarmingly when tax is included in the price. This is, however, only applicable to those areas where shopkeepers bother to pay taxes—outside of the cities, especially in Berber communities, taxes are typically something that happens to other people. You may be required to pay an export tax when you are leaving the country, though, especially if you are conspicuously laden with high-value goods.

Shops & Stores

Due to the informal, marketlike nature of most Moroccan commercial activity, it's hard to provide practical listings for individual stores. The following list of stores represents only a small fraction of Morocco's shopping opportunities. For many, the act of exploring the medina is the most exciting part of shopping in Morocco.

Art Galleries

Morocco's reliable sunshine, vibrant traditional design, and exotic charm have been attracting Western artists for centuries. In addition to these foreign settlers, there is a healthy and rapidly expanding native arts scene, especially in cities like Casablanca and Essaouira.

Athar

12 rue Ibnou Khalouiya, Casablanca
Tel (0522) 29 95 36
New and old works of art from Morocco and neighboring countries.

Galerie Bazar Kasbah

4 rue Tétouan, Essaouira
Tel (0524) 47 61 23
Art gallery showcasing the best of young local artists.

Galerie d'Alice
Résidence Tiguemi, avenue des
FAR Agadir
Tel (0528) 85 30 91
www.alice-galerie.com

Galerie Dar d'Art
6 rue Khalil Metrane, Tanger
Tel (0539) 37 57 07
A gallery of contemporary art and
sculpture from Morocco and the
region.

**Galerie des Arts de Frédéric
Damgaard**
Avenue Oqba, Ibn Nafiaa, Essaouira
Tel (0524) 78 44 46

Galerie Jama
22 rue Ibnou Rochd, Essaouira
Tel (0524) 78 58 97

Galerie Jamil des Beaux Arts
11 Zankat Sbetriyine, Seffarine,
Medina, Fès
Tel (0535) 74 02 07

Galerie La Kasbah
4 rue de Tétouan, Essaouira
Tel (0524) 47 56 05
Art gallery and crafts store selling
everything from modern paintings
to antique carpets.

Galerie Nadar
5 Rue Al Manaziz, Maarif,
Casablanca
Tel (0522) 23 69 00
Galerie Nadar is a Casablanca
institution, recently reopened after
having been closed for many years.

Galerie Othello
9 rue Mohamed Layachi,
Essaouira
Tel (0524) 47 50 95

Bookshops
Most of the stock carried by
Moroccan bookshops is in French,
with a smaller proportion of books
in Arabic. Given the sheer number
of languages spoken in Morocco,
however, it's hardly surprising that

many bookshops also have small
English-language sections. You're
not likely to find a particularly wide
range of books in these stores,
but they'll do if you're looking for
something to read on the train or
for a musty exotic old volume to
put on your shelves.

Librairie Colonnes
54 boulevard Pasteur, Tanger
Tel (0539) 93 69 55

Librairie Farraire
43 rue Oraïbi Jilali, Casablanca
Tel (0522) 22 63 38

Librairie Internationale de Rabat
70 rue T'Ssoule, Rabat
Tel (0537) 75 01 83

Librairie Jack's
Place Moulay Hassan, Essaouira
Tel (0524) 47 55 38

Librairie Papeterie Gillot
44 avenue Mohamed V, Marrakech
Tel (0524) 43 40 40

Librairie Populaire
53 boulevard Mohamed V, Fès
Tel (0535) 62 04 58

Clothing & Accessories
From the brightly colored foutas of
the Riffan Berber tribeswomen to
the simple pointy-hooded djellabas,
worn by both men and women,
Moroccan traditional clothing has a
unique style, loose and breath-
able for the hot weather, while
being sufficiently modest to meet
Islamic customs. The stores listed
below sell a wide range of beautiful
handmade clothes and accessories
for men and women.

Akbar Delight
45 place Bâb Fteuh, Medina,
Marrakech
A wide selection of brightly
colored, traditionally made Moroccan clothes and fabrics, made using
traditional methods.

Beldi
9–11 rue Mouassine, Medina,
Marrakech
Tel (0524) 44 10 76
An upmarket boutique selling
handmade Moroccan clothing.

Bijouterie al Afrah
34 Rass Charratine, Medina, Fès
Tel (0535) 23 17 06
A jeweler that sells a wide range of
traditional and modern items.

Bijouterie el Fath
280 Souk el Kifah, Medina, Fès
Tel (0668) 10 44 59
A traditional Moroccan jewelry
store that specializes in Berber-style
items made with semiprecious
stones and coral.

Boutique Volubilis
15 Petit Socco, Medina
Tel (0539) 93 13 62
A well-established store that sells
finely made men's clothing in the
heart of Tanger's medina.

Carolin Kaftans
33 boulevard Pasteur, Tanger
Tel (0539) 93 37 94
Sells handmade traditional clothing
and accessories.

J'nan Beldi
24 rue Saint-Louis, Fès
Tel (0535) 60 91 92
An outpost of traditional style in
the center of Fès's ville nouvelle.

Kenza Melehi
41 passage Ghandouri, Guéliz,
Marrakech
Tel (0524) 42 26 41
Sells a beautiful range of unique
handmade Moroccan clothing.

Place Vendôme
141 avenue Mohamed V, Guéliz,
Marrakech
Tel (0524) 43 52 63
A small boutique that specializes
in locally made leather accessories,
such as bags.

Rafia Craft
82 rue d'Agadir, Essaouira
Tel (0524) 78 36 32
Stylish, handmade sandals and
accessories.

Cosmetics & Perfumes
Herboriste Bou Inania
Derb Moulay Abdellmalik,
Medina, Fès
Tel (0535) 63 87 60
Sells argan oil– and olive oil–based
cosmetics, as well as many other
exotic lotions, soaps, and traditional
medicines.

Le Sens de Marrakech
18 Zankat Sidi Ghanem, Marrakech
Tel (0524) 33 69 91
Sells argan oil soaps and other
locally made beauty products.

Parfumerie Madini
Boulevard Pasteur, Tanger
Tel (0539) 37 50 38
A long-established perfumery that
specializes in traditional Moroccan
scents.

Surf Stores
The southern town of Essaouira,
on the Atlantic coast, is the heart
of Moroccan surf country. While
it is a long way from some of the
best waves, its relatively large
size and proximity to many good
surf beaches allows it to sustain a
number of surfing-related stores
year-round.

Explora
2 place Chrib Atay, Rue Laalouj,
Essaouira
Tel (0611) 47 51 88
www.exploramorocco.com

Gipsysurfer
14 rue de Tétouan, Essaouira
Tel (0524) 78 32 68

Moga Surf
Bâb Doukkala, place des Artistes,
Essaouira
Tel (0660) 40 94 78

Ocean Vagabond
Boulevard Mohamed V, Essaouira
Tel (0524) 78 39 34
www.oceanvagabond.com

Traditional Crafts & Antiques
For visitors who do not have the
patience or the energy required to
spend hours rummaging through
the backstreets and souks of the
big cities, there are a growing
number of boutiques with small,
carefully selected collections of art
and antiques. These places have
good working relationships with
skilled local craftsmen and typically
offer higher quality products than
the stalls in the souks (albeit at a
significantly higher price).

Akkal
322 Zankat Sidi Ghanem,
Marrakech
Tel (0524) 33 59 38
Ceramics and locally produced
crafts of high quality.

Amira Bougie
277 Zankat de Sidi Ghanem, Sidi
Abbad, Marrakech
Tel (0524) 33 62 47

Art Berbère
Rue Omar Alhayam, Agadir
Tel (0528) 21 50 10

Coin Berbère
67 Talaâ Kebira, Medina, Fès
Tel (0535) 63 69 46
Three adjacent stores, owned by
the same family. The first sells
antique decorative items, ceramics,
and furniture. The second sells
traditional handmade carpets,
while the third sells silver and coral
jewelry.

Complexe Artisanal
23 Abis Lot Municipate, Quartier
Industriel, Agadir
Tel (0528) 22 09 48

Cooperative des Patrons Potiers
Rue de Sidi Harzeme, Ain Nokbi
Tel (0535) 64 92 25

Darkoum
5 rue de la Liberté, Guéliz,
Marrakech
Tel (0524) 44 67 39
Sells arts and crafts from all over
Africa and India.

Dinanderie d'Art Rza
Rue Jabir Ibn Hayane, Fès
Tel (0535) 64 37 16
The workshop of master craftsman
Abdellatif Hazzaz, who specializes
in zellij mosaics.

Made in M
246 Talaâ Kebira, Medina, Fès
Tel (0611) 05 48 63

Romanos Antiquités
30 rue Jallal-Eddine Essayouti,
Casablanca
Tel (0661) 08 35 68
Sells antiques, lamps, and furniture.

Entertainment

Due to the traditional restrictions on alcohol, permanent entertainment venues such as bars and clubs are a relatively rare sight in Morocco. The few bars that exist are mostly men-only dives where the only entertainment is smoking. This does not mean that there is no entertainment to be had, however; it's just that entertainment venues tend to be temporary, informal places.

Ordinary Moroccans are rightly proud of their rich and diverse cultural history and despite the country's rapid modernization, traditional festivals and entertainments do not struggle to find enthusiastic participants. This does not mean, however, that Moroccan culture is backward-facing or stagnant. Standing as it does on the fringes of Europe and the Arab world, Moroccan culture has always been defined by its fusion of disparate cultural traditions. This practice of combining new or foreign elements into traditional art is still alive and well, leading to such things as *electro-gnaoua*, *raï* (a mixture of Western pop and traditional North African music), and Moroccan modernist painting. While most tourist itineraries focus on traditional performances and events, exploring Morocco's contemporary culture—whether it is independent film, Arabic hip-hop, or conceptual art—can give a better insight into the character of modern Morocco.

Cultural Festivals

Festivals, traditionally known as *moussems,* have always played an important role in Moroccan culture. For centuries, the Moroccan cultural calendar has been marked by these events, typically centered on the shrine of a saint or mystic, where thousands will gather for entertainment and a sense of religious and social community. It is perhaps this long history that has led to annual festivals becoming the preferred venue for cultural activities in Morocco—while there are few permanent theaters, art galleries, or music venues in the country, it can seem like every single town has a festival of some kind or other. These events can range from low-key local events to major international music festivals, attracting acts and audiences from around the world.

Essaouira Gnaoua Festival

www.festival-gnaoua.net
Though its focus is still very much on gnaoua music, this festival—held every July—has grown in recent years, and now attracts dancers and musicians from across the world.

Fès Sacred Music Festival

www.fesfestival.com
Every June, theaters and other venues around Fès house a week of performances of religious music from around the world. Many of the acts are drawn from Morocco's own diverse history of sacred music, which includes songs from the Jewish and Muslim tradition.

Festival National des Arts Populaires

www.marrakechfestival.com
Lasting a week every summer in Marrakech, this festival celebrates traditional Moroccan music and performance.

Jazz au Chellah

www.jazzauchellah.com
Held in the ruined Roman town of Chellah, just outside Rabat, during June each year, this jazz festival has been growing steadily more musically adventurous and popular since its founding in 2005.

Tanjazz Festival

Italian Palace, rue Moulay Idriss, Ville Nouvelle, Tanger
Tel (0539) 93 91 03
www.tanjazz.org
A four-day jazz festival held every September in the old Italian consulate in Tanger.

Live Music

Live-music venues are still something of a rarity in Morocco. A few bars and restaurants do have regular live-music nights, but these musicians seldom reach the sublime heights of Morocco's traditional street performers. In that regard, the Djemaa el Fna in Marrakech is probably the country's finest music venue, even if there isn't a stage to be seen.

Movie Theaters

A legacy of 1930s European occupation, Morocco has no shortage of movie theaters. Many of these art deco edifices are now rather run-down and disreputable, although they still draw decent audiences. Unless noted otherwise, these places usually show a range of international releases with French subtitles. If you've got some time to kill, the traditional B-movie double-bill of a Bollywood musical and a Hong Kong kung-fu movie is an authentically Moroccan experience. In addition to these grand old movie houses, many big cities now have large modern multiplex cinemas on the outskirts of town that show the latest releases.

Cinéma A B C

12 avenue Nehrou, Meknès
Tel (0535) 52 17 81

Cinéma Caméra
Rue de Paris, Meknès
Tel (0535) 52 20 00

Cinéma Fayrouz
63 avenue Hassan II, Rabat
Tel (0537) 72 49 59

Cinéma Le Colisée
281 avenue Mohamed V, Rabat
Tel (0537) 76 62 67

Cinéma Renaissance
266 avenue Mohamed V, Rabat
Tel (0537) 72 21 68

Cinéma Rex
45 avenue Mohamed Slaoui, Fés
Tel (0535) 62 24 96

Cinéma Rif Essaouira
Rue Moulay Youssef, Essaouira
Tel (0524) 47 50 25

Cinéma Royal
Zankat Al Amal, Rabat
Tel (0537) 72 41 18

Cinéma Sahara
Place Talborjt, Agadir
Tel (0528) 84 00 25

Cinéma Sahara
Rue Al Majazir, Rabat
Tel (0537) 69 14 92

Cinémathèque de Tanger
place de 9 Avril 1947 (Grand
Socco), Ville Nouvelle, Tanger
Tel (0539) 93 46 83
www.cinemathèquedetanger.com
The Cinémathèque de Tanger
is a movie theater and cultural
center founded with the aim
of "promoting world cinema in
Morocco, and Moroccan cinema
in the world." It shows a diverse
range of movies and documenta-
ries from Morocco and abroad.

Megarama de Casablanca
Boulevard de la Corniche,
Casablanca
Tel (0522) 79 71 84

Megarama Marrakech
Entre route de l'Ourika et
boulevard Mohamed VI,
Marrakech
Tel (0890) 10 20 20

Rialto Cinema
Rue Mohamed Quory, Casablanca
Tel (0522) 26 26 32

Théâtre National Mohamed V
Avenue Al Mansour Addhabi,
Rabat
Tel (0537) 70 73 00
www.tnmv.ma
A multipurpose cultural venue
incorporating theaters, concert
halls, and a well-appointed
cinema that shows high-profile
new releases.

Theater & Performance
In addition to the performances
at Morocco's many cutural festivals, there are a small number
of permanent theaters in the
country. Most of them are gathered in the city of Casablanca,
which is the home of Moroccan
contemporary culture.

Ballet Théâtre Zinoun
21 rue Najib Mafoud, Casablanca
Tel (0522) 27 59 52

Théâtre 121
121 boulevard Mohamed Zerktouni, Casablanca
Tel (0522) 77 98 70

Théâtre du SOC
Route d'El Jadida, Casablanca
Tel (0522) 25 40 23

Théâtre Mogador
515 boulevard Ghandi,
Casablanca
Tel (0522) 23 60 89

Théâtre Municipal
140 avenue des FAR, Casablanca
Tel (0522) 31 12 64

Théâtre National Mohamed V
See "Movie Theaters"

Théâtre Royal Marrakech
40 boulevard Mohamed VI,
Guéliz, Marrakech
Tel (0524) 43 15 16

Outdoor Activities

Morocco is currently most popular as a destination for exotic city breaks or relaxed beach holidays, but away from the crowds of the souks and beaches, there is a whole other Morocco, wild and rugged, just waiting to be explored. The infrastructure needed for some outdoor activities is still in development, so don't expect the newest technology or the most luxurious accommodations.

Morocco's varied landscape and pronounced seasonal variation allows for a wide variety of outdoor activities, from desert camel treks to snowboarding. On the Atlantic coast, there are ample opportunities for surfing, windsurfing, and kiteboarding, while the rugged landscapes of the Rif Mountains and the Middle Atlas are ideal places to explore in an off-road vehicle or on horseback. You do not have to venture far from the major tourist centers before you find yourself in pristine, untouched landscapes ripe for exploring. Whenever you go, and wherever you choose to stay, you will find that there is much more to do in Morocco than sit on the beach or shop in the souks.

In addition to the companies listed below, many hotels and *riads* are willing and able to organize excursions for their guests, so make sure to ask if you're looking for something to do.

Fishing

Morocco has some of the most abundant fish stocks in the world, a fact that is clearly apparent to anyone who has stood down by the docks in Essaouira, Agadir, or Mohammedia when the day's catch is brought in. At the moment, however, few businesses have realized the potential for sportfishing excursions in the country. Inland, the story is similar—the country's many rivers and reservoirs are well stocked with fish, but largely untroubled by hooks and lures.

Hotel Bin el Ouidane
Bin el Ouidane
Tel (0523) 44 26 00
www.hotelbinelouidane.com
This small hotel on the banks of the huge Bin el Ouidane reservoir (east of Marrakech) offers equipment rental, small boats, and advice for those who want to fish in the lake. It is not unheard of for carp as large as 70 pounds (30 kg) to end up in angler's nets here.

Maroc Sport Fishing
Agadir
Tel (0528) 82 39 52
http://joudat.iliass.free.fr
Run by French expats Patricia and Claude Crouzet, Maroc Sport Fishing is one of the only specialized deep-sea fishing companies in Morocco. With their purpose-built vessel and experienced crew, they offer the chance to fish for shark, tuna, and swordfish.

Golf Courses

The late King Hassan II's enthusiasm for golf bred a minor industry in Morocco, with green fairways popping up on the outskirts of towns across the country. While these courses are a valuable economic boost to many areas, they are also a divisive feature of the landscape. Away from the verdant north of the country, the green grass of the fairways and greens requires constant irrigation to keep alive, using more than 300,000 gallons of water a day. This drives up the price and availability of water in this already parched country.

Cabo Negro Royal Golf Club
Tétouan
Tel (0539) 97 83 03
Ppened in 1972, this British-designed course offers spectacular views of the Rif Mountains. It's quite a challenging course surrounded by dense shrubbery and swept by unpredictable coastal winds.

Fès Royal Golf Club
Km 15, route d'Imouzzer, Fès
Tel (0535) 66 52 10
A technically challenging course that first opened in 1924. The course offers impressive views of the Middle Atlas and cunningly positioned obstacles to catch out even the most experienced golfer.

Marrakech Royal Golf Club
Ancienne route de Ouarzazate, Marrakech
Tel (0524) 40 47 05
Designed in the early 1920s, this course has hosted famous figures such as Winston Churchill and Dwight Eisenhower during its long history.

Meknès Royal Golf Course
Jnan al Bahraouia, Ville Impériale, Meknès
Tel (0535) 53 07 53
www.royalgolfmeknes.com
A compact course designed to fit neatly into the grounds of Moulày Ismail's grand royal palace. Formerly the private course of Hassan II, it is now open to the public and relatively cheap. A few rounds of golf here provide the only way to see inside the royal enclosure of the Ville Impériale.

Royal Golf Dar Es Salam
Km 9, avenue Mohamed VI/
Road of Zaers, Souissi, Rabat
Tel (0537) 75 58 64
www.royalgolfdaressalam.com
This course hosts several major
international competitions
every year and was a longtime
favorite of King Hassan II. The
fairways are dotted with some
rather unusual obstacles, including ancient Roman pillars from
nearby Chellah.

Tanger Royal Golf Club
Tanger
Tel (0539) 93 89 25
Designed for Tanger's prosperous British population in 1917,
this is Morocco's oldest golf
course. The course is laid out
on the slopes of the northern
Rif, among stands of cypress
and pine. The fairways and clubhouse offer panoramic views
across the Strait of Gibraltar.

Horseback Riding & Off-Road Excursions

One of the best ways to see the
beautiful Moroccan countryside
is by traveling on horseback or
by camel (more atmospheric,
perhaps, but less comfortable).
Off-road vehicle tours allow you
to cover more ground, especially
in the southern desert, but it's
worth mentioning that the dust
and sand these vehicles churn
up is doing significant damage
to the delicate ecosystems on
the fringes of the desert.

Atlas Cheval
932 Résidence Al Massar, route
de Safi, Marrakech
Tel (0524) 36 86 10
www.atlascheval-marrakech.net

Atlas Sahara Trek
6-bis rue Houdoud, Quartier
Majorelle, Marrakech
Tel (0524) 31 39 01

Fax (0524) 31 39 05
www.atlas-sahara-trek.com

Club Farah
www.clubfarah.com
Based just outside the city of
Meknès, Club Farah has been
organizing horse-trekking
holidays in Morocco since 1982.
The company can arrange
anything from a day's riding in
the country outside Meknès,
to a weeklong trek through the
Atlas Mountains, sleeping in
Berber tents.

Le Cavaliers de Atlas
La Palmeraie, Marrakech
www.lescavaliersdelatlas.com

Maroc Rando Cheval (Horse Trekking Morocco)
Domaine Equestre Aïn Amyer,
2.5 km, route d'Imouzzer, Fès
tel (0535) 94 21 18
www.marocrandocheval.com

Morocco Explored
Tel (0667) 70 52 12
www.moroccoexplored.com
This Marrakech-based company
organizes guided horse and
camel treks, as well as off-road
vehicle tours in the Atlas Mountains and beyond.

Mountain Voyage
5 avenue Mohamed V, 2nd floor,
Guéliz, Marrakech
Tel (0524) 42 19 96
Fax (0524) 42 19 95
www.mountain-voyage.com

Nature Trekking Maroc
www.maroctrekking.com
BP 8107 Mhamid, Marrakech
Tel (0524) 43 24 77
Fax (0524) 44 81 68

Pur Sang Nomade
Taroudant
www.pursangnomade.com

Ranch Les 2 Gazelles,
Sidi Boulfdail, Province de Tiznit
www.les2gazelles.com

Trekking in Morocco
Asni, south of Marrakech
Tel (0662) 15 41 89
www.trekkinginmorocco.com
This company, based in the Atlas
Mountains, offers a wide variety
of activities, including cycle
touring, mountain climbing, and
off-road adventures, as well as
horse and camel treks.

Zouina Cheval
Diabat, near Essaouira
www.zouina-cheval.com

Hot-air Ballooning

Ciel d'Afrique
15 rue de Mauritanie, Guéliz,
Marrakech
Tel (0524) 43 28 43
www.cieldafrique.info
An unorthodox but breathtaking
way to see the landscape of the
Atlas Mountains. Operating from
a site a few minutes south of
Marrakech, Ciel d'Afrique offers
hot-air balloon flights over and
around Marrakech. The flights
are piloted by Maurice Otin, an
experienced balloonist who has
been operating in Morocco since
1990. Prices start from around
$250 per person for a flight.

National Parks

National parks are a relatively
new addition to the Moroccan
landscape. Several have now been
opened in Morocco to protect
areas of outstanding natural
beauty or biodiversity from the
impact of Morocco's overzealous
logging industry.

Al Hoceima National Park
Rif Moutains Tourism Board,
19 rue Ajdir, Al Hoceima
Tel (0667) 14 05 80
www.parquenacional
alhucemas.com

Talassemtane National Park
Direction du Parc National de
Talassemtane
Tel (0539) 98 91 78
www.parctalassemtane.com

Tazekka National Park
Tel (0535) 28 00 96
www.tazekka.com

Toubkal National Park
Al Haouz, route de l'Ourika,
Setti-Fatma
Located 50 miles (80 km) south
of Marrakech, this national park
is centered on Jebel Toubkal, the
Morocco's tallest mountain. The
park encompasses 146 square
miles (380 sq km) of some of the
country's finest mountain scenery.

Rock Climbing

For those who want something
a little steeper than the fairly
leisurely approaches to Jebel
Toubkal, the Todra Gorge—
located in the mountains east of
Marrakech—is the place to go.
First scouted by a French climber
in the 1970s, this rocky valley
contains dozens of well-bolted
sport climbs that attract expert
climbers from around the world.
The locals know the routes well,
and the hotels nearby have plenty
of information for climbers.
Guided expeditions to the area
can be organized through **Cosley
and Houston** (www.cosley
houston.com) or through **K-one**
(www.k-one-pianetamontagna.it).

Surfing

Surfing is not an activity that
many would associate with
Morocco, but the sport is rapidly
growing in popularity here. The
country's long Atlantic coastline
has many good surfing spots,
and the supporting infrastructure is developing fast. While
you won't get any Hawaii-size
waves here, the relatively gentle

swell is an excellent place for
learners and beginners. The area
around Essaouira is popular with
windsurfers and kitesurfers, while
other surfers prefer to head
farther south. Those looking for
big waves venture to the hard-
to-reach resort of Dakhla in the
Western Sahara.

**Association de Planche a Voile
(Windsurfing Association)**
Boulevard Mohamed V,
Essaouira
Tel (0670) 57 74 11
The Moroccan windsurfing association is based, unsurprisingly, in
the windy city of Essaouira. Come
here to get information about
tutors, conditions, and the best
places to go in the area.

Dynamic Loisirs
Villa Argane, Tamrhakht (near
Agadir)
www.surf-maroc.com
Based in the heart of Morocco's
surfing coast, this small company offers equipment rental,
beachside accommodations, and
transport for surfers who want to
see all this area has to offer. They
can arrange an eight-day "surfari"
for more experienced surfers.

École de Surf: Vagues et Vents
4-bis plage d'Agadir, Agadir
Tel (0661) 21 57 46

Essaouira Kitesurf
Tel (0567) 20 67 25
www.essaouirakitesurf.com
For those who want to kitesurf,
this store is your one-stop shop.
The company offers lessons,
equipment rental, and guides for
the more experienced surfer.

Explora
2 place Chrib Atay, rue Laalouj,
Essaouira
Tel (0611) 47 51 88
www.exploramorocco.com
Run by a group of local surfers

who have been riding the waves
off Essaouira for decades.

Ocean Vagabond
Boulevard Mohamed V,
Essaouira
Tel (0524) 78 39 34
www.oceanvagabond.com
With branches in Essaouira and
Dahkla, this company caters to
both the serious surfing com-
munity and those looking to hire
a teacher and a board.

Ooudayas Surf Club
http://edu.ac.ma/transitions/
surfing/index
Located in a large white building
down by Oudaïa Beach in Rabat,
this surf club offers lessons and
board hire.

White-water Rafting & Kayaking

Despite Morocco's stunning
rivers and mountainous terrain,
white-water rafting and kayaking
are not common activities here.
Interest is growing, however;
there are now several international tour operators that offer
such activities.

**Splash White Water Rafting
Morocco**
7 Derb Gnaoua, Ben Saleh,
Medina, Marrakech
www.moroccoadventure
tours.com
Tel (0618) 96 42 52
This British company operates
tours around Morocco's rivers
from its private riad in Marrakech.

Water by Nature
Tel (303) 988-5037 (in U.S.)
www.waterbynature.com
This U.S.-based company offers
kayaking and white-water rafting
expeditions in the Atlas Mountains, as well as kayaking lessons
on the lake Bin el Ouidane, east
of Marrakech.

Language Guide

The history of Morocco is marked by numerous waves of migration. Peoples and cultures from all over the world have converged on this corner of North Africa, each bringing its own languages and dialects. Although the most obvious outside influence is French colonialism, a quick examination of the languages spoken in Morocco shows that they were by no means the first.

Darija

The official language in Morocco is Modern Standard Arabic, the same language, more or less, that is spoken formally throughout the Middle East and North Africa. Any Arabic speaker stepping into Morocco's noisy streets, however, will soon realize that the reality is rather different. The de facto primary language of most Moroccans is a distinctive dialect of Arabic commonly known as Moroccan Arabic or, locally, Darija.

While it is fundamentally the same as the language that is spoken as far away as Iraq, the influence of European colonialism, indigenous Berber languages, and many centuries of distant relations with the heartland of Arabia have led it to develop a unique vocabulary, grammar, and pronunciation that make it almost unintelligible to anyone who learned Arabic in the Middle East.

Even within Morocco, the dialects vary considerably, often reflecting the impact of different spheres of colonial influence and local minority populations. While there are some phrase books and guides available for Darija, it is almost impossible to render many aspects of Darija pronunciation in phonetic English. Unless you have some prior knowledge of Arabic, it's unlikely you'll be able to make yourself understood using any of these books.

Berber

Morocco is a much more linguistically diverse country than its official statistics would imply. For various reasons—some political, some cultural—the state of Morocco tends to downplay the number of its citizens that speak minority languages and the diversity of spoken Arabic in the country.

Although it is not officially acknowledged, a significant proportion of the Moroccan population (some estimates place it as high as 15 percent) speak Berber as their first language. The Berber-speaking population is mostly confined to rural areas, particularly in the mountains and southern desert. There are three main dialects: Riffan Berber is spoken in the Rif Mountains and along the Mediterranean coast, Shilha Berber is spoken in the south of the country and along the Atlantic coast as far as Essaouira, while Tamazight Berber is spoken primarily in the High Atlas and Middle Atlas Mountains. For many years, the Moroccan state has attempted to suppress the Berber language, enacting laws that, for example, make it essentially illegal to give children Berber names. In recent years, however, the government's attitude has relented somewhat, although Berber speakers are often discriminated against in urban areas.

Second Languages

To further complicate Morocco's already confusing linguistic landscape, most Moroccans have a decent grasp of at least one other language in addition to their mother tongue. For the country's Berber population, this second language is typically Darija, although some Berbers speak a European language in addition to this. For the rest of the population, however, this second language is usually French. Under the French colonial regime that controlled the country during the first half of the 20th century, French was the language of government, business, and the media.

Although the government funded an extensive Arabization process during the 1960s, French still pervades many aspects of everyday life. Habit plays a large role in this—people will still refer to streets by their old French names, for example, long after the signs have been rewritten in Arabic—but there is also the language's relative convenience in a country where there are so many different dialects.

All Moroccans are taught French in school, and there are still plenty of expensive private schools that conduct their teaching entirely in French. Although English is making inroads here (it's the third language of choice in the big cities), French is still the language of choice for many online services, radio stations, and businesses. In most parts of the country, and particularly in the cities, a few words of French are more likely to be useful than attempts at Darija or trying to find someone who understands English.

French as spoken in Morocco is typically grammatically simpler and easier to understand than French spoken in France itself.

INDEX

ILLUSTRATIONS CREDITS

2-3, Brigitte Merle/Photononstop/Photolibrary; 4, Nicolas Pitt/Photolibrary; 8, Ray Hub/Shutterstock; 11, David Norton Photography/Alamy; 12 istockphoto; 14-15, Thomas Stankiewicz/Look-foto/Photolibrary; 16, KFS/Imagebroker/Photolibrary; 18-19, Lee Frost/Robert Hading World Imagery/Photolibrary; 20, Sébastien Boisse/Photononstop/Photolibrary; 22-23, Duncan Maxwell/ Robert Harding World Imagery/Photolibary; 25, Pierre Andrew Hoffman/Picture Press/Photolibrary; 27, Antonello Lanzellotto/Tips Italia/Photolibrary; 28, Martin Harvey/Peter Arnold/Photolibary; 30, fotolincs/Alamy; 33, Gavin Hellier/Robert Harding World Imagery/Photolibrary; 34-35, Bruno Morandi/age fotostock/Photolibrary; 37, Bruno Morandi/age fotostock/Photolibrary; 38, Stefan Auth/Imagebroker/Photolibrary; 40, Dallas and John Heaton/Corbis; 43, Sygma/Corbis; 45, Ruthven Carstairs/Alamy; 46, Shepherd Sherbell/Corbis; 49, Richard Duebel/Imagestate/Photolibrary; 50, Bill Lai/Index Stock/Photolibrary; 52, Tolo Balaquer/age fotostock/Photolibrary; 56, Walter Bibikow/age fotostock/Photolibrary; 58, PCL/Alamy; 60, Andrew Watson/John Warburton-Lee Photography/Photolibrary; 62, Olivier Diqoit/Imagebroker/Photolibrary; 64, Bruno Morandi/age fotostock/Photolibrary; 65 Floris Leeuwnberg/The Cover Story/Corbis; 67, Xabier/Richer/Photononstop/Photolibrary; 68, Steve Vidler/Imagestate/Photolibrary; 72, Bruno Morandi/age fotostock/Photolibrary; 75, Nicolas Thibault/Photononstop/Photolibrary; 76, Paul Thompson/Ticket/Photolibrary; 78, J. D. Dallet/age fotostock/Photolibrary; 81, Ethel Davis/Robert Harding World Imagery/Photolibrary; 83, Guy Bouchet/Photononstop/Photolibrary; 84, Bruno Morandi/Robert Harding World Imagery/Photolibrary; 87, Gerrit de Vries/Shutterstock; 88, Emilio Suetone/Hemis/Photolibrary; 90, J. D. Dallet/Photolibrary; 92, Gonzalo Azumendi/Photolibrary; 96, Ken Gillham/Robert Harding World Imagery; 98, Julian Love/John Warburton-Lee Photography/Photolibrary; 100, Ming Tang-Evans/Ticket/Photolibrary; 103, Gary Cralle/Tips Italia/Photolibrary; 104, Ludovic Maisant/Hemis/Photolibrary; 107, Nicolas Thibault/Photononstop/Photolibrary; 108, K.M. Westerman/Corbis; 110, Philippe Saharoff/Photononstop/Photolibrary; 112, Roger-Viollet/Topfoto; 114, Paul Thompson Images/Alamy; 117, Keren Su/Corbis; 119, Michael Schaef/F1 Online/Photolibrary; 120, Witold Skrypczak/Alamy; 123, Imagestate/Alamy; 124, Hugo Canabi/Icontec/Photolibrary; 127, Christopher Rennie/Robert Harding World Imagery/Photolibrary; 128, David Bartruff/Indexstock/Photolibrary; 130, Alvaro Lelva/age fotostock/Photolibrary; 133, J D Dallet/age fotostock/Photolibrary; 134, J D Dallet/age fotostock/Photolibrary; 138, Sven Randebrock/Photolibrary; 140, Bruno Morandi/Hemis/Photolibrary; 142, Randebrock/Alamy; 144, Mark Hannaford/John Warburton-Lee Photography/Photolibrary; 146, Robert Harding World Imagery/Photolibrary; 148, Nicolas Thibault/Photononstop/Photolibrary; 150, Bruno Morandi/Robert Harding World Imagery/Photolibrary; 151, Roland T. Frank/Mauritius/Photolibrary; 152, Hugo Canabi/Icontec/Photolibrary; 154, Michael Boyny/Look-foto/Photolibrary; 158, Steve Vidler/Imagestate/Photolibrary; 161, Tibor Bognar/Photononstop/Photolibrary; 162, Pat Behnke/Alamy; 164, Bruno Morandi/age fotostock/Photolibrary; 166, Walter Bibikow/Mauritius/Photolibrary; 167, Nicolas Thibault/Photononstop/Photolibrary; 169, Jean Dominique Dallet/Alamy; 170, AFP/Getty Images; 172, Jacques Bravo/Photononstop/Photolibrary; 174, Roger Eritia/OSF/Photolibrary; 175, Michael Tarrier/age fotostock/Photolibrary; 176, Walter Bibikow/age fotostock/Photolibrary; 180, Tol Balahuer/age fotostock/Photolibrary; 182, Paul Nevin/Ticket/Photolibrary; 186 KFS/Imagebroker/Photolibrary; 189, Kevin Foy/Alamy; 190, Nicolas Thibault/Photononstop/Photolibrary; 192, Stefan Auth/Imagebroker/Photolibrary; 195, Andrew Newey/The Travel Library/Photolibary; 196, Targa/age fotostock/Photolibrary; 200, Xavier Richer/Photononstop/Photolibrary; 202, KFS/Imagebroker/Photolibrary; 204, Kevin Foy/Alamy; 205, Simon Reddy/Alamy; 207, Gilles Rigoulet/Hemis/Photolibrary; 208, istockphoto; 209, Jean Pierre Lescourret/Corbis; 228, John Warburton-Lee Photography/Alamy; 213 Realimage/Alamy; 214, K M Westermann/Corbis; 216, Christian Kober/John Warburton-Lee Photography/Photolibrary; 218, Hidalgo & Lopesino/age fotostock/Photolibrary; 220, Xavier Richer/Photononstop/Photolibrary; 222, Andrew Watson/John Warburton-Lee Photography/Photolibrary; 224,Bruno Perlousse/age fotostock/Photolibrary; 228, Walter Bibikow/age fotostock/Photolibrary; 230, Jean Du oisberrenger/Hemis/Photolibrary; 232, Alan Keohane/Imagestate/Photolibrary; 235, Joachim Hiltmann/Imagebroker/Photolibrary; 237, E G Pors/Shutterstock; 239, Walter Bibikow/Jon Arnold Travel/Photolibrary; 240, Antonello Lanzelloto/Tips Italia Photolibrary; 242, blickwinkel/Alamy; 245, Rob Crandall/Alamy; 246, JTB Photo/Photolibrary; 249, Camille Moirenc/Hemis/Photolibrary; 250, Nicolas Thibault/Photononstop/Photolibrary; 253, Xavier Richer/Photononstop/Photolibrary; 254, Vladimir Wrangel/Shutterstock; 257, Alan Keohane/Imagestate/Photolibrary; 258, Pascal Parrot/Sygma/Corbis; 261, Bildagentur/Tips Italia/Photolibrary; 263, AFP/Getty Images; 266, Nedko Dimtrov/Alamy.

National Geographic

TRAVELER
Morocco

Published by the National Geographic Society

John M. Fahey, Jr., *President
and Chief Executive Officer*
Gilbert M. Grosvenor, *Chairman of the Board*
Tim T. Kelly, *President, Global Media Group*
John Q. Griffin, *Executive Vice President;
President, Publishing*
Nina D. Hoffman, *Executive Vice President;
President, Book Publishing Group*

Prepared by the Book Division

Barbara Brownell Grogan, *Vice President
and Editor in Chief*
Marianne R. Koszorus, *Director of Design*
Barbara A. Noe, *Senior Editor*
Carl Mehler, *Director of Maps*
R. Gary Colbert, *Production Director*
Jennifer A. Thornton, *Managing Editor*
Meredith C. Wilcox, *Administrative Director, Illustrations*

Staff for This Book

Lawrence M. Porges, *Project Manager*
Kay Kobor Hankins, *Art Director*
Jane Sunderland, *Copy Editor*
Al Morrow, *Design Assistant*
Michael McNey, David Miller, *Map Production*
Jack Brostrom, Jackie Attwood-Dupont, Olivia Garnett,
Linda Makarov, *Contributors*

Manufacturing and Quality Management

Christopher A. Liedel, *Chief Financial Officer*
Phillip L. Schlosser, *Vice President*
Chris Brown, *Technical Director*
Nicole Elliott, *Manager*
Rachel Faulise, *Manager*
Robert L. Barr, *Manager*

The Brown Reference Group Ltd.

Lindsey Lowe, *Editorial Director*
Tim Harris, *Managing Editor*
David Poole, *Design Manager*
Supriya Sahai, *Senior Designer*
Joan Curtis, *Designer*
Sophie Mortimer, *Picture Manager*
Martin Darlison, *Cartographer*
Clive Carpenter, Joe Fullman, Alastair Gourlay,
Leon Gray, Ben Hollingum, Sally McFall, *Contributors*

National Geographic Traveler: Morocco
ISBN 978-1-4262-0706-8

The National Geographic Society is one of the world's
largest nonprofit scientific and educational organizations. Founded in 1888 to "increase and diffuse
geographic knowledge," the Society works to inspire
people to care about the planet. National Geographic
reflects the world through its magazines, television
programs, films, music and radio, books, DVDs, maps,
exhibitions, live events, school publishing programs,
interactive media and merchandise. *National Geographic*
magazine, the Society's official journal, published in
English and 32 local-language editions, is read by more
than 35 million people each month. The National
Geographic Channel reaches 320 million households
in 34 languages in 166 countries. National Geographic
Digital Media receives more than 13 million visitors a
month. National Geographic has funded more than
9,200 scientific research, conservation, and exploration
projects and supports an education program promoting geography literacy. For more information, visit
nationalgeographic.com.

For more information, please call 1-800-NGS LINE
(647-5463) or write to the following address:

National Geographic Society
1145 17th Street N.W.
Washington, D.C. 20036-4688 U.S.A.

Visit us online at www.nationalgeographic.com

For information about special discounts for bulk
purchases, please contact National Geographic
Books Special Sales: ngspecsales@ngs.org

For rights or permissions inquiries, please contact
National Geographic Books Subsidiary Rights:
ngbookrights@ngs.org

The information in this book has been carefully
checked and to the best of our knowledge is accurate.
However, details are subject to change, and the
National Geographic Society cannot be responsible for
such changes, or for errors or omissions. Assessments
of sites, hotels, and restaurants are based on the
author's subjective opinions, which do not necessarily
reflect the publisher's opinion.

Printed in China

10/TS/1

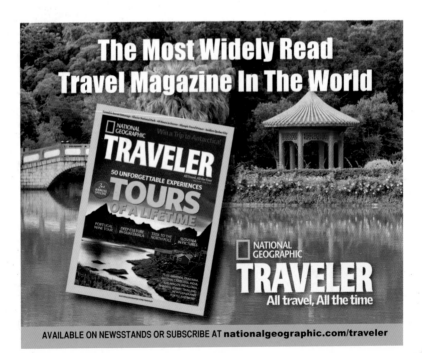